Histories of Leisure

Leisure, Consumption and Culture

General Editor: Rudy Koshar, *University of Wisconsin at Madison*

Leisure regimes in Europe (and North America) in the last two centuries have brought far-reaching changes in consumption patterns and consumer cultures. The 1980s and 1990s have seen the evolution of scholarship on consumption from a wide range of disciplines but historical research on the subject is unevenly developed for late modern Europe, just as the historiography of leisure practices is limited to certain periods and places. This series encourages scholarship on how leisure and consumer culture evolved with respect to an array of identities. It relates leisure and consumption to the symbolic systems with which tourists, shoppers, fans, spectators, and hobbyists have created meaning, and to the structures of power that have shaped such consumer behaviour. It treats consumption in general and leisure practices in particular as complex processes involving knowledge, negotiation, and the active formation of individual and collective selves.

Editorial Board

Histories of Leisure

Edited by
Rudy Koshar

Oxford • New York

First published in 2002 by
Berg
Editorial offices:
150 Cowley Road, Oxford, OX4 1JJ, UK
838 Broadway, Third Floor, New York, NY 10003-4812, USA

Berg is the imprint of Oxford International Publishers Ltd.

Library of Congress Cataloging-in-Publication Data
Histories of leisure / edited by Rudy Koshar.
    p. cm. -- (Leisure, consumption, and culture)
Includes bibliographical references (p.) and index.
    ISBN 1-85973-520-7 -- ISBN 1-85973-525-8 (pbk.)
    1. Leisure--Social aspects--Europe--History--19th century. 2. Leisure--Social
aspects--Europe--History--20th century. 3. Consumption
(Economics)--Europe--History. 4. Europe--Social life and customs. I. Koshar,
Rudy. II. Series.
  GV73 .H57 2002
  306.4'812--dc21
                                                                    2002000202

British Library Cataloguing-in-Publication Data
A catalogue record for this book is available from the British Library.

ISBN 1 85973 520 7 (Cloth)
     1 85973 525 8 (Paper)

Typeset by JS Typesetting, Wellingborough, Northants.
Printed in the United Kingdom by Biddles Ltd, Guildford and King's Lynn

Contents

Contents

Preface and Acknowledgments

This volume brings together a substantial range of essays on the history of European leisure culture from the late eighteenth century to the present. As the contributors make clear, although the historiography of leisure is quite developed, it is also uneven, with respect both to the time periods and countries it has studied as well as to the subjects it has emphasized. This volume does not claim to be a comprehensive rejoinder to the oversights or exaggerations of previous scholarship. Indeed, a central premise of the volume is that the history of leisure culture eludes a fully definitive or synthetic treatment; it consists of multiple temporalities and concatenations whose shape and content shift with reference to an array of political, social, cultural, economic, and environmental forces. Nonetheless, broad patterns of change and continuity do appear, and the tripartite structure of seeing, traveling, and consuming offers one approach to discerning them, at least for the purpose of categorization and discussion. This volume brings together some of the most innovative scholarship in the historical study of leisure practices available at present. It is hoped that it will serve readers as a kind of benchmark for current thinking on a most lively and changing topic.

This project would have been impossible without Maike Bohn, who suggested the idea, and Kathryn Earle, who has encouraged, advised, and recruited with characteristic energy and insight. I thank them both, as well as the editorial staff of Berg, for their valuable and unflagging assistance.

Rudy Koshar

Contributors

Leora Auslander, Associate Professor of History, University of Chicago

Christopher Breward, Reader in Historical and Cultural Studies, London College of Fashion

Robert Goodrich, Assistant Professor of History, Northern Michigan University

Stephen Gundle, Head of Department of Italian, Royal Holloway, University of London

Stephen L. Harp, Assistant Professor of History, The University of Akron

Matthew Hilton, Lecturer in History, University of Birmingham

Erik Jensen, PhD Candidate in History, University of Wisconsin at Madison

Pieter Judson, Associate Professor of History, Swarthmore College

Rudy Koshar, DAAD Professor of German and European Studies, University of Wisconsin at Madison

Marius Kwint, Lecturer in History of Art, Oxford University

Esther Leslie, Lecturer in English and Humanities, Birkbeck College, University of London.

Jan Palmowski, Lecturer in German, King's College London

Nick Prior, Lecturer in Sociology, University of Edinburgh

Christopher S. Thompson, Assistant Professor of History, Ball State University

Patrick Young, Instructor, Core Curriculum, Boston University

Seeing, Traveling, and Consuming: An Introduction

Rudy Koshar

Not long ago, the critical theory of social philosophers Theodor Adorno and Max Horkheimer achieved an almost canonical status in scholarly interpretations of leisure culture in the twentieth century. "Amusement under late capitalism is the prolongation of work," they wrote in *Dialectic of Enlightenment*, published first in Amsterdam in 1947 but then reissued more than twenty years later at the height of the European student protest movement.[1] Leisure was an "escape from the mechanized work process," but it was an escape whose content and form was so indelibly stamped by the exigencies of capitalist production that one's "experiences are inevitably after-images of the work process itself." "What happens at work, in the factory, or in the office can only be escaped from by approximation to it in one's leisure time."[2] These passages occurred in a more elaborated analysis of the so-called "culture industry," the name for which captured the philosophers' larger point that time spent away from labor was inextricably caught by the demands of mass production and mass consumption. On both sides of the Atlantic, this approach not only shaped much New Left thinking about late modern society, most notably in countercultural classics such as Herbert Marcuse's *One-Dimensional Man* and *Eros and Civilization*, but also later left its mark on the emergent field of "cultural studies."[3]

The historical moment in which Horkheimer and Adorno wrote explains something of the sharp despair with which they castigated modern society. Exiled from his position as founder and director of the famous Institute for Social Research in Frankfurt, Horkheimer joined Adorno in Los Angeles during World War II to write most of *Dialectic of Enlightenment*. It is unsurprising in this context that the uprooted scholars focused on American cinema and radio to demonstrate how "enlightenment" reverted to ideology, and how the modern media, organized around principles of mass production, had come to perpetuate "mass deception" on consumers. But what is striking is how comprehensive their analysis was: "automobiles, bombs, and movies keep the whole thing together," they remarked.[4] In their perspective, the world of leisure, whether symbolized by the motorized hordes of Sunday drivers and vacationers, or by the movie-going audiences in southern California cinemas, was directly continuous with the world of capitalist production. That capitalism was now producing more bombs than cars was only an accident of the historical situation. Indeed, for Horkheimer and Adorno, Hitler, Mussolini, and their many imitators were not products of militarism or war as such, but rather specific European manifestations of a deeper trend in industrial society. Politics, leisure, popular culture, music, cinema, tourism, advertising, shopping, consumer society – all bore the indelible mark of the social hierarchy that manipulated them, that obliterated the last traces of criticism or at least of a tragic worldview, and that finally subsumed everything in a totalitarian system of capitalist domination. In contrast to those who argued that the dissolution of religion and growing bureaucratic specialization had fragmented social experience, Adorno and Horkheimer argued that an impressive degree of coherence existed in society. "Culture now impresses the same stamp on everything," they claimed.[5] Movies simply provided the requisite advertising to further the totalitarian colonization of everyday life.

The Frankfurt school philosophers had not stepped into a theoretical vacuum, of course. Before Horkheimer and Adorno, intellectuals in Europe and North America worried aloud about the effects of mass production and consumption on established hierarchies of cultural influence. Georg Simmel, Sigmund Freud, Max Weber, Thorstein Veblen, José Ortega y Gasset, and many others contributed to an often anxious conversation in which scholars bemoaned what appeared to be the dissolution of the work-oriented, rational, liberal individual of the nineteenth century. *Dialectic of Enlightenment* was only one of the most totalizing and pessimistic statements in this genre, though its popularity after the 1960s gave it much influence beyond the world of scholarship – especially among student radicals, who were more willing than most to accept the radical pessimism of its writers. In the first half of the twentieth century, other thinkers reacted more positively to the world of mass leisure, although they assumed, like the pessimists, that classically trained intellectuals should direct the process of educating consumers to make proper use of the new opportunities for time spent away from labor.[6] Almost all wrestled with the fact – if not the full realization – that the commodity form was dominant in the United States and much of Europe by the 1920s, and that time spent outside the factory or office was molded increasingly by commercial society.

The challenge that this situation represented was enormous, as Bertrand Russell understood when he wrote "to be able to fill leisure intelligently is the last product of civilization."[7] Russell's observation contained at least three unspoken assumptions, critical rejoinders to which are central to this volume. The first was that "leisure" is something that can be defined as a more or less identifiable thing or practice, to be "filled" with content just as a vase is filled with water. The second is that someone – in Russell's case, the arbiters of good taste as seen from the rather narrow view of the renowned English philosopher, but just as easily from the perspective of exiled German-Jewish Marxists – could determine what was an intelligent use of leisure and what was not. Third, Russell expressed what has been a common, if often unacknowledged, assumption about the qualities of leisure that place it in the "after" – after a degree of automation (and hence lessened work time) has been achieved in the sphere of production; after societies have gone through a learning process whereby the feel for what constitutes proper use of time away from labor becomes "second nature"; after enough discretionary income has been accumulated to purchase "non-necessary" goods and services; or, most simply, after paid work has been done. This putative quality lent an aura of subsidiarity to leisure that is reinforced again and again in public discussion as well as some parts of academic discourse, where the thematic canon often remains fixed on power, production, and the public sphere rather than on that "private" experience that is usually assigned (misleadingly) to the realm of leisure. None of these assumptions are indisputably "wrong," to be sure. But neither do they stand up without deep qualification against the now substantially accumulating research on the history of leisure, for which this collection may stand as illustrative of the complexities of the subject.

The *Oxford English Dictionary* contains sixteen definitions of leisure, some rare or obsolete, drawn from sources going back to the early fourteenth century.[8] Of the many definitions offered, it is the idea that leisure is "the state of having time at one's own disposal; time which one can spend as one pleases; free or unoccupied time," which comes closest to contemporary understandings. But some of the other entries are revealing precisely for their obsolescence. We rarely think of leisure as "duration of opportunity" and "time allowed before it is too late," but well into the nineteenth century (and perhaps into the twentieth) it was common to hear of someone "having the leisure" to undertake something before something else occurred. This notion stands diametrically opposed to the now regnant sense of leisure as coming "after." Even rarer is the idea of regarding leisure as a specific "opportunity" to carry out a defined task. Mentioning such definitional permutations reflects the protean quality of the subject, for which there is abundant evidence in the following pages. But even when we settle on the more up-to-date notion of leisure as "free or unoccupied time," the predominant impression is that this stands in considerable contrast to the argument of leisure's subsidiary quality. After all, something constituted by "free" time would, it seems, be not only prior to that which is "unfree," but also in liberal societies premised on the development of individual personalities at some distance from the state, superior in nature to time or action not characterized by this quality. The contemporary understanding is so expansive, in any case, that it suggests there is not just one history of leisure but rather only a multiplicity of temporalities, histories of concatenated pleasures and practices, and narratives of variable experiences and expectations. This, too, is an important premise of this volume.

Historical scholarship offers an abundance of evidence for the idea that leisure is not only central to modern history but also truly centrifugal in its influences and manifestations. Even so, some patterns do emerge in the scholarship that suggests there are correspondences and similarities across very dissimilar activities. One theme, important for the historical background of this volume's subject, is that the chronologies in question are much longer than contemporary discussions of "leisure society" would suggest. Although Adorno and Horkheimer concentrated on the first half of the twentieth century, they introduced their subject by claiming that the modern culture industry had occupied the social space once captured by religion.[9] This view situated contemporary leisure in an elongated chronology the contours of which the philosophers only barely touched on. But consider also recent debates over the "invention" of leisure in the early modern period.[10] The important factor here is not so much whether before the coming of industrial capitalism people were fully aware of their leisure. Rather, it is that histories of leisure (or play, as the early moderns might have put it, or "recreation," as many Americans say) belong as much to the fourteenth as they do to the late nineteenth or twentieth centuries. But the point is not only that leisure practices have very long temporal reaches, but also they describe important transformations over time. An activity closely associated with the aristocratic warrior class in earlier ages, fencing was later transformed into a sport that can now be taken as a class on just about any US university campus. Moreover, some leisure practices gained stunning popularity in particular times and regions, only to be found on the margins of society later. The history of cockfighting in American or British culture is one such example.[11] On the other hand, some leisure practices are strikingly new – web-surfing for example – and bear little or only the most indirect resemblance to free-time activities in earlier ages.

Yet scholarship also indicates that not only the meaning and form of time free from work but also the significance of recreation in constituting individual identities has shifted dramatically in the past 150 years. Leisure time was relatively strictly tied to the dominant social hierarchies in earlier historical periods, just as clothing and other objects were. Festival culture offered opportunities for the momentary inversion of this hierarchy, to be sure, but it was an inversion that always reinscribed the legitimacy of social and religious power. That which was deconstructed eventually only reaffirmed authoritative construction. By contrast, in the late modern era, leisure, though restricted by income and many other social factors, took on a more dynamic character in relation to identity formation. One became increasingly identified with what one did at play, and what one did at play was relatively less determined by systems of status, social power, and cultural expectation than by individual choice. As noted below, such choices also came to be associated with *consumption* choices, and with both the purchase and use of commodities such as clothes, jewelry, furniture, cars, and food. There is much evidence for this theme in the chapters of this volume, though the cumulative effect of the book is also to push the discussion somewhat beyond what scholarship on consumption has achieved to date. Conversely, there is little evidence in the following chapters for the interpretation Horkheimer and Adorno would have proposed, namely that individual choice was only the modus operandi of a capitalist culture industry whose dominance was total.

The history of leisure has been inextricably intertwined with the history of work, and it is primarily the social history of the manual laboring classes that has directed attention to the way in which the advent of industrial capitalism created new conflicts over the control of time. New forms of work discipline demanded new apprehensions and disciplines of time, as E.P. Thompson once so elegantly argued.[12] Manufacturers and workers debated the possibilities and effects of shortened work time, the former fearing its consequences for the devotion to labor, the latter divided both as to its place in the political struggle and to the way in which working-class organizations could direct members' lives when away from work.[13] Such debates have continued throughout the history of industrial capitalism, from the moment when "Taylorist" forms of labor discipline first made inroads in the United States and later Europe, to the present, in which "instantaneous time" and other concepts spark disagreement and confusion over the proper relation between work and non-work.[14] The group of chapters assembled here do not delve into issues of work time and short hours movements, partly because there is already a developed scholarship on them, but partly also because our project was to concentrate more on the experience and meaning of leisure itself.

If control over the length and quality of work time was one of the central conflicts in the history of leisure, control over the content of time spent away from work was equally as significant. The relationship between leisure and consumption has been constitutive here. For many policy-makers and academics over the twentieth century, to fill leisure intelligently was by definition to avoid or severely control the blandishments of consumer society. To fill leisure intelligently, moreover, was often something for which only the most demanding individual could hope. Adorno and Horkheimer placed their belief in a complex practice of "negation," the requirements and procedures of which only the most disciplined and ideologically correct intellectuals could fathom. Gary Cross's history of the making of consumer culture discusses debates over whether "time," defined as "duration from both income-producing work and from consumption," or "money," discretionary income for non-essential goods, were to be preferred for wage earners in Britain, the United States, and France in the twentieth century.[15] The advocates of more "democratic" forms of leisure time set their sights somewhat lower than the Frankfurt School philosophers did, but they were often no less concerned about limiting or attacking the beachheads constructed in daily life outside the workplace by consumer industries. Among Victorian "recreationists," such efforts included not only consideration of the content of leisure but also the design of recreational spaces, from the home to seaside resort, to ensure that certain proper forms of leisure took place while others were marginalized.[16]

Significantly, gender history has dealt with the issue of leisure-consumption only gingerly. Although social history recognized the gender division of labor as a constitutive element of working-class experience, the gender division of consumption has received much less scholarly attention. One concern was that scholars, by studying women as purchasers of commodities, would reproduce regnant cultural assumptions about women's allegedly proper (and secondary) status as consumers rather than producers. There are of course now classic accounts of women as consumers in US and British society.[17] Such scholarship is less prevalent but by no means absent in the social and cultural history of the Europe. But a recent excellent volume on consumption and gender identity reveals how much more remains to be done in this genre.[18] Several of the chapters in *Histories of Leisure* touch on women's history, but this is not our primary focus. In contrast to most recent scholarship, however, there is considerable evidence here for a more explicit and focused history of masculinity as it relates to spectatorship, travel, clothing, drinking, and smoking. Compared to the historiography of women's consumption, only partially developed as it may be, the topic of men's leisure-time consumption is both understudied and undertheorized.[19]

Individual, class, and gender identities have been linked in scholarship to the history of leisure and consumption, but national identities have received much less explicit attention in this regard. Victoria De Grazia's seminal analyses of "bourgeois" and "Fordist" modes of consumption imply, but do not explicitly address, the question of whether or how national communities gain a sense of collective selfhood through patterns of leisure shaped by the act of purchasing commodities and services. The relatively less developed nature of scholarship on this topic has to do in part with the inattention with which historians have treated the national state's role in promoting, regulating, or dampening consumption in its subject population.[20] Scholarship on the United States' cultural impact on Europe – and on European responses to "Americanization" – is perhaps one of the most promising areas of research on the national dimensions of consumption.[21] Popular sport[22], from soccer matches to skiing[23], offers a rich area of research on leisure's role in the building of national identities. Such research remains rather scattered and unfocused for historians of late modern Europe, however, and some of it takes the national dimension for granted. What precisely is the relationship between individual or group patterns of consumption and national culture? When do national or state imperatives shape consumption choices, and how? Do chances for the expression of national differences through consumption increase or decrease with accelerating transnational flows of goods and people under (post-) modern conditions? In the present volume, the chapters by Auslander, Gundle, Judson, Palmowski, Thompson, Young, and Prior have evidence on national styles of leisure practice, while Hilton, Prior, Koshar, and Auslander offer information on the national state's interventions into leisure culture.

The chapters collected here have a tripartite structure based on active human agents seeing, traveling, and consuming. Of course, practices associated with each category overlap considerably, but the distinctions are useful nonetheless because they draw attention to meanings and forms with their own specificities. In the first category, the visual elements of leisure culture take center stage. Vanessa Schwartz and others have directed our attention to "spectacle" in urban culture in the late modern era, an argument that is relevant not only for this section but also for the material on tourism and consumption.[24] Wherever economic and cultural capital accumulated to become an image for mass consumption – in urban spaces, on the stage, in museums, in natural environments, in cinema – there one finds evidence for the growing power of the eye in shaping and directing leisure time. One recent study demonstrates how urban "surface values" contained in film, architecture, shop window displays, and advertising in Weimar Germany had a formative influence on what we understand as the culture of modernity.[25] Yet this development, so often associated with the nineteenth and twentieth centuries in particular, is not entirely new, though the forces and exigencies driving it in recent decades may be. Rather, a form of spectacle, or the determinant force of "surfaces," was not unknown to medieval and early modern Europe.

In Nick Prior's discussion of the museum and Marius Kwint's analysis of nature in the circus, we find examples of visual display whose origins may be located in the eighteenth century but whose influence resonates right into late modern history. In the case of the museum we find a characteristic "double-bind" of modernity in which aspirations to social exclusivity and expert control vied with what were increasingly more inclusive strategies of public mobilization and "improvement" coordinated by state agencies. This double bind was coterminous with the formation of mass leisure and urban cultures in which groups previously excluded from the halls of (artistic) learning gained increased access to the cultural capital deployed for visual consumption in museums and other venues. Marius Kwint's chapter focuses on the circus, a cultural production that from the beginning appealed to social elites and the popular classes alike, but which underwent a transformation in which the rowdier practices of the crowd were purged or regulated. Built in part on human mastery over animals – and more broadly on humankind's complex negotiations with its own natural history – the circus reformed the sights and sounds of carnival and other popular celebrations in a way that made it more palatable to the sensibilities of Victorian England.

If museums and circuses revealed important practices and assumptions about spectatorship, then Esther Leslie's chapter on flâneurs in Paris and Berlin and Erik Jensen's discussion of boxing crowds in 1920s Berlin provide even more direct information on this subject. Partly fact, partly fiction, the flâneur inhabited the changing public spaces of nineteenth-century Paris, scrutinized the streets and stores, and melted into the burgeoning crowds. Though usually allied to the figure of the artist or poet, the flâneur could also be the journalist-writer, the author of city feuilleton, or the critical leisure traveler– part tourist and part dandy. In some respects, as Leslie argues, the idle vigilance of the flâneur's gaze became common property for the urban dweller, at least for those who were determined to read urban spectacle as a play of potentially meaningful (or dangerous) surfaces.[26] Fittingly, Leslie concludes with Adorno and Horkheimer's insistence that the critical edge of the flâneur's activity was no longer possible in the age of the culture industry, but that predictions of the flâneur's demise were rife in the previous century as well. Does the flâneur's idle-critical gaze live on in the choices and appropriations of individuals in modern leisure culture?

The flâneur's existence was a comment on proper forms of spectatorship, with tourism as the foil against which the flâneur measured his (or her)[27] actions. Yet there were many other commentators and professionals who not only voiced concern about spectators but also tried to shape their behavior and educate them. Boxing crowds in 1920s Berlin were part of the new urban mass culture that made the German capital such a fascinating cauldron of activity before Hitler came to power. But Jensen notes that most scholarship on spectatorship has concentrated on the flâneurs and the movie-goers rather than on sports fans, who were certainly as numerous as any other type of spectator in this important era of a burgeoning leisure culture. Commentators in Weimar Germany were wary of the behavior and composition of sports crowds, and boxing crowds in particular seemed to offer much grist for their mill, since boxing had been associated since before World War I with crass sensationalism and blood lust. Yet there were also many members of the middle and upper classes who flocked to the boxing matches, some of Weimar's avant-garde cultural luminaries not the least among them. Sports writers and feuilletonists tried to exercise influence over these diverse crowds, advocating a form of spectatorship that downplayed boxing's violence or salaciousness in favor of highlighting technical skill and expert knowledge. Opinion makers' anxiousness over the proper form of boxing viewership was, argues Jensen, a reflection of broader anxieties about how German society fit together on the eve of the disastrous economic and political crisis that led to Adolf Hitler.

Leisure travel might include attendance at museums, circuses, or sports events, and the eye of the traveler is not so far removed from the restive and vigilant gaze of the flâneur. The chapters in Part II concentrate more directly on the practice of tourism as a significant element of late modern leisure culture. Of all the texts and markers that give significance to the tourist experience, travel guidebooks are among the most significant.[28] Fittingly, it was in the first half of the nineteenth century that such publications became more standardized and accessible to a touring public that increasingly included not the sons and daughters only of aristocratic or high bourgeois elites but also members of the professional and business middle classes. These tourist-readers needed reliable guidebooks that allowed the traveler to cover a good deal of ground on a relatively limited budget in a shorter time span than that which had been available to the comfortable scions of European elites as they took their leisurely Grand Tour. Jan Palmowski discusses the venerable Baedeker guidebooks to Europe and their relationship to middle-class consumers. He argues that the history of the guidebook reveals much about not only the class and gender identities of English travelers abroad but also their sense of national belongingness. But he also maintains that the English bourgeoisie derived a strong sense of identification with the European continent through the use of the Baedeker guides; leisure travel created a kind of layered identity through which both national and broadly European sensibilities were formed. Palmowski's discussion reveals how a still rather underutilized historical source, the travel guidebook, offers a rich and complex window through which cultural assumptions and social practices may be explored.

If an important figure of late modern leisure culture was the newly ambulatory traveler, then the bicycle was one of his or her most important machines. Considered by many to be a force for democratization, the bicycle aroused fears of social disruption, especially among the bourgeoisie, who worried that when the "lower orders" used the new vehicle they would flout the sporting etiquette of the "bicycling gentleman." Of course, bourgeois women raised fears of social upheaval as well when they used the bicycle as a source of emancipation – spatial, social, sexual, and sartorial. But Christopher Thompson's discussion focuses on bicycling culture's relationship to shifting class tensions and identities, and thereby pinpoints some of the important ways in which leisure activity had direct political and social consequences in Belle Epoque France. What comes through clearly is how much bourgeois elites wanted to control the burgeoning population of working-class cyclists – and how uneven their success was in light of the fact that only 5.5 percent of French bicyclists belonged to clubs that might have come under official supervision. With close to 3 million cyclists traveling on French roads before World War I, the chances that bicycling culture could be directly shaped or dominated by state officials or the social elite seem to have been slim indeed.

For some, bicycling represented a mass sport that created the opportunity for national cohesion and cultural solidarity. Precisely these values were in the forefront of efforts by German-speaking nationalist organizations in the Austro-Hungarian empire on the eve of World War I to use tourism for political gain. Pieter Judson offers a rich analysis of Austrian groups that used "nationalist tourism" to promote their particular vision of national identity in a situation fraught with ethnic and political conflict. Urging tourists in Cisleithania (the non-Hungarian half of the Dual Monarchy, or Austria-Hungary) to plan and measure their trips according to nationalist criteria, the promoters of nationalist leisure travel had a diverse and often unintended impact in the regions in which they worked. Whereas tourist industries were built up in areas such as the Bohemian Woods, it was unclear if this was due primarily to an increase in national enthusiasms, or to a careful assessment of the economic gains to be had by bringing in more tourists. In one direction, the activists of nationalist tourism contributed to that paralysis at the center of the Empire that pitted different ethnic communities against one another and that strengthened the state's allergic reactions to all expressions of national identity. But at the "periphery," in the towns and villages where leisure travelers attended local festivals, bought souvenirs, and ate in local restaurants, nationalist tourism broadened economic development and mobilized local populations to participate in community decision-making. The intertwining of leisure culture and politics thus operated in very different ways at different levels of state and society.

Nationalist tourism was of course not at all unknown to other European countries, though its effects in the multiethnic Dual Monarchy were strikingly complex. Even so, in France, where, as Patrick Young writes here, a growing network of bourgeois promoters built up French tourism with the intention not only of making money but also renewing the nation, a kind of nationalist tourism also had multifaceted results. The focus of Young's chapter is the Touring Club de France, which, more forcefully than other similar associations, articulated a highly modern vision of tourism in which moral, physical, cultural, economic, and political motivations were embedded.[29] One of the central ambitions of the tourist associations was to create new tourist attractions other than those that had attracted attention up to 1890, such as spas and beaches. This task entailed developing and promoting *la France profonde*, the traditional regions of the country that offered scenic vistas and a greater sense of authenticity than Paris or the crowded beaches offered. This vision, encompassing geography, cuisine, climate, history, peasant culture, and architecture, was based on an "ethic of reconciliation" conducive to the project of republican state-building. Class, regional, and political differences ideally dissolved in this perspective, as French tourists, consuming the spectacle of regional and local peculiarities, discovered their profound connectivities as members of a republican community. One could argue that the gap between vision and social reality was not as great in the French touristic vision of the nation as it was in Austria, to take an obvious contrast. But Young's conclusion leaves little doubt that the ideal of national reconciliation through leisure travel in the regions was above all an urban middle-class ideal increasingly stamped by the exigencies of consumption and state-building.

It is useful in this context to recall Christopher Thompson's discussion of the way in which a notionally inclusive leisure activity such as bicycling raised severe doubts about national and social cohesion. In Stephen Harp's account of early-twentieth-century French tourism and the Michelin Red Guides, we receive another important reminder of how tourism, as an act of desired reconciliation, was open to a whole array of social tensions. In this instance, however, not the train or bicycle but the automobile is the primary means of transportation, and gastronomy is the focus of the travel experience. Unlike the venerable Baedeker guides, which gave short shrift to the automobile until the 1930s, the *Guide Michelin*, published first in 1900 and free of charge, was based on the vision of the bourgeois head of household traveling for pleasure with his family by car – and preferably riding Michelin tires. Such mechanized patriarchal tourism befit France not only because French roads were higher in quality than those of any other European country before World War I, but also because the French automobile industry produced more cars than all other European countries combined from 1902 to 1907.[30] Beside emphasizing repair shops and tire suppliers, the Michelin guides paid close attention to hotel prices, the availability of gasoline, the hygienic quality of overnight accommodations, and (especially after 1918) food. Gastronomic tourism had of course always been available to the well-heeled devotees of the Grand Tour, but throughout the nineteenth century, and now more forcefully just before and after World War I, food came to play a greater role in leisure travel than ever before. Not only the wealthy bourgeoisie, but now also an expanding caravan of middle-class motorists were interested in dining while traveling, and the Michelin guides became the central authority in this area. Guidebook itineraries focused on different classes of restaurants allowed the automobilist family to conduct a *tour de la France gastronomique*, literally eating their way through the country. That food-based touring was seen by the guidebook publishers as an essential part of Frenchness was reflected in the fact that they ignored foreign cuisine, even in the French empire, where it was assumed (usually correctly) that in Morocco, Algeria, and Tunisia, French people ate French food. Harp demonstrates that the Michelin guides amounted to a most sophisticated form of advertising, which on the one hand reinforces criticisms of the culture industry's totalizing influence on free time. Yet Harp concludes with the point that we do not yet understand the problem of reception and use when it comes to historical study of travel guidebooks. Moreover, insofar that these publications were developed in close conjunction with the perceived needs and interests of their readers, their history suggests a complex intertwining of production and consumption, authorship and reception, rather than a one-way imposition of values from above.

My own contribution to this volume also deals with motorized tourism, but this time in Germany between the world wars. Germany, the country in which the internal combustion engine was invented and pioneers such as Carl Benz and

Gottlieb Daimler produced cars that would become (*pace* Cadillac) the standard of world automotive engineering, nonetheless ranked far behind France and England in the production and use of the car. After World War I, the automobile was still primarily used for leisure in Germany, and Hitler's radical-populist vision of a motorized nation derived much of its force from the idea of cars and roads that gave unprecedented numbers of Germans access to a modern forms of travel and consumption. The exigencies of planning for war, always foremost in Hitler's mind, called for controls on both automobile production and tourism, but this did not mean that Germans themselves gave up the hope of driving for pleasure. The building of the Autobahn, envisioned and planned before Hitler but realized in part under the Nazi regime, did much to further popular hopes of motorized leisure. The Autobahn was regarded by the regime as an important constituent of Nazi propaganda, but some drivers insisted that it called for new, more socially sensitive, driving practices, and new forms of interaction between Germans themselves. While the sense of social engagement spawned by driving the new superhighways was finally based on Nazi concepts of racial identity and "blood," writers such as Heinrich Hauser were also determined to emphasize the participatory qualities of the experience. Leisure driving demanded reciprocity, a sense of citizenship, from which many (like the Jewish literature scholar Viktor Klemperer) were agonizingly excluded, but which also connoted involvement and selfhood. Not for long could the Autobahn be used as an instrument of totalitarian domination, the efforts of the Nazi culture industry notwithstanding. Closely intertwined with the visions and practices of political community, motorized leisure travel in National Socialist Germany revealed a multiplicity of meanings and contingencies over which the regime had only imperfect control.

All the chapters in this volume deal in one way or another with modern consumption practices, but in Part III the contributions put the emphasis more directly on specific commodities, material objects, images, and modes of consumption. Robert Goodrich discusses alcohol consumption among Catholic workers in Cologne and other Rhenish cities in Imperial Germany, analyzing drink as a social boundary. Goodrich demonstrates that working-class drink cultures were part of a "whole way of life," to use Raymond Williams's still evocative term.[31] Drink cultures were rooted in a *habitus*, the term deployed by Pierre Bourdieu to analyze mediations between the inherent limiting and enabling features of cultural practice. In some respects, Goodrich's analysis parallels that of Thompson's discussion of French bicycling culture. Just as bourgeois cycling groups tried to delimit and shape working-class sports in Belle Epoque France, Cologne municipal and religious authorities as well as Catholic working-class officials tried to deflect the worker from his *Kölsch* beer or schnapps. But just as Thompson's conclusion leads to doubt as to the broader success of cultural control, Goodrich's chapter presents evidence of the durability of working-class drinking patterns. Moreover, Goodrich shows that workers distinguished between different kinds of drinking, in contrast to bourgeois and working-class reformers, who made a more coarsely grained connection between alcohol and dissolution. Above all, mediation rather than determinacy belongs at the center of a theory of leisure consumption, Goodrich argues.

Much the same point could be made about masculine clothing, according to material presented by Christopher Breward in the only contribution in this volume that has been published elsewhere.[32] Breward's detailed explication shows how suburban middle-class and lower-middle-class men, alongside working-class consumers, either integrated the "fashionable commodity" and its imagery into local "fashion systems" or used it for more resistant and subcultural aims in turn-of-the-century London. The point of mediation in this process of purchase, appropriation, and subversive reuse was the music hall, which relied on a kind of grammar of fashion knowledge to which performers and audience subscribed. On one level, Breward's discussion offers a finely elaborated study of how material culture had become a dynamic element in the building of masculine social identities in the rapidly changing fin-de-siècle metropolis, where just about all markers of social distinction were up for grabs. On another level, he shows how particular points in the leisure culture spectrum, in this case popular song and the venues in which it was performed, served as switching points and "archives" in the use of material objects. That the making of masculine identities relied as much on consumption as feminine identities did is of course a seemingly obvious but still overlooked argument in contemporary social history writing. That such male consumption also often revolved around personal appearance and adornment – a kind of aesthetic repertoire – is an even less widely recognized point for which the historiography of leisure culture ought to have particular sensitivity.

The aesthetic repertoire of Jews in Paris and Berlin from just after World War I to the Holocaust is the subject of Leora Auslander's innovative discussion. Here the concept of an aesthetic repertoire refers to the furnishings and other everyday objects with which Jews living in Paris and Berlin surrounded themselves. The evidence for this piece is culled not only from memoirs, diaries, and photographs,[33] but also from an unlikely and disturbing source, namely the Nazi record of expropriation and auction of real estate and personal belongings from Paris and Berlin Jews in World War II. Auslander argues that everyday objects were used by Jews to signal likenesses and differences between themselves and non-Jews and between different groups of Jews. She points out significant differences in the manner in which Parisian and Berlin Jews responded to the greater presence of the poorer and more obviously "Jewish"-looking Eastern European Jews in the French and German capitals. Whereas the Jews of Paris seem to have reacted defensively to the newcomers from the East, the Jews of Berlin were less anxious about them, revealing perhaps that a strong sense of conformity in everyday habit and taste was not required of them. She theorizes that the power of the nation did much to determine such responses, although she wisely notes that the full complexity of this issue must await a fuller discussion elsewhere. That variations on the dominant pattern of purchase and use of everyday objects can be explained by reference to individual, rather than "Jewish taste," is a further significant result of Auslander's interesting comparison.

In his study of tobacco use, Matthew Hilton addresses a social practice that is unlike other forms of leisure consumption such as sports spectatorship or drinking insofar that it was not confined to a particular site or time of day. Moreover, he uses tobacco, just as Breward uses male fashion systems and Goodrich "confessional drinking," to make a point about how the *experience* of leisure has an important role to play in the making of broader political identities and social movements. Smoking was a ubiquitous practice, enjoyed by 80 percent of the adult male population and 40 percent of the adult female population in Britain in 1950. That it had a multiplicity of meanings is not too surprising, but Hilton demonstrates that liberal, bourgeois values of independence and individuality came to represent most authoritatively the appeal of smoking in the course of the twentieth century. Significantly, this occurred even when the standardized cigarette became widespread between the world wars, and it explained much of the reaction with which male and female smokers responded to mounting evidence of the disastrous effects their habit had both for themselves and those around them. Although the habit-forming effects of cigarettes and the tobacco companies' advertising and propaganda contributed to smokers' resistance to health warnings, it was finally the idea, reinforced in daily use, cinema, and popular literature, that smoking had much to do with individual identity that proved to be most central. In Europe and North America, the evolution of consumer consciousness is regarded as a positive step, but what if consumers defend leisure practices, such as cigarette smoking and excessive automobile use, that harm the environment and the population? The history of tobacco usage, seen by many as a last refuge of individualism in the face of state power and health professionals' grasping intrusion in daily life, offers a rich test case for such a question.

Like Hilton's chapter, Stephen Gundle's handling of the history of "glamour" in Italy brings the volume into the post-World War II era. Gundle discusses not a specific commodity or practice but rather what might be called an "aura" of glamour constituted by style, commodities, physical beauty, architecture, spectacle, fashion, celebrity, and even body language and attitude. When represented in illustrated magazines and the cinema, glamour became an important point of entry for American influences among an Italian population hungry for new goods and images after the ravages of war. It had important political consequences because it worked to feed individual dreams of consumption and pleasure that seemed to erode the old class rigidities while simultaneously reinforcing hierarchies of social power. Hollywood, the heart of the culture industry for which Adorno and Horkheimer reserved such vituperation, was the wellspring of glamour in the twentieth century. For Europeans, of course, Hollywood was a two-edged sword, representing both modernity's promise and the threat of American domination. After World War II, such fears notwithstanding, many Italians were ready to embrace things American, just as many other Europeans were. American cinema and American film stars like Rita Hayworth and Tyrone Power were the seductive representatives of the glamorous life. While Italian culture eventually produced its own stars, it could not have done so without the American example, argues Gundle. When Italian glamour developed home-grown images of pleasure and consumption, represented by the uncrowned Italian queen Gina Lollobrigida, not only were they not identical to American prototypes, but also they were not without their similarities to the original. In the working out of such differences, both in film and in the growing fashion industry, in the urban spectacle provided by Roman celebrities living *la dolce vita*, and in the turn to mass consumption, Italian glamour and its audiences still held to older notions of family, land, and craft tradition. Substance rather than image still held primacy even when the language of glamour spoke (broken) American English.

The cumulative effect of the chapters reinforces the argument of the impressive multiplicity of histories embedded in leisure culture. This point may seem obvious, perhaps, but scholarship has done relatively little to map these varied temporalities and narratives, or to understand their historical dimensions and interrelationships. Such a mapping will lead to the conclusion that the study of leisure allows for a much less dichotomized view of social relationships than the topic usually implies. Leisure practices cannot be assigned to the "private" sphere, for example, in whatever form scholars render that problematic concept. Nor can tried and true divisions between work and leisure be maintained in a historical analysis that does justice to the complexity of the subject. Concepts and experiences of leisure have always interacted with definitions and practices of work; it is not labor as such that defines how leisure is conceptualized, either by expert observers or actual participants, but rather labor and leisure are intertwined, the one reciprocating the other's contradictions and tensions. Max Weber argued before 1914 that the modern work experience had become so debilitating that leisure was necessarily seen as an antidote to work, or as a necessary escape to steel one for the rigors of continuous and enervating drudgery in factory, office, and school.[34] Even if one were to accept this interpretation, it is logical to argue that the historical evolution of a "leisure society," to use a misleading but perhaps indispensable notion, reversed the earlier terms of the relationship between work and free time. It was no longer the character (or duration) of work that carved out new social spaces for leisure practice but rather leisure that changed how we defined work, what we expected from it, how long it should last, and how it should be regulated. Social history's privileging of the work experience may have been defensible when the topic was early industrialization, when leisure time was a precious commodity for the majority of laborers. As the historian's view moves closer to the present, however, it is the *full* interdependence of notions of work and leisure that offer a better conceptual point of departure. It was precisely this interdependence that led some interwar British commentators to claim that their country's slow decline in industrial efficiency was caused in part by the working man's overdeveloped interest in sport and hobbies.

Beyond this, the preceding chapters suggest that political, economic, cultural, social, and environmental factors are embedded in the history of leisure practices. To disentangle them analytically is part of the project of historical mapping as well. As Stephen Harp notes, the history of tourism cannot dispense with the history of labor, since leisure travel is made possible by the labor of others. Environmental history enters the picture at every turn, whether the subject is motorized tourism on the German Autobahn, train travel through the "unknown France" of the provinces, or smoking habits of British men and women. In the United States, leisure often operated as the point of mediation between the social and the natural. "Factories and cities took humans away from nature," writes Richard White of American perceptions, "leisure brought them back."[35] What variations on this theme existed for Europeans? Politics, too, play a role in the story, and not only because identities formed in leisure activities often provide the basis for political and social movements, an important subject to which we return below. Leora Auslander's sources are the direct result of a policy of genocide, it must be remembered, and here too the historical analysis of leisure leads the scholar directly to questions of the distribution of power, of winners and losers, of perpetrators and victims, and of trauma and pleasure. Scholarship often recognizes such interconnections, but the continuous tendency of historical research to place leisure culture "after" other categories, whether those categories are derived from economic, political, or social history, suggests that the point needs explicit reinforcement.

The mapping of the histories of leisure needs to be done in a more practical sense as well. What are the proper subjects? This volume cannot claim to offer a comprehensive overview of the vast sphere of leisure practices, to be sure. Among the areas we have not explored are cinema going, mass sporting spectacles such as soccer or rugby, and hobbies. Some themes are obvious, and have received adequate attention, but what of activities such as smoking, which, as Hilton notes, is not confined to specific sites or times, or listening to music on MP3 players, which can be done at work, at home, or even (to teachers' dismay) in classrooms? Some of the more standard topics have gained increased attention in the 1990s, but even these are rather unevenly mapped. Travel is now one of the best researched topics, but it still has not made it into the historical "canon."[36] But what of virtual travel and web-surfing? Such "imaginative mobilities" may engender radical transformations in contemporaries' understanding of the public sphere and civil society.[37] Or television, for which systematic historical research palls in the face of this medium's enormous cultural impact? The study of radio listening habits in German society, a topic full of possibility for researching women's identities in the early twentieth century, to say nothing of the importance of its use for political propaganda, came under really serious scrutiny from scholars only recently.[38] One could mention many other areas. The rejoinder here may be predictable: that leisure practices are generally comparable across types, and that analysis of each specific genre may be likened to carrying so many coals to Newcastle. But the chapters here and other research makes one skeptical about such criticism. It is the historical inassimilability of various leisure forms to larger interpretative models, whether derived from theories of the "culture industry," from narratives built around the idea of the "society of the spectacle," or even from the work of now popular theorists such as Pierre Bourdieu, that comes through most clearly in the preceding contributions. This sheer centrifugality is to be welcomed, for it suggests that beneath it all there is still much room for individual initiative, for resistant or subversive practice, or simply for a degree of pleasure and self-satisfaction that can still not be tapped by projects of social domination – or by an overarching conceptual framework that finally does much violence to the historical actors and experiences it purports to illuminate. In German historiography, the operative term in this context is *Eigensinn*, which Alf Lüdtke has used to analyze the self-affirming words, gestures, pauses, pranks, or actions of workers on the shopfloor as they choose to conform to or dissent from their lifeworld.[39]

If recognition of such self-expressive variety raises the issue of what forms of leisure still need to be studied, then a similar assessment also applies to the historical and political location of various leisure practices. In this book readers are presented with an impressive range of examples drawn from late Georgian to late-twentieth-century Britain; from Imperial, Weimar, and Nazi Germany; from Third Republic and Vichy France; and from the Austro-Hungarian empire and post-World War II Italy. What significance does leisure have in these different political contexts? What impact does political culture have on prevalent meanings of pleasure or desire? Our examples suffice to demonstrate that in general we have much more information about a practice such as leisure travel as it evolved in relatively free, liberal societies than in fascist or Communist dictatorships. It is not insignificant that leisure and consumption are among the least researched topics in the history of Nazi Germany even though these twelve dramatic years have given rise to a veritable cottage industry of popular and scholarly writing built around the dire narratives of war and genocide. As for post-1945 socialist states of Eastern Europe, it is in the history of leisure practices (the desire for them, the perceived need to have more of them, and the disgruntlement felt at being denied them) that we find some of the sources of opposition to Communist rule that finally brought 1989 into the historical pantheon.[40]

The contributors to this volume are less given to the kind of anxiousness that once characterized so much scholarly opinion about the relationship between leisure and consumption. But this does not mean that the authors regard processes of commercialization or commodification as unproblematic. Nor should it imply that the march of consumer society through contemporary history was a foregone conclusion. Rather, the growing authority of a culture of commodity purchase and display within leisure activities was the result of specific decisions taken in the past by a variety of actors, whether travel entrepreneurs in provincial France, the organizers of the eighteenth- and nineteenth-century circus, or consumers themselves. To study the history of leisure is in some respects to ask the same questions that historians of consumption have asked: what degree of agency should be attributed to shoppers, travelers, or spectators? What is more, scholars who focus on relations between the commodity form and leisure have a rather mixed bag with which to work if they turn to the research on consumer societies. The historiography of consumption is quite uneven, with areas of rather bright illumination and impressive detail, but also with many time periods, subjects, and historical processes very much underdeveloped. The United States and early modern Britain have received much attention, for instance, while mainland Europe is much less richly researched. As with the history of leisure travel, socialist consumerism is still very much *terra incognita*. Finally, whereas there is considerable correspondence between the historical map of leisure and that of consumption, there are also disparities. For example, in the social history of continental Europe, the history of nutrition and working-class household budgets, which is to say the history of certain necessary forms of social reproduction, is much more thoroughly worked out than is the history of the purchase and use of "non-essential" goods and practices.[41]

The historiography of consumption has been dominated by either the process of mediation (as in advertising) or by the study of the act of purchase itself.[42] The actual social use of material objects has come in for much less historical scholarship. This disparity exists across a range of cognate areas, for example, the history of technology, which has been dominated until recently by narratives of invention and production rather than of use.[43] This is by no means a logical consequence of the focus on objects since, as Hannah Arendt once noted, consumption connotes not only the act of buying but also the process of "using up."[44] How commodities are deployed in daily life, how they come to be embedded in the complex interstices of the family or the workplace, and how they may be discarded or passed on to future generations are topics that need much more attention in research on leisure culture than they have received. Leora Auslander's chapter, as well as her work on furniture and power in France,[45] illustrate the possibilities of such research for understanding how leisure culture is constituted in part by the positioning and manipulation of "things." From a more theorized perspective, Dick Hebdige's interesting studies of the Italian motor scooter and other artifacts of European youth culture also merit attention in this context, as does Arjun Appadurai's seminal collection of essays on the "social life of things."[46] Just as we have little in the way of an empirically satisfying and properly theorized history of consumption as cultural "production,"[47] so there is precious little scholarship that shows how the work of leisure is often dependent on artifacts and objects brought to bear on it. What "things" circulate most prominently in the history of certain leisure practices? How do human users perceive and manipulate those things to create webs of meaning?

Not all "things" are equal, to be sure. Some material objects can be manipulated ad infinitum, it would seem, but others have a more constitutive character in everyday life. The question of technology and leisure culture has barely been addressed in the literature, for example, even though theoretical perspectives and public opinion earlier in the century would logically have made this one of the first areas of research. The impact of technology not just in urban life or industry but in everyday rhythms and practices was an important part of Horkheimer's and Adorno's concern. In *Dialectic of Englightenment*, they insisted that leisure had become organized according to the tempos and exigencies of the assembly line, a perspective that drew in part on the interwar observations of critics such as Siegfried Kracauer. Kracauer thought he depicted the forms and temporalities of modern industry in stadium spectacles and cabaret dance troupes such as the Tiller Girls, though he was careful not to reduce these cultural forms to epiphenomena of capitalist production techniques.[48] But there is an even deeper issue of the character of the machine itself, and of its power to determine the physics of human action. Having discussed everything from refrigerator and car doors to sliding window frames, Adorno wrote in *Minima Moralia*, published in 1944, "the movements machines demand of their users already have the violent, hard-hitting, unresting jerkiness of Fascist maltreatment."[49] It would have been illuminating to ask Adorno which machines, in his opinion, educed "movements" that were democratic or liberating. But the general point was clear enough: the Frankfurt School scholar envisioned a universe in which the physical motions and perceptions associated with "free" time were shaped by an industrial-technological matrix of which fascism was the most recent and dangerous political emanation. The progressive or emancipatory potential of machinic culture was, in this view, eviscerated by an insidious geometry of repression.

Clearly, the issue of how people related to technology during leisure time is an important issue. One could make this point with reference to obvious topics, such as the impact of radio (in the 1930s) or television (in the 1950s) in the home. But it is not only an issue of the passivity with which moderns reacted to the penetration of technology or mass media in their private lives. In Europe and North America, the 1950s and 1960s saw an increase in the "do-it-yourself" movement, which included gardening, woodworking, and the like, but also included much popular technology, especially among people who built their own radios, or worked on cars. In many parts of the United States after World War II, but also in Europe, entire subcultures grew up around the appropriation and modification of automotive technologies.[50] This history continues, of course, and now includes a transnational dimension even more pronounced than in earlier decades of the twentieth century. For example, "tuning culture" began in Japan in the 1960s but soon made its way into the United States, first on the West Coast but then in other parts of the country. It includes automotive shops, magazines, websites, and countless social interactions among young men (and not a few women) who customize, display, and race Hondas, Acuras, Toyotas, Nissans, and other Asian automobiles. This is a rich – and massively overlooked – chapter in the history of social assertion over technologies in daily life.

Questions of passivity or agency go directly to the problem of the history of experience and emotion. How people experience leisure time has much to do with the meanings they derive, the memories they preserve, and the anticipation with which they approach the future. Recently, scholars of modern German history have called for closer attention to how the history of pleasure weaves itself through the violence of the twentieth century. This issue derives much of its moral energy not only from the history of genocide but also from the extraordinary bifurcation of German history in the twentieth century between an age of war and an age of unprecedented prosperity. One of the most surprising aspects of an otherwise deeply troubling memoir of life in Nazi Germany is the record of the Jewish professor Viktor Klemperer's experiences with learning how to drive a car, a subject taken up in my chapter on German driving practices.[51] Klemperer's enjoyment of the automobile symbolized a degree of freedom at a moment when German Jews' ability to act as normal citizens was being cut away on a daily basis by the Nazi regime. For the German "Aryan" population, however, the interpenetration of persecution and pleasure was of a different nature. Regime policies of persecution and genocide rested in part on the Nazis' capacity to maintain a relatively normal standard of living for most of the population, and postwar economic well-being derived much of its initial energy from the buildup of industrial capacity under the Nazis. From the demand side, meanwhile, Germans, supported in part by a tradition of bourgeois self-cultivation, could easily regard consumption as an important function of identity formation without troubling themselves about the larger exploitations on which it rested.

But the concatenation of pleasure and pain in the twentieth century is a subject for other histories as well, as suggested in Eric Hobsbawm's synthesis of modern world history, an "age of extremes."[52] One topic in which the extremes of contemporary history come to light most forcefully is in the European experience with imperialism and colonialism. Kristin Ross's evocative study of French popular culture in the 1950s and 1960s makes an explicit link among France's past as an imperial power, decolonization, and the compensatory reordering of French society as an Americanized culture based on specific consumption and leisure practices. In this analysis, modernized France derives its identity from forgetting a history of colonial exploitation, and thereby creates a social formation in which new forms of racism and discrimination against Algerians and North Africans, most notably, but also other ethnic groups, are made possible. Cars, cinema, and notions of cleanliness in everyday life all play a role in this process whereby a violent colonial past is "replaced" by a modern leisure society built around not only desire for commodities but a process of demarcation against groups that are deemed unworthy of inclusion.[53]

The relationship of the pleasure/pain nexus to the project of mapping histories of leisure returns us to the questions raised by Adorno and Horkheimer, if not to the answers they offered. The history of leisure culture is clearly also the history of political culture, indeed of citizenship in the broad sense of social participation. As the chapters in this volume demonstrate, this is not a matter only of the development of a sense of citizenship that includes the right to leisure, however defined, though this is an important and still largely unwritten part of the story. As definitions of citizenship are transformed under conditions of transnational movement and exchange, narratives of leisure history, in both exemplary and cautionary modes, will undoubtedly play a key role. But it is also a question of how our experience of leisure may lead to particular and often diametrically opposed political positions. Not an epiphenomenon of state and political action, leisure is seen as a set of practices and connectivities that gives rise to notions of community, rights, and belonging that are constitutive of how individuals situate themselves in their societies. For the Frankfurt School exiles from Nazi Germany, modern individuals were always "the situated," never agents of their own lives. The contributors to this volume do not deny the possibility of this critical or negative analysis of leisure culture, but they do find it constricting and narrow, and they present evidence demonstrating that it is far too dismissive of nuances and variations in the historical fabric. That this fabric is made up of many other strands and patterns than those examined in this volume, many other ways of practicing leisure through seeing, traveling, and consuming, should spur further research in this rich field of study.

Notes

1. Max Horkheimer and Theodor W. Adorno, *Dialectic of Enlightenment* (New York: Continuum, 1999), p. 137.

2. Ibid.

3. See Simon During (ed.), *The Cultural Studies Reader* (London and New York: Routledge, 1993), pp. 31–2.

4. Horkheimer and Adorno, *Dialectic of Enlightenment*, p. 121.

5. Ibid., p. 120.

6. See Gary Cross, *Time and Money: The Making of Consumer Culture* (London and New York: Routledge, 1993), pp. 15–75.

7. Quoted in Pauline Madow, "Introduction," in *Recreation in America* (New York: H.W. Wilson, 1965), p. 9.

8. "Leisure," *Oxford English Dictionary Online* (Oxford: Oxford University Press, 2001).

9. Horkheimer and Adorno, *Dialectic of Enlightenment*, p. 120.

10. Peter Burke, "Viewpoint: The Invention of Leisure in Early Modern Europe," *Past and Present* 146 (February 1995), pp. 136–50; Joan-Lluis Marfany, "Debate: The Invention of Leisure in Early Modern Europe," *Past and Present* 156 (August 1997), pp. 174–97, and Burke's reply in the same issue, pp. 192–7.

11. For these and other examples: Gary Cross, *A Social History of Leisure since 1600* (State College, PA: Venture, 1990).

12. E.P. Thompson, "Time, Work Discipline and Industrial Capitalism," *Past and Present* 38 (1967), pp. 59–91; Peter N. Stearns, *European Society in Upheaval: Social History since 1750*, 2nd edn (New York: Macmillan, 1975), pp. 163–5.

13. Cross, *Time and Money*, pp. 76–98; for a review of Cross and other literature on the subject, see Richard Weight, "The Politics of Pleasure: The Left, Class Culture, and Leisure in England, 1918–1960," *Journal of Urban History* 20, 2 (1994), pp. 252–70.

14. On "instantaneous time," see John Urry, *Sociology beyond Societies: Mobilities for the Twenty-First Century* (London and New York: Routledge, 2000), ch. 5.

15. Cross, *Time and Money*, p. 5.

16. See for example, Mark Billinge, "A Time and Place for Everything: An Essay on Recreation, Re-Creation and the Victorians," *Journal of Historical Geography* 22, 4 (1996), pp. 443–59.

17. For a useful overview of the literature: Mary Louise Roberts, "Gender, Consumption, and Commodity Culture," *American Historical Review* 103, 3 (1998), pp. 817–44.

18. Victoria de Grazia (with Ellen Furlough) (eds), *The Sex of Things: Gender and Consumption in Historical Perspective* (Berkeley and Los Angeles: University of California Press, 1996).

19. See the argument and citation of literature in Mark A. Swienicki, "Consuming Brotherhood: Men's Culture, Style, and Recreation as Consumer Culture, 1880–1930," *Journal of Social History* 31, 4 (1998), pp. 773–808; see also Christopher Breward, *The Hidden Consumer: Masculinities, Fashion and City Life 1860–1914* (Manchester: Manchester University Press, 1999), ch. 6 of which appears as Chapter 13 in this volume; Mike J. Huggins, "More Sinful Pleasures? Leisure, Respectability and the Male Middle Classes in Victorian England," *Journal of Social History* 33, 3 (2000), pp. 585–600. For examples from German working-class history, see the review essay by Nicholas Stargardt, "Male

Bonding and the Class Struggle in Imperial Germany," *Historical Journal* 38, 1 (1995), pp. 175–93.

20. See De Grazia, "Introduction," in *Sex of Things*, pp. 1–10, as well as her introductions to the individual sections of the collection; see also De Grazia, "Changing Consumption Regimes in Europe, 1930–1970: Comparative Perspectives on the Distribution Problem," in Susan Strasser, Charles McGovern, and Matthias Judt (eds) *Getting and Spending: European and American Consumer Societies in the Twentieth Century*, (Cambridge: Cambridge University Press, 1998).

21. Erica Carter, *How German is She? Postwar West German Reconstruction and the Consuming Woman* (Ann Arbor, MI: University of Michigan Press, 1997); Richard Kuisel, *Seducing the French: The Dilemma of Americanization* (Berkeley and Los Angeles: University of California Press, 1993); Kristin Ross, *Fast Cars, Clean Bodies: Decolonization and the Reordering of French Culture* (Cambridge, MA: MIT Press, 1996); Reinhold Wagnleitner, *Coca-Colonization and the Cold War: The Cultural Mission of the United States in Austria after the Second World War* (Chapel Hill, NC: University of North Carolina Press, 1994).

22. John Lowerson (ed.), *Sport and the English Middle Classes, 1870–1914* (Manchester: Manchester University Press, 1993).

23. See for example Sverker Sorlin, "Nature, Skiing and Swedish Nationalism," *International Journal of the History of Sport* 12, 2 (1995), pp. 147–63.

24. Vanessa Schwartz, *Spectacular Realities: Early Mass Culture in Fin-de-Siècle France* (Berkeley and Los Angeles: University of California Press, 1998); M. Christine Boyer, *The City of Collective Memory: Its Historical Imagery and Architectural Entertainments* (Cambridge, MA: The MIT Press, 1994); the classic statement is by Guy Debord, *La Société du spectacle* (Paris: Buchet/Chastel, 1967).

25. Janet Ward, *Weimar Surfaces: Urban Visual Culture in 1920s Germany* (Berkeley and Los Angeles: University of California Press, 2001).

26. Peter Fritzsche, *Berlin 1900* (Cambridge, MA: Harvard University Press, 1996).

27. Female flânerie is an understudied topic: see Anke Gleber, *The Art of Taking a Walk: Flanerie, Literature, and Film in Weimar Culture* (Princeton, NJ: Princeton University Press, 1999), pp. 171–213.

28. See Rudy Koshar, *German Travel Cultures* (Oxford and New York: Berg, 2000).

29. For discussion of an analogous organization, see R.J.B. Bosworth, "The *Touring Club Italiano* and the Nationalization of the Italian Bourgeoisie," *European History Quarterly* 27 (1997), pp. 371–410.

30. James J. Flink, *The Automobile Age* (Cambridge, MA and London: MIT Press, 1988), p. 19.

31. Raymond Williams, *Marxism and Literature* (Oxford: Oxford University Press, 1977), pp. 11–20.

32. Breward, *Hidden Consumer*, ch. 6.

33. Family photographs are a ubiquitous but underutilized source for the history of everyday leisure. See Oddlaug Reiakvam, "Reframing the Family Photograph," *Journal of Popular Culture* 26, 4 (1993), pp. 39–67.

34. See John Patrick Diggens, *Max Weber: Politics and the Spirit of Tragedy* (New York: Basic Books, 1996), pp. 17–44.

35. Richard White, *The Organic Machine* (New York: Hill and Wang, 1995), p. 34.

36. John K. Walton, "Taking the History of Tourism Seriously," *European History Quarterly* 27 (1997): 563–71.

37. Urry, *Sociology beyond Societies*, pp. 66–76.

38. Kate Lacey, *Feminine Frequencies: Gender, German Radio, and the Public Sphere, 1923–1945* (Ann Arbor, MI: University of Michigan Press, 1996); Inge Marssolek, "Radio in Deutschland 1923–1950: Zur Sozialgeschichte eines Mediums," *Geschichte und Gesellschaft* 27, 2 (2001).

39. See Alf Lüdtke, "What Happened to the 'Fiery Red Glow'? Workers' Experiences and German Fascism," in Lüdtke (ed.), *The History of Everyday Life: Reconstructing Historical Experiences and Ways of Life*, (Princeton, NJ: Princeton University Press, 1995), esp. pp. 234–7.

40. There is virtually no developed scholarship on leisure travel in Communist states, for example. See József Böröcz, *Leisure Migration: A Sociological Study on Tourism* (Oxford: Elsevier Science, 1992).

41. Alon Confino and Rudy Koshar, "Regimes of Consumer Culture: New Narratives in Twentieth-Century German History," *German History* 19, 2 (2001), pp. 135–61.

42. Susan Strasser, Charles McGovern, and Matthias Judt, "Introduction," in Strasser *et al.* (eds) *Getting and Spending*, pp. 1–7.

43. See Ronald Kline and Trevor Pinch, "Users as Agents of Technological Change: The Social Construction of the Automobile in the Rural United States," *Technology and Culture* 37, 4 (1996), pp. 763–95; Eric Schatzberg, *Wings of Wood, Wings of Metal: Culture and Technical Choice in American Airplane Materials, 1914–1945* (Princeton, NJ: Princeton University Press, 1999).

44. Hannah Arendt, *The Human Condition* (Chicago and London: University of Chicago Press, 1958), pp. 136–9.

45. Leora Auslander, *Taste and Power* (Berkeley and Los Angeles: University of California Press, 1996).

46. Dick Hebdige, *Hiding in the Light* (London and New York: Routledge, 1988); Arjun Appadurai, (ed.), *The Social Life of Things: Commodities in Cultural Perspective* (Cambridge: Cambridge University Press, 1986).

47. The point is made by Daniel Roche, *A History of Everyday Things: The Birth of Consumption in France, 1600–1800* (Cambridge: Cambridge University Press, 2000).

48. Siegfried Kracauer, *The Mass Ornament: Weimar Essays*, ed. by Thomas Y. Levin (Cambridge, MA: Harvard University Press, 1995).

49. Theodor Adorno, *Minima Moralia: Reflections from Damaged Life* (London and New York: Verso, 1974), p. 40.

50. For two recent studies dealing with the "social life" of cars, see Sean O'Connell, *The Car in British Society: Class, Gender, and Motoring 1896–1939* (Manchester: Manchester University Press, 1998); Daniel Miller (ed.), *Car Cultures: Materializing Culture* (Oxford and New York: Berg, 2001). On a related topic, see H.F. Moorhouse, *Driving Ambitions: An Analysis of the American Hot Rod Enthusiasm* (Manchester and New York: Manchester University Press, 1991).

51. Viktor Klemperer, *I Will Bear Witness: A Diary of the Nazi Years*, vol. 1: *1933–1941* (New York: Random House, 1998).

52. Eric Hobsbawm, *An Age of Extremes: A History of the World, 1914–1991* (New York: Pantheon, 1994).

53. Ross, *Fast Cars, Clean Bodies*.

Part I

Seeing

2

Museums: Leisure between State and Distinction

Nick Prior

To be modern is to live a life of paradox and contradiction.

Marshall Berman, *All that is Solid Melts into Air*[1]

The history of the museum is an elusive tale not least because the air of neutrality and permanence exuded by the institution today veils its multivalent genesis. Museums were (and are) ambiguous spaces. In the nineteenth century the marriage of museums with discourses of taste, connoisseurship, and high culture connected them with the struggle for a refined identity that was so crucial to the historical position of the bourgeoisie. Hence, the museum became a contributory badge of quality fought for by ascendant social groups in the struggle for symbolic power. For this reason, museums tended to exclude in the act of distinction, symbolically purifying themselves of lower historical tendencies and visitors.

Yet, museums also catered for shifts in the structure of governance, peeling away older remnants of monarchical or aristocratic grandeur and religious servitude. Through this process they opened up to the emerging space of the nation, with its origins in "civil society" and a representative generality. National publics were now encouraged to exploit the operation of new leisure regimes and partake of the moral benefits offered by the museum as a repository of civilization's highest values. Governing forces also recognized the role that museums could play in the regulation of social behavior, "civilizing" the population as a whole and making the visit an instance of self-amelioration. All this happened at different speeds and according to different social and political conditions throughout Europe and, later, North America.

This chapter is addressed to the emergence of museums both in general historical terms and in terms of the specific relationship between state, class and culture in nineteenth-century Europe. To understand the nature of the museum and its publics, I shall suggest, one must grasp the institution as an allotrope – an element with dual properties. Like modernity itself, the museum is Janus-faced, double-coded, ambivalent. Historically, it has oscillated between contrasting sets of values and exhibited apparently self-contradictory behavior – inward-looking elitism and populist democratic pedagogy, religiosity and secularism, tradition-alism and modernity.[2] The coupling of these cultural and political coordinates has had particular implications for the function of the museum visit and to the meanings attached to the social groups who have participated – willfully or not – in the museological encounter.

The first section of the chapter will utilize a Bourdieusian framework to deal with how the museum had been constructed as a sanctuary of high culture and refinement, elevated to an exclusive position beyond the collective. The second section will detail the opening up of museums at the behest of nation-states, integrating their populations into national culture via utilitarian programmes of social regulation and improvement. The institutional space opened up by this latter process, it will be argued, was enough to allow a certain leakage of the popular into the museum in a way that fissured the project of the museum even further.

In the course of this chapter, I will not enter into nuanced particularities on the mechanics of specific nations, their museums, or visitors. I hope, instead, to sketch a broader canvas that takes in the early history of the museum in Europe in order to reveal the two defining principles of power which gave the museum its modus operandi in the nineteenth century. Of course, not all museums in Europe functioned in quite the same way; meaningful differences exist, for instance, between provincial museums and national museums, continental European museums and British picture galleries, early-nineteenth-century museums and late-nineteenth-century museums. Still, there is some merit in capturing the general strokes that patterned the evolution of many large-scale museums in Europe. The fact that nearly all major European countries possessed a large, public museum by the first few decades of the nineteenth century must at least alert us to the unifying contours that link different European cases. There is also a burgeoning critical literature, born of interdisciplinary urgencies, charting the genesis and development of specific museums and art galleries.[3]

In his short essay, "The Problem of Museums," the French poet and essayist Paul Valéry defines museums as places "where Aphrodite is transformed into a dossier."[4] It is absurd, complains Valéry, to reduce the "marvellous actuality" of things to a singular tableau in which is gathered together disparate objects that do most damage to each other when they are forced to be alike. Museums, by their very nature, fail to kindle much in the way of delight because they belong to the order of taxonomy, conservation and public improvement. Direct feelings are quashed, to be replaced by a calculated superficiality and frigidity. "At the first step that I take toward things of beauty," he writes, "a hand relieves me of my stick, and a notice forbids me to smoke." As he proceeds the museum is revealed in all its ambiguous glory and Valéry is "smitten with a sacred horror":

My pace grows reverent. My voice alters to a pitch slightly higher than in church, to a tone rather less strong than that of every day. Presently I lose all sense of why I have intruded into this wax-floored solitude, savouring the temple and drawing room, of cemetery and school . . . Did I come for instruction, for my own beguilement, or simply as a duty and out of convention? Or is it perhaps some exercise peculiar to itself, this stroll I am taking, weirdly beset with beauties, distracted at every moment by master-pieces to the right or left compelling me to walk like a drunk man between counters.[5]

And he is clearly not alone in his loneliness before art, in his veneration for the vastness of the galleries. The first visitors to museums in the late eighteenth and early nineteenth centuries were struck with a similar reverence within the new temples of art. When Goethe visited the Dresden gallery in 1768, for example, his impressions were that of a man caught in the "profound silence that reigned . . . a solemn and unique impression, akin to the emotion experienced upon entering a House of God."[6] The processional routes, the monumental architecture, the great stairs, all circulated the requisite values of this new secular temple – a cultural sanctuary which, by the nineteenth century, had been set aside from everyday life and culturally appointed for a special kind of contemplation and decorum.

Museums, in short, were imposing places, caught in a logic that belonged to previous centuries of dynastic splendor and religious contemplation. Their origins in historical models such as monastic libraries, churches, cabinets of curiosities and princely galleries, fostered conditions of consecration and solemnity which placed the visitor in the position of subaltern before the auratized ensemble.[7] Before the nineteenth century, for instance, princely collections like those of Philip II of Spain and Cardinal Mazarin, were visually ordered according to a principle of quantity and excess, a "spectacle of treasures" that interiorized the personal worldview of the prince. Pictures were arranged, floor-to-ceiling, in a tapestry-like style, manifesting the magnificence of the ruler in a system of superabundance. The visitor – in effect the prince's guest – viewed this spectacle in relation to the symbolic presence of the prince, rather than to the objects themselves.[8] Access-ibility was therefore secondary. Although some collections were open to the public before the mid-eighteenth century (usually on payment of a fee or by strict appoint-ment and on restricted days only), visitors, as Hudson affirms, "were admitted as a privilege, not as a right and consequently gratitude and admiration, not criticism was required of them."[9]

By the late eighteenth and early nineteenth centuries, the gradual transformation of the princely gallery and other museological precursors into the public art museum fed off, and into, the struggles between competing social groups. Museums were, after all, the storehouses of Western civilization's most cherished objects, set aside for scientific progress, civil refinement and moral betterment. The upheavals of the French Revolution were the clearest and most dramatic locus of these struggles, resulting in the opening of the Louvre as the first large-scale public national museum in Europe. But throughout Europe, by the early nineteenth century, museums had become the cultural signposts of a middle-class struggling to inherit, overturn or outgrow previous monarchical and aristocratic systems of rule.[10] As a realm of high culture, in other words, the museum was a chief institutional site through which bourgeois elites could elaborate their own signifiers of cultural distinction, articulate a distance from other social groups, and select appropriate categories for inclusion or exclusion.

What is indicated in much of the material on the interface between the public and the museum from the nineteenth century is that, far from being a total or complete translation of Enlightenment values concerning universal edification, the museum was based on a limited conception of what "the public" consisted of.[11] The modes of behavior associated with the popular classes were emphatically precluded from the museum in a way that marked a division between the groups that seemed to belong to the museum and those that were alien. Hence, from internal regulations on the prevention of vandalism, the touching of pictures, and the carrying of babies, to proscriptions against spitting, drinking, and dirty footwear, the museum demonstrated the type of visitors and behavior to be discouraged. This paralleled the situation in the literary circles, debating societies, and coffee houses of the "public sphere" generally.[12]

Certainly, the museum had been set up in opposition to places of popular assembly such as fairs and taverns. These realms of the "carnivalesque" (to borrow Bakhtin's phrase) were negatively coded as "vulgar," "barbaric," and hence as "other."[13] As Stallybrass and White argue, certain codes of behavior were elevated in places like museums and debating societies as "part of an overall strategy of expulsion which clear[ed] a space for polite cosmopolitan discourse by constructing popular culture as the 'low-Other,' the dirty and crude outside to the emergent public sphere."[14] "Public," in this sense, belonged to the restricted space set aside for higher-rank modes of consumption, rather than *tout le monde*. The "civilization process" had marked itself in the leisure practices of these groups, whose standards of restraint and decorum distinguished them from the crowds at the fair.[15]

A few examples may be instructive here. Despite all the rhetorics of universal access and popular education which underpinned the Louvre, as McLellan observes, its internal functioning actually helped to exclude the uneducated and privilege the initiated, particularly the "bourgeois amateur."[16] Very little help was given to inexperienced visitors by way of guides and there was no education department. Similarly, Sherman notes that in late-nineteenth-century France, provincial museums lacked descriptive labels that would instruct the public. Instead, pictures were arranged in the cluttered Baroque style, without differentiation or an attempt at democratic pedagogy.[17] According to Telman, limitations redolent in the organization of the Altes Museum in *Vormärz* Berlin spoke of a logic of separation and exclusion in the nineteenth century. The Altes Museum served to establish the authority of the political administrators of cultural reform as the arbiters of taste and distinction. This separated the refined from the common, engendering in the latter "an attitude of awe, wonder and quasi-religious respect."[18] Indeed, an artifice used by Schinkel to promote such a mood of "sacred solemnity" was to arrange his classical sculpture on very high pedestals in order to place the visitor on a plane spiritually inferior to that of the sacred objects.

In other museums, undifferentiated public access was fiercely countered by artists and curators faithful to the idea that unmediated or popular access spoilt the silent contemplation of the works of art. As Thackeray was to write in 1841: "Genteel people . . . do not frequent the Louvre on a Sunday. You can't see the pictures well, and are pushed and elbowed by all sorts of low-bred creatures."[19] Across Europe, museums still implemented restricted hours of opening that discouraged working people from attending and audience screening was a widely used method of discriminating between the studious and the plebeian, favor lying with scholarly and artistic patronage.[20] Sir Henry Ellis's belligerent response to suggestions that the British Museum might be opened to the "vulgar classes" on popular holidays in 1835, for instance, is telling: "I think," he replied, "the most mischievous portion of the population is abroad and about at such a time . . . the exclusion of the public is very material, inasmuch as the place otherwise would really be unwholesome."[21]

When the lower ranks were admitted they were done so in carefully regulated conditions. In Edinburgh, the Royal Museum of Scotland opened on New Year's Day in 1852, experimentally, to "the working classes." Groups of one hundred were shepherded into the museum space and a bell rung after twenty-five minutes signaling them to leave, to be replaced by a proceeding group.[22] Admission was free, but only on possession of a ticket – a condition intended to bar "improper individuals." Several years later guards at the National Gallery of Scotland were asked to be particularly vigilant towards children and "disorderly visitors" who might attempt to "ascertain the surface" of the pictures (clearly, those who could not control the limits of their bodies were not "civilized"); while officers were empowered to refuse admittance to "suspicious characters."[23] In London, connoisseurs and critics of the National Gallery such as Cockerell, Unwins, and Waagen riled against "persons, whose filthy dress tainted the atmosphere with a most disagreeable smell."[24] And in Russia, looking the part was a precondition of acceptance into the Hermitage up until the 1860s, initial directives stipulating that visitors had to acquire an admission ticket and wear regimental or aristocratic attire.[25]

For Bourdieu, such museological discriminations make sense if we recognize the role of high culture as fulfilling certain social functions of legitimizing social differences and thereby reproducing power relations. *The Love of Art* was Bourdieu's initial attempt at an empirically based study of museums which assaulted Kantian and other essentialist theories of taste which assumed certain a priori faculties towards aesthetic pleasure.[26] The sensitivity to experience higher artistic pleasures, a facet that may be experienced by any human being, as Kant had it, is revealed by Bourdieu as the privilege of those who have access to the conditions in which "pure" and "disinterested" dispositions are acquired. Hence, museum visiting is unveiled as a socially differentiated activity resting on the possession of educational and cultural dispositions towards art practices and products and, as such, almost the exclusive domain of the cultivated classes.

Cultural competence, for Bourdieu, is a precondition for the classification and organization of artistic knowledge. Individuals can decipher works of art "aesthetically" as it were, only if they have a mastery of the codes and systems of classification which are able to process styles, periods, techniques, and so on. Repeated contact with high culture via informal and formal education processes encourages the accumulation of these instruments of appropriation, leading to an "unconscious mastery" of art and its discourses. Having a "feel for the game" (*sense pratique*), or a familiarity with art objects is the outcome of culturally acquired systems of perception, not something naturally or universally programmed. However, this sense is expressed in a form which emphasises its natural, quasi-instinctual and pre-reflexive quality, in the dispositional form of the cultured *habitus,* itself an expression of favorable material conditions of existence.[27]

Cultural proficiency, then, appears as a gift of natural talent and taste, available to all on an equal basis. It is not recognized as accumulated outcomes of differential learning and training, requiring, at least, some distance from material necessities and leisure time. Members of the initiated classes, from this perspective, accept as a "gift of nature a cultural heritage which is transmitted by a process of unconscious training."[28] The "masters of judgement and taste" appear as rising above the vagaries of material processes, even though they are definite products of such processes. Culture, in short, is achieved by negating itself as culture (i.e., acquired) and presenting itself as nature (or grace).

It is to this extent that the museum and its objects remained the natural appurtenance of middle-class elites. The museum comprised a "pure" space, symbolically opposed to the vulgarities of the carnival, where the values of civilized bourgeois culture were coded and decoded by this class itself. As Sherman does, we can make sense of a seemingly trivial instance such as the refusal to give up umbrellas at the doors of nineteenth-century French provincial museums as an important illustration of the bourgeois urgency to retain the objects and codes of its distinction. The umbrella was a particularly resonant object of middle-class apparel, carried even in clement weather. Its shape and possession codified the *habitus* and deportment of this class to itself and to others within the museum. Its function was to effect a visible mechanism of differentiation of the holder from other competing groups by speaking of his or her refinement, aloofness, or delicacy.[29] Equally, we could identify events such as the expulsion of Punch and Judy shows in the 1860s from the site of the National Gallery of Scotland as evidence of the extrication of carnival from the visual field, leaving an unsullied space where bourgeois recognized bourgeois, in relative hush.[30]

Such movements had, by the early nineteenth century, crystallized into the normative and institutional distinctions subtending systems of cultural production arranged around two poles: restricted/high culture versus large-scale/popular culture. High art was the symbolically potent system of classification valorized by the appropriate cultural experts, discourses and nationally consecrated institutions that included orchestras, theaters, and other "serious" civic institutions with established conventions of public demeanor and cultural restraint. Museums emerged within this system as an organization of cultural authority, based on the collective action of elites that bounded them ever closer to consecrated culture. All this underpinned the sense of belonging of some social groups over others in the museum – a feeling that was reinforced in the minute details of its internal functioning:

> Everything, in these civic temples in which bourgeois society deposits its most sacred possessions, that is, the relics inherited from a past which is not its own, in the holy palaces of art, in which the chosen few come to nurture a faith of *virtuosi* while conformists and bogus devotees come and perform a class ritual, old palaces or great historic homes to which the nineteenth century added imposing edifices, built often in the Greco-Roman style of civic sanctuaries, everything combines to indicate that the work of art is as contrary to the world of everyday life as the sacred is to the profane. The prohibition against touching the objects, the religious silence which is forced upon visitors, the puritan asceticism of the facilities, always scarce and uncomfortable, the almost systematic refusal of any instruction, the grandiose solemnity of the decoration and decorum, colonnades, vast galleries, decorated ceilings, monumental staircases both outside and inside, everything seems done to remind people that the transition from the profane world to the sacred world presupposes, as Durkheim says, 'a genuine metamorphosis.'[31]

Free entrance, in short, was also optional entrance, in practice put aside for those who felt at home in the museum's confines. The founding of art museums was inseparable from the struggle of the bourgeois class to elevate its own worldview while appearing to rise above the realities of material life from the early nineteenth century. As the bourgeoisie reconciled the stylistic demeanor of the aristocracy with instrumental reason, it used the aesthetic (one tool among many, incidentally) to define a space for itself, a sanctuary of high culture that served to produce and reproduce this class's claim to the status of cultural superiors of the social system.

But does this emphasis on exclusion and severance really exhaust the nature and function of the museum in the nineteenth century? Is the museum really such a hermetically sealed space? And what about the role of the nation-state and the casual nature of leisure and consumption among the metropolitan crowds? As already indicated, a thorough grasp of the historical trajectory of the museum can be based only on acceptance of historically conceived ambiguities. In particular, while exclusion and distinction were clearly central to the historical becoming of the museum, its imbrication with the complex priorities and workings of the nation-state pulled the institution towards more open conditions of reception. In other words, while Bourdieu's effort to chip away at the rhetorics of universal accessibility are worthy, the nineteenth-century museum should not be reduced to the ideologies of a fully constituted bourgeois class without consideration of some countervailing tendencies. Not only had museums become significant to a moral economy of leisure in the city, a better place to consume than pubs, inns, and taverns, but also they had been opened up to the possibility of popular use by more amorphous metropolitan crowds.

For a start, then, the museum could not work without the participation and agreement of the public, even if this agreement guaranteed the popular sovereignty of the liberal state. At the beginning of the nineteenth century a host of European nation-states were recognizing the role of public museums as instruments of national consciousness, while royal collections were turned over to state or semi-state administrations. The augmentation of state-sponsored art museums in the early nineteenth century represented a new urgency to concentrate national pride in the populace at large. National museums, in this sense, took on a similar role to nationalism in general – political cohesion and the constitution of the nation as an "imagined community."[32]The museum's emergence thereby demonstrated the new value accorded to the national collection, framed in a museum, as a cultural asset for the expanding apparatus of governance.

Carol Duncan has argued that institutions such as museums "made (and still make) the state look good: progressive, concerned about the spiritual life of its citizens, a preserver of past achievements and a provider for the common good."[33] Nineteenth-century museums were ideal monuments to democracy. As such they produced and reproduced a set of key values, including citizenship, public participation, and common humanity – all ideological food for the modern state in its role as guardian of a nation's artistic heritage. This was most explicit with the Louvre, the prototypical public art museum and symbol of the bourgeois state as it evolved in the age of democratic revolutions.

Opened in August 1793, the Louvre displayed in dramatic form the glory of the Republican Government. Once a private palace of kings, the Louvre was now a leitmotif for the overthrow of the *ancien régime* and homage to the French nation-state. The nationalized museum was intended to "nourish a taste for fine arts, please art lovers and serve as a school to artists," in the words of the Minister of the Interior, who continued:

> It should be open to everyone. This will be a national monument. There will not be a single individual who does not have the right to enjoy it. It will have such an influence on the mind, it will so elevate the soul, it will so excite the heart that it will be one of the most powerful ways of proclaiming the illustriousness of the French Republic.[34]

In 1803, the Louvre was renamed the "Musée Napoleon" in honour of the Emperor's contribution to its formation. The layout of the collection now fell in with the procedures established in the Enlightenment and followed by other museums. Pictures were organized into schools (Italian, French, Dutch, and Flemish), each work was given an explanatory text and a catalogue was provided – the first to be aimed at the average citizen, according to Hudson.[35] France now had a museum which appeared fully secular, public, and national: a monument to democracy, civilization, and international cultural domination. As a "Universal Survey Museum" the Louvre recodified the exhibition space to suit the visibility of the French Republic by transforming the signs of luxury, status and splendor of the *ancien régime* into objects of a universal spirit (genius), embodied most gloriously in the particulars of French art.[36]

A visit to the Louvre was "scripted" accordingly as a ritual of national glorification, with the interior space forming "an ensemble that functions as an iconographic programme."[37] The visitor was now addressed as an idealized citizen of the state and inheritor of the highest values of civilization. The visitor was the recipient of the nation's most profound achievements, beneficiary of the state's ideals of democracy, not the subordinate of the prince or lord. Social relations between the visitor and the collection had shifted, in other words, away from those pertaining to the absolutist space of representation, where the visitor was the prince's guest, towards notions of equal access, giving every citizen, in principle, universal rights to art. In short, the state, as an abstract presence, replaced the king as host, and stood as "keeper of the nation's spiritual life and guardian of the most evolved and civilized culture of which the human spirit is capable."[38]

Such was the Louvre's influence on other nations that museum-building accelerated markedly from the early nineteenth century, often with the consent of heads of state in those nations. Napoleon's excursions into Spain, Italy, and The Netherlands provided a climate in which new national galleries could be formed in subject cities such as Madrid, Milan, Naples, and Amsterdam, founded on French-inspired principles of nationhood. In the Netherlands, the foundation of the Rijksmuseum dates from 1808, the year in which Napoleon's brother transferred his court from Utrecht to Amsterdam with the aim of making it a center for art and learning. On Dutch independence the museum was once again elevated into a state institution, with a national purchase grant. However, religious divisions (the north remained Protestant, the south Catholic) and foreign military occupation made for an uncertain sense of national unity in the Netherlands. Despite having one of the richest fields of visual art in Europe, as well as a powerful bourgeoisie, The Netherlands suffered a form of syncopated rule which undermined the project of the museum and militated against expansion in its collections. As it was, the Rijksmuseum remained, ceremonially, under the charge of the sovereign prince, albeit on behalf of the people, as was the case in other nation-states.[39]

In Germany, and to a lesser extent Italy, the princely kingdom was administratively proactive. In the former, nationhood lacked the vital political dimension and Germany's system of divided states made for a less integrative structure of rule, precluding the idea of a single state-sponsored gallery (Germany had no single capital city, for instance).[40] Yet the Altes Museum in Berlin was opened in 1830 on return of the paintings acquired by France, and helped articulate a national identity in Prussia after the Napoleonic Wars. The works inside no longer served as expressions of the private wealth of the Hohenzollern family, but came to symbolize Prussian national heritage. Elsewhere in Germany, the collections of the Alte Pinakothek and the Glyptothek, both in Munich, opened in the 1830s and a Bavarian national museum was established in 1867. In Prague, the rise of nationalism underpinned the founding of a museum in 1818 given over to the concentration of cultural identity and the study of Czech and Slovak history. In Russia, despite functioning as a royal museum up to the revolution, the Hermitage, opened in 1852 by Nicholas I, is said to have fulfilled most of the functions of a national museum. And in France, as well as the Louvre, Lenoir's *Musée des Monuments Français,* formed during the early stages of the Revolution, was devoted partly to art and partly to national history.[41]

Notwithstanding local idiosyncrasies, then, what is clear is that the museum had been decked out in its national costume by the early nineteenth century. The museum indexed the urgencies and interests of the nation-state, but it also mobilized these interests, providing a powerful cultural base where official ideologies were made and remade. This implied a breaking down of the restrictions on access that characterized collections of the previous century and the opening up of new publics. The eighteenth-century public sphere now had a place at the very heart of the nineteenth-century constitutional system, constructed in such a way as to actively require popular participation and engagement. Indeed, what gave the nineteenth-century project of the state effective momentum was the idea of the "nation" itself, the "named human population sharing an historic trajectory, common myths and historical memories, a mass, public culture, a common economy and common legal rights and duties for all members."[42] In short, the museum, as a state-sponsored institution had commingled with citizenship, as a system of political expression and mass participation.

In Britain, projects like the Great Exhibition of 1851 (the first of many world fairs in Europe) and the complex of museums subsequently founded around South Kensington demonstrated a more open and cacophonous regime of leisure.[43] A general public had been invited to partake of the moral benefits offered by the mix of amusements, educational displays and trade fair stands at Crystal Palace, support for which was found in an English social-democratic tradition that willed the encounter between the masses and higher pleasures.[44] Figures such as John Stuart Mill, William Morris, and John Ruskin all believed in the transformative effects of art and the purposeful function of culture in elevating the moral status of the worker; while reformers such as Joseph Hume argued strenuously for museums and galleries to widen their accessibility and thereby improve the lives of the lower orders.

Late-nineteenth-century museums and exhibitions, then, were conceived on instrumental lines: not only to broaden public education and raise the profile of British design and manufacturing, but also to specify norms of individual conduct. Indeed, throughout Europe, as nation-states expanded and sought to extend their control over society, they increasingly designated norms of individual behavior by example and enforcement. Increasing daily bonds were forged between citizen and state in areas such as education, welfare, and policing. States no longer wanted to merely educate, they needed to govern the populace, particularly that section of the populace which could pose a threat to their new-found security.

Museums were, to this extent, institutions which fitted neatly into the project of what Gramsci called the "ethical state" as it sought to "raise the great mass of the population to a particular cultural and moral level, a level (or type) which corresponded to the needs of the productive forces for development."[45] Like other "improving" spheres such as libraries and public parks, museums were enlisted as instruments of social management which, as Bennett has explained, exemplified a new form of "governmental" power. This aimed "at producing a citizenry which, rather than needing to be externally and coercively directed, would increasingly monitor and regulate its own conduct."[46]

Statements on the moral efficacy of museums from the founders of these institutions constituted the museum as a tool of public enculturation. As "antidotes to brutality and vice," as Henry Cole was to put it in 1874, museums were believed to improve the moral health of the subordinate classes by improving their "inner selves," their habits, manners, and beliefs.[47] Hence, the value of rational pro-grammes of education in science and history museums in the nineteenth century rested on their promotion of forms of pedagogy and noble feelings. In Britain, a visit to the museum was considered to be a "rational recreation" which might lift popular taste, improve the industriousness of the population and help prevent disorder and rebellion – especially in the wake of Chartism and the Luddite disturbances of the 1810s. [48]

Not (just) museums as elite distinction, then, but as appropriation and rational calculation. Schemes of education and statements on moral improvement were servitors for new forms of self-management and social cohesion that absorbed the problematic "masses" within the legitimate confines of liberal power. In Foucauldian terms, the political rationality of the museum illuminated a technology of power that governed by seeming not to govern. The state worked at a removed distance to shape mental and moral behavior, to regulate conditions of life of individuals and populations. "Governmental" power, in this sense, worked in contrast to the modalities of absolutist, visible force, by investing itself in populations which governed themselves. Or as Bennett puts it:

> Rather than embodying an alien and coercive principle of power which aimed to cow the people into submission, the museum – addressing the people as a public, as citizens, aimed to inveigle the general populace into complicity with power by placing them on this side of a power which it represented to it as its own.[49]

For Bennett, it is this new principle of power which accounts for the discourse of museum reform in the nineteenth century. Clearly, new technologies of power and governance could be effective only if the museum doors were open to those at whom the technologies were aimed. The museum had to be refashioned in the nineteenth century to give its civilizing role priority, detaching the museum from ethics of royal splendor and placing it firmly within the realms of popular enlightenment and social regulation. Hence, the reordering of objects in the museum according to historicist tropes of evolution was a program of public instruction which called up the citizen as a "progressive subject" who would be "auto-tuned to the requirements of the new forms of social training."[50]

The problem, of course, is how to coordinate this program once the population enters the hallowed doors of the museum. The state, after all, could not guarantee its aims would work: it could provide the conditions of possibility for wider audiences but could not specify exactly who entered the museum and for what reasons. As the cities of Europe expanded, urbanism as a "way of life" was increasingly based on the denseness and heterogeneity of metropolitan populations, constituting a mix of social groups who had not previously shared the same leisure spaces.[51] The jostling metropolitan crowds could now wander around museums in a relatively unregulated fashion, their gaze circulated through a casual form of consumption in the nineteenth century.

Though the Great Exhibitions between 1851 and 1871 were devised according to governmental tropes of improvement, for instance, organizers were perturbed by evidence indicating that the masses were seizing the event as a popular holiday ritual. The audience, particularly after 1862, had not been anchored by the well-meaning intentions of officialdom, but had appropriated the occasion for its own avocation. The most popular attractions were those that belonged to the sphere of entertainment rather than high art. Indeed, according to Greenhalgh, the more culturally "refined" areas such as the fine arts had been subsidized by the entertainment facilities. By the late nineteenth century the British government capitulated in the face of this failure and began to plan its international exhibitions with leisure in mind. This was a move partly motivated by international rivalry – the French Expositions being more spectacular and festive affairs than those of Britain – but it was also in recognition of the fact that popular leisure patterns had changed to accommodate modern industrial society.[52]

Throughout Europe, in fact, visual consumption in the metropolis had been informed by and skewed towards popular pastimes and recreations as the "leisure industry" took off. The city (and its popular delights) had become a kind of performance or urban exhibition enjoyed by increasingly undifferentiated publics. Metropolitan life centered upon the circulation of commodities and the concentration of spectacle, fashion, and pleasure. Inevitably, the gaze used to contemplate such a drama had seeped into the museum as well, despite the fact that the museum had been intended for a more contemplative order. Many visitors either expected the same pleasures of entertainment that they found in popular exhibitions, shows and street dramas or "misread" the intentions of cultural philanthropists according to their own metropolitan class realities.[53]

During the 1880s and 1890s, for instance, exhibitions were organized in Whitechapel, London, to promote urban renewal and make a reality of Ruskin's ideas regarding the cultural education of the working class. The exhibition promoters believed that, if arranged in an accessible style, with a straightforward catalogue and guidance from committed educators, art objects could be understood by the working-class public. By this act of seeing, it was reasoned, the lower orders would be exposed to a system of moral aesthetics and products of beauty guaranteed to attenuate despair and class hatred. Conditions inside the parish church at Whitechapel were arranged to allow a degree of noise, and the paintings were carefully chosen – narrative paintings, portraits of the famous and depictions of the city of London – in order to "connect" with the everyday lives of the public.

As Koven notes, however, the working-class public "read against" this exhibitionary text, often contesting the meanings given to the exhibition by the philanthropists. Some visitors focused on the probable monetary value of the paintings and their frames, while others resisted the spiritual and grandiose interpretations of labor depicted in the pictures. More commonly, visitors generalized their experiences of industrial commodities to high cultural production. One visitor, for instance, suggested that a rendition of three classical maidens by Albert Moore called *Waiting to Cross* "reminded her of nothing so much as the United Kingdom Tea advertisement."[54] Portions of the audience had interpreted the exhibition as a substitute for the cultural commodities of industrial capitalism, such as pubs, music halls and billboard advertisements.[55] The meanings attached to exhibitions in Britain's capital, in other words, were refracted by the conditions of mass leisure and twisted by the everyday realities of class and consumption.

Hence, while the foundation of the National Gallery in London had been achieved through the progressive purification of the gallery space as a realm of polite assembly, commentators, by the 1850s, had noted that the metropolitan crowds were using the space to eat lunch and shelter from the rain.[56] The uncanny congruence of different modes of cultural use and forms of assembly had been guaranteed by the sheer physicality of urban crowds. For Trodd at least, this made the National Gallery less a controlling or disciplinary space and more of a "fluid, ambivalent or disordered environment."[57] It certainly points to the fact that the museum was not a single text, read in the same way by all, but meant different things to different social groups. It also suggests that the museum was both *structured* and *structuring*, both constraining and enabling.

Directives regarding the "correct" use of leisure time were often undermined by the nature of modern urban relations and the complex points of articulation between class, culture and leisure. The dramatic tension between regulation and transgression mapped itself onto everyday urban relations, including patterns of museum visiting already layered with elite aspirations towards purity and refinement. The tensions between these poles constituted the ongoing process of state formation, class distinction, and mass leisure. The museum's ambiguous trajectory through the nineteenth century was thereby bound up with complex social upheavals, political directives and unintended consequences which accumulated from the sixteenth century to deliver the museum in all its paradoxical glory.

Museums were placed between two modalities of power that pulled the institution in different directions, at times resulting in potentially critical tensions. On the one hand, the museum (particularly the art museum) was the basis to forms of social exclusion, a tool to naturalize the social and cultural dominance of the *cognoscenti* by appearing to fit naturally with the bourgeoisie's social being. While not causing social differences or inequalities, the museum nevertheless helped to sustain them. On the other hand, the museum represented the interests of increasingly bounded European nation-states. National art museums reflected and sustained an array of important official ideologies and popular identities by integrating mass populations into the nation-state via utilitarian programs of social regulation and improvement. Nationalization was, furthermore, coterminous with the development of increasingly public and heterogeneous leisure regimes, allowing a certain leakage of the popular into the museum in a way that reversed the intentions of official discourse. This placed the museum at a point of perpetual oscillation between constraint and enfranchisement, regulation and transgression, and between state and distinction.

These are, indeed, the very tensions that characterize the museum today as it grapples with the historical dilemmas of double-coding: whether to be shrines for the few or educators for the many, to appeal to the popular (often attacked as "dumbing down") or connoisseurial (charged as "elitism"), to be arenas for secular research or churches for the auratic object. In fact, it is testament to the museum's resilience that it has dealt with the fabric of ambiguity and paradox which lies behind its history, accommodating these tensions into its very being. Hence, most of the European examples mentioned – the National Gallery in London, the Rijksmuseum, the Altes Museum, the Louvre – continue to flourish as national but, also, respectable, middle-class institutions of fine art, coping with various modes of social assembly and political directives. Thinking the museum, then, involves the acknowledgment of the ambivalent nature of modernity, the ability to conceive of paradox as an essence of modern life. This has been the historical double-bind of the museum.

Notes

1. Marshall Berman, *All that is Solid Melts into Air: The Experience of Modernity* (London: Verso, 1982), p. 13.

2. Or, as Nochlin condenses it: "As the shrine of an elitist religion and at the same time a utilitarian instrument of democratic education, the museum may be said to have suffered schizophrenia from the start": Linda Nochlin, "Museums and Radicals: A History of Emergencies," *Art in America* 54, 4 (1971), p. 646.

3. See, for example, Carol Duncan, *Civilizing Rituals: Inside Public Art Museums* (London: Routledge, 1995); Andrew McLellan, *Inventing the Louvre: Art, Politics and the Origins of the Modern Museum in Eighteenth-Century Paris* (Cambridge: Cambridge University Press, 1994); Marcia Pointon (ed.), *Art Apart: Museums in North America and Britain since 1800* (Manchester: Manchester University Press, 1994); Nick Prior, *Museums and Modernity: Art Galleries and the Making of Modern Culture* (Oxford and New York: Berg, 2002); Gordon Fyfe, *The Social Construction of British Art Institutions, 1750–1950* (Leicester: Cassell, 1998); Vera Zolberg, "American Art Museums: Sanctuary of Free-for-All?" *Social Forces* 63, 2 (1984), pp. 377–92; Jesus Pedro Lorente, *Cathedrals of Urban Modernity: The First Museums of Contemporary Art, 1800–1930* (Aldershot: Ashgate, 1998).

4. Paul Valéry, "The Problem of Museums," in *Degas, Manet, Morisot,* collected works vol. 12 (London: Routledge and Kegan Paul, 1960), p. 205.

5. Ibid., pp. 202, 203.

6. Johann Wolfgang Goethe, quoted in Germain Bazin, *The Museum Age* (New York: Universal Press, 1967), p. 160, n. 4.

7. On the ritual quality of various museums see, for example, Duncan, *Civilizing Rituals*; Cesar Graña, "The Private Lives of Public Museums," *Trans-Action* 4, 5 (1967), pp. 20–5;

P. Lee, "The Musaeum of Alexandria and the Formation of the Muséum in Eighteenth-Century France," *Art Bulletin* 79, 3 (1997), pp. 385–412.

8. On the visitor's relationship to the princely gallery see, for example, Duncan, *Civilizing Rituals;* Bazin, *Museum Age;* Gordon Fyfe, "Art Museums and the State," *University of Keele Working Papers* no. 2 (1993).

9. Kenneth Hudson, *A Social History of Museums: What the Visitors Thought* (London: Macmillan, 1975), p. 6.

10. A decent exploration of museums and social class can be found in Carol Duncan and Allan Wallach, "The Universal Survey Museum," *Art History* 3, 4 (1980), pp. 448–69; Bazin, *Museum Age;* Daniel Sherman, "The Bourgeoisie, Cultural Appropriation and the Art Museum," *Radical History* 38, spring (1987).

11. For a discussion of this relationship, Robert Lumley, *The Museum Time-Machine: Putting Cultures on Display* (London: Routledge, 1988); Gordon Fyfe and Max Ross, "Decoding the Visitor's Gaze: Rethinking Museum Visiting," in Gordon Fyfe and Sharon Macdonald (eds), *Theorizing Museums* (Oxford: Blackwell, 1996); Tony Bennett, *The Birth of the Museum* (London: Routledge, 1995); Nick Prior, "The High Within and the Low Without: The Social Production of Aesthetic Space in the National Gallery of Scotland, 1859–1870," *Cultural Logic: An Electronic Journal of Marxist Theory and Practice*, http://eserver.org/clogic, 2, 2, spring 2000.

12. Geoff Eley, "Nations, Publics and Political Cultures: Placing Habermas in the Nineteenth Century," in Nicholas Dirks, Geoff Eley, and Sherry Ortner (eds), *Culture/Power/History: A Reader in Contemporary Social Theory* (Princeton, NJ: Princeton University Press, 1994).

13. Mikhail Bakhtin, *Rabelais and his World* (Cambridge, MA: MIT Press, 1968).

14. Peter Stallybrass and Allan White, *The Politics and Poetics of Transgression* (London: Methuen, 1986), p. 87.

15. Norbert Elias, *The Civilizing Process*, vol. 1: *The History of Manners* (Oxford: Blackwell, 1978); *The Civilizing Process*, vol. 2: *State Formation and Civilisation* (Oxford: Blackwell, 1982).

16. McLellan, *Inventing the Louvre.*

17. Daniel Sherman, *Worthy Monuments: Art Museums and the Politics of Culture in Nineteenth-Century France* (Cambridge, MA: Harvard University Press, 1989).

18. Jeremy Telman, "The Creation of Public Culture in Pre-1848 Berlin," conference paper, The Nineteenth Century City: Global Contexts, Local Productions, Interdisciplinary Nineteenth Century Studies, University of Santa Cruz, CA, 1996, pp. 10–11.

19. William Makepeace Thackeray, quoted in M. Moriarty, "Structures of Cultural Production in Nineteenth-Century France," in P. Collier and R. Lethbridge (eds), *Artistic Relations: Literature and the Visual Arts in Nineteenth-Century France* (New Haven, CT: Yale University Press, 1994), p. 27.

20. See, for example, A. Wittlin, *The Museum: Its History and its Tasks in Education* (London: Routledge and Kegan Paul, 1949).

21. Sir Henry Ellis, quoted in Richard Altick, *The Shows of London* (Cambridge, MA: Harvard University Press, 1978), p. 248.

22. Geoffrey Swinney and David Heppel, "Public and Privileged Access: A Historical Survey of Admission Charges and Visitor Figures for Part of the Scottish National Collection," *Book of the Old Edinburgh Club* 4 (1997), pp. 69–84.

23. Prior, "The High Within and the Low Without."

24. Gustav Waagen, quoted in Colin Trodd, "Culture, Class, City: The National Gallery, London and the Spaces of Education, 1822–57," in Marcia Pointon (ed.) *Art Apart*, p. 42.

As with galleries elsewhere, the National Gallery in London became a symbolically loaded space, cleansed at the behest of the bourgeoisie. Once the space was dedicated solely to the love of art, the gallery was marked by its function to contain objects of purity and to exclude both the anachronism of mere possession and, as far as possible, the disruptive forces of the "impure" and "vulgar." "To attempt to draw distinctions between the objects for which admission was sought, to limit the right of admission on certain days might be impossible," admitted Sir Robert Peel, "but the impossibility is rather an argument against placing the pictures in the greatest thoroughfare of London the greatest confluence of the idle and unwashed": cited in Trodd, "Culture, Class, City," p. 33.

25. Geoffrey Lewis, "Collections, Collectors and Museums: A Brief World Survey," in John Thompson (ed.), *Manual of Curatorship: A Guide to Museum Practice* (London: Butterworth, 1992).

26. Pierre Bourdieu and Alain Darbel, *The Love of Art: European Art Museums and their Public* (Cambridge: Polity, 1991).

27. Pierre Bourdieu, *Outline of a Theory of Practice* (Cambridge: Cambridge University Press, 1977).

28. Pierre Bourdieu, *The Field of Cultural Production: Essays on Art and Literature* (Cambridge: Polity, 1993), p. 234.

29. Sherman, "Bourgeoisie, Cultural Appropriation and the Art Museum."

30. Prior, "The High Within and the Low Without."

31. Bourdieu, *Field of Cultural Production*, p. 237.

32. Benedict Anderson, *Imagined Communities: Reflections on the Origin and Spread of Nationalism* (London: Verso, 1983).

33. Carol Duncan, "Art Museums and the Ritual of Citizenship," in I. Karp and S. Lavine (eds), *Exhibiting Cultures: The Poetics and Politics of Museum Display* (Washington, DC: Smithsonian Institution Press, 1991), p. 93

34. Quoted in Duncan and Wallach, "Universal Survey Museum," p. 454.

35. Kenneth Hudson, *Museums of Influence* (Cambridge: Cambridge University Press 1987).

36. Duncan and Wallach, "Universal Survey Museum." On the ceiling of the vestibule of the Louvre, for instance, four medallions symbolized the key art historical schools, each personified by a female figure holding a famous example of its sculpture. For Egypt, a cult statue was used; for Greece, the Apollo Belvedere; for Italy, Michelangelo's Moses; and for France, Puget's Milo of Crotona. France, in this schema, became the telos of human-kind's most civilized achievements.

37. Duncan and Wallach, "Universal Survey Museum," p. 451.

38. Duncan, *Civilizing Rituals*, p. 26.

39. M. Westermann, *The Art of the Dutch Republic 1585–1718* (London: Everyman, 1996). In 1810, Napoleon decreed the formation of a Museum of Painting in Madrid, using funds, partly, from religious orders. This project never materialized, but the seeds had been sown and the Prado was opened to the public in 1819 by Ferdinand VII, and consisted of 311 paintings, with a catalogue

40. Detlef Hoffmann, "The German Art Museum and the History of the Nation," in Daniel Sherman and Irit Rogoff (eds), *Museum Culture: Histories, Discourses, Spectacles* (Minneapolis, MN: University of Minnesota Press, 1994).

41. Edward Alexander, *Museums in Motion* (Nashville, TN: American Association for State and Local History, 1979); Lewis, "Collections, Collectors and Museums."

42. Anthony Smith, *National Identity* (Harmondsworth: Penguin, 1991), p. 14.

43. The South Kensington Museum was opened in 1857 and offered extended opening hours to maximize working-class attendance. Its success is indicated by the recording of over 15 million visits between 1857 and 1883, nearly half of which were made in the evenings, the most popular time for working-class visitors: Altick, *Shows of London.*

44. Paul Greenhalgh, "Education, Entertainment and Politics: Lessons from the Great International Exhibitions," in Peter Vergo (ed.), *The New Museology* (London: Reaktion, 1989).

45. Antonio Gramsci, *Selections of Cultural Writings,* edited by G. Forgacs and G. Smith (Cambridge: Cambridge University Press, 1971), p. 258.

46. Bennett, *Birth of the Museum*, p. 8.

47. Henry Cole, quoted in Simon Tait, *Palaces of Discovery: The Changing World of Britain's Museums* (London: Quiller, 1989), p. 9.

48. It is no accident that the fear of popular disorder attended the wake of unsettlement on the continent, the rise of working-class movements and the semantic shift in the word "mass" to connote "mob" and "unruly crowd": Raymond Williams, *Keywords: A Vocabulary of Culture and Society* (London: Croom Helm, 1976).

49. Bennett, *Birth of the Museum*, p. 95.

50. Ibid., p. 47.

51. Louis Wirth, "Urbanism as a Way of Life" (1938), reprinted in Richard LeGates and Frederic Stout (eds), *The City Reader* (London: Routledge, 1996), pp. 189–97.

52. Greenhalgh, "Education, Entertainment and Politics"; Peter Bailey, *Leisure and Class in Victorian England* (London: Routledge and Kegan Paul, 1978).

53. Altick, *Shows of London*; Georg Simmel, "Metropolis and Mental Life" (1903), in *On Individuality and Social Forms*, edited by Donald Levine (Chicago: University of Chicago Press, 1971).

54. Seth Koven, "The Whitechapel Picture Exhibitions and the Politics of Seeing," in Sherman and Rogoff (eds), *Museum Culture*, pp. 22–48.

55. Ibid., p. 38.

56. Trodd, "Culture, Class, City."

57. Colin Trodd, "Being Seen: Looking at the National Gallery in Mid-Victorian London," unpublished conference paper, ESRC Museum and Society Seminar, University of Keele, 1998, p. 13.

3

The Circus and Nature in Late Georgian England

Marius Kwint

You at command make brutes obey,
Walk, work, or dance, with movement gay.
Your horses far excel report,
Whose minuet might grace a Court;
Their hornpipe quick to music true,
They seem as if each step they knew,
But all the art and skill's with you.
The monkey, though of race despis'd
Unequall'd must by all be priz'd
His excellence excites surprise;
For e'en with man for fame he vies.
The dancing dogs, where Lady Flaunt
In chariot plac'd to take a jaunt
With flirting airs so perfect seen,
She seems to move a fairy queen.
The hunting, where the taylors chace,
A fox with mirth o'er spreads each face.

> *"lines . . . addressed to Mr. Astley by a Lady, on
> seeing his performances" (1785)*[1]

The modern circus has a rather different form and content from the chariot races of its ancient Roman namesake because it is the product of more recent times. It was invented chiefly around London during the 1760s and 1770s by a new breed of plebeian equestrian who possessed extraordinary skills of gymnastic trick riding.[2] Several of them had learned their techniques while training as cavalrymen in the British army during the Seven Years War (1756–63), which left Britain with a vastly expanded empire. Once demobilized, they sought to turn their skills to profit by performing stunts (such as headstands in the saddle or bestriding three cantering horses at once) at pleasure gardens and fairgrounds across Britain, continental Europe and sometimes further afield. Calling themselves "riding masters," they also offered riding lessons and set up arenas for the purpose. This was a time not only of unprecedented expansion and prosperity in leisure markets, but also of increasing reaction to them in the form of the Movement for the Reformation of Manners. Concerns about the limits of acceptable play have of course been perennial. But the years of Enlightenment and Industrial Revolution saw a new level of concerted efforts by Parliament and local magistrates to purge popular amusements of the most disorderly elements – the petty crime, vice and frequent cruelty towards animals – that had long attended the gathering of crowds.[3]

In this context a particularly talented and enterprising riding master, an ex-sergeant major from the light dragoons named Philip Astley, thought to intersperse his arduous feats on horseback with the more traditional fairground and interlude elements of tumbling and clowning.[4] He opened his own "riding school" in a field in Lambeth, on the southern fringes of London, in April 1768. It proved popular with a broad social range of audiences, but was forced to weather the jealousy of West End theater-managers and harassment from local magistrates before it won general recognition as a respectable form of family entertainment.[5] It was, however, by no means exclusively family-oriented. Partly because it was based in the common appreciation of the horse, the show transcended the normal differences of class and cultural outlook, and enjoyed the custom of prosperous working classes and aristocracy alike, although in segregated accommodation. Making a reported 40 guineas a day, Astley was within the next 20 years able to build permanent covered "amphitheaters" in Paris and Dublin as well as Lambeth. He then used these as headquarters from which to tour smaller towns in winter. Competition mounted, not least from the "Royal Circus," which opened near to Lambeth in 1782.[6] The Royal Circus not only coined a name for the genre, but also erected a fine stage next to the ring, bringing circus close to the world of drama for much of the next century. Astley's and the Royal Circus began to emulate each other in producing swashbuckling horse-borne melodramas known as "hippodramas."[7] Based on recent news of imperial exploits or Gothic legends, they were set with lavish scenery in exotic locations, and usually ended in massed battle scenes in front of burning castles complete with crashing timbers. Then the "scenes in the circle" would begin. Astley died in 1814 but his company in London went on to survive the Royal Circus, the introduction of the big top tent to Europe by a visiting American company in 1842, and the proliferation of many smaller touring companies without stages. Astley's Amphitheatre became a cherished institution of Victorian Britain and a standard brand for the circus business. However, after being immortalized in the writings of Dickens and Thackeray and lampooned in the pages of the satirical magazine *Punch*, it began to suffer from a decline in the taste for hippodrama and increasing competition from the music halls.[8] The Amphitheatre was finally demolished in 1893.

This chapter concentrates upon the founding example of Astley's in order to analyze the attitudes to the environment that the circus inherited, and with which it played. The circus is, after all, basically about nature, testing its limits by dwelling on spectacular and exceptional things. Most of these performances are obviously gained through training and cultivation, but some are presented as natural anomalies. My method is borrowed from structural anthropologists, notably Claude Lévi-Strauss and Edmund Leach, who have studied the way that humans tend to order the world into fundamental categories, regardless of place or time.[9] These categories fall into a sequence as one moves from the familiar realm of the self and the home, through the ambiguous zone of "vermin" and "game," to the threatening domain of "the other," the exotic, and the wild. Corresponding sequences apply to all phenomena: thus humans may be (and frequently are) subjected to the same criteria of domesticity, wildness or ambiguity as other animals. Indeed the chief lesson of this approach is that statements about the differences *between* species actually reflect our perceptions of difference *within* our own, and our evaluations of them.

It may seem inappropriate to use such an avowedly anti-historical doctrine as structuralism as a tool of historical analysis. But I see no reason why the foundations of human thought cannot be shown in their relationship to the more *super*structural, ideological elements of belief and practice that changed over time. Indeed a more chronologically inflected application of structuralist thinking can be seen in the work of the famous Soviet critic Mikhail Bakhtin, who saw revolutionary potential in the grotesque symbolism employed by the French sixteenth-century writer Rabelais, especially in his story of the gluttonous and incontinent giants *Gargantua and Pantagruel*.[10] These literary idioms stemmed, Bakhtin argued, from an ancient and pervasive culture of the carnival that, ironically, reached its peak in the repressive and religiose world of the late Middle Ages and early Reformation. Humans tend to punctuate periods of normalization and restraint (in this case Lent) with outbursts of misrule, when the social lid is lifted off and the world seems temporarily to be turned upside down. Night becomes festive day, women dominate men, boys are dressed up as bishops and swing censers filled with human excrement, animals dress up as humans and vice versa. Authority is lampooned; hierarchies and taboos are suspended in a phase of Dionysiac excess. The lofty realm of the mind is temporarily subverted by the base physical interests of the genitals and the guts – the "lower bodily stratum," as Bakhtin called it.

Much of this symbolism is of course traceable in the modern circus, most particularly in the nonsensical trickster-figure of the clown, but in a comparatively etiolated form. There is no spilling over into the mass participation that characterizes the carnival proper. This is partly because the circus is a *reformed* form, shaped by the moral and political campaigns of late Georgian and Victorian

Britain. The circus packaged up the vestiges of carnival in within an orderly commercial space, and added feats of human discipline and demonstrations of how animals should be cared for and cultivated. By these means it helped to rescue certain popular traditions from a world that had begun to look unacceptably rough, disorderly, and cruel to many opinion-formers. This remained the rationale of the circus, even though its precepts were deeply archetypal, and even arcane. How the circus negotiated these tensions provides much of the substance of the following account.

As far as we know, the robust figure of Philip Astley rarely intellectualized his art, except in his early "Prologue on the Death of the Horse" of June 1768. His steed would play dead in the ring while Astley announced that this was to show, "how brutes by heaven were design'd / To be in full subjection to mankind." Then, referring to a famous general in the recent Seven Years War with the French, Astley bellowed: "Rise, young Bill, & be a little Handy / To serve that warlike Hero, [the Marquis of] Granby."[11] Whereupon the horse would of course briskly stand up. Circuses went on frequently to stage the death of the horse in order to elicit astonishment at the ability of riding masters to train their animals. Equestrian performers had, after all, founded the circus, and remained its hub. So the relationship between human and horse is likely to be the first key to the logic of the genre.

It is widely accepted that the natural world is fundamental to human identity by allowing awareness of ourselves as a species. Animals in the human environment provide instruments for categorical thought: they are, in the words of Lévi-Strauss, "things to think with."[12] Onto them we project our visions of human difference and moral character, and hence our emotions. It is nonetheless surprising that an influential genre of mass urban entertainment should be sustained by an equestrian cult that lacked the appeal of competition or gambling. Some circus historians have suggested that the ubiquity of the horse in pre-automotive society had the effect of heightening the audience's astonishment at what the riding masters could do.[13] This may have been true, but was hardly a new factor by the time that the modern circus was founded in the 1760s. Other circumstances must have helped to make the dramatic potential of the horse so apparent.

In his splendid book *Realizations*, the cultural historian Martin Meisel attributes the circus firmly to an emerging Gothic and Romantic sensibility that captured the imaginations of elite intellectuals and popular pleasure-seekers alike.[14] Meisel takes Astley's famous hippodrama *Mazeppa; Or, The Wild Horse of Tartary* (first performed there in 1833) as an example. The play was based upon Lord Byron's poem of the same title, in which a low-born Polish youth who dares to love the daughter of the king is lashed naked to the back of a "fiery untamed steed" and sent galloping off across the Steppe. He survives to raise an army, avenge his punishment and win both the kingdom and his love. Meisel, noting the prevalence of fiery horses in parallel mid-nineteenth-century imagery, notably the paintings of Rosa Bonheur and Eugene Delacroix, rightly perceives that the "image of the horse apparently spoke to this age with a special eloquence." He goes on to claim that "[b]oth the mastery of embodied passion and energy, and the pure passion and energy itself, ready to shake off or run away with the presumptuous human will, were part of the fascination with the horse and its drama."[15] The steed, in other words, was a metaphor for the restless forces of history that had been unleashed by revolution, and a true embodiment of the sublime. The language used to describe and promote equestrian spectacles certainly took on clear political overtones: in 1827, for example, the great performer and manager of Astley's Andrew Ducrow staged a gladiatorial combat of "Ferret Horses" in the ring, who seized and flung each other "as when in a Wild Ungovernable State of Nature."[16] This was, of course, a time when the radicals and conservatives were battling to present their preferred forms of government – republican on the one hand or monarchic on the other – as the most "natural," virtuous, and correct. By the 1830s the craze for the display of nature red in tooth and claw was sweeping even the august stage of the major London theaters, arousing much controversy from the critical guardians of serious drama. As well as horses, these formulaic melodramas began to feature wild exotica including elephants, camels, zebras, and big cats, with the plot usually hinging on their apparently miraculous "taming" on stage. Fairly plainly, the oriental settings of such spectacles as *Hyder Ali; Or, The Lions of Mysore*, shown at Drury Lane in 1831, switched the focus of anxieties about domination and control away from post-Napoleonic Europe and towards the colonial frontier.

The Romantic fondness for the wild or barely controlled horse was a deliberate attempt to subvert the animal's traditional meaning as a sign of gentility and property: a meaning that had been aquired and given a rich patina during many centuries of husbandry. As living proof of the power of nurture over nature, of reason over passion, the horseman – not bound and naked but poised and armed – normally served as an emblem of conquest and indeed of civilization itself. Since the Renaissance it had, after all, been standard practice throughout Europe for rulers to commemorate themselves with an equestrian statue at the heart of their city. Moreover, even during the industrial revolution the horse still served as the most spectacular source of muscular power for the building of commercial society. Like the painter George Stubbs, who depicted on the one hand shiny hunters and thoroughbreds standing with their masters in English pastoral idylls, and on the other Arab stallions wide-eyed and rippling with fear and arousal in the wilderness, the circus traversed the full range of interpretations of the horse during its time.[17] In the early days, however, the conservative and genteel message predominated, partly because that was simply the way things were in *ancien régime* society, and partly thanks to Astley's own military background, personal disposition, and desire to prove the social usefulness and cultural legitimacy of the circus in the face of doubts about its legal status. By demonstrating that his horse would volunteer its life for its master and country, Astley was making a fairly straightforward ideological point about the need for loyalty to the crown in a time of frequent war and apparent sedition.[18]

Nevertheless, during Astley's time several new and important complexities were emerging in the prevailing world view. As Keith Thomas has shown in his book *Man and Natural World*, orthodox accounts of human supremacy over the brute creation were no longer taken for granted by the latter half of the eighteenth century.[19] By the later 1780s, scientists and sentimental observers alike were beginning to credit the beasts with sympathetic intelligences of their own, no longer simply regarding them as benchmarks of human beings' comparative greatness, as God-given exemplars of certain moral characteristics from which people should learn (as in the medieval bestiary book), or as mere objects to be exploited. Astley's and his colleagues' achievements seem to have contributed a little to the shift in perceptions during this decade. Conventions of horse-breaking had themselves been modified by humanitarianism since the later seventeenth century, and Astley strongly advocated the newer wisdom. Choose a horse, he advised in his best-selling riding manual *The Modern Riding-Master* of 1775, "with Eyes bright, lively, resolute and impudent; that will look at an Object with a Kind of Disdain. We may discover by the Eye his Inclination, Passion, Malice, Health and Indisposition; the Eye is the most tender Part of the Frame." Any obedience was to be valued, "therefore if somewhat tractable the first Morning, take him into the Stable, and caress him; for observe this as a golden Rule, *mad Men and mad Horses never will agree together*."[20] The calm of a good horse reflected well upon its owner, although those animals that rebelled against this contract and their supposedly docile natures became all the more liable to savage punishment.

Even before the advent of the sublime aesthetic in the circus arena during the 1800s, there were moments when the apparently intractable horse was to be welcomed. One of the most enduring clowning routines from the early circus was *The Taylor to Brentford*. This was a parody of a foppish and jumped-up tailor who had, according to urban legend, failed to persuade his horse to carry him to vote for the radical John Wilkes in the Middlesex election in 1768. Ending with the horse chasing the tailor round the ring, it became a standard in circuses until the late nineteenth century, being adapted to various national and topical contexts.[21] *The Taylor* was also adopted more widely as a figure of speech about the supposed relations between master and servant. One memoirist of English high politics in the reign of George III, for example, explained that he knew from the start that the joint ministry of the radical Charles James Fox and Lord North would never last, "for he was court when Mr Fox kissed hands, and he observed George III turn back his ears just like the horse at Astley's when the tailor he had determined to throw was getting on him."[22] The satirical point, of course, was that radicals were morally and intellectually inferior to the beasts and, as such, would be sniffed out by the latter in the proving-ground of the circus, where the natural order of things was to be tested and reestablished. As Edmund Leach has stressed, the invidious comparison of humans with animals has always provided the basis for insult and derogation.[23] Speciesist jokes abounded in the circus. During the age of hippo-drama, press commentators often contrasted the histrionic talents of the "quadruped" actors with their "biped" counterparts, taking a swipe at the taste of the audience in the process. "People do not care much about fine acting at Astley's," wrote the author of one guide to London in 1827, "the horses are esteemed to be the principal performers, and if they do their parts well, the whole house – 'pit, boxes and gallery, egad' – is content."[24] As Andrew Ducrow famously said, audiences were usually eager to "[C]ut the cackle and get to the 'osses."[25]

The words pertaining to horses were usually printed in the largest font on circus posters, and accompanied by bold woodcut images of the creatures rearing or galloping, often with fiery manes, wild eyes and dilating nostrils in the manner of Delacroix.[26] One poster from 1829 effectively presented a manifesto for the entire cult of the circus horse:

[D]emonstrations of HORSEMANSHIP and HORSE-TUITION . . . afford contribution towards the Amusement and Instruction of Holiday Folks and Juveniles to a degree ever-remembered after a first visit, as the vivid emotions of surprise and delight arising from their exhibition . . . inculcate a love for that noble Animal, the Horse, and a kindly feeling for his welfare, which we are taught to interest ourselves in next to our own on account of his sagacity, usefulness, strength & beauty. The Art of Tutoring and Managing him is here converted to the object of recreation, & proves a . . . source of pleasurable contemplation, as it is one of powerful & undiminished attraction.[27]

A few years earlier, shortly before the first animal protection act was passed by Parliament in 1822, Astley's took a sentimental look at the plight of horses in its hit pantomime *The Life, Death and Restoration of the High-Mettled Racer*. This catalogued the decline of a celebrated thoroughbred, which ended its days as a dray at the Elephant and Castle in London and was eventually dispatched on a knacker's cart, only to find heavenly reward in a "Grand Palace of the HHOUYNMS" [*sic*].[28] In order to conclude that horses were a nobler species than the supposedly civilized humans who debased them, the last scene drew upon Jonathan Swift's satirical fantasy novel *Gulliver's Travels* (1726), where a nation of horse-like creatures called Houyhnhnms stands out as the most rational and sympathetic of all the strange societies that Gulliver visits. Similar points were raised in much anti-slavery rhetoric and in the related myth of the "noble savage."

Evidence of audience responses to these shows, although heavily mediated by graphic artists and fiction-writers, suggests that the "emotions of surprise and delight" were indeed "vivid." Charles Dickens fondly recalled taking his seat at Astley's as a part of childhood Christmas ritual, the "vague smell of horses suggestive of coming wonders."[29] He later elaborated in *The Old Curiosity Shop* on the way that one working-class matriarch in the gallery wore out the tip of her umbrella after hammering it on the floor in her excitement at the hippodrama. Throughout the classes, behavior at the theatre was generally more casual than it is today, allowing plenty of opportunity for socializing, eating, drinking, and showing off, including wise-cracks and collective banter with certain star performers.[30] However, the equestrian routines appear to have been moments for comparative rapture. Much of the wonder seems to have stemmed from the transfigured quality of the horses, which escaped their typical roles as beasts of burden and labour, becoming ethereal and, as many critics commented, appearing almost to fly along with their riders in acts of gleeful freedom and transcendence. "One of his horses – a short tailed bay," wrote one commentator of Ducrow, "is a beautiful creature – 'a beast for Perseus; he is pure air and fire; and the dull elements of the earth and water never appear in him'."[31]

As in all circus turns, whether such thrilling effects were the result of nature or nurture was deliberately left ambiguous, since it is a fundamental technique of spectacle to obscure the historical origins of what one displays. Conjuring – or, in Astley's words, "Natural Magic" – was, after all, a central part of the circus repertoire.[32] This was all the more the case in a culture that was coming to terms with curiosity as something of both commercial and intellectual value, and spent much time toying with the distinctions between "natural" and "artificial" phenomena.[33] Much literate commentary indicates that Astley's captivated many of the *cognoscenti* as well as the populace, demonstrating feats of cultivation that were widely thought to be a credit to the present age of intense scientific and technological experiment. However, circus performers remained coy about their techniques and disclosed them only in calculated fragments. Some newspaper readers were informed that Astley's horses were the product of at least six months and sometimes two or three years' painstaking work, but ultimately it did not matter whether the effects were known to be natural or artificial. Humankind was so powerful as to make the artificial seem natural.

In a similar spirit, but with added ideological irony, equestrian culture congratulated itself on its achievements in training and selective breeding while treating those differences as divinely ordained. This vagueness about the origins of hierarchy was useful for representing the human class system, as circuses purported to give lessons on social deference and duty. The supreme arbiter of equestrian culture was the gentleman on horseback, so the riding master (originally his servant) served as teacher of stewardship and duty. His sensitive work contrasted the vicious attacks sometimes made by proletarians on the prized horses of the rich, as he strove to educate the people in the importance of physical fitness and martial skills.[34] "When mounted on his beautiful grey, in the centre [of the ring]," eulogized the *Morning Post* in 1807, "the veteran ASTLEY, apparently in the flower of his age, still conserves the extraordinary management of the horse . . . What a noble example to the heads of families, civil and military, and to the rising generation in general, is to be witnessed every evening!"[35] And as with cars today, there was a horse for almost every status and occupation, and the circus displayed a full range, from "high-bred racers," through sturdier Hunters, horses "for Ladies," "Forest Racers" for children ("only 39 ins high"), to the broad-backed Hanoverian Creams used in the ring.[36]

Although the performing arts have often served as an avenue of social opportunity, equestrianism also helped to reinforce the norms of class, race, and gender. The essential horse required the quintessential man: in the early years circus horsemanship was headlined as "manly" (and hence English) in reaction to the worrying influence of French foppishness. Astley's own "System of Equestrian Education," on which he published a highly successful manual in the early nineteenth century, was presented as a plain and sensible home-grown rival to the previously dominant and supposedly simpering French and Neapolitan schools of horse-riding.[37] Horsemanship was the ultimate test of integrity, so for the early riding master Dingley in 1766, the feats of a female rider were proof that "The fair sex were by no means inferior to the male, either in Courage or Ability."[38] Despite the fact that horsemanship was held to be a "science" and therefore problematic for women, feats by them, including the spouses of Philip Astley and his rival Charles Hughes, were presented without particular qualification in the early 1770s. While the spotlight was on masculinity, exceptional women could use such activities to break free of tradition: there were swordswomen, female pugilists, and occasional jockeys into the Napoleonic period. During the nineteenth century, however, the need to define masculinity seems to have given way to a greater anxiety about the display of femininity, with commentaries on female performers usually stressing their prettiness, elegance and desirability to men. In 1818, a handbill for circus riding lessons (now segregated by sex) assured readers that "The most timid Lady need not be under the least Apprehension in Learning this most useful and necessary Art ."[39]

For ethnographic demonstrations, one could look at an increasing range of imported styles of riding during the nineteenth century; not only the classical Haute Ecole and Viennese, but also more stirring choices: "The kind of companionship and attachment between Greeks, Arabs, and their Horses," claimed a bill for Ducrow during the period of Ottoman war in 1826, "furnish[es] full scope for the managed Horses."[40] On the stage, a horse conferred worthiness on a foreign character, whether Cossack ally or Saracen foe, whereas the irredeemable savage always fought on foot. The horse as a mirror of humanity could also be reflected back upon certain grades of human, as well as other species: apart from the rope-dancer described as "a beautiful young female" in 1789, a play of 1785, for example, was about a cobbler's attempt "to bring his Wife to Proper Submission."[41] Not only did the different uses of the horse serve as metaphors for the vicissitudes of class, gender and ethnicity, but the equestrian setting also made for a brisk narrative. "The spectacle," in the words of one Astley's poster, "embodies Life as it Gallops."[42]

The species was the ultimate parameter of judgment in the circus: as one newspaper wrote in 1785, Astley's "endeavours" had been "to procure . . . various . . . phænomena both from the human and animal species."[43] However, the definition of species remained unclear, and the term was often confused in fairground rhetoric with such other categories as class, race, and nation: menagerie posters, for example, frequently talked of different "races" of animals. The resulting anxieties about the boundaries of the human species were seen most clearly in the presentation of human and animal oddities, or what twentieth-century American carnivals called freaks. Since the Renaissance they had been viewed as curiosities – clues to the grand puzzle of the cosmos – and as such could be legitimately displayed as both entertaining and of serious scientific interest. Errant or playful nature produces, said a fairground advertisement for a hermaphrodite in 1818, "a Magnet of Irresistible and Universal Attraction."[44] According to a modified Aristotelian view, such phenomena were misassembled from components from different species, indicating the units by which nature worked. Freaks, sometimes described as "creatures" to enhance their strangeness, thus threatened the orthodox divide between humans and the brute creation on the one hand, while at the same time often reassuring viewers of their relative normality on the other. As Robert Bogdan has argued, there have, as a result, been two alternative modes for presenting freaks, either normal and domesticated or alien and wild.[45] Wybrand Lolkes, "The Friesland Dwarf" was successfully exhibited at Astley's in the former manner in 1790, with souvenir publicity presenting the unremarkable bourgeois lifestyle that he sustained despite his unusual stature. However, such shows were already becoming controversial in polite circles and therefore tended to be avoided by the respectable circus unless they were comparatively tasteful.

More typically, the circus displayed artificial anomalies. Sufficient training could not only counteract the natural order, but also apparently reverse it. In what became a staple circus act, Astley's "Little Learned Military Horse" would simply fire "a pistol at the word of command."[46] By firing the pistol itself, not just withstanding one being fired nearby, this horse went against common knowledge about the nervousness of its species. Astley later gained a royal patent for his method of habituating horses to the sound of gunfire.[47] During the mid-1780s a wave of pigs, dogs, and monkeys momentarily upstaged Billy's equine conjuring and other tricks, with a more sensational impact upon the perceived gap between humankind and animals. The Learned Pig, the only really new admission to the ranks of the sapient, enchanted the salons of a credulous London between 1784 and 1788 with his apparent ability to speak with the aid of letter cards, as well as mind-reading and card tricks.[48] Writing in 1788, the year after Astley had shown his own version, the children's moralist Sarah Trimmer credited the act with real influence in the gradual dethronement of humankind:

> "I have," said a lady who was present, "been for a long time accustomed to consider animals as mere machines, actuated by the unerring hand of Providence, to do those things which are necessary for the preservation of themselves and their offspring; but the sight of the Learned Pig, which has lately been shown in London, has deranged these ideas and I know not what to think."[49]

Even a trainer, writing in 1805, claimed to be amazed by the animal's abilities. One could, he said, eventually abandon the subtle cueing signals, "for the animal is so sagacious, that he will appear to read your thoughts."[50] The pig, hitherto a byword for the bestial, touched a raw nerve in human–animal relations, sparking concerns and controversy about training methods, and becoming a satirical emblem for Romantics including Wordsworth and Burns.

Animal acts therefore sought to imply that the creatures had human-like motivations and reasoning: in 1770, the Little Learned Military Horse behaved "as if he understood" his instructions "word for word," and by 1799 Astley had developed the "LITTLE SPEAKING HORSE."[51] Astley's horse Billy was the progenitor of the now standard circus "Liberty Act," such a notion of freedom having been, of course, a definitively human aspiration. The significance of Astley's "really clever" dancing horses was that dance – an extension of manners – was seen as another crucially human attribute.[52] The *Morning Herald* in 1785 was not alone in saying that "The encrease of *learned animals* of the *brute species*, as horses, dogs, pigs, &c. must touch the feelings of every humane heart, when it is known that the tricks they perform are taught by the most excruciating torture."[53] Trainers warned the public that results were to be obtained by encouragement only, but it became known that Dancing Dogs at Astley's were kept hungry, and stormed a miniature castle on stage with such alacrity only because food was placed on the other side.[54] The acts played upon, as well as contributed to, an emerging bourgeois sensitivity towards the brute creation.[55] The restoration of a prelapsarian harmony within the animal kingdom was a powerful subtext for animal acts throughout the history of the circus.

Clothing became a basic tool of manipulation in these often anthropomorphic spectacles. The rope-dancing monkey General Jackoo, miming his own little interlude, needed only "the gift of speech" to make his appearance complete and, "while he is so laughably brandishing his sword, cry – 'Who's afraid?'"[56] In a genteel precedent to the chimps' tea party, Jackoo took an elaborate public breakfast with a canine Mme de Pompadour, which included a glimpse of a world truly upside down when they were waited on by humans. In similarly topsy-turvy and grotesque fashion in 1829, two ponies would sit down to eat at the table, dressed as Darby and Joan. Such acts provided comic antidotes to the adoration of the horse as an object of beauty. As well as animals stepping into human shoes (and sometimes vice versa), there were more complex exchanges between species. In 1785, Astley travestied the horse with a "large" and "richly caparisoned" dog, ridden by General Jackoo in a "Triumphal Entry" of 1785.[57] In 1788 he used "a surprising Real Gigantic Spanish Pig, Measuring from head to tail 12 feet, and 12 hands high, weighing 12 cwt. Which," again, was "rode by a MONKEY."[58] Anthropomorphism tended to suppress the usual differences between species, choosing instead to stress their common abilities as actors. In the Dancing Dogs, for instance, dogs and monkeys played humans together in the same scenes: mongrels carried monkeys to masquerades in sedan chairs, and simian executioners dispatched canine deserters. Illustrations made it hard to distinguish them. Other categories of human figured in the formula too: the child jockeys of the 1795 pony races at Astley's were, by 1848, supplanted by "5 Highly-Trained Monkeys."[59] In the circus, the *category* of the species became so important that *actual* species frequently was not.

What always mattered, however, was the mental map of the natural world, which defined the roles that animals could take. Animals (including people) were generally categorized by their apparent closeness to, or distance from, the gentlemanly norm. Horses or dogs, for example, qualified for the virtually human class by merit of their domesticity, while monkeys obviously did so on the basis of their anthropoid appearance. With its naked, pink skin, the pig conformed to some extent on both counts. The closest animals were given the most versatile roles: familiarity (as well as actual easiness to train) bred apparent complexity of character. Indeed the whole spectrum – from domestic to wild – could be encapsulated *within* a single species in the case of horses and dogs. Horses, most of all could be "devils" or heroes; actors who could portray emotions from "distorted fury" to "calm obedience."[60] By contrast unfamiliar animals – "the beautiful zebra," the "elegant" camel – tended to be typecast as aesthetic objects or irredeemable, if beautiful, monsters.[61]

Here the logical structures have been separated out for the purpose of analysis, but in reality they followed each other in quick succession, with interpretations adjusted to political fashion and perceived audience taste. The circus was the sequential version of the same fairground aesthetic that struck William Wordsworth, in his famous passage on "Bartholomew Fair" in *The Prelude* of 1816. To him the fair revealed the perceptual disorder at the heart of industrial modernity ("The Horse of Knowledge, and the learned Pig . . . All jumbled up together, to compose, / A Parliament of Monsters . . .).[62] These were "All," he said, the products of a single "Promethean" impetus; a panoply of infinite technological and political possibilities for the self-recreation of humankind and its environment. Wordsworth seems not to have been the first to notice this. "What cannot man," demanded a press doggerel-writer after Astley's tour to Dublin in 1790:

> . . . – the wonder of whose hand,
> The well-earned plaudits of this night command?
> When brutes the works of reason seem to find
> Glow into thought, and nearly change their kind;
> When the fleet courser proves obedient skill,
> And moves conformant to the master's will?
> Thus from instruction can perfection flow,
> And ev'ry grace of polished pleasure show,
> Admiring circles ever justly draw,
> And raise e'vn brutes beyond the brutal law.[63]

Hackneyed and deeply traditional circus acts were, at this revolutionary moment, reinterpreted in a semi-serious way. They became optimistic signs that modern human beings could transcend, by secular and enlightened discipline, the fallen state that had always appeared natural.

Notes

1. Hand-dated press cutting (hereafter ct.), June 19, 1785: British Library (hereafter BL), Th. Cts. 35 ("Astley's Cuttings from Newspapers"), item 673.

2. This chapter is based on a section of my 1995 Oxford University D.Phil. thesis, "Astley's Amphitheatre and the Early Circus in England, 1768–1830," forthcoming as a book with Oxford University Press. For an accessible factual introduction to the field, see George Speaight, *A History of the Circus* (London: Tantivy Press, 1980); for a cultural-historical survey that quotes several of my findings, see Helen Stoddart, *Rings of Desire: Circus History and Representation* (Manchester: Manchester University Press, 2000).

3. For a useful summary of these events and some of the debates they have generated (though I disagree with its slant), see Susan Easton *et al.*, *Disorder and Discipline: Popular Culture from 1550 to the Present* (Aldershot: Temple Smith, 1988); on the general growth of leisure consumption, especially in more elite circles, see John Brewer, *The Pleasures of the Imagination: English Culture in the Eighteenth Century* (London: HarperCollins, 1997).

4. See Marius Kwint, "Philip Astley (1742–1814)," *New Dictionary of National Biography* (Oxford: Oxford University Press, forthcoming); for detailed coverage of the early years also Kwint, "Astley's Amphitheatre," ch. 1.

5. See Marius Kwint, "The Legitimization of the Circus in Late Georgian England," *Past and Present: A Journal of Historical Studies* (February 2002); and for further information Kwint, "Astley's Amphitheatre," chs. 2, 3.

6. See George Palliser Tuttle, "The History of the Royal Circus, Equestrian and Philharmonic Academy, 1782–1816, St. George's Fields, Surrey, England" (Ph.D. thesis, Tufts University, 1972).

7. See Arthur H. Saxon, *Enter Foot and Horse: A History of Hippodrama in England and France* (New Haven, CT: Yale University Press, 1968).

8. See, for example, Charles Dickens, "Astley's," *Sketches by "Boz,"* vol. 1 (London, 1836); Charles Dickens, *The Old Curiosity Shop* (London, 1841), ch. 34; William Makepeace Thackeray, *The Newcombes: Memoirs of a Most Respectable Family* (London, 1854), ch. 16; for further literary and journalistic references see Raymond Toole Stott, *Circus and Allied Arts: A World Bibliography*, 4 vols (Derby: Harpur and Sons, 1958–71); Paul Schlicke, *Dickens and Popular Entertainment* (London: George Allen & Unwin, 1985); Stoddart, *Rings of Desire*, ch. 6; also Jacqueline Bratton and Jane Traies, *Astley's Amphitheatre* (London: Chadwyck-Healey, 1980), pp. 15, 60.

9. See, in particular, Edmund Leach, "Anthropological Aspects of Language: Animal Categories and Verbal Abuse," in E.H. Lennenberg (ed.), *New Directions in the Study of Language* (Cambridge, MA: MIT Press, 1964); Edmund Leach, *Humanity and Animality*, 54th Conway Memorial Lecture (London: South Place Ethical Society, 1972); Claude Lévi-Strauss, *Structural Anthropology*, 2 vols (London: Allen Lane/Penguin, 1968).

10. Mikhail Bakhtin, *Rabelais and his World,* trans. Helene Iswolsky (Cambridge, MA: MIT Press, 1968); for applications of his theories to other phenomena see Terry Castle, *Masquerade and Civilisation: The Carnivalesque in Eighteenth-Century Culture and Fiction* (London: Methuen, 1986); Peter Stallybrass and Allon White, *The Politics and Poetics of Transgression* (London: Methuen, 1986).

11. Transcript of advertisement, *Gazetteer*, June 11, 1768: BL, Th. Cts. 35, item 14.

12. Quoted in Edmund Leach, *Lévi-Strauss* (London: Fontana, 1985), p. 43.

13. Bratton and Traies, *Astley's Amphitheatre*, p. 11.

14. Martin Meisel, *Realizations: Narrative, Pictorial and Theatrical Arts in Nineteenth-Century England* (Princeton, NJ: Princeton University Press, 1983).

15. Meisel, *Realizations*, p. 216; on *Mazeppa*, see Saxon, *Enter Foot and Horse*, ch. 7; see also Whitney Chadwick, "The Fine Art of Gentling: Horses, Women and Rosa Bonheur in Victorian England," in Kathleen Adler and Marcia Pointon (eds), *The Body Imaged: The Human Form and Visual Culture since the Renaissance* (Cambridge: Cambridge University Press, 1993), pp. 89–107.

16. Astley's playbill, July 27, 1829: Astley's file, Theatre Museum, Covent Garden, London (hereafter TM); for an erudite biography of Ducrow in his context see Arthur H. Saxon, *The Life and Art of Andrew Ducrow and the Romantic Age of the English Circus* (Hamden, CT: Archon, 1978).

17. For a culturally insightful discussion of Stubbs see Stephen Deuchar, *Sporting Art in Eighteenth-Century England: A Social and Political History* (New Haven, CT: Yale University Press, 1988).

18. For this context see, especially, Linda Colley, *Britons: Forging the Nation, 1707–1837* (London: Pimlico, 1994); also Gillian Russell, *Theatres of War: Performance, Politics*

and Society, 1793–1815 (Oxford: Clarendon Press, 1995); Kwint, "Legitimization of the Circus."

19. Keith Thomas, *Man and the Natural World: Changing Attitudes in England, 1500–1800* (Harmondsworth: Penguin, 1984).

20. Philip Astley, *The Modern Riding Master; Or, A Key to the Knowledge of the Horse and Horsemanship, with Several Necessary Rules for Young Horsemen* (London, 1775), introduction.

21. The stereotyping of tailors seems to have had varied origins, some perhaps because they were perceived as slippery purveyors of social identities as well as being prominent radical agitators. See George Speaight, "Some Comic Circus Entrées," *Theatre Notebook* 32 (1978), pp. 24–7; John Towsen, "The Clown to the Ring: The Evolution of the Circus Clown, 1770–1975" (Ph.D. thesis, New York University, 1976), pp. 1–26.

22. George Townshend, c.1802, source untraced, quoted in Joanna Innes, letter to the author (November 30, 1999).

23. Leach, "Animal Categories."

24. [William Clarke], *The Every Night Book; Or, Life After Dark* (London, 1827), pp. 22–3; see also Saxon, *Enter Foot and Horse*, p. 8.

25. Saxon, *Life and Art of Ducrow*, p. 179.

26. On the graphic rendition of the horse see Kwint, "Astley's Amphitheatre", pp. 169–90.

27. Astley's playbill, June 8, 1829: TM.

28. Astley's playbill, April 10, 1820: TM; see also Saxon, *Enter Foot and Horse*, pp. 73–6.

29. Dickens, *Old Curiosity Shop*, ch. 34, quoted in Bratton and Traies, *Astley's Amphitheatre*, p. 60; see also Dickens, *Sketches by "Boz,"* p. 301.

30. See Kwint, "Astley's Amphitheatre," p. 244.

31. Clarke, *Every Night Book*, p. 24; for a discussion of the symbolism of flight and lightness in the circus, which some have argued betrays shamanistic archetypes, see Kwint, "Astley's Amphitheatre," pp. 268–72; also Stoddart, *Rings of Desire*, ch. 8.

32. See Astley's conjuring manual: Philip Astley, *Natural Magic; Or, Physical Amusements Revealed* (London, 1785).

33. See, for instance, Barbara M. Benedict, *Curiosity: A Cultural History of Early Modern Enquiry* (Chicago: University of Chicago Press, 2001), esp. ch. 5.

34. See Thomas, *Man and the Natural World*, p. 184.

35. Ct., Morning Post, 1807: BL, C. 103.k.11 (Lysons Collection), vol. 5, fo. 64.

36. Ct., September 15, 1791: BL, Th. Cts. 36, item 56 D; ct., April 10, 1770: BL, Th. Cts. 35, item 27; ct., *Morning Post*, November 27, 1810: BL, C. 103.k.11, vol. 5, fo. 64.

37. See Philip Astley, *Astley's System of Equestrian Education, Exhibiting the Beauties and Defects of the Horse; With Serious and Important Observations on his General Excellence, Preserving it in Health, Grooming, etc.* (London, 1801).

38. Quoted in Maurice Willson-Disher, *Greatest Show on Earth: Astley's (Afterwards Sanger's) Royal Amphitheatre of Arts* (London: G. Bell, 1937), 13.

39. Ct., November 2, 1818: BL, Th. Cts. 37, item 738.

40. Astley's playbill, April 10, 1826: TM.

41. Astley's playbill, November 25, 1844, for W.T. Moncrieff's *The Royal Fox Hunt and the Race Horse, and Life's Course of Man and Steed!:* Bodleian Library (hereafter Bod. Lib.,) John Johnson Collection, "Theatres A–C" portfolio.

42. BL, Th. Cts. 35, item 1112 (June 10, 1789), 692 (October 1, 1785).

43. Ct., October 20, 1785: BL, Th. Cts. 35, item 698.

44. Advertisement for Mlle Lefort, with a beard, h.d. 1818: BL, C. 103.k.11, vol. 1, fo. 75. During the eighteenth century scientific orthodoxy moved from the theory of "sports of nature" (*lusus naturae*) induced by God for our puzzlement and edification, to a more secular view of natural error. See, for example, Joseph Levine, *Dr. Woodward's Shield: History, Science and Satire in Augustan England* (Berkeley, CA: University of California Press, 1977), ch. 1.

45. Robert Bogdan, *Freak Show: Presenting Human Oddities for Amusement and Profit* (Chicago: University of Chicago Press, 1988) 206, ch. 4, *passim*.

46. Astley's playbill, 1770: BL, 1879 c. 13 ("Miscellanea Collection").

47. See Public Records Office, London, Patent Rolls, IND:16806.

48. See Gerald Stanley Eames, "The Freaks of Learning: Learned Pigs, Musical Hares, and the Romantics," transcript of lecture, Toronto Public Library, February 4, 1980: Bod. Lib., John Johnson Collection, "Animals on Show," box 2; also Ricky Jay, *Learned Pigs and Fireproof Women* (London: Robert Hale, 1986), pp. 8–21; Richard Altick, *The Shows of London* (Cambridge, MA: Belknap, 1978); Stallybrass and White, *Transgression*, ch. 1.

49. Sarah Trimmer, *Fabulous Histories Designed for the Instruction of Children, Respecting their Treatment of Animals*, 3rd edn (1788), p. 71, quoted in Thomas, *Man and the Natural World,* p. 92.

50. William Pinchbeck, *The Expositor; or Many Mysteries Unravelled . . . comprising The Learned Pig, . . . Invisible Lady* [etc.] (Boston, MA, 1805), p. 26, quoted in Eames, "The Freaks of Learning", p. 14.

51. Astley's playbill, 1770: BL, 1879 c. 13; ct., May 2, 1799: BL, Th. Cts. 36, item 176 C.

52. Ct., August 9, 1768: BL, Th. Cts. 35, item 863; see also Thomas, *Man and the Natural World,* p. 37.

53. *Morning Herald*, September 5, 1785, *Morning Post*, April 17, 1785: BL, C. 103.k.11, vol. 2, fo. 127.

54. Astley, *Natural Magic*, pp. 27, 36; for later evidence of Astley's alleged training methods see *Report from the Select Committee on Performing Animals, Together with the Proceedings of the Committee and Minutes of Evidence* (London: HMSO, 1921), p. 22, min. 641.

55. On this issue see Harriet Ritvo, *The Animal Estate: The English and Other Creatures in the Victorian Age* (Harmondsworth: Penguin, 1990), p. 27, chs. 2 and 3; Thomas, *Man and the Natural World*, ch. 4; Brian Harrison, *Peaceable Kingdom: Stability and Change in Modern Britain* (Oxford: Oxford University Press, 1982), ch. 2.

56. Ct., April 16, 1785: BL, Th. Cts. 35, item 648.

57. October 6, 1785: BL, Th. Cts. 35, item 750.

58. Advertisment, quoted in Thomas Frost, *Circus Life and Circus Celebrities* (London, 1875), p. 33.

59. Astley's playbill, January 10, 1848: Bod. Lib., John Johnson Collection, "Theatres A–C" portfolio.

60. Saxon, *Enter Foot and Horse*, p. 212; Astley's playbills, September 14, 1829, "*Third Week! . . . Oscar & Malvina*," 1812: TM.

61. Ct., November 24, 1780; playbill, September 25, 1822: both TM.

62. William Wordsworth, *The Prelude* (1816), 8.11. 685–723.

63. *Dublin Morning Post*, March 15, 1788: BL, C. 103.k.11, vol. 4, fo. 30.

4

Flâneurs in Paris and Berlin

Esther Leslie

The flâneur is a figure of rumor, perhaps larger in fiction than in life, more often described and defined than glimpsed walking on city streets. But if the flâneur has indeed paced real city streets, he would have been hard to spot, for unobtrusiveness is his aim. The flâneur is likely to be a black-suited insubstantial presence, out and about, snooping on the bustle of the world, then moving on. (The pronoun and the attire are apposite – fictional and factual flânerie is, in the main, a male pursuit – though recently female flânerie has been discussed and delineated).[1] The flâneur is allied to the dandy, but where the usually aristocratic dandy is known for his immaculate attention to dress and a desire for self-display (and self-publicity, hence renowned individuals such as Count Alfred D'Orsay, Prince de Sagan, and Beau Brummel), the flâneur is anonymous, passing by unnoticed, a product of hearsay. Or, he never appears simply as a flâneur, but in other guises: as poet, journalist, critic, detective, spy, shopper, gambler or crook. Flânerie may be a pretext – the promenade is for information-gathering, a reconnaissance, a stimulus to create, an excuse for a story. Perhaps he lives only to *flâner* or maybe his dallying is a temporary pursuit, and tomorrow he resumes his routine. Little is certain about the flâneur, and much is gossip, often put in circulation by the flâneur himself.

The first flâneurs were native to France, indeed Paris alone, and thrived best in the nineteenth century. The flâneur's special way of inhabiting the streets is not exported in those years – English dictionaries translate the word as "idler," unaware of the sheer energy and initiative that it takes to dwell in the streets in his way. In 1862 a study of France in the Second Empire, aimed at English speakers, appeared under the title *Ten Years of Imperialism in France: Impressions of a Flâneur*. The anonymous author describes himself as a flâneur, but in his preface finds it necessary to gloss the term:

In offering his impressions to the public, the "Flâneur" must apologise for his foreign name, and explain its meaning. His apology is that no word exists in the English language which would convey a correct idea of a Flâneur. He is not an "Idler" as is generally supposed; on the contrary, intense activity of all faculties is one of the most necessary qualifications of a Flâneur. Nor is he an "Observer;" for this would imply the concentration of his faculties towards a definite aim and in a certain direction. The true Flâneur has a horror of all definite aim; he never seeks – he trusts to chance. His mind is like sensitive blank photographic plate, ready for any impression which may present itself.[2]

Intensity of experience, openness to coincidence, a dread of all intention: these are all characteristics in many descriptions of flânerie. The photographic metaphor is noteworthy. The flâneur has a camera-eye, as befits an archetypal inhabitant of the century of optical devices, and in Paris, a prime location for their invention.

The flâneur was able to flourish as species only after the French Revolution. His existence is inseparable from the changes in urban public space, post-1789, that accompanied the establishment of bourgeois rule: industrialization, commodity production and democratization. The burgeoning arenas of bourgeois life – notably shops, public parks, cafés and then, later, railway stations, museums, exhibition halls – are essential for the flâneur's leisured and curious inhabitation of the urban realm. These are the "despised everyday structures" which attract the flâneur, places where the masses enter the stage of history, sites to scrutinize, spaces to hide in a crowd, open to chance encounters and always with one foot in the salon and an ear to the ground, from where all noteworthy commotion swells up.[3]

After the revolution, the new citizen of France acquired political interests, which, in turn, bred the desire for discussion and a curiosity about public affairs. A bourgeois public sphere took shape. Until the 1830s newspapers, available only on subscription, could be read otherwise in the cafés, among gamesters and smokers. And, since the revolution, many chefs having lost their aristocratic retainers, opened restaurants in Paris. Such were the places where a person might kill time, not detached from the world, but participating in its novel forms of citizenship. The flâneur inhabits these locations of modernity. And now his star rises, at least in certain interested circles, for he becomes, according to the periodical *Le Livré des cent-et-un*, not merely the "premier need of an advanced age" but also "the highest expression of modern civilisation."[4] The 1830s are the flâneur's golden years. The favored spots for haunting, the arcades, are built, for the most part, in the decade and a half after 1822. These covered walkways were lined with trading outlets and were a development out of the Galeries of the Palais Royal. With their jumble of diverse commodities from across the Empire, they offered much in the way of display. A guide from 1852 describes each glass-roofed and marble-lined passageway as "a city, a world in miniature."[5] They were perfect sites in which to linger.

The arcades gave way in time to department stores. Modes of purchase, ways of shopping were being reinvented through the century. On the way to the café or restaurant, a stroller passed through busy streets where, in a new bourgeois-capitalist environment, commerce had come to signify vitality – busi-ness. The city streets were bustling – hence their appeal to the flâneur desirous of haphazard, condensed sorties. In 1857, Adolf Stahr's survey of the Second Empire *Nach Fünf Jahren* illustrated in a vignette the Parisian technique of inhabiting the streets. Men are repairing the pavement and laying a pipeline. An area in the middle of the street is blocked off, but covered with stones.

> On the spot street vendors had immediately installed themselves, and five or six were selling writing implements and notebooks, cutlery, lampshades, garters, embroidered collars, and all sorts of trinkets. Even a dealer in second-hand goods had opened a branch office here and was displaying on the stones his bric-a-brac of old sups, plates, glasses, and so forth, so that business was profiting, instead of suffering, from the brief disturbance.[6]

Trade thrives in city disorder. Spaces of commerce and intercourse open up in the turmoil of the streets, and temporary sites of transaction emerge alongside the latest dazzling rows of shops with plate-glass windows, vitrines, mirrors, and artificial lighting (which allowed shops to open late into the night). These trading zones slinking through the metropolis are a facet of an enticing cityscape that offers many opportunities for looking, investigating, and speculating without having to commit to buy. Disinvestment from the displays is important, for the flâneur hopes to maintain a curious but uncommitted attitude, intense but not absorbed. The flâneur's experience is concentrated. Balzac links the flâneur to the artist, the person who experiences life in a heightened fashion: "to stroll is to vegetate, to *flâner* is to live," says Balzac's flâneur.[7] The flâneur lives passionately, but he also attempts to retain an intellectual mastery over the flux of spectacle and event. As Victor Fournel's *Ce qu'on voit dans les rues de Paris* states in 1858:

> Let us not, however, confuse the flâneur with the rubberneck (*badaud*): there is a subtle difference . . . The average flâneur . . . is always in full possession of his individuality, while that of the rubberneck disappears, absorbed by the external world, . . . which moves him to the point of intoxication and ecstasy.[8]

The flâneur approaches the city with faculties alert. He is a reader. For him, the city is a text, an array of signs ready for decipherment and interpretation. Scrutiny is directed at buildings and street furniture, but also at passers-by, men of the crowd. In 1840 Edgar Allen Poe's London-based "Man of the Crowd" appeared as an enigma demanding to be cracked. This followed on from Balzac's observation, in 1830, of the need for *vestignomie*. Reading clothing as signs was a response to a pace of life in which it seemed that there was no longer time to get to know the whole man. To a certain extent, such a "science" was developed in the spate of "physiognomies" and "physiologies" of eccentric or remarkable urban types presented to the public. The perplexing city scene provides the flâneur with much to see, but he too is a part of the spectacle. The flâneur is awarded his own handbook: *Physiologie du Flâneur* written by Louis Huart in 1841. Such books allowed the identification of social types, a guide to their clothing, mien or slang, and a key to their habitat and milieu. Surfaces are on show, but they may not be decipherable without further ado. Guides and experts are indispensable. This certainly appeared to be the case with commodities, in Marx's view, as intimated *Das Kapital* (1867), his guide to the nineteenth century's economic regime. One section is titled: "The fetishism of commodities and their secret." Marx's phrase conjured up detection and intrigue, and likewise many have written of the flâneur as a detective investigating modernity. The modern scene needed constant reinvestigation, for it was in permanent flux. As the author of *Ten Years of Imperialism in France* put it in 1862: "Another week or two, and another leaf will have been torn out of the book of historical Paris."[9] The city kept changing, most notably in the grand restyling of Paris by Baron Haussmann from the late 1850s onwards. The texts of the city, in turn, had to be ever revised. As Walter Benjamin notes in *The Arcades Project*, his uncompleted study of Paris, "the capital of the nineteenth century":

> Few things in the history of humanity are as well known to us as the history of Paris. Tens of thousands of volumes are dedicated solely to the investigation of this tiny spot on the earth's surface.[10]

The city as text, the city become decipherable signs, or words and stories, chock-a-block with secrets, stimulates the flâneur to activity. His activity is like that of an artist, a writer or a journalist-writer who records the scenes that he witnesses, the impressions that he snatches on his wanderings through city streets. That conversion of flâneuristic experience into an output – first freely generated as artistic pursuit, a by-product of leisured activity, later a mode of wage-labor – becomes a necessary part of the flâneur's remit over time. The flâneur is drawn into earning a wage. An 1808 dictionary of vulgar usage defined the flâneur as "a lazybones, a dawdler, a man of insufferable idleness, who does not know where to carry his trouble and his ennui."[11] This flâneur contrasts with a definition from a pamphlet in 1806, which presents the vision of a leisured type who submits to the daily rounds of salon visits in the guise of reviewer.[12] One is the dandyish idler without any purpose, the other a creature of habit, oriented to the cultural scene. A quarter-century later the flâneur cuts a quite different figure. Indolence is banished and regularity is his enemy. He is a hunter in search of the unexpected, the special, the affective. For the flâneur the city is akin to what untamed nature was for the Romantic soul: a place to wander and reflect. The flâneur approaches the city as if it were a landscape. The flâneur goes "botanizing on the asphalt," as Benjamin quips.[13] The city is a hunting ground, risky and bizarre. Gas lamps and lampposts appear as coconut palms, and the Arcade of Cairo, through its name and its emporia, imports marketable foreignness into the city. There is no Romantic sentimentality about lost nature. The city is more foreign and dangerous than the colonies or wild nature, according to Charles Baudelaire's morbid anthropology of man as hunter:

> What are the perils of jungle and prairie compared to the daily shocks and conflicts of civilisation? Whether a man embraces his dupe on the boulevard, or spears his prey in unknown forests, is he not eternal man – that is to say, the most highly perfected beast of prey?[14]

Primitivity is spied at the heart of civilisation: the urban scene as landscape. But Walter Benjamin is keen to pinpoint the dialectical flipside of the city as wild plain, identifying in nineteenth-century accounts of Parisian life reference to the street as interior, where glossy enameled shop signs function as wall decoration, newspaper stands as libraries, mailboxes as bronze busts, café terraces as balconies and the sections of the railway tracks where rail workers hang up their jackets as vestibules.[15] This is an exploded interior, for it is not an isolated shelter for privatized domestic bliss. The flâneur is the tenant most at home in this city as house, a world turned inside-out, where privacy is sneered at in favor of the life in the mêlée:

> The street becomes a dwelling for the flâneur; he is as much at home among the façades of houses as a citizen is in his four walls. To him the shiny, enamelled signs of businesses are at least as good a wall ornament as an oil painting is to the bourgeois in his salon. The walls are the desk against which he presses his notebooks; news-stands are his libraries and the terraces of cafés are the balconies from which he looks down on his household after his work is done.[16]

To the flâneur, the city, its arcades and streets, formed a vast world in miniature, through which the flâneur could wander unaccosted: Walter Benjamin labeled the spatial sensation "now landscape, now a room."[17] The coming of the department store provided another version of this doubled scale, being both a space that seemingly contains the whole world, an endlessly roamable landscape, varied as the jungle, and yet, at the same time, comprised of rooms, with intimate, domestic niches. The department store signals the generalization of flânerie as a mass affair, for, as Benjamin points out, the palaces of commodities "made use of *flânerie* itself in order to sell goods."[18] The point was to wander, circumspectly, among crowds, to tarry, to push past, to explore, and, above all, to see. In the city everyone is on show behind plate-glass windows and on café terraces. As much as they look, they are looked at. Resplendent nineteenth-century Paris reflects in countless passing eyes, transferring onto mobile crowds the gleaming brilliance of shop-windows, lit cafés and bistros, reflective façades and, after road surfacing, the "glassy smoothness of the asphalt on the roads," all performing as screens that mirror subjects back to themselves as objects. Paris is dubbed the "looking-glass city," and within its bounds the crowd turns spectacle and the flâneur its spectator and chronicler.[19] Such reportage presupposes detachment, even while in the midst of the crowds. Anonymity is an advantage.

Flâneur-poet Charles Baudelaire relished the sense of anonymity that the bustling streets provided. He hoisted the flâneur's sense of self to the ideal of anonymity in a crowd, a figure borne along by the waves of human activity. A defining article was that on Constantin Guys, published in the Parisian newspaper, *Figaro*, in 1863, titled "The Painter of Modern Life." Here Baudelaire describes Guys, an illustrator, as a superior relation of the "mere flâneur." This superior flâneur participates fully in modern life:

> The crowd is his element, as the air is that of birds and water of fishes. His passion and his profession are to become one flesh with the crowd. For the perfect flâneur, for the passionate spectator, it is an immense joy to set up house in the heart of the multitude, amid the ebb and flow of movement, in the midst of the fugitive and the infinite. To be away from home and yet to feel oneself everywhere at home; to see the world, to be at the centre of the world, and yet to remain hidden from the world – impartial natures which the tongue can but clumsily define. The spectator is a prince who everywhere rejoices in his incognito.[20]

The flâneur is "the lover of universal life" who "enters into the crowd as though it were an immense reservoir of electrical energy." Baudelaire scrambles for other metaphors to express the multifaceted and symbiotic relation of flâneur and crowd: "we might liken him to a mirror as vast as the crowd itself; or to a kaleidoscope gifted with consciousness, responding to each one of its movements and reproducing the multiplicity of life and the flickering grace of all the elements of life." What is this life he seeks that twinkles so enticingly, dispelling boredom?

> Be very sure that this man, such as I have depicted him – this solitary, gifted with an active imagination, ceaselessly journeying across the great human desert – has an aim

loftier than that of a mere flâneur, an aim more general, something other than the fugitive pleasure of circumstance. He is looking for that quality which you must allow me to call "modernity"; for I know of no better word to express the idea I have in mind. He makes it his business to extract from fashion whatever element it may contain of poetry within history, to distil the eternal from the transitory . . . By "modernity" I mean the ephemeral, the fugitive, the contingent, the half of art whose other half is the eternal and the immutable.

The flâneur treks the streets and boulevards in pursuit of the modern. He rummages among bourgeois ordinariness, encountering the modern everyday. The flâneur is a native, not a tourist, and he must live among everyday structures, for they are crucial to the flâneur's mode of seeing. As Benjamin noted:

> For it is not the foreigners but they themselves, the Parisians, who have made Paris the promised land of the flâneur – the "landscape built of sheer life" as Hofmannsthal once put it.[21]

The flâneur does not seek out beauty or ancientness, the exotic or the picturesque – indeed such things would distract him or overwhelm his attention. He searches rather for the modern quotidian, in order then to sniff out the fantastic in the ordinary. By now though, in Baudelaire's account, the flâneur appears to be less a man pursuing leisure, and more definitely an artist seeking material.

Baudelaire's study of Guys – which was also a self-conscious delineation of an epoch – was written for a newspaper, which is to say it was penned for money. Baudelaire is a mid-nineteenth century flâneur, and characteristic of such flânerie is the need to earn money in a more edgy, cut-throat marketplace. As the century progresses flânerie becomes less a leisure practice and more a mode of laboring, or at least turning leisure activities (walking, observing) into written copy in order to provide the material to occupy other people's leisure time. Or, perhaps, as the fine art of flânerie declines, a more mass version of its practices develops. This was certainly the way in which the word entered Anglophone usage. *Harper Magazine* spoke of the flâneur in 1854, asking its audience whether they too had not wasted a couple of hours in the metropolitan city window-shopping, as they "played the flâneur."[22] This is the flâneur as leisured type, yet also a potential consumer. In 1872 Braddon's *Life in India* ascribes a more purposeful activity to flânerie, mentioning the "knowledge of London life that comes to the active regular flâneur after years of active experience." E. Cobham Brewer's *Dictionary of Phrase and Fable* of 1894 makes flâneur synonymous with a lounger or gossiper, derived from *flâner,* to saunter about. *Websters Revised Unabridged Dictionary* of 1913 underlines this, calling the flâneur "one who strolls about aimlessly; a lounger; a loafer." But in France, once the numbers of flâneurs in fact and fiction had dwindled, a heroization reserved for the lost sets in. Pierre Larousse's *Grand Dictionaire Universel* in 1872 includes an entry on the flâneur of Paris:

> This city marked by a vitality, a circulation, an activity without equal is also, by a singular contrast, the place where one finds the most idlers, loungers, and rubbernecks.[23]

It continues, identifying the flâneur resolutely with the artist:

> His eyes open, his ear ready, searching for something entirely different from what the crowd gathers to see. A word dropped by chance will reveal to him one of those character traits that cannot be invented and that must be drawn directly from life; those physiognomies so naively attentive will furnish the painter with the expression he was dreaming of; a noise, insignificant to every other ear, will strike that of the musician and give him the cue for a harmonic combination; even for the thinker, the philosopher lost in his reverie, this external agitation is profitable: it stirs up his ideas as the storm stirs the waves of the sea . . . Most men of genius were great flâneurs – but industrious, productive flâneurs . . . Often it is when the artist and the poet seem least occupied with their work that they are most profoundly absorbed in it. In the first years of this century, a man was seen walking each and every day – regardless of the weather, be it sunshine or snow – around the ramparts of the city of Vienna. This man was Beethoven, who, in the midst of his wanderings, would work out his magnificent symphonies in his head before putting them down on paper. For him, the world no longer existed; in vain would people greet him respectfully as he passed. He saw nothing; his mind was elsewhere.[24]

This was a retrospective description of something deemed to be bygone. The flâneur-artist of the early nineteenth century was conceived as a man of regular habit – every day he walked, as did Kant – and as he paced he dreamt up creative schemes. But the likes of Beethoven would be jostled too much as the years progressed. The city has to come to serve the flâneur in another way. Indeed, in time, its Pandemonium and multiplicity becomes a creative spur. A symbiosis develops between the city with its teeming crowds and the production of flâneur-istic copy. The city becomes the only place that can generate material for the modern novel. Illustrative of this is Charles Dickens's comments in letters written in 1846 to John Forster from Lausanne. When in the mountains, Dickens missed the lack of street noise, indispensable to him for his writing.

> I can't express how much I want these [streets]. It seems as if they supplied something to my brain, which it cannot bear, when busy, to lose. For a week or a fortnight I can

write prodigiously in a retired place . . . and a day in London sets me up again and starts me. But the toil and labour of writing, day after day, without that magic lantern, is immense . . . My figures seem disposed to stagnate without crowds about them.[25]

Once more an optical metaphor – the city appears as a sort of screen, its throngs a phantasmagoria of half-perceived figures, obscurely going about their business. Dickens's social comedies, serialized in newspapers and journals, relied on his street observations. He also, in the persona of Boz the voyeur, lurked around the slums and market stalls of St Giles Circus, sketching farcical and tragi-comic encounters between individuals, which he then sold on to magazines.

The flâneur's experience, converted into creative output, is welcomed by the newspapers and magazines that are ever-more important vehicles of commun-ication and, especially, distraction. From the beginning of the nineteenth century, "feuilleton" was a part of what the newspaper offered. Feuilleton – from the French for "little leaves" – may refer to a particular rubric in a newspaper, perhaps marked off from the main copy by appearing underneath a line across the page or it may be a supplement to the main newspaper. Feuilleton can also denote a special mode of writing, a genre with a particular philosophical-aesthetic approach to the world and everyday life. It arose in the early 1800s in Paris and spread shortly afterwards to Germany. The Oxford English Dictionary records its slippage into the English language in 1845, in a quotation from the *Athenaeum*, but it remains a word for a peculiarly French activity: "The tendency of the newspaper feuilleton, in France, to absorb the entire literature of the day." In 1840 the *Blackwood Magazine* observes that: "The number of young feuilletonists . . . is now very considerable in France." The practice spread across Europe. In 1863 the *Macmillan Magazine* notes that a lot of Russian journals are carrying feuilleton. Feuilleton becomes a substantial part of the newspaper, as the newspaper market expands, and being informed about city life becomes a leisure pursuit. Gabriel Guillemot notes, in *Le Bohème* in 1869, that the introduction of the absinthe hour is connected to the growth of feuilletons.[26] As they sipped their green potion, drinkers relished the gossipy, frivolous and flamboyant feuilleton contributions: book reviews, fashion and the like, but also gleaned information about the latest events and most fashionable haunts in town. In this way the city itself becomes an object of interest, and the flâneur its expert witness. Observation has turned into a skill.

The flâneur has a keen eye for the market. But he is a participant too. In the guise of writer or journalist, he is also a supplier of commodities. Walter Benjamin records that the intelligentsia came into the marketplace as flâneurs. They thought that they were only observing the vitality of the market but soon they had to seek purchasers for their writing.[27] According to Benjamin this grouping became the *bohème*, and the corollary of its members' curious dependence on, but simult-aneous rejection of, the market, a double-bind formed by the uncertainty of their economic position, corresponded to the uncertainty of their political function. In his view, they become hacks, available to the highest buyer – an offshoot of their cultivated cynicism. Flânerie mutates into journalism: where the writer strings out sentences for cash, the artist illustrates for commercial purposes. The contemplation of the crowd, the impressions of urban seducement are rendered into currency. To this extent the flâneur is little different from any other person who sells his or her self, for he is inextricably linked in to the universality of exchange in commodity society. The flâneur, like the worker, is subordinated to the market. The peculiarity of capitalist commodity production is its all-engulfing nature. None can escape, and, in time, the flâneur succumbs to the clutches of that which had initially fascinated him but from which he had retained a certain distance. For Walter Benjamin it is their surrender while protesting that makes the flâneur, along with the poet, the dandy, the collector, the gambler, the worker, the rag-picker and the prostitute, a modern hero.[28] The modern hero is tragic, skewered on the contradictions of capitalist modernity. However, he is not nostalgic or sentimental about the past, rather he is engaged in finding strategies to survive the present. The world had changed so much since the flâneur's first gentle steps. Once upon a time the flâneur strolled leisurely through the city, in order to imbibe the visual delights of the urban display. His protest was to use idleness as a rebuke to a burgeoning economy of commodity manufacture and increased productivity.[29] Benjamin writes:

> There was the pedestrian who wedged himself into the crowd, but there was also the *flâneur* who demanded elbow room and was unwilling to forego the life of the gentleman of leisure. His leisurely appearance as a personality is his protest against the division of labour which makes people into specialists. It was also his protest against their industriousness.[30]

The flâneur's pace had been slow as a matter of principle. Of the arcades there developed a rumor that it was fashionable in 1839 to have the walking pace set by a turtle on a lead.[31] Gérard de Nerval preferred the more outlandish display of a lobster in the Palais Royal. Such behavior is bound to draw attention – and is, as such, perhaps, more dandyish. And even in the department store, where flânerie generalizes, restrooms, washrooms, and entertainments such as theatrical spectacles and fashion shows were part of a strategy to ensnare the shopper for a day. But this luxurious position becomes more and more difficult to sustain. The flâneur's position is seen to be ever more shaky as the century progresses, reaching a critical situation in the 1860s. The anonymous flâneur-author of *Ten Years of Imperialism in France: Impressions of a Flâneur* (1862), in his chapter titled "Money Mania," identifies an acceleration of Parisian life, and it is clear that as much as this pace of change stimulates urban fascination, it also threatens to destroy the very conditions of existence of the flâneurs and their ilk.

> There is a feverish activity perceptible in everything that surrounds us, strangely contrasting with that regular gentler current which once gave Paris the reputation for being the place above all others for *flâneurs*, *badauds*, and pleasure-seekers.[32]

The flâneur's habitat (like that of wild species) is under threat. The flâneur is a type whose very existence is in crisis, and yet there is something appropriate about this – for he is experiencing the crisis of the modern world, which is that world's very modus vivendi. The flâneur is an unstable figure, not one who indulges in a full mastery over the city that he traverses and the objects he examines. There can be no stable dominance over something that is in permanent flux. In the permanent revolution of metropolitan modernity, new experiences can be had, not least of which are the newly invented modes of transportation. These in turn compel overhaul of the roads, the flâneur's habitat. Benjamin notes a challenging situation:

> With the steady increase in traffic on the streets, it was only the macadamization of the roadways that made it possible in the end to have a conversation on the terrace of a café without shouting in the other person's ear.[33]

These were improvements that threatened the very existence of flâneuristic activity. While the possibility of conversation might have encouraged leisurely hours on the terrace, the new road surfaces led to an even greater increase in traffic, and so a general quickening of city life, such as militated against flâneuristic wandering. The arcades, which had once been a loitering zone protected from the traffic, are largely destroyed in Haussmann's replanned Paris, where wide boulevards slice through the space, allowing trams and military vehicles unimpeded movement. Haussmann was appointed by Louis Napoléon as the prefect of the Seine between 1853 and the fall of the Emperor Louis Napoléon in 1870. His restructuring shifted the working classes out of the city center to the east and gave the west over to the bourgeoisie. Impromptu urban growth on an arrondissement basis was replaced by authoritarian, centralized planning. This produced a pompous city of sweeping wide roads with monumental neo-classical façades that walled out the wanderer who did not possess wealth or status. The anonymous flâneur of 1862 detected this crisis in Second Empire Paris:

> the Old Town is still the heart and centre of Paris life, to which the Flâneur resorts, who wishes to participate in this life. After pacing up and down those large wide thoroughfares, a feeling of weariness comes over him. Those endless straight lines, those broad

boulevards which seem empty in spite of the crowd, that general resemblance of houses and shops so well calculated to strike at first sight and impress with an idea of grandeur, all contribute to benumb every sense after a short time, and to produce a kind of half-conscious stupor equally unfavourable to receiving impression or making observations. Almost without perceiving it, the flâneur branches off into one of the sidestreets, and a feeling of relief comes over him instantly.[34]

Perhaps then, at this point, the flâneur detaches himself from the progress of modernity, seeking instead the mud and the turmoil of the still remaining alley-ways. In these back-streets the crowd is not a listless mass, but alert, mastering its path through the streets, rather than traipsing down them, subjected to the brutish blows of modern life.

In Baudelaire the crisis of the flâneur and the pedestrian (as well, indeed, of modernity) finds aesthetic shape. The crisis that the flâneur comes to experience and register in his writing (in Baudelaire's case in his poetry and prose poems) is a shock experience, the crushing impact of city provocations, the elbowing of the crowd and the violence of market relations. Jostled by the urban crowd, the city dweller is forced to develop an exhaustingly vigilant stance, a military *on guard* that screens and judges and evaluates stimuli. But in this case, such city negotiation is less the dull street-traipsing that the 1862 observer noted and more a nervous watchfulness that forbids reflection or procrastination or leisured strolling. A prose poem from the late 1860s called "Loss of a Halo" expressed the new tensions well and cheekily. In the prose poem "Perte d'auréole" from *Petits poèmes en prose* (1869) Baudelaire mocks the idea of the aloof Romantic poet who muses on beauty. Instead the new poet must find material in his city dwelling. He must translate into poetry the streets, brothels, tarmac, traffic, noise, and commotion. He comes to this realization after a dangerous encounter while crossing the busy road. This causes him to drop his halo – his poetic laurel – onto the "mire of the macadam." He refuses to go back and reclaim it, happy now to walk incognito and be vulgar. Such a demotion can become burdensome. The poet-flâneur pays for his everydayness by becoming a wage-laborer like any other. He sells his poems. The streets are his routes to moneymaking. Eventually, notes Benjamin, the product – the poem, the feuilleton contribution – will be unnecessary, once the very act of walking becomes the way to earn some cash: as a sandwichman with an advertising board weighing on his shoulders, elevating the commodity he advertises while burdening the human being.

The major metropolises of the world had changed over a century and continued to change. Order gradually replaced disorder. In 1882 New York City, for example, was darkened by ugly bundles of overhead wires on wooden poles along all the main thoroughfares. The communication circuits of rival telegraph and telephone companies, burglar alarms and other amenities were strung without restriction or supervision, forming a criss-cross of decaying wires, some of which were no longer in use. The protruding wires of the arc lights were dangerous to the touch. In addition there were overhead circuits for distributing electrical energy to motors for lifts and driving machinery. Eventually this system of wires broke under its own weight and underground conductors were probed. Here Thomas Edison played a part in reforming the city, for he had long promoted the underground flow of electricity, just like water and gas. The system reached Paris.[35] A rationalized city emerges: well supplied with amenities and functionally planned boulevards. In certain respects the environment for walking was improved, and yet, at the same time, what had once attracted the flâneur diminished: the sense that something unexpected might occur, the chance encounter, the excuse to wander randomly. Those who can still afford to be flâneurs by the end of the century – that is, those do not have to find ways to make money from their leisure activities – retreat into the interior to build fantastic worlds of sensation and adventure. Here Huysmann's decadent hero D'Esseintes, with his perfumed experiments and luscious exotic interiors, is germane. But perhaps, at the point at which city planning and the intrusion of wage-labor made flânerie difficult to pursue in any serious and full-time way, it generalized as a part-time leisure activity, one largely linked to shopping and modes of seeking distraction. If this figure was no longer to be found loitering in arcades or bobbing in the mêlée, he had become a little part of every city dweller.

In any case the flâneur was not long absent and returned with some force – self-consciously, that is to say, with a theoretical armory – when, in the 1920s, the Paris-based Surrealists undertook a fantastic journey into the past that lurked in the present. Surrealism revived the art of strolling through a cityscape made of everyday peculiarities and chance encounters. They enjoyed the enclaves of anomaly that still nestled in the rationalized city. These niches, with their remnants of the past or ludicrous juxtapositions of objects, operated according to a different rhythm to that of the ordered rational city.[36] In particular, the Surrealists cherished the remaining arcades, as if they were passages into the unconscious of the city. Louis Aragon wrote in *Paris Peasant* in 1927:

> And how easy it is, amid this enviable peace, to start daydreaming. Reverie imposes its presence unaided. Here surrealism resumes all its rhythms.[37]

The Surrealists emphasized the reverie that could befall a flâneur wandering through the streets, disconnected from the purposiveness of regular daily life. This dreamstate was, of course, as is so often the case with flânerie, a precondition for poetic production. Saint-Pol Roux was said to display a sign on his bedroom door as he retired to sleep after a night on the tiles: Poet at work.[38]

It was not just in Paris that the art of flânerie was reinvigorated in these years. 1920s Berlin and Frankfurt hosted their share of wanderers, and this time in the guise of critics, rather than artists. Just as nineteenth-century flânerie had emerged hand-in-hand with the feuilleton press, in Germany too it was most definitely connected to new media. The deluge of magazines and journals that emerged in Germany after World War I incubated a type of journalism known as the "kleine Form," the little form. In this quasi-art form, literature met journalism in the form of poetic considerations of the "micro" and the "macro": everyday experiences, walks through favored parts of the city, remarkable and chance encounters and the like. The popular success of these short pieces was evidence of the widespread attraction of reading about big city life in the 1920s. The writings were matched by the visually striking city-documentaries of Walter Ruttmann and others. Indeed the connections to film were closer, for it seemed as if some of the short form pieces developed a sort of camera vision or cinema aesthetic, in tribute to the premier leisure activity of the epoch. For example, Siegfried Kracauer's observations on city scenes in Berlin and Frankfurt refer to literary translations of devices such as montage, superimposition, and dissolve. Moreover, Kracauer's feuilleton practice reflected on the place of film (alongside other leisure activities such as dance clubs and fairgrounds) in the lives of "white-collar workers."[39] Furthermore, the short form comes to be an analogue of modernity itself. It accommodated such elements as were found in Baudelaire's delineation of modern life: the ephemeral, the fugitive, the contingent, abruptness, fragmentation, superficiality.

Greater Berlin was formed in 1920 with 4 million inhabitants of an important industrial city and a cultural metropolis. It was immediately affected by the European trend for Americanism, in productive industry and in the cultural industries. The cityscape changed rapidly too. Berlin was electrified, the streets and department stores flooded by illumination. City observers picked up on novel experiences of time and space made technologically possible by mechanization and electrification and made concrete in modes of transport, telephones, telegraphs, conveyor belts, and the like. The new flâneur processes this dislocation and accelerated tempo. The new flâneur gives it back to the city inhabitants in the little sketches, harvested daily. Berlin was a difficult city to map, for it altered so quickly. It subsisted, thought Kracauer, in unhistorical space and empty historical time. In "Street Without Memory," December 16, 1932, he notes of a sortie into the everyday, that the façades on the old West End apartments are without ornament. This makes graphic for him a frightening loss of memory – "the bridge to yesterday" is cut away. He relates his searches for two favorite cafés on the Kurfürstendamm. All that is left of one is a hollowed-out interior, and the other, now a confectioner's, so represses the earlier memory of the café that it is as if it had never been there. Only the present exists.[40] The flâneur records a rapidly disappearing past, but the recording – the newspaper – is chucked away at the end of each day anyway. The flâneur's critical task has become an arduous and, maybe thankless, one. In an article for *Le Temps*, on May 22, 1936, the critic Edmond Jaloux conceded that the flâneur's days were over. The city is simply too hazardous for the chance-filled stroll. The streets are too noisy, too busy, and too policed.[41] Benjamin had another account of the decline of flânerie. It was the war on leisure itself, or at least leisure's industrialization through the adoption of Americanism. He affirms an observation in Georges Friedmann's *La Crise du progrès*, from 1936:

> Taylor's obsession, and that of his collaborators and successors, is the "war on flânerie."[42]

After F.W. Taylor comes Henry Ford and more speed-ups in an "efficiently" structured production process. With Ford comes Fordism, the rationalization and industrialization of leisure that would so irritate Benjamin's testy friends Adorno and Horkheimer in their 1940s analyses of "culture industry." With the arrival of the "culture industry," new types of culture-makers are needed for new audiences, all spontaneity and chance is said to disappear in the absolutely accounted-for, and all self-determined meandering apparently forbidden to the conformist "culture consumer" immobilized, under a dim light, in a plush chair.[43] But, then again, the death-knell of flânerie has been sounded repeatedly since the flâneur took his first ever steps.

Notes

1. In the 1980s the figure of the flâneur/flâneuse was the focus for an argument between feminists about the position of women in modernity, in modernism, and in "male" accounts of the modern. At stake was whether the concept of the flâneur offers women a subject position. Key contributions include: Janet Wolff, "The Invisible Flâneuse: Women and the Literature of Modernity," first published in *Theory, Culture and Society* 2, 3 (1985). Republished in Andrew Benjamin (ed.), *Problems of Modernity* (London: Routledge, 1989), pp. 141–56, and Janet Wolff, *Feminine Sentences: Essays on Women and Culture* (Cambridge: Polity, 1990); Elizabeth Wilson, *The Sphinx in the City: Urban Life, the Control of Disorder, and Women* (London: Virago, 1991) and "The Invisible Flâneur", *New Left Review* 191 (January–February 1992), pp. 90–110; Patrice Petro, *Joyless Streets: Women and Melodramatic Representation in Weimar Germany* (Princeton, NJ: Princeton University Press, 1989). For a discussion of English modernism and female flânerie, see Deborah L. Parsons, *Streetwalking the Metropolis: Women, the City and Modernity* (Oxford: Oxford University Press, 2000).

2. Anon., *Ten Years of Imperialism in France: Impressions of a Flâneur* (Edinburgh and London: William Blackwood and Sons, 1862).

3. See Walter Benjamin, *The Arcades Project* Cambridge, MA: Belknap, 1999), p. 55.

4. Quoted in Richard D.E. Burton, *The Flâneur and his City: Patterns of Daily Life in Paris 1815–1851* (Durham: University of Durham, 1994), p. 1.

5. Benjamin, *Arcades Project*, p. 31.

6. Ibid., p. 421

7. Quoted in Priscilla Parkhurst Ferguson, "The Flâneur on and off the Streets of Paris," in K. Tester (ed.) *The Flâneur* (London: Routledge, 1994), p. 29.

8. Benjamin, *Arcades Project*, p. 429.

9. Anon., *Ten Years of Imperialism in France*, p. 7.

10. Benjamin, *Arcades Project*, pp. 82–3.

11. *Dictionnaire Du Bas-langage, des manieres de parler usitees parmi le peuple* (Paris: Imprimerie De L. Hausmann Pour d'Hautel and F. Schoell, 1808), 2 vols. See also Ferguson, "The Flâneur on and off the Streets of Paris," pp. 24, 39.

12. See Ferguson, "The Flâncur on and off the Streets of Paris," p. 26.

13. Walter Benjamin, *Charles Baudelaire: A Lyric Poet in the Era of High Capitalism* (London: New Left Books, 1973), p. 36.

14. Benjamin, *Arcades Project*, p. 445.

15. Ibid., p. 423.

16. Benjamin, *Charles Baudelaire*, p. 37.

17. Ibid., p. 170.

18. Ibid., p. 170.

19. See Walter Benjamin, "Paris, die Stadt im Spiegel" (1929), in Benjamin, *Gesammelte Schriften* vol. IV.1, (Frankfurt/Main: Suhrkamp, 1989), p. 358.

20. This quotation and following ones stem from Charles Baudelaire, "The Painter of Modern Life," in Charles Baudelaire, *The Painter of Modern Life and Other Essays*, (London: Phaidon, 1964), sec. 3–4, pp. 5–15.

21. Benjamin, *Arcades Project*, p. 417.

22. See Oxford English Dictionary entry for flâneur.

23. Benjamin, *Arcades Project*, p. 451.

24. Ibid., pp. 453–4.

25. Cited in Benjamin, *Arcades Project*, p. 426, and in Forster's *The Life of Charles Dickens*.

26. Benjamin, *Arcades Project*, p. 430.

27. See Benjamin, *Charles Baudelaire*, pp. 170–1.

28. Ibid., p. 54.

29. See Benjamin, *Arcades Project*, p. 427.

30. Benjamin, *Charles Baudelaire*, p. 54.

31. Benjamin, *Arcades Project*, p. 422; Benjamin, *Charles Baudelaire*, p. 54.

32. Anon., *Ten Years of Imperialism in France*, p. 120.

33. Benjamin, *Arcades Project*, p. 420.

34. Anon., *Ten Years of Imperialism in France*, pp. 28–9.

35. Frank Lewis Dyer, *Edison, his Life and Inventions*, ch. 16: "The First Edison Central Station," http://www.cybernetbooks.com/edisonsamp.html

36. Benjamin, *Arcades Project*, pp. 100, 524.

37. Louis Aragon, *Paris Peasant* (London: Picador, 1971), p. 94.

38. See Walter Benjamin, *One-Way Street and Other Writings*, (London: New Left Books, 1979), pp. 226–7.

39. See Kracauer's various studies, including *The Mass Ornament*, (Cambridge, MA: Harvard University Press, 1995) and *The Salaried Masses: Duty and Distraction in Weimar Germany*, (London: Verso, 1998).

40. Kracauer, "Straße ohne Erinnerung," in *Straßen in Berlin und Anderswo* (Berlin: Das Arsenal, 1987), pp. 15–18.

41. Quoted in Benjamin, *Arcades Project*, pp. 435–6.

42. Quoted in ibid., p. 436. This "war on dawdling" is also identified in Benjamin, *Charles Baudelaire*, p. 129n.

43. See Theodor W. Adorno and Max Horkheimer, *Dialectic of Enlightenment* (London: Verso, 1995), pp. 120–67.

5

Crowd Control: Boxing Spectatorship and Social Order in Weimar Germany

Erik Jensen

Boxing launched the modern era of spectator sports in Germany during the Weimar Republic, a sport consumed by the masses, mirrored in film, newspapers, music, and literature, and celebrated in the highest social circles. With the possible exceptions of soccer and the six-day races, professional boxing resonated in the popular culture of the age far beyond any other sport, and it melded elements of both athletic competition and show business into a modern, hybrid form of popular entertainment that the public could afford. The allure of a top fight drew sold-out crowds in Berlin and other major cities, and discussions of the most recent bouts peppered everyday conversation. A 1925 poem evoked the trendiness and fashionability of professional boxing during this heyday: "A big fight beckons today . . . whether you ride or whether you sail . . . whether you flicker or [whether you] fox-trot – you have to go there: – there will be boxing!"[1] The public, in other words, not only wanted to watch the fights, but also had to watch. Boxing was "in."

This poem tellingly emphasized the viewing of the sport, rather than its practice. Despite tireless campaigning on the part of boxing associations, boxing never achieved the status of a *Volkssport*, a sport in which a large segment of the population actively engaged. Whereas both soccer and cycling attracted large numbers of weekend hobbyists and amateur players, as well as viewers, boxing enjoyed popularity primarily as a spectator sport, an activity that one cheered, analyzed, and discussed, but did not actually do.[2] A network of local boxing clubs certainly established itself throughout Germany in the 1920s, but the sport appealed to audiences out of all proportion to the numbers who actually practiced it.

Despite this mass following that boxing, and sports in general, enjoyed in Germany's larger cities in the 1920s, scholars have largely overlooked the social and cultural impact of this new form of spectatorship.[3] Pierre Bourdieu paved the way for examining the social significance of sports viewership as early as the

1970s,[4] but the growing literature on the history of leisure has generally concentrated instead on flânerie and the daily spectacle of the metropolis.[5] To the extent that it does address the phenomenon of spectatorship, it generally does so in the context of movie-going.[6] Adrian Shubert provides an exception, though, and points the way to a more thorough exploration of the influence of sports spectatorship on the broader society. In *Death and Money in the Afternoon*, Shubert examines the influence of bullfighting as "a form of commercialized mass leisure, a cultural industry" and emphasizes the social significance of spectating.[7]

Shubert and other historians also examine the crowd in modern history from a new perspective, no longer as the revolutionary, political instrument of the nineteenth century, but rather as a fundamental aspect of the twentieth-century growth of mass culture and leisure. As Vanessa Schwartz argues, in the context of France, the crowd did not disappear at the turn of the century, "their collective violence did."[8] Nonetheless, commentators in Weimar Germany remained wary of the social composition of sports crowds, and concern over how to discipline and educate this new group of leisure consumers emerged as one of the central topics in the German sports press after the First World War. In fact, the very mass appeal of boxing itself occasionally hindered the efforts of boxing officials to showcase the sport as a serious and respectable pastime.

Boxing in Germany had suffered from a reputation as something less than a full-fledged sport since the nineteenth century, and this continued in the years immediately after the First World War. Ernst Haberlandt expressed this common bias in 1920, when he wrote:

> It must be clear to everyone that six-day races, championship boxing, dance tournaments and similar contemporary developments have just as little to do with sport as skat tournaments, hunger artists, premieres of the fattest man, the thinnest woman and so forth. They are purely society enterprises designed to fill the pockets of the organizers.[9]

Many sports reporters associated boxing with crass sensationalism, and the spectacular growth of boxing spectatorship in the 1920s did not elicit unqualified cheers even from Germany's boxing associations. From the beginning of the Weimar Republic, the various associations, journals, and officials affiliated with German boxing tried to control the image of the sport and to encourage a certain kind of spectatorship, a proper form of viewing that fit with their vision of boxing as a serious athletic discipline, demanding appreciation of its grace and technical skill. The principal fear of this group, that boxing would attract only those fans looking for a cheap thrill, prompted frequent articles in both the journal *Boxsport* and the general-interest sports magazines.

In an effort to counteract this association between boxing and low-brow stuntmanship, the boxing press sought to attract and groom a sophisticated, informed, and sports-savvy viewing public. At the same time, and partly because of boxing's action-packed allure, the sport achieved a remarkable public following throughout the 1920s and early 1930s. In this chapter, I look at some of the reasons for the phenomenal popularity of boxing in Weimar Germany, and I examine the gap between an ideal notion of proper spectatorship, advanced by the boxing press, and the ways in which the German fans themselves enjoyed the sport. In particular, I focus on gender and social background in this analysis.

The hand-wringing over the public image of boxing stemmed partly from the sport's shadowy reputation prior to the First World War. Although no nationwide law prohibited boxing in Imperial Germany, police chiefs in the larger cities repeatedly imposed bans on public fights, and many early fights ended with police raids and fleeing spectators.[10] Whereas Britain and the United States had cultivated strong boxing traditions since at least the nineteenth century, only a few clubs in Germany managed to establish even a low-profile presence by the eve of the First World War, a situation that accounted for boxing's shallow roots in the postwar German population.[11] After the universal lifting of police bans on boxing in 1918, though, the sport spread rapidly,[12] popularized largely by a young generation of German boxers who had learned their craft in British prisoner-of-war camps during the war. These so-called "Knockaloe-Boxers," named after the internment camp on the Isle of Man, included such early German boxing stars as Hans Breitensträter, Kurt Prenzel, and Adolf Wiegert.[13] After the war, British occupation troops in the Rhineland further promoted the sport, and the future world heavyweight champion, Max Schmeling, recalled this region as an early hotbed of talented German fighters, although Berlin had eclipsed it by mid-decade.[14] Despite boxing's skyrocketing popularity, its promoters struggled throughout the 1920s to legitimize the sport and to overcome its image as a raw pursuit on the fringes of legality. As late as 1926, a judge in Baden declared boxing to be a *Roheitsdelikte* (brutal crime) in the guise of a sport.[15]

The sheer novelty of boxing surely accounted for much of its initial following, as promoters staged large events openly for the first time and hooked the public on their drama and visual spectacle. The well-publicized fights fed a postwar society hungry for excitement and diversion. Already, within a year of its complete legalization, people swarmed to boxing matches. A 1920 article in *Illustrierter Sport* wrote:

Anyone who observed the throngs of people on Wednesday night who headed for the small cycling arena in southeastern Berlin by streetcar, commuter train, automobile or foot and shoved their way before the small entrance must have automatically asked themselves how it is possible that boxing has achieved such a popularity with us in one year and that it has so many admirers.[16]

The very venues in which boxing matches took place in the 1920s indicated the sport's close relationship to the entertainment industry. Lunapark, an amusement park, hosted boxing programs that consisted of six or seven bouts and drew crowds of several thousand, as did music halls, theaters, and beer gardens, such as Zirkus Busch, the Admiralspalast, the Bockbrauerei, and the Berliner Prater.[17] In Hamburg, a theater presented boxing matches at the end of each night's dramatic performance, and some Berlin movie theaters considered introducing boxing matches during the intermissions of films. The journal *Boxsport* criticized this form of boxing promotion even though it accounted for much of the sport's public acclaim. One reporter feared that the coupling of boxing and show business would cause the public to "see boxing as a type of variety-show number."[18]

Some contemporary observers attributed the growth in spectatorship to a general dependence on comforts associated with the industrial age. Egon Erwin Kisch, a prolific commentator during the period, emphasized the passivity of the viewer in a 1928 article:

> The industrial era has mechanized and specialized everything . . . and when one has hot running water instead of having to heat the water oneself, why should one exhaust one's own body through sport – down on the track or up in the ring they, who you pay by purchasing your ticket, do it for you.[19]

Where Kisch saw the lazy ease of spectatorship, other writers discerned a collective effort, in which the crowd often determined the outcome of the fight itself. A 1927 article in *Boxsport* insisted that fans did actively participate in the contest by encouraging the boxer to give his best performance: "Just as the actor can only give his best before a sold-out house, the boxer cannot fight before empty seats."[20] Bertolt Brecht even wanted theater audiences to mimic sports fans and watch the drama unfold as if watching an athletic contest,[21] and he erected, on several occasions, a stage in the form of a boxing ring.[22]

Boxing spectators not only cheered the match itself, but also prepared for it ahead of time by honing their knowledge of the sport, and they read about it voraciously after the fact. Fritz Giese, in the 1925 book *Spirit in Sport*, distinguished between theater-goers, who appreciated the play without background information, and sports fans, who needed precisely that information to derive any sort of appreciation: "If he does not know the rules, the performance probably bores him beyond belief – he also remains unable to join in with the collectivity!"[23]

The press fed this demand for detailed information and simultaneously groomed well-informed spectators by devoting expanded coverage to sporting events and to instructions in their rules, strategies and finer points. On some Sundays, the sports section comprised over 50 percent of the newspaper.[24] A 1925 article in

Deutsche Presse advocated including sports coverage in the main section of the newspaper in order to arouse the athletic passions of those who normally skip over the sports section.[25] Because of its quasi-underground existence in Wilhelmine Germany, boxing, in particular, benefited from this increased sports coverage in the Weimar Republic, which acquainted greater numbers of people with the techniques, rules, and strategies of the sport. The two largest newspapers in Berlin, the *BZ am Mittag* and the *Morgenpost*, for example, organized introductory courses in the fundamentals of boxing.[26]

The press did not provide the only mass communications outlet for acquainting people with, and drawing them to, the fights. The 1920s witnessed the advent of radio and the proliferation of cinema, and the media industry capitalized on public enthusiasm for boxing, while further fueling it. Even audiences in smaller towns could watch footage of the greatest bouts of the day at their local movie theater,[27] or listen to radio broadcasts of the big fights, which debuted on German radio in 1925, from the comfort of their living rooms. Birk Meinhardt, an historian of boxing, argues that boxing fit neatly with the mission of early German radio. Stations broadcast all of the important fights not necessarily because the audience for them already existed, but because boxing provided a simple form of entertainment that would build its audience, "bringing to the German people some excitement and happiness," as the radio commissioner Hans Bredow put it.[28] Radio broadcasts greatly expanded boxing's already diverse audience to include rural populations and entire families, rather than predominantly urban men and women, and it created a form of virtual spectatorship. A 1932 account of the huge listenership for the radio broadcast of Max Schmeling's world-heavyweight-championship fight from New York noted the family nature of the event and the rapt attention with which fans across Germany sat glued to their radios at 3 A.M. to hear the results:

> Everywhere the two German announcers in New York are blaring from the windows, our entire half of the street is brightly lit. In Berlin W in a small villa on the top floor, an entire family in pajamas and bathrobes sits around the shrieking loudspeaker, while at the same time burglars downstairs are packing up 5,000 Marks in silver and carpets unnoticed.[29]

For those who could not attend the fights in person, radio, and to a lesser extent cinema, provided accessible substitutes.

Boxsport, the principal journal of the boxing associations, envisioned its role, and that of the press and mass media in general, as one of teacher, not only explaining the sport, but also showing how best to appreciate it. It tried, for instance, to soften the brutal image of boxing in a 1921 article:

The large part of the public that still remembers the talk of boxing's brutality from before the war has no idea of the refinement of this sport. It is worth enlightening people; reading materials must be created that discuss boxing glowingly and in layman's terms, that describe its rules, that outline the hard training and that demonstrate good, athletic fights in words and pictures.[30]

As early as 1919, *Illustrierter Sport* advocated "Sportliche Erziehung" (the rearing of good spectators, as if by parents) in an article that decried the unappreciative boxing crowds who simply wanted to watch a slugfest: "Hopefully the time is not so far off when our public has gathered a true knowledge of boxing, recognizing the subtleties of this sport and no longer going there in order to see bloody noses."[31] The magazine entitled the article, fittingly, "More self-control at boxing matches." Because of boxing's regulated violence and its very recent emergence in Germany as a fully sanctioned sport, boxing reporters often went to great lengths to dampen the baser emotions on display at fights and hoped to instill, instead, an appreciation of the subtleties of the sport.

Although radio and the press played potentially positive roles in the promotion of informed spectatorship, their attention also had a flip-side that made some boxing commentators, themselves members of the press, wary, since the media also attracted sensation-seeking spectators and accelerated the sport's commercialization. Socialist and communist journalists regularly decried the market-driven side of boxing, but even the mainstream boxing press criticized the drive for greater sensationalism and larger crowds. Many linked this commercialization directly to the growing US influence on German society and pointed to the United States as a frightening sign of things to come. A reader of the mainstream sports journal, *Der Leichtathlet*, for example, warned in 1927 of the encroaching Americanization of German sport: "One should not forget that America in its athletic development . . . has taken paths that are anything but exemplary and that our avoidance of these paths can only be deemed a positive outcome."[32] Americans thought of sport solely in business terms, he argued, and he pointed to the professionalization of sport and the high salaries for top players in the United States as examples. The editors of *Der Leichtathlet* commented that the reader had described a well-known situation, but that his letter served as a necessary reminder and dire warning.

If boxing owed much of its success to its sheer novelty and to its active promotion by the media industry, it also attracted an immediate following in the early years of the Weimar Republic partly because the very nature of the physical struggle resonated with large numbers of Berliners. The actor Fritz Kortner, both a fan and practitioner of boxing in the 1920s, stated: "What plays itself out in the ring mirrors life. As mercilessly, as furiously as the boxers go at one another, so bitterly do we all fight for our existence."[33] Not only did boxing provide a nice metaphor for the turbulent times in which postwar Germany found itself, but it also provided urbanites with a safe and controlled form of violence, in stark contrast to life on the streets. Birk Meinhardt, an historian of boxing, writes:

> Since brass knuckles and rubber truncheons counted as everyday pieces of equipment in the country, the people must have seen boxing as normal. It hardly appeared alarming in light of the conditions outside of the hall or stadium. Quite the opposite, it appeared orderly. The order of events were known, and the dangers, too. Violence, yes, but divided into tolerable doses. And most important: you weren't drawn into it, you remained a spectator.[34]

Boxing counteracted the irrational violence of the First World War and of the turbulent postwar German society by refracting it through the prism of sport, a "rational" form of violence. As the sociologist Karl Raitz notes, regarding the attraction of sport, "the rules create an order, both social and spatial, that is not found outside the playing site."[35] At the same time, boxing federations vigorously assailed the depiction of boxing as violent and emphasized instead its graceful athleticism. Boxing, then, could appeal both to those who sought an ersatz form of violence to that which surrounded them and to those who sought an escape from that violence altogether.

Boxing not only reflected the struggle of daily life, but also offered a ray of hope in the figure of the boxer himself, who represented a modern success story. Because most of the early boxers in Weimar Germany came from modest backgrounds, boxing developed a reputation as a blue-collar sport that attracted its best talent from the raw youth of working-class neighborhoods. Rags-to-riches boxing stories rapidly became a staple of Weimar popular culture.[36] The popular image of the champion fighter who had pulled himself up by his bootstraps contributed to the mystique of the boxer and lent a powerful element of heroism to the sport of boxing. Working-class fans, at least, flocked to boxing matches partly to see one of their own, someone who had "made it." And those who had made it attracted a loyal following.

Fans identified closely with their favorite boxers, and the personality and charisma of top fighters in Weimar Germany drew ever larger crowds to the big matches. The public idolized boxers to a degree witnessed in few other sports of the time. *Boxsport* championed boxers as "the embodiment of a modern national hero,"[37] and boxing's popularity grew as German boxers achieved international success in the late 1920s and early 1930s. As the fortunes of one boxer fell, several new boxers emerged to take his place in the national pantheon. In the early 1920s, boxers such as Hans Breitensträter, Kurt Prenzel, and Paul Samson-Körner captivated the public. By the late 1920s, Franz Diener and, especially, Max Schmeling had eclipsed these former greats. A poll of 14-year-olds taken in 1930 showed that Max Schmeling had the highest name recognition in Germany, placing well ahead of Gustav Stresemann, Karl May, and Henry Ford.[38]

Boxing placed the body on display more than most other sports, and its unabashed display of physical development and the human form also drew many spectators to the sport.[39] In an attempt to capitalize on this draw, boxers occasionally incorporated some sort of flirting with the crowd as a part of their in-ring persona. A report from a 1920 fight, for example, noted that one of the contestants threw kisses to spectators before the first round.[40] In a press report describing the arrival of Breitensträter in Vienna in 1922 for his fight against Bruno Schmidt, the reporter wrote:

> The main interest of the evening was palpably focused on the blond German heavyweight champion, who was greeted loudly and excitedly . . . Representatives of the boxing associations, press personnel, sports enthusiasts and also excited female fans awaited the blonde Hans on the train platform.[41]

This article repeatedly called Breitensträter by his nickname, "the blonde Hans," and practically fetishized his golden hair, referring at one point to "Schmidt's blonde opponent" and to "[Breitensträter's] open, honest face with its crowning shock of hair." By focusing on this boxer's general attractiveness, the reporter underscored the presumable reason for his popularity among most female and, undoubtedly, a fair number of male spectators.

A satirical boxing lexicon published in *Boxsport* in 1925 gave the following "definition" for Breitensträter: "Hans = box-office magnet, darling of the people, honored citizen of Biesenthal, holder of the longest record as well as the blondest hair."[42] By referring to Breitensträter as the "darling of the people," the passage employed language associated with film starlets, whose popularity also depended a great deal on their looks. It also implied that the boxer's blonde hair contributed a great deal to his status as a "box-office magnet." A 1921 article paid direct homage to Breitensträter's well-developed body and the devoted following that it attracted: "Admiration from untrained bodies surrounded him like soft babbling, him and his strong chest, his elegant legs."[43] In a 1932 article in *Der Querschnitt*, Breitensträter himself acknowledged the number of fans drawn to his good looks and warned of the strain that this could have put on a marriage.[44]

Because boxing appealed to the public on a number of different levels, as the above-mentioned examples show, it attracted a remarkably broad audience. This audience, however, did not share a universal appreciation for all types and levels of boxing. Whereas the *Großkampfabende*, the professional events that featured champion fighters, played to packed houses in Berlin, only true boxing aficionados regularly attended amateur events or fights sponsored by local boxing clubs. The fact that these contests had a hard time filling even small venues indicated, perhaps, that a regard for the technical aspects of the sport itself accounted for only a small part of professional boxing's popularity during the Weimar Republic. In a 1921 article, *Boxsport* bemoaned the fact that only the big fights achieved any sort of public notice, and then largely thanks to the "stylish advertisements." It also portrayed boxing as largely a Berlin phenomenon, clearly rooted in the fashionable milieu of the metropolis and passing by most Germans "with more or less complete indifference."[45]

Boxsport lobbied for more club fights and for less emphasis on the sensationalism and commercialism of the big events. In a 1927 front-page article, it wrote, "What differentiates us from other major boxing centers are the establishment of permanent small or mid-sized rings. The entire development of boxing in Berlin is always attuned only to the big fights."[46] The article criticized the Berlin fans for focusing on the crass showmanship of these spectacles, and it implicitly blamed them for the underdeveloped network of boxing clubs and amateur contests.

Boxing commentators regularly criticized this public fixation on showmanship rather than technique and attributed it to the social background of the spectators. Kisch, for one, lampooned the perceived spirit of many boxing fans in Weimar Berlin, who just wanted to see a good scrap, with lots of punches and little attention to the rules. In one piece, he published a cacophonous pastiche of dialog from a boxing match, in which fans hurled insults, threw bottles and shouted, "Down with the referee."[47] Physical punishment impressed these fans more than the question of who displayed the best footwork. The journal, *Die Leibesübungen*, conceded in 1927 that some spectators at boxing matches truly appreciated the sport and attended, in part, to enrich their own knowledge of boxing, but it characterized the majority of spectators as "this mass of beer-drinking, spitting, cigarette-smoking, loud-mouthed sensation-seekers."[48] Curt Gutmann, in a 1928 article, bemoaned the fact that most spectators still did not understand the sport of boxing:

> How little the broad masses actually understand about boxing, its essence and its art can be seen anew with the deepest regret at each fight. They want to see k.o.'s; blood must flow; they want to see pounding, grabbing, until one or the other boxer or, better yet, both collapse; the high point would be a 'double k.o.'[49]

Gutmann's appraisal indicated, perhaps, the limited pedagogical value of press and radio coverage and even implicated the media in the generation of precisely this violent thrill-seeking that the boxing crowds exhibited.

The popular Berlin feuilletonist, Rumpelstilzchen, painted an even darker picture of boxing spectators and their motivations for attending the matches. He wrote in 1922, "The eyes of the spectators glimmer. They want to see blood . . .

These people, nine-tenths of whom belong to the lower-middle and working classes, read daily in their press the pacifistic lead articles, but they thirst for fighting and knockouts."[50] In contrast to the desired audience, presumably well-heeled, or at least middle class, Rumpelstilzchen depicted an overwhelmingly working-class crowd, and one that definitely favored the rawer side of the sport. In a 1931 piece, he again disdained the working-class origins and crude reactions of the fans in attendance: "The intellectual or the person hungry for new knowledge cowers shyly in this crowd, for to him they seem like low-life."[51]

Whereas Rumpelstilzchen held the working classes responsible for the blood-thirsty spectatorship at boxing matches, the socialist journal, *Arbeitersport*, predictably offered an opposing interpretation. The workers' sport movement criticized the crass commercialism of mass spectator sport in Weimar Germany, as well as the self-promotion of its star athletes and the craven desire for spectacle among its followers. A 1929 article by Fritz Wildung implied that the market-driven competition for audiences inherent within capitalist society stoked spectators' demands for violence and sensation:

> The sensation-seeking public wants to have its thrill and lusts for increasingly neck-breaking feats. That becomes glaringly apparent at boxing matches and six-day races. A large part of the public that visits such events in exchange for steep entry fees wants to see blood at all costs. Split lips, swollen eyes of the boxers, life-threatening spills by the cyclists, such fine people enjoy that.[52]

Interestingly, this critique closely resembled those presented by the mainstream boxing associations – that the big fights perverted boxing's athletic origins and pushed the sport toward baser forms of mass entertainment.

Just as the middle-class boxing associations did, Wildung also differentiated between *der wirkliche Sportfreund* (the true sports friend) and the thrill-seeking spectator at boxing matches, and he argued that the true fans rejected both the brutality and the commercialism of professional boxing:

> For [the true friend of sports] it is really scandalous when a boxer, who knocks out his opponent with his hard fist . . . not only makes more money than a scholar earns over his entire life, but is also hailed as a wonder of the world.[53]

Wildung carefully placed the blame for boxing's glorification of violence and its unjust distribution of wealth on bourgeois sport, not on sport in general. His "true sportsman," found in the *Arbeitersportbewegung* (workers' sport movement), possessed the strength of character to resist such sensationalist exploitation of physical culture. "It is continually shown that none of the degeneration [in sport] is accidental, but rather of a societal – a capitalistic, societal – character," he declared.[54] In Wildung's estimation, boxing – perhaps the sport most closely associated with the new economic order in Weimar Germany – emerged as the most salient example of a degeneration of the athletic spirit.

Even Rumpelstilzchen, one of the most vocal critics of the thrill-seeking spectatorship that he attributed to the working-class background of boxing crowds (itself an inaccurate generalization), occasionally and grudgingly sided with Wildung in applauding the sensibility of working-class fans. In a 1931 piece, for example, Rumpelstilzchen described a fight at which an African American entered the ring, eliciting both curiosity and sympathetic solidarity from the crowd.

> [the black boxer] has it hard because he is frozen out, so to speak, by the white American teammates. "The nigger stinks," they say. But the German gallery, who in true Marxist fashion stand up for the equality of everything that has a human face, showered him with thunderous applause.[55]

Rumpelstilzchen attributed this show of support to the socialist upbringing of these working-class Germans, but he also mocked the hypocrisy of these same socialist fans who allowed the excitement of a good fight to get the best of them. He referred to the "hundreds of thousands [of fans] who perhaps scream 'No more war!', but go gleefully berserk over a wounded jaw bone."[56]

Rumpelstilzchen's impression of the blue-collar nature of boxing crowds reflected a general assumption that the sport attracted unrefined spectators, those too coarse to appreciate the fighters' skill and technique. Such assumptions, however, probably reflected the expectations of the press regarding working-class behavior more than it did the social composition of many boxing crowds. The size and status of the fight significantly determined its audience, and indeed, the diversity of boxing's fan base distinguished it from many other spectator sports. The championship fights, in particular, attracted Berliners from all backgrounds, and these events quickly established themselves as socially acceptable pastimes.

Contrary to the rough-around-the-edges image of boxing, it gained a substantial following among the middle and upper classes, including educated professionals, wealthy business people, and the artists, actors, and brokers of Berlin's thriving cultural scene. The sport enjoyed such a strong following among regular theater-goers, generally middle- and upper-class, that a Berlin theater postponed the premier of a play in 1928 because it fell on the same night as a Max Schmeling–Franz Diener fight.[57] Alfred Flechtheim depicted the crowd at a 1926 fight as a veritable who's who of Berlin's cultural elite: "The Sportpalast doesn't recruit its public from beer-deliverymen and drivers alone; – all of Berlin's fine society is there, princes and princesses, painters and sculptors, literati . . . and all the actors who aren't working this evening."[58] Flechtheim, himself a prominent art dealer and founder of the journal *Der Querschnitt*, avidly followed the sport of boxing, as did Bertolt Brecht, Vladimir Nabokov, George Grosz, the sculptor Rudolf Belling, the conductor Leopold Stokowski, and a host of other artists, writers, and intellectuals.

Max Schmeling recalled in his memoir how he gained entrance as a 22-year-old into the highest cultural circles of Berlin partly through the doting patronage of Flechtheim. In his biography of Schmeling, Matthias Forster highlighted the centrality of boxing in the cultural life of Berlin and suggested a certain see-and-be-seen mentality, as well: "[Schmeling] made the German boxing of his day into a socially acceptable event, moreover, he made it so that attendance was *de rigeur* when there was good boxing."[59] Schmeling himself remarked in 1930, "It is part of good social form that prominent actors go to every boxing match (even if it means skipping their rehearsals and performances)."[60] Contrary to its reputation as an exclusively blue-collar sport, boxing had evolved into a cultural happening for the fashionable set.

Rumpelstilzchen himself refined his one-dimensional characterization of boxing crowds in a 1922 column about a Berlin *Großkampfabend*:

> No person, not even the pale-as-moonlight Tauentzien-aesthete, still talks about . . . the Einstein-eclipse or the exchange rate of the dollar, but about a hook to the chin and a clinch and fighters and kidney punches. I would bet anything that the small tot from Acker Street knows more about Dempsey and Breitensträter and Carpentier than about Hindenburg and Goethe and Derfflinger.[61]

According to Rumpelstilzchen, even the so-called "Tauentzien-aesthete," the sophisticate of Berlin's main café district, regularly followed boxing. The passage further maintained that those middle- and upper-class intellectuals and business-men, who might otherwise discuss physics or currency fluctuations, instead conversed enthusiastically about the most recent fights.

A 1922 article from *Sport im Bild* drew a distinction between two types of upper-class spectators at one of Berlin's big fights:

> Thin, elegant men with sleek heads, sports people, cosmopolitans who fit in everywhere and are familiar with everything to do with sport . . . next to them others who are bull-necked and overweight and who have claimed title to a seat in the first row solely on account of their new wealth.[62]

By portraying this latter group as bloated parvenus, the article evoked a very clear image of newcomers who lacked the breeding and refinement of the traditional upper class. The term "new wealth" also touched on a lingering resentment of those perceived to have profited from the First World War while the rest of the nation sacrificed, an attitude often loaded with anti-Semitic overtones, as well. The article revealed that the distinction between proper and improper spectatorship did not always break down along lines of economic status. It further contrasted the manner in which the two groups of privileged viewers watched the fight:

> The sportsman follows every fight with the understanding of an expert and enjoys every finesse in the lead of the fist or in self-defense like an exquisite work of art; the other, whose judgment is shaped in no way by a knowledge of the sport, wants to see hard punches and – let's be honest – blood; he also does not want an undecided fight and feels cheated if the evening does not bring at least one or two knockouts. He needs that for stimulation and does not otherwise have an appetite afterwards. What naturally would be a shame![63]

The commentator contrasted the civilized self-control of the former spectator with the coarse abandon of the latter. The "sportsman" elevated boxing to an art form, appreciated the necessary skill, and accorded the contest the proper level of respect. The parvenu, on the other hand, unleashed his venal appetites and debased boxing to the level of a carnival sideshow.

Boxing's appeal transcended not only class and social lines, but also gender lines. Women composed part of every boxing crowd in the 1920s, especially at the big professional fights that had established themselves as staples of the social scene. This female presence in the audience not only challenged traditional notions of proper entertainment for women, but also made boxing itself more socially acceptable. If female fans formed a tiny minority in the early years of the Weimar Republic, their numbers increased over the course of the decade. Although reliable attendance figures categorized by sex do not exist, some early accounts noted that only a few women ventured into the boxing arena. A 1921 article by Rumpelstilzchen stated: "This is not for delicate sensitivities. Here and there one sees a gangster with his diminutive girlfriend, but men fill the rows of benches almost exclusively."[64] Another of his columns, two years later, also noted the low number of women in attendance and inferred that the brutal nature of the sport frightened many women away: "One has to say it again: it [boxing] is truly a brutal craft. For every 100 male spectators there is one woman."[65]

Other articles from the early 1920s, however, registered larger contingents of female fans, and this attendance grew as boxing gained in both popularity and acceptability. A 1922 article from *Sport im Bild*, for instance, highlighted the presence of women at a boxing match:

And the eternally feminine! They are also here, some as coolly non-engaged spectators, because one simply must be there, some enthusiastic, excited to the tips of their fingers, lustful, inflamed for the slender one or the blond or the strong one. They are entirely absorbed and never take an eye off the fighters once they have . . . figured out what boxing is really about.[66]

This article advanced several explanations as to why women attended boxing matches, including social pressure and the attractiveness of the boxers, referred to in the article solely by their physical attributes. According to this reporter, even the enthusiastic female fans arrived at an understanding of boxing only belatedly, and the overall tone implied that few women truly understood the sport's strategy or appreciated its technique.

The suspicion that women watched boxing for reasons other than a high regard for the sport lingered. A 1928 article in *Sport und Sonne*, for example, reported that even the female custodial staff at the arena snuck a glimpse of the proceedings in the center ring. The reporter suggested, however, that they watched the fight more for the social cachet that attending such a popular and socially "in" event conferred upon them than out of any true enthusiasm for the sport: "I was able to push myself between a small herd of cleaning women, who also wanted to catch a glimpse . . . [and] want to be able to tell their neighbors the next morning that they were there."[67] In a 1925 article in *Boxsport*, Erwin Petzall analyzed the kinds of women who attended boxing. The wives of boxers, managers, and fans constituted one category, a reflection of the fact that many women attended boxing matches with a male escort, and usually at his behest. Indeed, an ideal evening for upper-class couples often included a visit to the fights. In the 1928 Fritz Lang film, *Spione* (*Spies*), the two main characters enjoyed a date at the fights, along with table after table of similarly elegant couples, all of them dressed in tuxedos and evening gowns.[68]

Petzall underscored the presence of many independent women, as well, those who attended either on their own or in the company of other women. Actresses and artists constituted a notable part of this category, a further indication of the popularity of boxing within the cultural circles of 1920s Berlin. Even working-class women, though, occasionally went to the fights alone. A 1924 column described a scene in which a woman spent all of her money on a ticket to a boxing match and, upon learning that her small boy could not accompany her into the arena, sent the boy home alone while she hurried inside for an evening of boxing.[69]

In his final category, Petzall placed those women who attended partly out of an interest in the proceedings, but equally out of sexual attraction for the boxers. "Sexual moments naturally also play a role with these women, who are moved by the athletic physiques of the protagonists."[70] Many commentators invoked this image of the impassioned woman when describing or explaining female boxing spectatorship in the 1920s. Fritz Giese argued that women were subconsciously attracted to the hyper-masculinity of boxers, to their brute strength and raw force:

> The women perhaps do not always know it, but the strong man and the boxer will always be the favorites of the unconscious feminine drive . . . The primitive instinct of the woman to detect love in masculine brutality . . . this and more influence the unconscious, primitive drive of the female spectators . . . and so women collect around the heroes like flies around a piece of sugar.[71]

Giese's pseudo-anthropological explanation for female boxing spectatorship hearkened back to the "ur-instinct" of pre-historic women, but he simultaneously highlighted a very modern phenomenon, that of sexually liberated women objectifying and eroticizing the male body.

The motif of the woman enamored of boxers surfaced again and again in the popular literature and cinema of the period, as the Weimar media industry updated its staple romance lines with a popular and timely twist. Films, such as *Die Boxerbraut* (*The Boxer's Bride*), *Liebe im Ring* (*Love in the Ring*), and *Knockout* (not released until 1934) focused on the erotic attraction of the leading woman to a boxer. In *Die Boxerbraut*, the heroine became so obsessed with boxing that her fiancé decided to pose as a professional boxer to ensure her affections.[72] In the short story, "Inge und der Boxkampf" ("Inge and the Boxing Match"), the protagonist fell in love with a boxer she had seen in a painting. Driven by repeated dreams, she attended her first boxing match, where the presence of the two contenders (her "two heroes") dazzled her.[73] Both the film and the short story clearly presented their main characters as "New Women," sporting bobbed hair and exuding an air of confidence and independence. For both of these stories, boxing represented not just modernity, but also a masculine world that these women breached, even co-opted. Interestingly, though, in both cases this co-optation proved only temporary, as the women ultimately recoiled from the violence and rawness of the sport.

As a flip-side to these story-lines of women's naive infatuation with boxers, another sub-genre of novels, films, and short stories took as its central plot device the seductive cabaret singer, actress, or dancer who lured the boxer away from his pugilistic calling or sapped him of his strength. In the 1926 short story, "Delila und der Boxer" ("Delilah and the Boxer"), for example, a young seductress's advances caused an up-and-coming boxer to neglect his training and jeopardize his fighting career.[74] The title itself underscored the feminine danger, alluding as it did to the biblical story of Delilah, who cut Samson's hair and rendered him impotent. The 1930 film *Liebe im Ring*, starring Max Schmeling, presented a talented boxer who fell under the sway of a sultry society woman and nearly lost an important fight as a consequence. In the film, Schmeling actually sang about the need for a boxer to remove himself from the influence of women:

> The heart of a boxer knows only one love: the battle for victory above all else . . . And once his heart beats for a woman, passionately and loudly: the heart of a boxer must forget everything, otherwise the next guy will knock him out.[75]

Boxing commentators, and boxers themselves, regularly asserted that one could not box at peak level and have a relationship with a woman at the same time. After the boxer Rudi Wagener began courting a film starlet in 1924, Rumpelstilzchen predicted, "She will gradually cause a weakening of his muscles!"[76] In a 1927 article from *Sport und Sonne*, the American champion Gene Tunney argued that women only divert the boxer's attention and weaken his resolve: "If all of his thoughts and everything within him is not concentrated on his retaining his crown . . . he will necessarily make mistakes and will probably be dethroned."[77] Many male spectators feared that women would inhibit the crowd, as well as the boxers. A letter published in *Boxsport* in 1925 declared, "We want to scream and yell to our heart's content at boxing matches and not be restrained out of respect for the weaker sex."[78]

According to some reports, though, these male spectators need not have expressed concern for the sensibilities of the "weaker sex." In fact, some writers described the female spectators as more enthusiastic about the violent aspects of the sport than their male colleagues. In the same 1929 *Arbeitersport* article that criticized the blood-thirstiness of boxing crowds, Fritz Wildung noted the significant numbers of equally exuberant women in the arenas.[79] In "Inge und der Boxkampf," even as the protagonist grew increasingly repulsed by the match, she noticed other women in the crowd enjoying themselves immensely. "There she saw the men's expressions, contorted with excitement and passion, and in the eyes of the women an expression that she had seen flare up only in Madrid at the bullfights."[80] In fact, commentators during the Weimar Republic noted a small, but vocal contingent of women at most matches who reveled in the violent displays and exhibited precisely the same behavior that boxing sophisticates had come to associate with working-class men and "improper spectatorship." Rumpelstilzchen wrote that many women, by nature, enjoyed a bloody fight, rather than feeling repelled by it:

> The forehead of one boxer has been beaten and the area around the left eyebrow ripped open. His opponent already has a shoulder that was beaten bloody by the second round. A pair of young women on the main floor, block A, lick their lips in deep satisfaction. This is nature, not decadence or perversion . . . I cannot understand how men, who certainly know this cruel feline instinct, can drag their girls with them to a boxing match at the Sport Palace.[81]

Here, Rumpelstilzchen contradicted some of his earlier comments from the 1921 article regarding women, boxing and "delicate sensitivities." Instead, he argued against women attending boxing matches not because it would offend their natures, but precisely the opposite – because it would arouse their natures and appeal to their basest desires. Contrary to the standard assumption that women would reject boxing after witnessing its true nature, the article feared that women would embrace it.

Other commentators also saw something in the female nature that drew women to the violent aspects of the sport. In a 1928 article in *Sport und Sonne*, boxing elicited the repressed, violence-loving side of its female spectators. Just as in the short story "Inge und der Boxkampf," the article invoked the bestial image of a bull fight:

> The women . . . Honor the women . . . but not at a boxing match. There the superwoman steels her gaze; nature reveals itself as cruel, cold and lascivious . . . 'Oh God, Hans, look, he's bleeding!!' I look at [the woman who just said that] . . . I suspect that this woman has only one regret: that we still do not have bullfights here.[82]

The woman described in this article wore an expensive fur and the latest fashions and clearly came from the upper class. Interestingly, reports generally characterized the women who attended fights as middle or upper class, whereas many of these same reports continued to portray the majority of the male spectators as working or lower-middle class. Commentators who decried male behavior at boxing matches attributed it primarily to the crowd's working-class origins. Descriptions of improper female spectatorship, however, attributed it to the nature of women themselves.

Due to the inhibitions and superstitions surrounding women's attendance and to the fear that the physical aggressiveness of the sport would either upset or arouse them, boxing associations in the 1920s often sought to restrict women's presence at fights. During a meeting of the *Boxsport-Behörde Deutschlands* (German Boxing Authority) in 1927, the council reminded officials not to seat women ringside at any fights.[83] The minutes mentioned no specific reason for this reassertion of existing policy, but it probably aimed both at safeguarding boxing from the presumed deleterious effect of women on the performances of the fighters, and at protecting the sensibilities of women from the violent scenes visible at such close proximity to the ring.

A very few boxing commentators, however, took the opposite stance. Rather than seeking to restrict women's access to boxing matches, they sought to increase it. Erwin Petzall, in his analysis of women at the fights, pushed for greater female attendance, arguing that this would encourage better behavior on the part of the men and revive appreciation of the sport. Petzall essentially saw women as instruments in fostering proper spectatorship. Working from the prevalent assumption at the time that primarily working-class men attended bouts and that they caused the disruptions, Petzall claimed that women would tame these unruly fans: "The very presence of the woman gives our sport the proper dignity, for her presence will contribute greatly to the disciplining of the male public."[84] Greater attendance by women would not just make an evening at the fights more decorous, however. Petzall further implied that female spectatorship could change the nature of the sport itself. He noted that the introduction by the *Verein Deutscher Faustkämpfer* (Association of German Fistfighters) of the six-ounce glove and soft bandaging at all national fights had reduced the number of knockouts and focused attention more on the technical prowess of the fighters. He estimated that this development would lead even more women to attend matches. This suggested the possibility that boxing federations would, in turn, respond to increased female spectatorship with further reforms in this direction – a gradual and market-driven feminization of boxing.

Petzall returned to the theme of class at the end of his piece with a direct appeal to the *Bildungsbürgertum* (the educated upper and middle classes) among male boxing fans:

> We desperately need women from precisely this social background [educated professional classes]. Therefore we must try by all means to win her for us. To our followers let it be said: bring your wives with you to the fights. They will and must learn to love our sport, the most beautiful that there is.[85]

This article served the larger project of many boxing officials in Weimar Germany to attract and groom a proper spectatorship for the sport. In Petzall's estimation, the presence of women not only would subdue the unruly fans that he attributed to the working classes, but also would gradually replace them with members of the professional classes, Petzall's ideal audience.

Petzall's article certainly provided one of the most explicit calls for a more refined spectatorship at boxing matches, but far from the only one. His voice joined a whole chorus of commentators who criticized the conduct and composition of boxing crowds throughout the 1920s. In a similar manner to the "taste professionals" that Leora Auslander describes in her history of furniture design in France, these commentators saw themselves as both able and obligated to shape the behavior of a growing group of sports consumers.[86] Although the criticisms of these commentators often varied significantly from one another, they shared a basic agenda that sought to solidify boxing's standing as a serious sport. These critics generally wished to purge the arena of its carnivalesque atmosphere, which smacked too much of American-style commercialism and a fixation on the knockout, and to encourage an appreciation of style, strategy and a victory by points.

In addition, the boxing press generally shared certain assumptions about social behavior. They often attributed to working-class spectators, for example, all of the traits and behaviors that most upset them at boxing matches. Other reporters disdained the bloated confidence and sense of entitlement of the nouveau riche, and they vented this derision in their columns, where they lampooned the group's base appetites and misunderstanding of the sport. The attendance of women received little support or encouragement from the boxing press, and its criticisms of female spectators reflected not only the traditional biases regarding women's natures, but also the growing anxiety over the increasingly assertive role of women in Weimar society. Even those few commentators who championed female spectatorship as a means of abetting the larger project of drawing an appreciative and well-behaved crowd to the big boxing matches played on well-worn stereotypes regarding the civilizing function of women.

This concern over proper spectatorship at the fights arose partly from the nebulous status of boxing itself. Boxing commentators wanted to present boxing as a "pure" sport rather than some hybrid form of mass entertainment. They hoped to encourage a stronger club-level boxing life that drew people to participate in the sport rather than simply observe it. This motivation proved especially true for the reporters of specialty boxing journals, such as *Boxsport*. By bolstering the respectability of boxing, of course, the commentators also bolstered their own status and cachet as serious sports journalists. Furthermore, the anxiety of the boxing associations over proper spectatorship represented a larger effort to keep the sport entirely legal and socially accepted. The danger existed that if boxing degenerated into a gladiatorial brawl, focused exclusively on the knock out, that municipalities might once again choose to restrict or ban the sport, just as many had done in Wilhelmine Germany.

More importantly, however, the anxiety over the nature of spectatorship at the big professional fights intersected with many of the larger social issues of the Weimar Republic. The lampooning of nouveau-riche boxing fans resonated with broader criticisms of the behavior of a new breed of profit-oriented business people in the 1920s. The debates surrounding women in the boxing arena mirrored the larger debates surrounding the emergence of the New Woman. As women achieved greater prominence in politics, business, culture, and even sports, social commentators grappled with these rapidly changing gender roles and sought continually to redefine exclusively male spheres. The outcry over the crass commercialization of boxing had equally broad significance in Weimar society, representing as it did yet another arena in the debate over Americanization and the uncertain consequences of *Massenkultur* (mass culture). Finally, concerns about the violence-loving nature of boxing fans echoed a much broader anxiety regarding violence in society, as indicated by sensationalized crime reporting, street fighting, armed militias and political assassinations. The quest for proper spectatorship represented, in many ways, the quest for a proper society, as well.

Notes

1. Theodor Frehse, "Es wird geboxt," *Boxsport* 5, 239 (1925), p. 13.

2. Christiane Eisenberg, "Massensport in der Weimarer Republik: Ein statistischer Überblick," *Archiv für Sozialgeschichte* 33 (1993), p. 168.

3. David Bathrick examines the image of the boxer in Weimar Germany, but he does not specifically address spectatorship: "Max Schmeling on the Canvas: Boxing as an Icon of Weimar Germany," *New German Critique* 51 (1990), pp. 113–36. Kasia Boddy explores female boxing spectatorship in the context of American film and literature: "Watching the Fight: Women Spectators in Boxing Fiction and Film," in Tim Armstrong (ed.), *American Bodies: Cultural Histories of the Physique* (New York: New York University Press, 1996), pp. 204–12.

4. Pierre Bourdieu, "How Can One be a Sports Fan?" (1978), in Simon During (ed.), *The Cultural Studies Reader* (New York: Routledge, 1993), pp. 339–56.

5. Vanessa R. Schwartz, *Spectacular Realities: Early Mass Culture in Fin-de-Siècle Paris* (Berkeley, CA: University of California Press, 1998). Judith Walkowitz, *City of Dreadful Delight: Narratives of Sexual Danger in Late-Victorian London* (Chicago: University of Chicago Press, 1992); Peter Fritzsche, *Reading Berlin 1900* (Cambridge, MA: Harvard University Press, 1996).

6. Patrice Petro, *Joyless Streets: Women and Melodramatic Representation in Weimar Germany* (Princeton, NJ: Princeton University Press, 1989); Jackie Stacey, *Star Gazing: Hollywood Cinema and Female Spectatorship* (New York: Routledge, 1994); Leo Charney and Vanessa R. Schwartz (eds), *Cinema and the Invention of Modern Life* (Berkeley, CA: University of California Press, 1995); Marsha Kinder, *Blood Cinema: The Reconstruction of National Identity in Spain* (Berkeley: University of California Press, 1993); Yuri Tsivian, *Early Cinema in Russia and its Cultural Reception*, trans. Alan Bodger (Chicago: University of Chicago Press, 1991); Heide Fehrenbach, *Cinema in Democratizing Germany: Reconstructing National Identity after Hitler* (Chapel Hill, NC: University of North Carolina Press, 1995).

7. Adrian Shubert, *Death and Money in the Afternoon: A History of the Spanish Bullfight* (New York: Oxford University Press, 1999), p. 14.

8. Schwartz, *Spectacular Realities*, p. 5.

9. Quoted in Gertrud Pfister and Gerd Steins (eds), *Sport in Berlin: Vom Ritterturnier zum Stadtmarathon* (Berlin: Verlag Forum für Sportgeschichte, 1987), p. 8.

10. For a full treatment of the history of professional boxing in Germany, see Knud Kohr and Martin Krauß, *Kampftage: Die Geschichte des deutschen Berufsboxens* (Göttingen: Die Werkstatt Verlag, 2000).

11. Leonhard Mandlár, "Entwickelung des modernen Boxsports in Deutschland und seine Organisation," *Boxsport* (October 13, 1921), pp. 1–3.

12. Ibid., p. 1.

13. Dieter Behrendt, "'Boxen mußt de, boxen, boxen,'" in Alfons Arenhövel (ed.) *Arena der Leidenschaften: Der Berliner Sportpalast und seine Veranstaltungen, 1910–1973* (Berlin: Verlag Willmuth Arenhövel, 1990), p. 84.

14. Max Schmeling, *Erinnerungen* (Frankfurt a/M: Verlag Ullstein, 1977), p. 29.

15. "Sport und Mensur," *Boxsport* 7, 325 (1926), p. 4.

16. "Eckeroth schlägt Spalla," *Illustrierter Sport* 8, 29 (1920), p. 547.

17. Behrendt, "'Boxen mußt de, boxen, boxen,'" p. 85.

18. "Der Boxsport im Theater und im Kino," *Boxsport* 7, 338 (1927), p. 2.

19. Egon Erwin Kisch, "Der Sportsmann als Schiedsrichter seiner selbst," in Willy Meisl (ed.), *Der Sport am Scheideweg* (Heidelberg: Iris Verlag, 1928), p. 7.

20. Max Leusch, "Boxer und Publikum," *Boxsport* 7, 329 (1927), p. 14.

21. Bertolt Brecht, "Das Theater als Sport" (1920), in Günter Berg (ed.) *Der Kinnhaken und andere Box-und Sportgeschichten.* (Frankfurt a/M: Suhrkamp Taschenbuch, 1998), pp. 23–4.

22. Franz Josef Görtz, "'Dichter, übt euch im Weitsprung': Sport und Literatur im 20. Jahrhundert," in Hans Sarkowicz (ed.), *Schneller, Höher, Weiter: Eine Geschichte des Sports* (Frankfurt a/M: Insel Verlag, 1996), p. 348.

23. Fritz Giese, *Geist im Sport: Probleme und Forderungen* (Munich: Delphin-Verlag, 1925), p. 62.

24. Birk Meinhardt, *Boxen in Deutschland* (Hamburg: Rotbuch Verlag, 1996), p. 46.

25. Walter Bergmann, "Frau und Sport," *Deutsche Presse* 15, 51/52 (1925), p. 12.

26. Schmeling, *Erinnerungen*, p. 86.

27. In October 1921, for example, the Scala Theater showed a film of the Dempsey–Carpentier world heavyweight championship fight: "Der Dempsey–Carpentier-Film in der Berliner Scala," *Boxsport* 1 (October 6, 1921), p. 5.

28. Meinhardt, *Boxen in Deutschland*, p. 47.

29. Rumpelstilzchen [Adolf Stein], Feuilleton from June 23, 1932 in *Nu wenn schon!* (Berlin: Brunnen-Verlag, 1932), p. 316.

30. "Wie gewinnt der Boxsport das Allgemein-Interesse?" *Boxsport* 1 53 (September 15, 1921), p. 1.

31. "Mehr Selbstbeherrschung bei Boxkampfen," *Illustrierter Sport* 7, no. 35 (1919), p. 687.

32. *Der Leichtathlet* 4, 19 (1927), p. 20.

33. Quoted in Meinhardt, *Boxen in Deutschland*, p. 11.

34. Ibid., p. 72.

35. Karl B. Raitz, "The Theater of Sport: A Landscape Perspective," in Karl B. Raitz (ed.), *The Theater of Sport* (Baltimore, MD: Johns Hopkins University Press, 1995), p. 12.

36. See, for example, Karl Heinz Grétschel, "Sein letzter Kampf!" *Boxsport* 6, 303 (1926), pp. 25ff; or the serialized novel by Hannes Bork, "Der Deutsche Teufel," *Boxsport* 5, 225 (1925), pp. 24ff.

37. "Der Kampf um die Amateurtitel in Hannover," *Boxsport* 5, 237 (1925), p. 16.

38. Max Schmeling enjoyed a 90 percent name recognition; Stresemann had 80 percent, Karl May 54 percent and Henry Ford 49 percent: "Vom Sportleben unserer Vierzehn-jährigen," *Die Leibesübungen* (June 20, 1930), p. 339.

39. David Bathrick addresses a related point, although he argues less that the boxer was an object of desire than that the boxer's body reflected the lean, competitive efficiency of the new age in which he lived: "Max Schmeling on the Canvas," pp. 113–36.

40. "Breitensträter und Naujocks besiegen ihre Gegner!" *Illustrierter Sport* 8, 17 (1920), p. 318.

41. "Breitensträters Debut in Wien," *Boxsport* 2, 96 (July 26, 1922), p. 6.

42. "Lustige Ecke," *Boxsport* 5, 224 (1925), p. 11.

43. H. von Wedderkop, "Hans Breitensträter," *Die Weltbühne* 17, 38 (1921), p. 298.

44. Hans Breitensträter, "Soll ein Sportsmann heiraten?" *Der Querschnitt* (1932), in Wilmont Haacke and Alexander Baeyer (eds), *Der Querschnitt: Facsimile Querschnitt durch den Querschnitt 1921–1936* (Frankfurt a/M: Verlag Ullstein, 1977), pp. 287–8.

45. "Wie gewinnt der Boxsport das Allgemein-Interesse?", p. 1.

46. "Weshalb hat Berlin so wenig Kämpfe?" *Boxsport* 7, 346 (1927), p. 1.

47. Egon Erwin Kisch, "Boxkampf im Radio, " *Prager Tageblatt* (May 7, 1925), in Günter Berg and Uwe Wittstock (eds), *Harte Bandagen: Eine Box-Anthologie in 12 Runden* (Munich: Verlag C.H. Beck, 1997), p. 103.

48. W. von Wasielewski, "Berufssport?" *Die Leibesübungen* 5/6 (March 20, 1927), p. 134.

49. Curt Gutmann, "Boxen als Geschäft und als Sport," *Der Querschnitt* 8, 8 (1928), p. 560.

50. Rumpelstilzchen [Adolf Stein], Feuilleton from January 19, 1922 in *Was sich Berlin erzählt*, essays published 1921–2 (Berlin: Brunnen-Verlag, 1923), p. 130.

51. Rumpelstilzchen, Feuilleton from October 22, 1931 in *Nu wenn schon!*, p. 61.

52. Fritz Wildung, "Der Rekord," *Arbeitersport* (1929), in Hajo Bernett (ed.), *Der Sport im Kreuzfeuer der Kritik: Kritische Texte aus 100 Jahren deutscher Sportgeschichte* (Schorndorf: Verlag Karl Hofmann, 1982), p. 53.

53. Ibid., p. 50.

54. Ibid., pp. 53–4.

55. Rumpelstilzchen, Feuilleton from October 22, 1931 in *Nu wenn schon!*, p. 62.

56. Rumpelstilzchen [Adolf Stein], Feuilleton in *Mecker' nich!* (Berlin: Brunnen-Verlag, 1926), pp. 347–8.

57. Schmeling, *Erinnerungen*, pp. 108–9.

58. Alfred Flechtheim, "Gladiatoren," *Der Querschnitt* 6, 1 (1926), p. 48.

59. Matthias Forster, *Max Schmeling: Sieger im Ring – Sieger im Leben* (Munich: Delphin Verlag, 1986), p. 26.

60. Max Schmeling, *Mein Leben, Meine Kämpfe* (Leipzig: Grethlein, 1930), p. 97.

61. Rumpelstilzchen [Adolf Stein], Feuilleton from September 28, 1922 in *Und det jloobste?* (Berlin: Brunnen-Verlag, 1923), p. 14.

62. "Impressionen im Ring," *Sport im Bild* 28, 11 (1922), p. 391.

63. Ibid., p. 391.

64. Rumpelstilzchen [Adolf Stein], Feuilleton from April 28, 1921 in *Berliner Allerlei* (Berlin: Verlag der Täglichen Rundschau, 1922), p. 188.

65. Rumpelstilzchen [Adolf Stein], Feuilleton from April 26, 1923 in *Und det jloobste?*, p. 227.

66. "Impressionen im Ring", p. 391.

67. "Wie Sie zusehen: Beobachtungen mit dem Rücken zum Ring," *Sport und Sonne* 1 (January 1928), p. 40.

68. *Spione*, directed by Fritz Lang (Germany: Ufa Production, 1927–8).

69. Joseph Roth, "Der Kampf um die Meisterschaft," *Frankfurter Zeitung* (March 3, 1924), in *Harte Bandagen*, p. 67.

70. Erwin Petzall, "Die Frauen und der Faustkampf," *Boxsport* 5, 243 (May 22, 1925), p. 9.

71. Giese, *Geist im Sport*, p. 81.

72. *Die Boxerbraut: Lustspiel in 5 Akten*, directed by Robert Liebmann (Germany: Ufa Production, 1926).

73. Mara Herberg, "Inge und der Boxkampf," *Sport im Bild* 32, 16 (1926), p. 697.

74. Georg Holmer, "Delila und der Boxer," *Boxsport* 6, 305 (1926), p. 25.

75. Quoted in Schmeling, *Erinnerungen*, pp. 142–3.

76. Rumpelstilzchen [Adolf Stein], Feuilleton from March 6, 1924 in *Bei mir – Berlin!* (Berlin: Brunnen-Verlag, 1924), p. 206.

77. Gene Tunney, "Darf ein Weltmeister heiraten?" *Sport und Sonne* 6 (June 1927), p. 330.

78. "Die Frauen und der Boxsport," *Boxsport* 5, 245 (1925), p. 6.

79. Wildung, "Der Rekord," p. 53.

80. Herberg, "Inge und der Boxkampf," p. 697.

81. Rumpelstilzchen [Adolf Stein], Feuilleton from October 16, 1924 in *Haste Worte?* (Berlin: Brunnen-Verlag, 1925), p. 42.

82. "Wie Sie zusehen: Beobachtungen mit dem Rücken zum Ring," pp. 39–40.

83. "Amtliches," *Boxsport* 7, 347 (1927), p. 9.

84. Petzall, "Die Frauen und der Faustkampf," p. 9.

85. Ibid., p. 9.

86. Leora Auslander, *Taste and Power: Furnishing Modern France* (Berkeley, CA: University of California Press, 1996), p. 195. In the case of furniture design, though, Auslander describes a class-specific definition of consumer behavior. In the case of boxing, the commentators conceived of a uniform code of behavior that would transcend class.

Part II

Traveling

6

Travels with Baedeker – The Guidebook and the Middle Classes in Victorian and Edwardian Britain

Jan Palmowski

What literary fame equals John Murray's? What portmanteau, with two shirts and a nightcap, hasn't got one Handbook? . . . Does he look upon a building, a statue, a picture, an old cabinet, or a manuscript, with whose eyes does he see it? With John Murray's, to be sure!

I cannot conceive anything more frightful than the sudden appearance of a work which should contradict everything in the Handbook . . . if we awoke one morning to hear that the "Continent" was no longer the Continent we have been accustomed to believe it, what a terrific shock it would prove.[1]

This sketch by Charles Lever reflects a growing phenomenon of the Victorian and Edwardian era, the "middle classification" of travel. No longer an exclusive prerogative of moneyed elites willing to spend months or even years on the "Grand Tour" of Europe, travel became more widespread as better turnpikes, railway travel, and steamboats greatly reduced the burdens of travel with regard to price, comfort, and length. In the early 1850s, Charles Dickens marveled at the speed and comfort with which the express train whisked him to Paris. "I feel as if I were enchanted or bewitched. It is barely eight o'clock yet . . . And yet this morning – I'll think of it in a warm-bath." "When can it have been that I left home? When was it that I paid 'through to Paris' at London Bridge, and discharged myself of all responsibility . . .? It seems to have been ages ago."[2] In a more sophisticated manner than Lever, Charles Dickens, too, was acutely aware of the connection between the guidebook and middle-class travel. Although fiercely hostile to the English traveler's slavish fixation on the guidebook whenever abroad, Dickens found his Murray's indispensable for his own continental journeys.[3]

Murray's handbooks for travelers, published from 1836, were the first in a new generation of guidebooks responding to the growth in middle-class travel. These guidebooks intended to "supply the traveler with all needful information, to point out the most interesting places and the best way of reaching them, to render him comparatively independent of the services of guides and others."[4] They profession- alized travel for the middle classes, and rationalized – and in this way directed – essential components of the tourist experience: the anticipation, perception, and memory of travel.[5] This close interrelationship with middle-class tastes makes the guidebook a unique and valuable historical source. Each of the twenty-five English editions of the Baedeker on Switzerland published before 1914, or the eighteen English editions of the Baedeker on Paris, presented an opportunity to enter into a dialogue with its audience. Up to now, the precise nature of that dialogue has remained relatively unclear.[6] This chapter will explore in greater detail the relationship between the middle classes and the guidebook, and the ways in which they influenced each other. This will suggest ways in which the travel guide was an essential, and hitherto neglected, determinant of middle-class culture.

Intensive research in recent years has significantly increased our understanding of the nature of the middle classes in a European and national context.[7] The greater appreciation of the extent to which the middle classes left their imprint on politics and society in late-nineteenth-century Europe has been concomitant with a realization of their complexity and diffuseness that defies easy generalization.[8] The middle classes are as difficult as ever to understand. Instead of adding to the exhaustive research on "objective" factors of middle-class definition (such as income, sociability, education), this chapter will use the guidebook to explore actual communities of feeling that existed among the middle classes. This can account for the spread of certain values and outlooks that bound the middle classes together and added to a shared sense of culture. A focus on the most popular British tourist destinations abroad will illuminate the guidebook's popularization of "high" culture and its implantation and prolongation of particular modes of thinking. This chapter will reflect on the ways in which handbooks for travelers influenced social trends, most notably relating to gender and class.

At the center of investigation are the relationship between middle classes of Victorian and Edwardian Britain, and two of their own most lasting creations, foreign mass travel and the "professional" guidebook. At the same time, foreign travel and the guidebook necessarily involved encounters both with the host culture, and, increasingly, the fellow travelers from other nations. Whereas in Frederic Harrison's younger days, three-quarters of the tourists to Switzerland were British, he estimated in 1908 that the relative number of British tourists at the most beautiful haunts had shrunk to one-fifth or even one-tenth of the total, with German tourists very much in evidence.[9] This contribution responds to some of the arguments raised by Rudy Koshar's work on the guidebook and national consciousness,[10] and considers questions about national identity in the ways travel and the guidebook were experienced by the middle-class traveler.

Large-scale travel was a Victorian phenomenon, participated in by virtually all sectors of urban society. As British cities expanded, their populations sought refuge on holidays in nearby resorts. The number of passengers transported from London to Margate and Ramsgate by the Margate Pier and Harbour Company rose from 17,000 in 1812–13 to 105,625 in 1835, after which the railways made access to these resorts even easier.[11] In the season of 1879, each day an average of 40,000 excursionists swamped Blackpool, which was already catering for 70,000 visitors on longer stays.[12] For the middle classes eager to take refuge from the traveling hordes so mercilessly caricatured in contemporary sketches, traveling abroad became increasingly de rigueur.

Even before the advent of the railway, greater speed in travel resulted in large increases of passengers: reflecting improvements in navigation from England to France, the journey from Boulogne to Paris, which took 35 hours to complete in 1814, took but 16 hours in 1848.[13] By 1840, around 87,000 passages (equivalent to 43,500 return trips) between Britain and the European continent were recorded. Following the completion of the railway link from London and Paris to the coast, the number of cross-Channel passages recorded rose to 165,000 in 1850, 238,264 in 1860, and 344,719 in 1869. Up to 80 percent of these journeys were undertaken by British passengers.[14] Many of these British passengers consisted of British residents in France or their visitors; as early as the 1840s, there were 66,000 British residents in France, with regular English church services being held in 25 towns.[15] A further group comprised commercial travelers, those going to Paris or other parts of Europe on business. This chapter focuses on a third group of travelers, vacationers, those who went abroad for any length of time, from a couple of days to several months. These formed the market for tourist guidebooks. It is impossible to determine accurately the relative size of these groups, but the significant increase from the 1840s in seasonal travel over the summer months suggests strongly that the lion's share of the growth of travel in Victorian and Edwardian Britain was the result of vacation travel. Whereas at the beginning of Victoria's reign (1837), 33 percent of annual travel through Dover occurred in summer (July to September) compared to 19.6 percent for the three winter months, by 1865, 40.5 percent of annual travel through Calais took place in summer, compared to the 15.4 percent using this route from December to February.[16] It is only with the growth of winter vacationing from the 1880s that the proportional number of passengers passing through the Channel ports in the winter months increased.[17]

The growth of vacationers during the 1850s and 1860s is directly reflected in the proliferation of guidebooks. After the publication of the first edition of Murray's guidebook to Switzerland in 1838, the sixteenth edition was published in 1879. In that year, Karl Baedeker published the eighth English edition of his guidebook to Switzerland, which followed the publication of his seventeenth German edition on Switzerland two years earlier. These two guidebooks had very similar origins, and in their erudite comprehensiveness were aimed at the same market. The differences between them were, however, unmistakable. The Baedeker was more compact, and much more sombre in its descriptions. In the same way that the Baedeker's German heritage was evident, the Murray was a book written by the British, for the British. Where Baedeker made its point with a brief quotation from Goethe, Murray retaliated with long passages from the English romantics, and Byron in particular.[18] Murray introduced the Bernese Oberland as the land of Tennyson and Byron, and proceeded to illustrate every sight with the appropriate quotation from "Manfred" or similar sources. Moving on to Chillon, the son of Byron's publisher referred to the "Prisoner of Chillon" for two pages. The Baedeker, by contrast, introduced the Oberland much less exuberantly, commencing its account with a warning precisely against the tourist trappings which Murray's tourists attracted (endless offerings of crystals, pistol shots to test the echo, yodeling, and the like). Baedeker could not avoid Byron in Chillon, but was nevertheless much briefer on the castle and its history.[19] Over the years, in its new editions Murray adopted a more sombre and factual style, but the differences between the two guidebooks remained unmistakable throughout.

More revealing is a comparison of the guidebooks' descriptions of sites intrinsically unrelated to romanticism. A random, if telling, example involves a comparison of the guidebooks' descriptions of Interlaken. This town evoked mixed emotions in most guidebooks, since it was at once beautiful and overrun with tourists and amusements. This ambiguity is clear in Murray's guide, which noted the contrast between Interlaken's bustling promenades and the sublimity of its surrounding Alpine panorama. Still, Murray advised that Interlaken "must not be disparaged"; it was a good, cheap base for tours in the surrounding Oberland, and afforded good views over the Alps. The Baedeker, by contrast, was positive without reservation, praising Interlaken as a "point of attraction to visitors from all parts of Europe." It recommended the town not just because of the surrounding countryside, but as a resting place in itself.[20] It was not the case, therefore, that Baedeker was always more critical than Murray. Both were full of practical advice, but whereas both guidebooks carried out their agenda to determine "what ought to be seen," Murray went a step further, showing more clearly not just what ought to be seen, but how it should be appreciated.

As more people traveled to Switzerland, guidebooks became more diverse.[21] In the 1860s, John Ball, the founding president of the Alpine Club, published his *Alpine Guide* in three volumes. In trying to appeal to a more "elevated" market "serious" about the Alps, it contained detailed descriptions of walks and paths, and included signed descriptions and recommendations by members of the Alpine Club, among them Leslie Stephen. With its clientele in mind, the guide despaired, for instance, at the average Interlaken visitors "incapable of deriving deep and continuous enjoyment from the sublime objects that surround them."[22] The other end of the popular spectrum was distinguished by the competition of two guides, one of which was Thomas Cook's *Handbook on Switzerland*, first published in 1874. This had no pretentions other than to describe the beaten track, and even then the sights it included were highly selective. In its appeal to popular instincts, its prose was marked by a more jocular style, introducing one resort thus: "Interlacken [*sic*] has been described as the Leamington, or Cheltenham, or Harrogate of Switzerland." Mocking the whey cure that had been the town's original attraction, the guide recommended, with unfailing drollery, the "tour-cure" instead, which consisted of the purchase of Cook's tourist ticket. Cook's handbook did not contain a description of the town's actual sights, but was nevertheless content to convey to the reader an altogether dismissive assessment of Interlaken.[23] The second consciously down-market popular guidebook was Henry Gaze's *Switzerland: How to See it for Ten Guineas*, available for just one shilling (compared to nine shillings for Murray's Swiss guide in the 1860s). It was part of a series covering the most popular English tourist destinations: Paris, northern Italy, and the Low Countries. As indicated in its title, the guidebook's emphasis was on price, its main function being the design of an itinerary whereby the sights of Switzerland could be experienced for the allotted sum.[24]

The proliferation of guidebooks to cater for the growing British tourist market confirmed rather than challenged the preeminence of Murray's and Baedeker's guides. John Ball was happy to copy verbatim passages from Murray into his own guide. Henry Gaze went further, recommending, for a "full enjoyment" of the scenes passed by, the Murray as an "invaluable companion"; to save space, at each point of interest Gaze's book referred to the relevant page number in the Murray for more detailed information.[25] Baedeker, in turn, was championed by Thomas Cook, whose guidebook highlighted its indebtedness to Baedeker through extensive quotations, without shying away from copying, without acknowledgment, Murray's extensive use of Byron in the Oberland or at Chillon.[26] Directly and indirectly, Baedeker's and Murray's handbooks maintained and extended a unique preeminence in the increasingly diverse market for guidebooks.

The spread and relative uniformity of travel guidebooks was an important precondition for the cultural impact of the Murray and the Baedeker, but this says little about the actual nature of their influence. Famously, when Lucy Honeychurch and her cousin Charlotte set out to discover the sights of Florence in E.M. Forster's *A Room with a View*, Lucy needed the Baedeker to tell her what was "really beautiful" in Santa Croce. On his first trip to Venice in 1869, it was perfectly natural for Henry James to rely on the Murray, and he decided to lodge in the first place recommended by the guidebook.[27] Beyond such illustrious examples from the literary world, up to now the close association between guidebook and readership has been more assumed than proven. This is surprising, for the wealth of published and unpublished travelers' journals of the period offers a genuine insight into the precise ways in which guidebook and audience interacted.

When Mrs Staley from Rochdale embarked on a trip to Switzerland in August 1862, she chose upon her arrival in Basle to stay in the "Trois Rois," the first hotel recommended in the Murray. In her published journal, she noted her excitement at the Rhine, which "rushes past in a full, broad flood of clear light green" – an image replicating verbatim that given in Murray's. In her impressions of the cathedral she appears as an incarnation of Foster's fictional character in Florence: the cloisters described in the Murray as "extensive and picturesque" she felt to be "extensive and remarkable." After visiting the cathedral, Mrs Staley walked up an elevated terrace behind the cathedral to enjoy, "under some magnificent chestnut trees at a great elevation," "an extensive and beautiful view of the Rhine, the city, and the neighbouring hills." This bore more than a striking resemblance to Murray's description of the terrace, "75 ft. above the river, planted with chestnut trees, and commanding a beautiful view over the Rhine, the town, and the Black Forest hills."[28] Throughout Mrs Staley's book, descriptions are enriched by observations which are not from the Murray, but, at every turn of the journey, Murray's prescriptive guidance is unmistakable.[29]

Even more striking is the journal kept by Jemima Morrell, one of the members of Cook's first tour to Switzerland. Morrell's description of the Giessbach was copied verbatim from the Murray. Her opinion on the valley of Sarnen that "neither of the lakes can boast of being surrounded by much decided Alpine scenery; its character is peaceful and pleasing, but not grand" was but an insignificant variation from Murray's view that "the valley of Sarnen, bounded by gently sloping hills, has nothing Alpine in its scenery; its character is quiet, and pastoral, and pleasing."[30] On the way from Chamounix to Martigny, Murray noted at a particular point the vegetation, the abundance of wild fruits. And so it was precisely at this point that Jemima noticed that "On the border of the path the vegetation was profuse and varied. Tufts of diantus, delicate ferns, harebells and wild strawberries and mosses, too." Such appreciative detail was clearly the product of Jemima's own observations; but the impetus to observe and form an impression came from Murray.[31] In fact, Murray's handbook could even create virtual impressions, experiences which were felt without actually having occurred. On the way from Geneva to Chamounix, Murray highlights the "valley of the Arve, in which the blanched stones mark by their breadth how furious the river must be after storms." This was enough for Jemima Morrell to feel overawed as "from the blocks of granite squandered in the vale, evidently rounded by the action of the water, we could form an idea of the force of that torrent when it ceases its summer play."[32] Of course, Jemima did not ignore the Baedeker altogether. Baedeker was relied on more (though, not exclusively) for practical information such as hotels and route planning. Yet it is Murray's guidance on how to appreciate her experience which metamorphosed into most of Jemima's personal impressions and formed her memory. She viewed the Wengern Alp not through the eyes of Goethe, but of

Byron.[33] These journals were usually written down in their final version only after the trip, clearly with the help of notes of impressions sketched out during the journey, and aided by the factual information provided by the guidebook. Not only did travel guides shape the actual impressions and assumptions, but also their function as an aide-memoire served to engrave the memory and experience of their readership.

There were those, of course, who resisted Murray's influence quite consciously. Jane Freshfield published her journal to give guidance for ladies on their Swiss travels, and she left her readers in no doubt that an important aim was to correct what she perceived to be the mistakes of the Murray. Yet in this very rejection, she testified to the cultural pervasiveness of the object of her scorn. Freshfield's book is a fascinating example of how the communication between guidebook and traveler worked both ways, of how the guidebook responded to its critical readership.[34] Throughout her account, Freshfield delighted in proving Murray wrong: at Mürren, she undertook an excursion which was not, as she noted, signposted in the Murray, and walked "up the hill (which Murray calls one of the summits of the Schilthorn)." The next, fully revised edition of the Murray duly responded and corrected its mistake. The Murray now recommended this "very interesting excursion," described the walk in detail, and pointed out that despite the difficulty of the ascent "it has been frequently accomplished by ladies."[35] In another instance of Freshfield's critical engagement with the guidebook, she explodes in the opening sentence of Chapter 4: "It is time that 'Murray' should qualify his assertion, that the Griess 'is not a pass for ladies'." This was, indeed, a correct quotation from the 1858 edition of the guidebook which she would have used. Once again, Murray responded in the handbook's next edition by assuring the traveler that "The pass is quite practicable for ladies."[36]

The guidebook was thus in intimate communion with the perceptions of its largely middle-class audience. It closely reflected middle-class views, and in turn determined them. While Henry Gaze and Thomas Cook brought tourists to Switzerland en masse, the guidebooks taught them what to see, and how to see it. There are, of course, exceptions, the main one being the serious Alpinists. These had other recourse to information through the Alpine Club and its journal, and, if they did make use of a guidebook, it tended to be Ball's *Alpine Guide*.[37] For the majority of travelers, the guidebook "domesticated" and familiarized a foreign environment not simply by providing information, but by appealing to, and strengthening, preconceived cultural norms. The guidebook became a mediator of "high" culture, as perhaps the most effective translator of the Romantics' notion of Switzerland into popular middle classes' awareness. Middle-class appreciation of the Romantics was not new, of course, but Murray's active advocacy of the Romantic poets at precisely the point at which Romantic emotions could be verified and authenticated "first hand," where they had first been felt, gave Byron and Shelley new levels of popularity. Images became internalized by the middle classes, such as Byron's impression of Mont Blanc as the "monarch of mountains," which is replicated not just in the guidebook, but in virtually every recorded traveler's sentiment.

In this way, the guidebook did everything to confirm and strengthen the religiosity of its mid-Victorian readership. The Alps were a place to meet God, and to encounter His power. This was not simply a consequence of romantic notions of Switzerland. Travel and religion had been connected ever since Thomas Cook's first excursion in 1841, and this link continued through to the 1890s, when the Evangelical Henry Lunn discovered the winter holiday.[38] Murray's handbook encouraged the Protestantism of its readers never crudely, but its admonitions to enjoy the Alps spoke for themselves.[39] The Catlow sisters, for instance, made a point of staying at the Weissenstein for more than just one day, refusing to leave until they had been able to witness the sunset promised them by the Murray. Eventually, they were rewarded with what was clearly, to them, a numinous experience, full of mystery, magic, and wonder. In the distance, they could make out the lakes of Neuchâtel and Bienne, which in their "misty loveliness" looked "as though they hardly belonged to the earth, while the shadowy mountains surrounding them were scarcely less ethereal."[40] These were religious experiences, personal encounters with God often recorded in travel journals through quotations from the Bible.[41]

Switzerland was usually perceived as a Protestant country in which God's work could be enjoyed by every individual, without distraction. To the guidebook and its readership, the assumed kinship with Protestant Britain was strengthened further by the lack of bureaucracy and military evident in public life, in marked contrast to the Catholic French Empire and Austrian-occupied Venice.[42] Upon their arrival in Dieppe, passengers were welcomed by two large crucifixes overlooking the harbor, making unmistakable France's religious flavour. In France, Victorian Protestant middle-class travelers encountered Roman Catholicism, often for the first time, through visiting the ornamental churches recommended by the guide-books. Indeed, visiting a Roman Catholic service became a tourist attraction in its own right.[43] In Italy, the Papacy, grandeur, and decline were so closely intertwined that Catholicism was a major theme in the Victorian's fascination with the country and its treasures. For this reason, the "Protestant" Murray had no hesitation to write in highest praise about Roman Catholic churches, while the Baedeker delighted in the sights of Paris, despite the anti-French leanings of the firm's founder.[44] The aim of the guidebook was necessarily to sell travel; its intrinsic professional interest lay in praising the beauty of the sights it covered, lest the guidebook be dispensable to its readership. Moreover, the buildings of Venice, Florence, and Rome were highly relevant to the present, and their treasures of Gothic and Renaissance, "Christian" and hedonist art, implied lessons for the observer which in the Victorian cultural and social context were not difficult to disentangle.[45] If, then, descriptions of Renaissance art and architecture connoted to Victorians the decline of Roman Catholic exuberance and the moral superiority of Protestant asceticism, the guidebook was not the major culprit, but an unwitting accomplice to the establishment of national, cultural middle-class norms.

As a mediator between "high" and popular middle-class culture, the guidebook (and the Murray in particular) offers an important key to understanding John Ruskin's popularity. Through the veneration of Rousseau's *Nouvelle Héloise*, Byron and Wilhelm Tell, Ruskin and the guidebooks appreciated the Alps in very similar ways, even though in practice they followed very different agendas.[46] For an audience increasingly familiar with the glories of Switzerland and northern Italy, the author of *The Stones of Venice* and *Modern Painters* simply expressed better than anybody else what scores of travelers experienced, and what they ought to experience, themselves. Ruskin, middle-class travel, and the guidebook are thus related, albeit indirectly. Many travel journals point to the importance of Ruskin in their vision of Switzerland, which Murray in turn enabled them to verify and deepen.[47] Jemima Morrell was alerted to a particular recognition of the landscape by Ruskin's descriptions, but at the same time she had no problem disagreeing with Ruskin if Murray's guidebook directed her appreciation in different ways.[48] By contrast, Sophia Holworthy's journal is a good example of how Ruskin appealed to the middle-class traveler simply through the tone and the sentiment of his writings. As a mark of her self-reliance, she chose to rely on the Baedeker, not the more prescriptive Murray. In her effort to encounter Italy and Switzerland free from preconceived notions, she did not even look at her objects of interest with noticeably Ruskinian eyes. And yet, Ruskin appealed to her deep sense of Christianity, which had propelled her to undertake the journey in the first place. And it was in Ruskin's words that she ended her book, admonishing the traveler to simplicity and spirituality along the journey.[49] It is impossible to understand the impact Ruskin had on the Victorian middle classes without their experience of travel, as mediated through the guidebook.

One of the participants of Thomas Cook's first tour to northern Italy in 1864, George Heard, was no exception in appreciating his Murray – indeed, he and a group of female travelers he met on the excursion spent much of the fifteen-hour trip from Switzerland to Italy comparing their guidebooks. When Heard arrived in Venice after parting with the group, he saw the city not only through Byron's, but also through Ruskin's, eyes. His day there was spent admiring much Titian and Tintoret, and everywhere he noted with sadness the city's decline. Heard's account of his day in Venice ended in a Ruskinian climax. He ventured to note with conviction that it would be impossible for the city to shake off its Austrian oppressors through force; what was needed instead was a moral regeneration of the city.[50] Only months later, Austria was defeated and Venice incorporated into the Kingdom of Italy.

Apart from influencing the frame of mind of so many Victorian travelers, Ruskin's engagement with tourists in northern Italy was formalized through his involvement with the revision of Murray's *Handbook to Northern Italy*. Its first edition, written by the eminent classical scholar, Francis Palgrave, had caused much controversy upon publication in 1842. Ruskin took a leading part in criticizing the work for the unusual subjectiveness in its judgment and its evaluation of classical and Renaissance art. In response to this barrage of criticism, the handbook was revised thoroughly for its second edition, which was published in 1847. To this edition, Ruskin made a number of contributions himself, mainly on works of art in Florence and Pisa.[51]

It would be beyond the scope of this chapter to examine further the irony of tourists "doing" Ruskin's Venice in a day, or the contradictions of Ruskin's contribution to the Murray, on the one hand, and his loathing both of the guidebook and the kinds of tourists it encouraged, on the other.[52] Murray's guidebook and Ruskin shared the intent to direct the appreciation of their readers towards particular objects and buildings, but in doing so they followed completely different agendas, the former encouraging general impressions, the latter directing particular views.[53] Ruskin did not just try to correct popular impressions created by the Murray, but in 1875–7 he even created his own, "alternative" guidebook. *Mornings in Florence*, a cheap, popular guidebook sold in six separate parts at 10 pence each, with each booklet providing a tour for a day through Florence: 3,000 copies of each part were sold by 1881, when another 3,000 copies each were printed.[54] Yet, in his very engagement with Murray and the middle-class traveler, Ruskin was fighting a losing battle. Whether written by Ruskin or by Murray, the guidebook helped to turn its own romantic notions of travel into a travesty. Miss Jemima's appreciation of the sunrise from the Rigi Culm was directed by her Murray's extensive description of the view and its importance. Yet, if in Byron's day in 1816 these impressions were enjoyed by 294 guests who had signed the visitors' book of the Rigi Culm's first Inn, by 1870, 40,000 annual visitors graced its peak. In 1874, following the completion of the railway line to the top of the mountain, that number had exploded to over 104,000 visitors.[55] The sunrise may still have been sublime, but its experience was no longer solitary.

What deserves to be borne in mind is the sheer numbers affected by the images communicated through the guidebook. In addition to its influence through Ball's and Gaze's guides, Murray's *Handbook to Switzerland* sold 44,250 copies between 1838 and 1874. If one assumes that the average size of each traveling party consisted of four people who shared one handbook, the Murray had been used by almost 200,000 British middle-class travelers to Switzerland alone.[56] In the 1860s, organizers such as Cook and Gaze brought Switzerland and northern Italy within reach of sections of the middle classes who would otherwise not have been able to travel thus far. Gaze's efforts rewarded those able to dispense with ten guineas, while Cook priced his twenty-one-day Swiss tour at seventeen guineas.[57] Jemima Morrell paid a total of £19 17s. 6d. for the journey. If one accepts the technical economic definition of the middle classes as all income-tax payers with annual incomes above £100, these were still considerable sums – but evidently not too much to pay for the experience of a lifetime. Anecdotal evidence suggests that two groups availed themselves disproportionately of the opportunity to travel: teachers and the clergy. These were not just people with sufficient vacations, but they also acted as prolific cultural multiplicators. They were the affirming witnesses to the "majesty" of the Mont Blanc, and the gloomy heroics of the prisoner of Chillon. If we add to this the readership of the flood of travel journals written for private and public circulation, which referred to the guidebook with such striking closeness, then the cultural significance of the guidebook for middle-class sentiment becomes evident.[58]

Through the promotion of foreign, and the facilitation of domestic, travel, the guidebook assisted in creating a national traveling culture which in turn contributed to a greater sense of national identity.[59] It is striking how travel in the second half of the nineteenth century acquired a British, as opposed to "English," flavor. Travelers abroad availed themselves of the English Murray in conjunction with the Scottish Bradshaw's railway guide. More importantly, the growth of a British national perspective from the 1840s may have been expressed through the establishment of Balmoral as a royal residence, and the "Britishness" of Gladstone,[60] but it acquired a popular dimension in that decade not least through the growth of popular travel. Thomas Cook's first commercial tour was to the Menai Straits, and this was followed by the organization of conducted tours in which he carried thousands of visitors every year to Wales and Scotland.[61] Aided and facilitated as always by the proliferation of guidebooks to these areas, the Celtic fringe of Great Britain (with the notable exception of Ireland) became experienced and known to an unprecedented degree.[62] Travelers to these places did note differences to England, of course, but these parts were clearly distinct from the European continent through their closeness to England in religion, government, and landscape. Without a doubt, the growth of "domestic" travel and the guidebook were crucial factors in the spread of a middle-class national identity which, in a century of peace with Britain's continental neighbors, served to highlight the communion of England, Scotland, and Wales, and their common distinctiveness *vis-à-vis* the continent.[63]

One of the most striking phenomena of middle-class travel abroad is that of the woman traveler. From the start, Thomas Cook advised "unprotected females" to join his tours, and throughout, more women than men took advantage of his vacation offers.[64] Travel offered to women the opportunity to escape the confines of Victorian domesticity and experience new horizons. This encouraged Emily Lowe, an experienced traveler, to state – not without some exaggeration – that "The only use of a gentleman in traveling is to look after the luggage."[65]

It is the guidebook that gave women the wherewithal to experience travel in complete independence.[66] In Forster's *A Room with a View*, what is most remarkable about Lucy's experience in "Santa Croce with no Baedeker" is that, on her own, it is only because she is without her guidebook that she is forced to seek the protection of two men whose company she would otherwise have avoided, that of the socialist Mr Emmerson and his son George. To the newly married Effie Ruskin, Murray's guidebook proved a godsend. Writing to her mother from Venice, she urged her to get one of Murray's guidebooks for herself, for "we use it constantly and when I want you to get a fuller description or more details of any particular Church than I have time to give you I will refer you to the particular page in Murray . . . Murray is invaluable and we never turn a step without its being useful."[67] Ignored by her husband for large parts of their stay in 1849–50, Effie relied on the Murray as an informed and independent guide which empowered her to explore the city on her own.[68] Effie's experience is highly reminiscent of Dorothea's lonely existence in Rome, with her new learned husband Mr Casaubon in *Middlemarch*, which George Eliot dated around 1830. Dorothea, too, was abandoned by Mr Casaubon in his search for the city's treasures, and she yearned for the countryside which she could comprehend, "where she could feel alone with the earth and sky." She admitted freely that Rome was probably the "spiritual centre and interpreter of the world" to those with "the quickening power of a knowledge which breathes a growing soul into all historic shapes." To Dorothea, however, without the necessary education and, one might add, without the guidebook, Rome meant nothing.[69] It was that guidebooks like the Murray and the Baedeker gave women the independence and the wherewithal to enjoy foreign cultures that was quite new. As Sophia Holworthy advised potential female imitators after her solitary travels through Europe for eighteen months, "Baedeker's guide books are most useful, and make you independent of men guides."[70]

Among its middle-class readership, the guidebook was a great leveler of knowledge and of culture. This was precisely the reason, of course, why the Murray or the Baedeker were such objects of scorn for many contemporary observers. By contrast, for those who had not received a good classical education, among them many women travelers, the guidebook was a great emancipatory tool. The travel journals described above, which were largely written by female authors, may not have been great literature, and were tedious for their plagiarism of the Murray. At the same time, the guidebook enabled the writing of such books in the first place. It was critical in establishing this genre of (largely female) writing, and provided these amateurs with a treasure of appropriate quotations and sensations which would make their impressions publishable. Moreover, even if these female travelers returned to a society that was little changed in their immediate context, their experience of self-reliance provided lasting memories, not least through the travel journal. Although most women stopped traveling on their own after marriage, this experience of independence contributed to the changing role of women and their greater freedom of maneuver within the family before 1914.[71]

If the guidebook became an emancipatory tool with regard to gender, the opposite was true with regard to class. This is surprising at first glance. One of the revolutionary aspects of travel in the railway age was, after all, that in theory it leveled class distinctions, as all classes boarded the same trains, from the same platforms, going to the same destinations.[72] It is true that continental travel was perceived to be too expensive and time-consuming for the British working classes.[73] Yet with growing numbers of travelers overseas, the idea of the European continent being a preserve of the middle classes became more of an illusion than a reality. In the early 1870s, the cumbersome passage from Newhaven and Dieppe, which would, depending on the tide, take between eighteen and twenty-four hours to complete,[74] thrived on its low cost, as it offered travel in third class which reduced the price for the cheapest return from London to Paris to 30s. (compared to 75s. via Folkestone). Just as the London Great Exhibition had made the experience of domestic travel truly popular throughout society, the Paris Exhibitions exposed new social groups to the continent, extending the social scale of travelers downwards. For the 1867 Great Exhibition in Paris, the number of cross-Channel passengers increased by 50 percent, from 295,000 (1866) to 457,000 (1867), before it fell to 305,000 in 1868.[75] Around 10,000 traveled under the auspices of Thomas Cook, whose cheapest ticket made it possible to travel from London to Paris, with four days there including accommodation, meals, and entrance fees, for 36s.[76] For the Great Exhibition in 1878 Cook sold 75,000 tickets between London and Paris, and in 1889 he arranged the sale of 200,000 tickets. Each time, it was the cheap passage from Newhaven and Dieppe which recorded the steepest rise in passengers.[77]

As the nineteenth century drew to a close, travel became cheaper, in relative and absolute terms. The commencement of Cook's tours to the European continent coincided with the growth of real incomes of the middle classes from the 1860s, which was especially pronounced from the 1880s.[78] At the same time, the travel industry became responsive to new groups. In 1900, Henry Lunn offered a week's trip to the Paris Exhibition for five and a half guineas, a nine-day trip to Lucerne for £6 6s., and an eighteen-days' tour through Switzerland for £11 5s. 6d.[79] Thomas Cook could offer a special rate to Switzerland for one week at five guineas for literary and other societies, polytechnics, and schoolteachers. In fact, cross-Channel travel was barely more expensive than vacationing in England. In 1899, Thomas Cook offered short trips to Calais and Boulogne including three nights' accommodation and full board for £2 2s., while the cheapest five-day excursion from London within England, to Brighton, cost £2 2s. 6d.[80] In this way, a small number of foreign resorts became refuges no longer exclusively for the British middle classes. In 1899, 951,078 passages were recorded across the Channel, a number which increased to over 1.5 million by 1911.[81] This figure did not even include the substantial number of day trippers to France, especially Boulogne, which became a regular feature from 1876. Their number peaked in 1899, when a total of 108,744 British day excursionists graced the town's streets, in addition to the vacationers spending several nights in the resort.[82]

By the end of the Victorian era, foreign travel had stopped being the exclusive preserve of the middle classes. And yet, it would be wrong to assume that this development replicated the experience of domestic travel where the middle classes had such difficulty in being among themselves. As more people traveled, the travel industry was quick to develop sophisticated ways of differentiation among its clientele. Luxury holidays in Egypt, Mediterranean cruises, the Orient Express, luxury hotels such as the Ritz, and educational trips restricted to, for instance, Harrovians and Etonians, all provided means of maintaining and even extending class barriers.[83] "High-class" vacations to popular Swiss resorts with emphasis on comfort and style were offered at more than double the price of the "cheap conducted tours."[84] Foreign travel entrenched and enriched differences not just between, but within, classes, and guidebooks were an important contributor to this development.[85]

Some guidebooks profited enormously from the travel boom. For the 1878 Paris exhibition, Thomas Cook sold 20,000 of his own guidebooks, and another 10,000 guidebooks issued by others.[86] Henry Gaze published one of his guidebooks for the 1867 exhibition at a cost of 1s., and by 1902, this was in its twenty-eighth edition.[87] Other guidebooks, by contrast, seemed little affected by the growth of popular travel in the late Victorian era. John Murray had published sixteen editions of his handbook on France by 1879, but the eighteenth edition did not appear until 1892, the boom in cross-Channel travel notwithstanding. This growth in traffic also left the Baedeker relatively unaffected, as eight editions of Baedeker's guide to Paris were published in the twenty years from 1874 to 1894, and a further eight in the following twenty years. Contrary to many a contemporary's objection that Murray or Baedeker made it possible for the lower orders to travel, in practice the "great unwashed" did not refer to these classic guidebooks. Day excursionists to Boulogne or Calais, or those on short vacations to such resorts, had no use for guidebooks which devoted but a tiny section to such destinations.[88] If they needed a guidebook at all, they would buy one concentrating on the locality or the region, such as Merridew's guide to Boulogne, which reached its fifteenth edition in 1911. Moreover, for such budget travelers, the cost of a Murray at 10s. would have represented a considerable proportion of the cost of their travels. Quite apart from the cost, these tourists did not have the leisure to "do" Paris in Baedeker or Murray fashion: even one whole day in the Louvre would seem like a luxury to such travelers. For this market, Black's guide to Paris with its three pages on the Louvre was much more apt than the Baedeker with thirty pages devoted to the museum in the 1873 edition.[89] These popular guides were only partly about what to see – Gaze devoted less than one-quarter of his guide to the actual sights of Paris – and were much more prescriptive in content, and simple in layout, than Baedeker and Murray: Gaze told his readers not just when to get up in the morning, but also what to eat where and at what time.[90]

The opening up of foreign travel to the petty bourgeoisie and the "respectable" working classes did not weaken the link between the Baedeker or Murray and its educated middle-class readership. In fact, it strengthened it. As educational tours or trips to the Palestine were directed at a middle class eager to distinguish and justify itself through culture, Baedeker and Murray came to act as further signposts to this section of the population. Having been scorned as facilitators of popular travel in the mid-Victorian period, in Edwardian England they were appreciated as works of education and learning. In 1850, *The Times* warned that it was Murray's handbook which enabled "the veriest cockney, the greenest school-boy, and the meekest country clergyman" to travel to the European continent.[91] By 1889, William Coolidge, one of England's greatest Alpinists, urged for a thorough revision of the Murray as the only book that gave justice to Switzerland's culture and heritage, among the glut of popular guidebooks swamping the market.[92] Guidebooks in their diversity reflected the growing class differentiation among British travelers abroad, and in turn strengthened it. By 1900, the Baedeker had become indispensable to the middle-class traveler eager to emphasize his or her cultural credibility. The communion between guidebook and readership had become closer than ever before.

This raises a final question, about the relationship between the Murray and the Baedeker. Whereas the two guidebooks first established themselves in their separate markets, from the 1860s Baedeker had his guidebooks translated into English and thus directly competed with Murray for the same readership. As shown earlier, in the 1860s the Murray more than held its own against its German rival, both in quantitative (as measured by the number of editions) and in qualitative terms – Murray was the guidebook which continued to be synonymous with English middle-class travel.[93] New editions of Murray's guide to Switzerland appeared regularly until the publication of the sixteenth edition in 1879. Thereafter, it sold with greater difficulty, and in 1891, W.A.B. Coolidge stood by his word and supervised thorough revisions of the eighteenth edition. This failed to revive sales, and the nineteenth edition did not appear until 1904. By 1851, John Murray had made a profit of £10,000 on his handbooks. In the 1880s, as Baedeker became acknowledged as the "prince of guide-book makers,"[94] Murray's handbooks had difficulties breaking even, and in 1901 almost the entire series was sold to Edward Standford, a publisher of low-budget guidebooks, for £2,000. Standford's reissue of many of the titles was not graced with more success, and after the outbreak of

World War I, he sold the series on to James and Findlay Muirhead, until the war the English editors of the Baedeker's guides, who published a new series of guidebooks in 1918 as the "Blue Guides."[95]

There are important commercial and technological reasons for Baedeker's success. The Baedeker was famous for the quality of its maps. It gained a reputation for being more reliable for the European continent, its own "backyard."[96] Even though the different language editions were in some areas adapted to the specific national markets, translating the guidebook into a number of languages achieved important economies of scale which made it possible for the Baedeker to be sold much more cheaply than the Murray. In the 1860s, Baedeker's English guidebook to Switzerland cost 5s. 6d. compared to 9s. for the Murray.[97] Murray's handbooks tended to be longer, bulkier, and less easy to carry around. Even though Murray was endorsed by Gaze and Ball, Baedeker was rigorously promoted by the market leader in travel provisions, Thomas Cook, not only in Cook's Guides, but also in his brochures and magazines.[98] These arguments go a long way to explaining why the Baedeker was more successful commercially, but they do not tell the whole story. In particular, they do not reveal why the Murray, which had been such a cultural icon despite its inferior maps and other shortcomings in the 1860s, had passed on that status to the Baedeker by 1900. In an age of mass travel, one might have expected that a high price and comprehensiveness would have been welcomed by a middle-class clientele eager to distinguish itself from the growing mass of budget travelers.

The key to the Murray's decline *vis-à-vis* the Baedeker towards the end of the century was the different values which the competitors presented to their readership. In its *Handbook to Paris*, for instance, Murray commended French food, but hastened to add that "there is perhaps no public dining establishment in Paris which can produce a first-rate dinner equal to that of a good London club." By contrast, Baedeker left no doubt that, "Paris is indisputably the cradle of high culinary art." There was no mention anywhere in the Murray of the city's theaters, whereas the Baedeker urged its readership to visit at least some of the theaters it listed as a characteristic aspect of Parisian life.[99] Together with the impressions gained earlier from a comparison of the guidebooks to northern Italy and Switzerland, it is difficult to escape the conclusion that it is precisely because the Murray was so patronizingly familiar in its assumptions and values that the middle classes in Britain came to prefer the Baedeker. In the 1860s, continental travel was still a relatively new phenomenon for the British middle classes, and it was all the more important to have a guidebook which reassured and reaffirmed in its familiarity. By 1900, foreign travel had ceased to be extraordinary, and the middle classes traveled abroad to experience something different. Despite their efforts to keep up with their readership, in the end Murray's handbooks could not deny their origins. In the 1860s, the Murray's unadulterated English flavor had been a clear advantage over the distinctly European Baedeker. By 1900, the Murray had failed to keep pace with the Edwardian middle classes. These now identified with the Baedeker.

The close identification between the travel guidebook and its middle-class readership makes tangible some of the salient features of the Victorian and Edwardian middle classes. The guidebook's popularization of "high" culture and its prescription of attitudes and experiences were particularly effective because of the great degree to which readers relied upon their guidebook in an otherwise unfamiliar environment. Byron was revered at the Drachenfels, the sunset admired at the Rigi Culm, and the torrent of the river Arve imagined because to so many travelers there was no alternative source for guidance and information. Popular travel and the guidebook affirmed a middle-class society ready and able to verify John Ruskin's meditations on morality and beauty on its travels, while the opening up of the middle-class horizon of experience was a quintessential factor in the popular impact of John Ruskin. Like many tour operators, Murray's values and assumptions were rooted in Victorian Protestantism. Through encouraging visits to continental churches and religious art, guidebooks encouraged a confrontation of the normally Protestant Victorian traveler with Roman Catholicism, urging him or her to show reverence and courtesy. At the same time, Puritan disgust at the morality of the French nobility in Murray's description of sights such as the Palais Royal,[100] or the romantic encouragement of an individual divine experience in the Alps, did much to deepen the Protestant inclinations of the Victorian middle-class traveler.

It is not possible in a single chapter to chart in detail the diversity of the guidebook's cultural impact on the Victorian middle classes. For instance, the way in which guidebooks (and the Murray especially) commented in detail upon flora and fauna, in contrast to relatively cursory observations about the host country's inhabitants, has to remain unexplored, even though this speaks volumes about the growing Victorian appreciation of the countryside over urban life. Where the guidebook undoubtedly did confirm current social trends was in the Victorian awareness of class. Whereas the Murray or Baedeker became a mark of distinction of the educated middle classes, a highly differentiated market for guidebooks catered for the growing diversity of travelers and their needs. At the same time, this chapter has shown how the guidebook could function as an important agent of change, through an investigation of the relationship between the guidebook and the lady traveler. It created a cultural and educational level playing field for independent female travelers and thus made possible the development of an entirely separate and distinctive sphere for women beyond previous conventions and norms.

For Britain, there is no question that guidebook-assisted travel promoted significantly the development of a greater sense of Britishness; an appreciation and understanding of distinctive British nations through domestic travel, and a sense of common distinctiveness *vis-à-vis* the European continent through foreign journeys. This makes the success of the Baedeker with its "Germanic" qualities of efficiency and reliability, over the recognizably Victorian Murray, all the more striking. Clearly, there was some unease about the success of the German product compared to its English rivals. On the publication of Baedeker's guidebook to Great Britain, the *Pall Mall Gazette* lamented the "melancholy" fact that a book of such quality should not have been produced in Britain. But, while it did refer to the context of economic rivalry between the two countries, it welcomed the "German Cicerone" on account of its clear superiority over its British rivals.[101] At one level, the Baedeker's German heritage was pronounced and unmistakable. Yet if by the 1880s it had become synonymous with "the" guidebook in Germany,[102] after 1900 this became true for Great Britain and the United States also. There, too, by 1914 Baedeker had established itself as the generic term for any book that claimed uncontestable reliability, authority, and cultural learnedness (*Bildung*).[103]

The Baedeker was not the product of German officialdom or Prussian militarism. Instead, it connoted "positive" German attributes; Edwardian travelers had no sense of economic threat or competition,[104] but were pleased to have a guidebook that was rigorously dependable, methodical, and cultured.[105] To recover from the stress of preparing Britain for war with Germany, Henry Asquith took to traveling, "lapping up Baedeker like Hippocreme" (according to his daughter). In 1913, he took one of his vacations with Winston Churchill on the Admiralty yacht *Enchantress* along the Dalmatian coast. It was a trip which Asquith found afforded "endless opportunities for the conscientious student of Baedekers, and after nearly a week's experience I can assure you need not fear the rivalry of my present trip-fellows." The Baedeker also gave the Prime Minister the opportunity to score over his First Lord of the Admiralty, whose only comment on seeing Dioclecian's Palace at Spalato was "I should like to bombard the swine."[106] Despite (and because of) its "clear" German characteristics, the Baedeker was simply not considered in reference to Anglo-German antagonism. It had become, effectively, a European cultural middle-class institution.

Travel and the guidebook did not necessarily create a better understanding between visitor and host, or between tourists of different countries. Baedeker's or Murray's guidebooks made it clear which hotels were frequented by which nationality, while cheaper guidebooks restricted their hotel recommendations to lodgings frequented by the English from the start.[107] Even when travelers did encounter other customs and nationalities, this could confirm as well as remove prejudice.[108] The aim of the first Baedeker guidebooks, after all, had been to provide a guidebook that served the distinctive taste of German travelers, and to liberate them from their reliance on the Murray. Baedeker's different language editions were careful to take note of the national peculiarities of their audience. In many descriptive details and guidances, Baedeker confirmed and encouraged its readership's cultural assumptions. At the same time, it created travel customs (not least the reliance on the Baedeker itself) which united the European middle classes in their experience of foreign travel and culture. Baedeker allowed for and encouraged national distinctiveness while, at the same time, connecting the British middle classes firmly to continental European culture.

Baedeker's adoption by the Edwardian middle classes is a reminder that it is important to arrive at a more complex understanding of national and cultural identities, in which there is room for different layers of experience and sentiment. By 1900, the Baedeker had become an essential component of the cultural canon of the British middle classes. Rejecting the insularity epitomized by the Murray, they wanted to experience travel in what they perceived to be a rigorous, continental, and uncompromisingly professional way. The guidebook's function as a litmus test for middle-class sensibilities suggests that, by the eve of World War I, the British middle classes identified much more closely with the European continent in outlook and culture than ever before. It was precisely this awareness of a common European heritage which contributed to the readiness of so many members of the middle classes to engage in a war in which this heritage seemed threatened.

Notes

1. [Charles Lever], *Arthur O'Leary: His Wanderings and Ponderings in Many Lands* (London, 1844), vol. 1, pp. 86–7.

2. Charles Dickens, "A Flight," in Charles Dickens, *The Uncommercial Traveler and Reprinted Pieces etc.* (Oxford: Oxford University Press, 1958), pp. 482–3.

3. Tore Rem, "*Little Dorrit, Pictures from Italy*, and John Bull," in Anny Sadrin (ed.), *Dickens, Europe and the New Worlds* (London: Macmillan, 1999), pp. 131–45; Andrew Sanders, "The Dickens World," in Michael Cotsell (ed.), *English Literature and the Wider World,* vol. 3: *Creditable Warriors 1830–1876* (London: Ashfield, 1990), pp. 131–42.

4. This quotation is taken from K. Baedeker, *Switzerland and the Adjacent Portions of Italy, Savoy, and the Tyrol,* 15th edn (Leipzig, 1893), p. v; Cotsell, *Creditable Warriors,* p. 12.

5. John Urry, *The Tourist Gaze: Leisure and Travel in Contemporary Societies* (London: Sage, 1990), p. 3.

6. Burkhart Lauterbach, "Baedeker und andere Reiseführer: Eine Problemskizze," *Zeitschrift für Volkskunde* 85 (1989), pp. 206–36.

7. J. Barry, "The Making of the Middle Class?" *Past and Present* 145 (1995), pp. 200–1; R.J. Morris, *Class, Sect and Party: The Making of the British Middle Class 1820–1850* (Manchester: Manchester University Press, 1990); W.D. Rubinstein, "The Size and Distribution of the English Middle Classes in 1860," *Historical Research* 61 (1988), pp.

65–89. In recent years, scholars have been particularly active in Germany, where the middle classes have acquired a pivotal position to a number of key debates. See esp. Jürgen Kocka, "The Middle Classes in Europe," *Journal of Modern History* 67 (1995), pp. 783–806; Jürgen Kocka and Allan Mitchell (eds), *Bourgeois Society in Nineteenth-Century Europe* (Oxford: Berg, 1993). For a different approach, see Lothar Gall (ed.), *Stadt und Bürgertum im Übergang von der traditionalen zur modernen Gesellschaft* (Munich: Oldenbourg, 1993).

8. Note especially the continued reluctance to investigate the bulk of the middle classes, the petite bourgeoisie. Laudable exceptions to this rule are Geoffrey Crossick and Heinz-Gerhard Haupt, *The Petite Bourgeoisie in Europe* (London: Routledge, 1995); Friedrich Lenger, *Sozialgeschichte der deutschen Handwerker seit 1800* (Frankfurt a/M: Suhrkamp, 1988).

9. J.A.R. Pimlott, *The Englishman's Holiday. A Social History* (Hassocks: Harvester, 1976), p. 210.

10. Rudy Koshar, "'What ought to be seen': Tourists' Guidebooks and National Identities in Modern Germany and Europe," *Journal of Contemporary History* 33 (1998), pp. 323–40.

11. Pimlott, *Englishman's Holiday*, p. 77.

12. K. Theodore Hoppen, *The Mid-Victorian Generation 1846–1886* (Oxford: Clarendon, 1998), pp. 367–8.

13. Georges Oustric, *Le Port de Boulogne-sur-Mer au XIXe siècle* (Boulogne, 1995), p. 89.

14. R.J. Croft, "The Nature and Growth of Cross-Channel Traffic through Calais and Boulogne 1840–70," *Transport History* 4 (1971), pp. 252–65, here p. 265; Laurent Tissot, "How Did the British Conquer Switzerland? Guidebooks, Railways, Travel Agencies, 1850–1914," *Journal of Transport History* 16 (1995), pp. 21–54, here Figure 2 on p. 30. The proportion of British travelers is taken from a rare set of statistics compiled for the years 1844 and 1845: Oustric, *Port de Boulogne*, p. 85. Similar (albeit tentative) conclusions about the proportion of British travelers are reached by R.J. Croft, "The Nature and Growth of Cross-Channel Traffic through Calais and Boulogne 1870–1900," *Transport History* 6 (1973), pp. 128–43, here p. 140. By contrast, J. Bernard contends that, by 1911, the proportion of British cross-Channel passengers was no more than 55 percent: J. Bernard, "Statistique du mouvement des voyageurs entre le Royaume-Uni et le Continent Européen," *Société Statistique de Paris* 53 (1912), pp. 232–7, here p. 234.

15. The best guide to the English-speaking community in Paris is *The Anglo-American Annual 1896–7: A Directory and Handbook for Residents of British and American Nationality in France* (Paris, 1897); John Murray, *Hand-Book for Travelers in France*, 3rd edn. (London: John Murray, 1847), p. xxxviii.

16. R.J. Croft, "Nature and Growth 1840–1870." The ports of Calais and Dover were the fastest and most expensive links to Paris, and were used disproportionately by business people. If anything, then, these figures underrepresent the seasonal variation across the whole of the Channel.

17. Croft, "Nature and Growth 1870–1900," pp. 138–9.

18. Note, for instance, the descriptions of the Staubbach in John Murray, *A Handbook for Travelers in Switzerland and the Alps of Savoy and Piedmont*, 10th edn (London: John Murray, 1863), p. 83; Karl Baedeker, *Switzerland and the Adjacent portions of Italy, Savoy, and the Tyrol: Handbook for Travelers*, 2nd edn (Coblenz, 1864), p. 112. On Byron and the Alps, see also Patrick Anderson, *Over the Alps: Reflections on Travel and Travel Writing* (London, 1969).

19. Murray, *Switzerland*, 8th edn (1858); 16th edn (1878). Note that in the 1860s, the revised 9th and 10th editions of Murray's guide did have a relatively short paragraph on the tourist trade, with an indirect reference to Baedeker: "A German writer has truly remarked that a traveler in the Oberland should be supplied with plenty of patience and small change." Murray, *Switzerland*, 9th edn (1861), p. 77. This paragraph is removed in the 1870s. Compare with the introduction to the Oberland in Baedeker, *Switzerland*, 6th edn (1873), pp. 99–100, and also Baedeker, *Switzerland*, 2nd edn (1864).

20. Murray, *Switzerland*, 10th edn (1863), pp. 80–1; Baedeker, *Switzerland*, 2nd edn (1864), p. 121.

21. A more detailed overview is W.A.B. Coolidge, *Swiss Travel and Swiss Guide-Books* (London, 1889).

22. John Ball, *The Alpine Guide*, 3 vols (London, 1863–68), here vol. 2, p. 58.

23. *Cook's Tourist Handbook for Switzerland* (London, 1874), pp. 88–91.

24. Henry Gaze, *Switzerland: How to See it for Ten Guineas* (London, 1866).

25. Ibid., pp. v, 16.

26. See, for instance, *Cook's Tourist Handbook*, p. 83 (Wengern Alp), p. 84 (Staubbach).

27. Hugh Honour and John Fleming, *The Venetian Hours of Henry James, Whistler and Sargent* (London: Walker, 1991), p. 20.

28. Mrs. Staley, *Autumn Rambles; or, Fireside Recollections of Belgium, the Rhine, the Moselle, German Spas, Switzerland, the Italian Lakes, Mont Blanc, and Paris. Written by a Lady* (Rochdale, 1863), pp. 104–6. Murray, *Switzerland*, 9th edn (1861), pp. 1–2.

29. Compare, for instance, the description of the journey the day they leave Basle. Staley, *Autumn Rambles*, pp. 106–11. Murray, *Switzerland*, 9th edn (1861), pp. 34–8, 210.

30. *Miss Jemima's Swiss Journal – The First Conducted Tour of Switzerland* (1863), also vol. 3 of *The History of Tourism: Thomas Cook and the Origins of Leisure Travel*, ed. Paul Smith (London: Routledge, 1998), pp. 70–1 (Giessbach), p. 74 (Sarnen). Murray, *Switzerland*, 10th edn (1863), p. 93 (Giessbach), p. 68 (Sarnen).

31. *Miss Jemima's Swiss Journal*, p. 35. Murray, *Switzerland*, 10th edn (1863), p. 401.

32. *Miss Jemima's Swiss Journal*, p. 21. Murray, *Switzerland*, 10th edn (1863), p. 381.

33. A further piece of evidence is provided by a comparison between Agnes and Maria E. Catlow, *Sketching Rambles. Or, Nature in the Alps and Apennines* (London, 1861), vol. 1, p. 145 (Staubbach) and pp. 165–71 (on Chillon), and Murray, *Switzerland*, 8th edn (1858), pp. 75–6, 162–4.

34. According to the Baedeker's English editor, evaluating the readers' correspondence was the essential first step in preparing a guidebook's new edition: *Pall Mall Gazette* (August 23, 1889), p. 1.

35. [Mrs. Henry Jane Freshfield], *Alpine Byways or Light Leaves Gathered in 1859 and 1860, by a Lady* (London, 1861), pp. 3–5, 8. Murray, *Switzerland*, 8th edn (1858), and Murray, *Switzerland*, 9th edn (1861), pp. 83–4. Freshfield's book would not have been published long before the revised 9th edition of Murray's handbook, but given her agenda set out in the introduction, and given the guidebook's very striking responsiveness, it is highly likely that Freshfield let Murray have her criticism before publication – after all, the Murray's actively encouraged readers' comments and criticisms.

36. Freshfield, *Alpine Byways*, p. 40. Murray, *Switzerland*, 8th edn (1859), p. 98. Murray, *Switzerland*, 9th edn (1861), p. 203.

37. See, for instance, Elizabeth Tuckett, *How we Spent the Summer or a Voyage en Zigzag in Switzerland and Tyrol, with Some Members of the Alpine Club* (London, 1864) – though some of the accommodation (e.g. in Bergün) used by the party was, of all the guidebooks, referred to only in the Murray.

38. On Lunn's Christian background, see Lynne Withey, *Grand Tours and Cook's Tours: A History of Leisure Travel 1750–1915* (London: Aurum, 1998), p. 215.

39. On Murray's Protestant inclinations, see also Coolidge, *Swiss Travel*, p. 78.

40. Catlow, *Sketching Rambles*, pp. 17–23.

41. *Miss Jemima's Swiss Journal*, p. 86.

42. Next to religion, soldiers and uniformed policemen were among the most striking curiosities noted in the Victorian travel journals of the 1860s. See, for instance, Heard, "My Journal," pp. 99, 105–6 (on Venice). Staley, *Autumn Rambles*, p. 3 (arrival in Calais). Murray, *Switzerland*, 10th edn (1863), p. xlv.

43. Heard, "My Journal," pp. 2–3, 4–7. William Miller, *Wintering in the Riviera with Notes of Travel in Italy and France*, 2nd edn (London, 1881), pp. 110–12. The Murray's even supplied advice for travelers how to behave in Roman Catholic services, urging the reader to show respect for the tradition. John Murray, *Hand-Book for Travelers in France: Being a Guide to Normandy, Brittany; etc.,* 3rd edn (London, 1847), p. xxxviii.

44. Alex W. Hinrichsen, *Baedeker's Reisehandbücher 1832–1990*, 2nd edn (Bevern: U. Hinrichsen, 1991), p. 13. For a different view, which suggests that Baedeker's "German" national agenda was more in the foreground in its description of sights, see Koshar, "'What ought to be seen?'," p. 333.

45. This theme is best explored in John Pemble, *The Mediterranean Passion. Victorians and Edwarians in the South* (Oxford: Oxford University Press, 1988), esp. pp. 31, 64, 193, 212, 225. John Pemble, *Venice Rediscovered* (Oxford: Clarendon, 1995), pp. 100–7. Michael Cotsell, "Introduction," in Cotsell, *English Literature*, pp. 30–2. In *Pictures from Italy*, Charles Dickens managed, as ever, to capture some of the themes concerning his fellow middle-class travelers. Sanders, "The Dickens World," pp. 134, 137. Rem, "*Little Dorrit*," esp. pp. 132–5.

46. For Ruskin's image of Switzerland, see Elizabeth Helsinger, "Lessons of History: Ruskin's Switzerland," in Cotsell, *English Literature*, pp. 187–208, here p. 192.

47. Note, for instance, George Heard's Ruskinian fascination with the "celestial hue on the towering mountains – those wonderous stepping stones from Earth to Heaven." Thomas Cook Archives, George Couch Heard, "My Journal: Or Three Weeks in Switzerland and North Italy," typescript, 1865, p. 182.

48. *Miss Jemima's Swiss Journal*, p. 37.

49. Holworthy, *Alpine Scrambles*, pp. 113–14.

50. Heard, "My Journal," pp. 183–6.

51. A summary of Ruskin's additions is in E.T. Cook and Alexander Wedderburn, *The Works of John Ruskin* (London: George Allen, 1912), vol. 28, pp. 326–30. Jeanne Clegg, *Ruskin and Venice* (London: Junction, 1981), pp. 175–6. W.B.C. Lister, *A Bibliography of Murray's Handbook for Travelers and Biographies of Authors, Editors, Revisers and Principal Contributors* (Dereham, Norfolk: Dereham Books, 1993), p. ix. Tim Hilton, *John Ruskin: The Early Years 1819–1859* (New Haven, CT: Yale University Press, 1985), p. 95.

52. Some discussion of these issues is in Piers Brendon, *Thomas Cook: 150 Years of Popular Tourism* (London: Secker and Warburg, 1991), pp. 81–2. See also the brilliant Pemble, *Venice Rediscovered*, esp. p. 132. This "problem" of mass middle-class travel was commented on by most contemporary observers. See, for instance, "Vacations," in *Men, Books, and Mountains: Essays by Leslie Stephen* (London: Hogarth, 1956), pp. 168–81 (written 1869).

53. J.G. Links, *The Ruskins in Normandy: A Tour in 1848 with Murray's Hand-Book* (London: John Murray, 1968). Inadvertently, this book shows just how contrasting Murray's and Ruskin's perceptions were.

54. John Ruskin, "Mornings in Florence," in E.T. Cook and Alexander Wedderburn, *The Works of John Ruskin* (London: George Allen, 1906), vol. 23, pp. 285–451, here esp. pp. 285–90. On the cultural impact of Ruskin's work on Florence, especially on the British travelers, see Pemble, *Mediterranean Passion*, esp. pp. 207–10.

55. Gustav Peyer, *Geschichte des Reisens in der Schweiz: Eine culturgeschichtliche Studie* (Basel, 1885), p. 190.

56. On the number of books printed, see Jack Simmons, "Introduction," *Murray's Handbook for Travelers in Switzerland 1838* (Leicester: Leicester University Press, 1970), p. 31. Bernard, *Rush to the Alps*, p. 95. This estimate of British middle-class travelers of the Alps would be affected negatively by foreign tourists availing themselves of the handbook, and positively by the Murray's being obtained in used condition.

57. As a guide, 12d. (pennies) = 1s. (shilling); 20s. = £1 (pound); £1 1s. = 1 guinea.

58. On the creation of new and "authentic" cultural symbols through tourism in general, see James Buzard, *The Beaten Track: European Tourism, Literature, and the Ways to Culture, 1800–1914* (Oxford: Clarendon, 1993), here p. 10. Ian Ousby, *The Englishman's England: Taste, Travel and the Rise of Tourism* (Cambridge: Cambridge University Press, 1990).

59. This confirms the important argument made in the German context by Koshar, "'What ought to be seen'," p. 332–3.

60. H.C.G. Matthew, *Gladstone 1809–1874* (Oxford: Oxford University Press, 1991), pp. 129–4.

61. W. Fraser Rae, *The Business of Travel: A Fifty Years' Record of Progress* (London: Thomas Cook and Son, 1891), pp. 33–40.

62. On guidebooks for domestic British travel, see John Gretton, *Essays in Book-Collecting* (Dereham, Norfolk: Dereham Books, 1985), pp. 20–5.

63. Another way of putting this is that travel and the guidebook encouraged the differentiation between mainland Britain, on the one hand, and Ireland, on the other. An excellent summary of debates about "Britishness" is in Hoppen, *Mid-Victorian Generation*, pp. 513–20.

64. Withey, *Grand Tours*, pp. 145, 158.

65. Jane Robinson, *Wayward Women: A Guide to Women Travelers* (Oxford: Oxford University Press, 1990), p. 117. This bibliography is a testament to the breadth of experience acquired by independent female travelers before 1914, and an excellent starting-point for further study in this area.

66. For a contrasting argument which emphasizes that the Murray's was an instrument to confirm and strengthen a masculine definition of English culture, and thus subjected women further, see Inderpal Grewal, *Home and Harem: Nation, Gender, Empire, and the Cultures of Travel* (London: Leicester University Press, 1996), pp. 103–4.

67. Mary Lutyens, *Young Mrs. Ruskin in Venice: Her Picture of Society and Life with John Ruskin 1849–1852* (London: John Murray, 1965), p. 73 (Venice, November 19, 1849). For further evidence of Effie Ruskin's use of the Murray's, see also pp. 89 and 134.

68. Clegg, *Ruskin and Venice*, p. 76; Links, *The Ruskins*, p. 37.

69. George Eliot, *Middlemarch* (Oxford: Oxford World Classics, 1996), p. 190.

70. Holworthy, *Alpine Scrambles*, p. 104.

71. In general, on the changing roles of women in marriage see Shani D'Cruze, "Women and the Family," in June Purvis (ed.) *Women's History: Britain, 1850–1945* (London: UCL Press, 1995), pp. 51–83, esp. p. 75.

72. On the difficulty of maintaining the social exclusivity of English resorts, see J. Christopher Holloway, *The Business of Tourism*, 4th edn (London: Pitman, 1994), pp. 21–2.

73. Pimlott, *Englishman's Holiday*, pp. 90–120; Pemble, *Mediterranean Passion*, p. 3.

74. Karl Baedeker, *Paris and its Environs*, 4th edn (Coblenz, 1874).

75. Croft, "Nature and Growth," p. 265.

76. Rae, *Business of Travel*, p. 90.

77. For the exhibitions of 1867, 1878, 1889 and 1900, travel on the inexpensive Newhaven–Dieppe route increased by an average of 127 percent: Bernard, "Statistique," p. 235.

78. Hoppen, *Mid-Victorian Generation*, pp. 78–9. On the growth of real incomes, see Charles Feinstein, "A New Look at the Cost of Living," in James Foreman-Peck (ed.), *New Perspectives on the Late Victorian Economy* (Cambridge: Cambridge University Press, 1991), pp. 151–79.

79. Henry S. Lunn, *Where to Spend the Summer Holidays* (London, 1900). Even before the advent of this travel boom set in, Charles Dickens, for one, was very fond of "his" watering place, Boulogne. Charles Dickens, "Our French Watering-Place," in Dickens, *Uncommercial Traveler*, pp. 400–12.

80. *Cook's Popular Tours to Italy and Switzerland* (London, Easter 1899), pp. 12–15.

81. Croft, "Nature and Growth," p. 128; Bernard, "Statistique," p. 234. One estimate suggests that in 1913, more than 750,000 return journeys to the European continent were made by British subjects: F.W. Ogilvie, *The Tourist Movement* (London: P.S. King and Son, 1933), p. 92.

82. Oustric, *Port de Boulogne*, pp. 187–8, 257–8. In 1885, a day trip by steamer from London to Boulogne, and back via Folkestone, cost 10s. *Travel*, August 8, 1885.

83. On the development of luxury travel, see Withey, *Grand Tours*, ch. 6; Pemble, *Mediterranean Passion*, p. 26; Brendon, *Thomas Cook*, pp. 227–32; Holloway, *Business of Tourism*, p. 22; Bernard, *Rush to the Alps*, pp. 108–11; Henry Lunn, *Cruises and Tours for Etonians, Harrovians and Other Public School Men* (London, 1903).

84. Compare, for instance, the enormous differences in price for very similar journeys between *Gaze's High-Class Conducted Tours* (London, May 1899) and *Gaze's Programme of Cheap Conducted Tours* (London, May 1899).

85. For an argument about the importance of class differentials in travel, see also Peter Bailey, *Leisure and Class in Victorian England. Rational Recreation and the Contest for Control, 1830–1885* (London: Routledge and Kegan Paul, 1978).

86. Rae, *Business of Travel*, p. 169.

87. Henry Gaze, *Paris. How to See it for Five Guineas* (London, 1867). Henry Gaze, *How to See Paris*, 28th edn (1902).

88. Baedeker's guide to Northern France, published in 1889, devoted two pages to Calais, and four to Boulogne.

89. By 1884, Baedeker's section on the Louvre had expanded to 65 pages, and in the 1904 edition it reached 75 pages. Adam and Charles Black concentrated on the Scottish and then British domestic travel market for their low-budget guidebooks, but exploited the popular demand for budget guidebooks during the Great Exhibitions by publishing a guide to Paris, for 1s., in 1867, 1787, 1889, 1900, and 1907. The later editions were largely based on *Black's Guide to Paris and the Exhibition of 1867*, ed. by David Thomas (Edinburgh, 1867).

90. Gaze, *Paris* (1867), pp. 67–8.

91. Gretton, *Essays in Book-Collecting*, p. 16.

92. Coolidge, *Swiss Travel*, pp. 115–6.

93. Pemble, *Mediterranean Passion*, pp. 70–2. Coolidge, *Swiss Travel*, p. 76.

94. *Pall Mall Gazette* (August 30, 1889), p. 2.

95. John Gretton, "Introduction," in Lister, *Bibliography of Murray's Handbook*, pp. iii, xxii–xxiv. John Murray, *The Origin and History of Murray's Handbooks for Travelers* (London: John Murray, n.d.).

96. W.B.C. Lister and Michael Wild, "The Baedeker–Murray Correspondence," *Baedekeriana* 13 (1990), pp. 2–20; *Baedekeriana* 14 (1990), pp. 16–31. *Baedekeriana* was a home-produced journal compiled by Michael Wild, which appeared for eighteen issues in sixty-five copies. Some copies are available both at the University Library, Cambridge, and the Bodleian Library, Oxford.

97. This price differential was also true for respective guides on Italy. Thomas Cook Archives, *Cook's Excursionist and European and American Tourist Adviser* (July 27, 1867). In 1865, Thomas Cook advertised the sale of Baedeker's Handbook to Paris for 4s. 6d., and the equivalent Murray's guide for 5s. Thomas Cook Archive, *Cook's Excursionist and International Tourist Advertiser* (May 22, 1865). Baedeker's first English guidebook, on the Rhine, cost 4s. 6d., while Murray's equivalent handbook was 9s. 4d. Hinrichsen, *Baedeker's Reisehandbücher*, p. 27.

98. See e.g. Thomas Cook Archive, *Cook's Excursionist and International Tourist Advertiser* (May 1, 1865).

99. Karl Baedeker, *Paris and its Environs*, 4th edn (Leipzig, 1873), pp. 8, 15; John Murray, *A Handbook for Visitors to Paris*, 6th edn (London, 1874), p. 28.

100. Murray, *Handbook for Visitors to Paris*, 6th edn (1974), p. 211. Compare with Baedeker, *Paris*, 4th edn (1973), p. 77.

101. *Pall Mall Gazette* (October 18, 1887), p. 3. A remarkably similar comment on the French edition on the "Sud-Est de la France" (1905) is in *Baedekeriana* 13 (1990), p. 22.

102. *Pall Mall Gazette* (August 23, 1889), pp. 1–2.

103. In the late 1880s, the Baedeker's predominance in the English market was not yet assured. For criticism of its cultural bias, see *Pall Mall Gazette* (August 31, 1889), p. 2. After 1900, though, scores of publications employed the Baedeker trademark. Ardern Beaman, *Travels without Baedeker* (London, 1913), refuted in its preface any "literary merit, nor any sort of accuracy, historical or otherwise." William George Jordan, *Little Problems of Married Life: The Baedeker to Matrimony* (New York, Chicago, Toronto, London and Edinburgh, 1910) claimed "Ciceronian" authority, while Carolyn Wells, *The Lover's Baedeker and Guide to Arcady* (New York, 1912) is a humorous American publication whose whole structure was modeled on, and could be understood only through knowledge of, the original. See also Koshar, "'What ought to be seen?'," p. 330.

104. Interestingly (and not necessarily paradoxically), the German view of the Baedeker as a symbol of German economic hegemony was not shared by those primarily affected, the British: Koshar, "'What ought to be seen'."

105. This view refines arguments about the inexorable rise of Anglo-German antagonism by pointing out that there were two Germanies in the British public perception, one militaristic, ruthless, and authoritarian, the other cultured and kindred. Paul Kennedy, *The Rise of the Anglo-German Antagonism, 1860–1914* (London: Allen and Unwin, 1982). Peter Pulzer, "Der deutsche Michel in John Bulls Spiegel: Das britische Deutschlandbild im 19. Jahrhundert," in *Jahrbuch des Historischen Kollegs* (Munich, 1998), pp. 3–19, here pp. 15–16. Peter Pulzer, "Vorbild, Rivale und Unmensch. Das sich wandelnde Deutschlandbild in England 1815–1945," in Hans Süssmuth (ed.), *Deutschlandbilder in Dänemark und England, in Frankreich und den Niederlanden* (Baden Baden, 1996), pp. 235–50, here 235–9.

106. Christopher Smith, "Asquith on 'Enchantress' with Churchill and Baedeker," *Baedekeriana*, 18 (1992), pp. 1–3 (insert).

107. In Frederic Harrison's opinion, contact between travelers of different nationalities even decreased towards the end of the nineteenth century: Pemble, *Mediterranean Passion,* p. 260.

108. Note Jane Freshfield's irritation at her snoring or talkative German neighbors with their heavy boots at one *Pension* where she spent the night. [Freshfield], *Alpine Byways,* pp. 16–17.

7

Bicycling, Class, and the Politics of Leisure in Belle Epoque France

Christopher S. Thompson

"[The bicycle] is going to revolutionize social relations, that is easy to predict, although the extent to which it will do so is still impossible to calculate."[1] This claim, made in 1894 by Dr Lucas-Championnière, one of cycling's most fervent enthusiasts, was an explosive one for French people of all social classes at the turn of the century, many of whom saw their nation as riven by political, social, and religious divisions. Under the impact of industrialization and urbanization, and with the reintroduction of universal male suffrage in the 1870s, the fledgling Third Republic faced the challenge of peacefully integrating the working classes into a society shaped by bourgeois norms and values. This "social question" was a particularly sensitive issue for the new regime, which owed its birth in part to the massacre of working-class Communards in 1871, itself a discomforting echo of the Second Republic's brutal repression of its working-class constituency in June 1848. In addition, republicans faced enemies to the right – Bonapartists, monarch-ists, and nationalists – as well as a divisive confrontation with Catholics over the institutional place of the Church in the Republic.

Many of his compatriots, seeking consensus and social peace, no doubt hoped that Dr Lucas-Championnière was correct when he claimed that cycling was a democratic sport that would "bring the nation's children together in common aspirations, by making them accomplish common efforts";[2] others, however, feared that the democratizing bicycle, far from being an instrument of national unity and social cohesion, raised the frightening specter of social disruption. These critics watched in dismay as the falling price of the bicycle in the 1890s made the new machine accessible to lower-class budgets, effectively challenging the virtual monopoly that middle- and upper-class practitioners of the new sport had enjoyed to that point. As lower-class cyclists discovered a world of speed and leisure that had traditionally belonged to their social betters, their appearance and conduct often flouted the cycling etiquette formulated by bourgeois experts of the bicycle, suggesting that new, unregulated forms of popular leisure posed a threat to the social order. Faced with this appropriation from below of their toy, the bourgeoisie elaborated a discourse of social distinction that contrasted the elegant ideal of the bicycling gentleman with his uncouth, working-class opposite. By the turn of the century, how one cycled, that is, one's behavior, posture, position, and attire on the bicycle, had become an important social marker.

Meanwhile, the republican regime, anxious to mend its relations with the increasingly visible, self-confident, and organized lower classes, sought to channel the latter's growing interest in cycling into activities and institutions – specifically, cycling clubs – that would instill in them republican civic values and bourgeois respectability. Battles over the social meaning and potential of the bicycle in fin-de-siècle France were thus intimately linked to class identities, class relationships, the rise of mass leisure, and a new consumer culture of plentiful and relatively inexpensive goods symbolized by the bicycle.

There is, of course, considerable scholarship on the social question, class formation, and class relations in nineteenth-century France. The focus of this scholarship has been essentially – and for good reason – on illuminating class identities, experiences, and relations through the dual prism of politics and work. Leisure – sport, in particular – has, however, until recently been relatively neglected. Yet for male workers broadly defined and for the young men filling the growing number of petty white-collar positions in commercial and government bureaucracies, the development of new leisure opportunities, especially new sporting activities such as bicycling, represented a significant improvement in their lives. The fact that these were *leisure* activities instead of work or politics did not of course render them politically or socially neutral; on the contrary, such activities and the organizations they spawned provided a new terrain, at the intersection of politics, civil society, and consumer culture, for the conceptualizing and playing out of class identities and relationships during the Belle Epoque. I have addressed elsewhere the case of female cycling in the Belle Epoque, specifically debates about the emancipation of bourgeois women by the bicycle;[3] here I shall focus on the ways in which contemporary perceptions of class and of political and economic interests both informed and were shaped by the realities and representations of male bicycling.

The Bourgeois *Cavalier Cycliste* versus the Working-Class *Vélocipédard*

Prior to the 1890s the bicycle's cost made it the virtually exclusive toy of the well-to-do; even so, bicycling faced elitists who dismissed the new sport because it was neither noble like fencing and riding, which, they noted, went back to the Crusades, nor well established like boating, gymnastics, foot races, and hunting.[4] As late as 1894, one defender of the bicycle noted the "disdain and pity," the "easy sarcasm" with which "fanatics of the horse of flesh" had until recently viewed the bicycle. These critics allegedly rejected the bicycle because it was a machine – an "inert and impersonal being" – which lacked the character and legitimacy of a living creature.[5] In the late 1890s, one head barrister forbade the lawyers under his authority to ride bicycles because he believed that cycling was incompatible with the personal dignity required of their profession. His successor relented but would not allow his lawyers to wear their cycling suits in the court's waiting area.[6]

To counter such prejudices, bourgeois proponents of the bicycle went to great pains to establish its social legitimacy in the final decades of the nineteenth century. To do so they conceptualized the bicycle as a mechanical horse, associating it explicitly with the traditional mount of the aristocracy: "The *Vélocipède* . . . is a mount for transportation, with an automatic biped structure, an upright position, rotating feet, moved and steered by the *Véloceman* who is its horseman [*cavalier*]."[7] The earliest *draisiennes*, the bicycle's pedal-less and gear-less ancestor, invented in the early nineteenth century, featured equine heads carved in wood protruding from the handlebars.[8] Late-nineteenth-century French cycling experts spoke of the *corps* (body) and of the "anatomy" of the bicycle,[9] which "quivers like an animal under its thin skin of nickel and enamel; it whinnies at times, . . . the screams and moans of steel being overworked . . . it has a soul."[10]

Such rhetorical gymnastics indicate the extent to which cycling enthusiasts were aware of and determined to undermine snobbish criticisms of bicycling. Yet even while they referred to the bicycle as a horse of steel or horse of iron,[11] some promoters of the new sport noted an important distinction that conditioned the bicycle's moral role and thus its social value: cycling, "the sport of the will," required a man to triumph over "his own flesh which protests and rebels," while a horseman had only to dominate the will of an animal.[12] Such claims were particularly relevant for a nation recovering from a military defeat widely attributed to the physical and psychological inferiority of the French *race*.

Defenders of cycling also borrowed from aristocratic equestrian etiquette to define an *équitation cycliste* intended to placate,[13] if not convert, elitist critics of the bicycle. The pedals were simply the cyclist's stirrups,[14] the handlebars were reins,[15] while the bicycle, according to an early instruction manual, "must appear to be moving on its own like a horse, with the pedals pulling one's feet along. It must be held on a normal ride by a single hand and pushed delicately with one's feet."[16] The impracticality and riskiness of such an approach to cycling illustrates how important the notion of elegance was in the elaboration of the ideal position and proper manner of riding the machine: "the cycling horseman [*cavalier cycliste*], like the horseman on a horse [*cavalier équestre*], has . . . an obligation to the public, the obligation of elegance."[17] All the experts, from Louis Baudry de Saunier to Dr Philippe Tissié (a leading figure of the burgeoning French sports and physical education movement), agreed that maintaining an upright position was essential to velocipedic elegance:[18]

besides its inelegance and the discomfort it causes our digestive functions, it [the inclined position] is perfectly useless for the cyclotourist . . . Supreme good taste currently calls for one to hold oneself almost straight: cyclists, male or female, who bend over their machines are by that very fact disqualified and shamefully called *pédalards* [cycling louts, ugly cyclists].[19]

Another doctor agreed, claiming that an overly inclined position was "inelegant, absurd, useless and harmful" for non-racers who leaned forward to reduce their wind resistance: "Just as a horseman out for a ride does not ride like a jockey, so too must a cyclist not ride like a bicycle racer."[20] Such class-based admonitions, reinforced by advertising posters portraying elegantly dressed, straight-backed bourgeois and aristocratic cyclists, were particularly apt in an age of Darwin-inspired self-consciousness: it was essential for bourgeois cycling enthusiasts to demonstrate that the highly evolved middle- and upper-class *homo cyclens* was a variation of *homo erectus* and thus eschewed "a position as depraved as it is inelegant."[21] The French medical community inveighed as much against the dangerous cultural and social implications of adopting a poor position on the bicycle as it did against the supposed physiological effects of such a position.[22] Physicians saw themselves not only as defenders of the French *race*, but as defenders of a social order in which they occupied a prominent place, a prominence reflected by the increasing parliamentary representation of doctors in the early Third Republic.[23]

The distinction drawn between the gentleman-cyclist or cyclo-tourist and the professional racer was pivotal.[24] Almost all professional cyclists came from the lower classes; their bent-over position on the bicycle was designed for maximum speed because maximum speed brought victories, which in turn earned them prize money and sponsorship contracts with bicycle and tire firms eager for good publicity. Erect posture distinguished bourgeois cyclists from working-class racers and the working-class youth who sped around town imitating their heroes, as well as from messenger boys and delivery men who now used the bicycle as a professional tool. For the bourgeois "[t]he art of cycling consists of skill, elegance and grace,"[25] not the pursuit of speed and efficiency. Physical elegance was closely correlated with moral rectitude: the ungraceful was disgraceful. Dr Lucas-Championnière might claim that the bicycle endowed everyone with elegance, further proof of its democratic nature,[26] but many bourgeois believed that the position one adopted on the bicycle reflected the position one occupied in society. As the price of the bicycle dropped and increasing numbers of male workers, shop clerks, and artisans acquired the new machine, these criteria of elegance allowed bourgeois advocates of cycling to draw sharp contrasts between their ideal of the gentleman-cyclist and a disturbing new working-class stereotype.

Until the 1890s cycling remained an expensive activity. A bicycle cost in the vicinity of 500 francs or the equivalent of two months lieutenant's pay or three months of a teacher's salary. The next two decades saw a dramatic fall in prices: in 1909, for example, it was possible to purchase a new Clément bicycle in the northern mining community of Longwy-Bas from 150 francs and used ones from only 50 francs.[27] According to bourgeois observers, as a result of this precipitous decline in prices, a new kind of working-class cyclist, the *vélocipédard* or *pédalard*, was giving respectable cycling a bad name: "The signs of the *vélocipédard* are: a striped jersey under his jacket; bared calves (outside the bicycle track); cap pushed back; feet in a false position on the pedals; a barking horn, a disorderly appearance, an always dry tongue and a definite fondness for wine merchants."[28]

Both the conduct and the clothing of the *vélocipédard* were considered inappropriate by the bourgeois standards of the day: the partial (and therefore excessive) nudity, the vulgar and arrogant nonchalance of the pose, the noise, the fondness for alcohol, and the overall impression of disorder all transgressed bourgeois norms founded on modesty, self-control, and respectability. Moralizing middle-class commentators – even some favorable to the bicycle – linked such cyclists to the socially disruptive cocktail of idleness and alcohol: "Alcohol is a poison . . . but . . . there are few cyclists who seem convinced of that fact, at least if one judges by the number of those one sees at the doors of the innumerable cabarets which too often dot the roadsides of our beautiful France."[29] Furthermore, these "ugly" working-class cyclists undermined bourgeois behavioral discourse on bicycling, suggesting by their very existence that there was another way to enjoy this new form of locomotion and leisure. The *vélocipédard* embodied and reinforced the fears of many members of the French middle and upper classes (including employers) that universal male suffrage, urbanization, and industrialization were spawning an increasingly autonomous, self-confident, and assertive working class that chose to reject the natural authority and superiority of its social betters even as it adopted the activities those betters had until recently monopolized.

No figure represented the autonomous, upwardly mobile worker challenging the social status quo more than the champion cycle racer. Dubbed "giants of the road" by a burgeoning sports press seeking to increase sales by praising their exploits, star racers quickly replaced earlier but now problematic national heroes, such as generals, emperors, and kings, and emerged as the new popular heroes of the day. Drawing huge crowds in newly constructed velodromes and along road race itineraries, celebrated in posters, postcards, novels, and songs, top racers earned sums that exceeded many middle-class incomes: the former chimney sweep who won the first Tour de France in 1903 earned prize money (not including his lucrative sponsorship contracts) in three weeks of racing equivalent to about five years' salary for many a provincial schoolteacher. And while only the best racers made such fortunes, many working-class youth succeeded in translating modest racing careers into their own café or cycle shop. Nicknamed "workers of the pedal" (*ouvriers de la pédale*), cycle racers were the first unskilled laborers to turn their physical capital (strength and endurance) into socioeconomic success (fame and fortune), thereby challenging the bourgeois social hierarchy which was founded on intellectual and social capital (education and relations).

Not all middle-class observers took such a dim view of the social implications of the democratizing bicycle. Rejecting its portrayal as a symptom and agent of social chaos and racial degeneration,[30] they claimed that the new machine offered at least a partial solution to the ongoing challenge of improving the lot of French working-class families and thereby reducing class tensions. This inexpensive, rapid mode of locomotion would decrease expenditures in the family budget, reinforce family unity, and improve personal hygiene by encouraging showers after a ride. The bicycle would also allow working-class families to move from their squalid, inner-city lodgings to less polluted suburbs, far from cabarets and cafés where the male head of household too often forgot his familial obligations and succumbed to alcoholism, tuberculosis, gambling, tobacco, and loose women.[31] The new sport led to "very moral distractions,"[32] allowing French youth to sublimate their passions and avoid precocious sexual activity while enhancing their health in the pure air of the outdoors: "is it not better to *get intoxicated* by the bicycle, than by tobacco, wine and love?"[33] Cycling fostered courage, prompt judgment, sobriety, initiative, self-confidence, and persistence;[34] it was "the great school of our character . . . hygienic not only for our flesh, but also for our minds."[35] Such hyperbolic claims suggest that for bourgeois commentators the stakes were high indeed.

The Citizen-Cyclist: Cycling Clubs and Social Integration

The challenge for middle-class bicycle enthusiasts, social and economic elites, and government officials was to monitor male, lower-class cyclists and reorient their energies, too often expended in morally and physically harmful – and therefore socially dangerous – environments and activities. Their search for a socially safe framework for lower-class cycling led them to promote and seek to control local cycling clubs. Their hope that these clubs would play a stabilizing social role raises a number of questions. Who were the members of these clubs? How did these clubs operate? What activities did they provide? And were efforts to control the expanding leisure opportunities of lower-class males successful in this instance?

The first French cycling clubs were founded in the final years of the Second Empire, but their creation stalled until around 1880. During the next three decades, however, the increase was spectacular: in 1910, there were 800 cycling clubs with a total of some 150,000 members. Areas of high concentration of bicycles included the Parisian region, Normandy, the North and a string of departments surrounding the Massif Central from the lower Loire to the Rhône. Conversely, the bicycle remained comparatively rare in the less prosperous, more isolated or more mountainous regions, as the absence of cycling clubs in a large part of Brittany and in the Lozère, Aveyron, Creuse, Nièvre, Hautes-Alpes, and Corsican departments illustrates. French cycling in the fin-de-siècle was essentially an urban phenomenon, with the exception of the western part of central France, where the establishment of a cycle industry countered the general pattern.[36]

Although the representation of specific trades and careers depended on local employment patterns, the members of these cycling clubs were largely drawn from the petty bourgeoisie and skilled artisans, such as locksmiths, mechanics, painters, masons, clock and watchmakers, jewelers, goldsmiths, glassworkers, mirror makers, tinsmiths, blacksmiths, gunsmiths, printers, engravers, decorators, cabinetmakers, lingerie makers, truss makers, photographers, and tailors. In addition, many members came from the food trades (grocers, butchers, bakers, wine merchants and millers), or from among hotel-, café- and restaurant-owners, tobacconists and retailers, particularly – and this comes as no surprise – bicycle and hardware shopowners. Employees such as shop assistants, municipal employees, bailiffs, clerks, tax collectors, insurance agents and office supervisors were also members as were pharmacists, barbers, schoolteachers, students and even soldiers from nearby garrisons.[37]

Frequently local notables, such as the mayor, a prominent industrialist, businessman or government official, assumed the highest positions in a cycling club. The honorary president of the Cyclistes Lunévillois was the town's mayor, its treasurer a local businessman. In Brittany, the president of the Vélo Cycle Rennais was a conductor of the Bridges and Roads department as well as president of the Rennes Choral. His vice-presidents were a businessman, an industrialist, and a traveling salesman, while his treasurer was not only an accountant, but also the son of a municipal councilor.[38] No doubt this tendency was in part due to the "natural" authority that came with these relatively exalted social, political and professional positions. But if clerks, students, artisans, and shopkeepers sought these people out to lead their clubs it was also because they represented a degree of respectability and political conformity that ensured the authorization from the departmental prefect required to found a club. In addition, clubs with such influential leaders could expect to benefit from municipal support (financial subsidies, authorizations, and assistance for club events) as well as from the generosity of local notables. In August 1910, for example, Baron Charles d'Huart offered the Union Cycliste de Longwy-Bas an excursion to the ruins of Orval, including a lunch for all participants for which he paid.[39] The previous year in the nearby town of Briey, the great industrialist François de Wendel had donated 100 francs to the Véloce-Club Briotin of which he was the *président d'honneur*.[40]

What is striking about the socio-professional identities of club members is the extent to which the bourgeoisie, petty-bourgeoisie, and artisans mingled within them, reproducing on a microcosmic scale the composition and hierarchy of local society. There were, however, some exceptions to this rule. Sometimes members of a given profession, generally located in a fairly large town or city, would form their own club, as, for example, the barbers of L'Union Vélocipédique des Coiffeurs de Rennes.[41] On the other hand, certain groups were conspicuous by their absence from cycling clubs, particularly agricultural workers who had little time or money to devote to organized leisure activities and who, because of their relative isolation, were exposed to the bicycle later than their urban compatriots. The case of industrial workers is more diverse: while they too had relatively little money and free time for such activities, some did participate in cycling clubs. In some cases, like the afore-mentioned barbers, industrial workers founded cycling clubs drawn exclusively from their own ranks: all seven members of the organizing committee of La Tucquegnieutoise were miners, strongly suggesting that the entire membership was drawn from that profession.[42] As for women, they were simply excluded from active membership but were usually allowed to participate in the club's annual banquet and family outings. Otherwise they were relegated to second-ary roles as spectators or club patrons.[43] Sport – particularly one as demanding as cycling – was seen as a largely masculine endeavor in Belle Epoque France.

The remarkable development of cycling clubs throughout France in the three decades preceding World War I cannot simply be explained by the increased access to leisure time among the lower classes of society and the steadily decreasing price of the bicycle. It was also the result of a concerted effort on the part of Republican politicians actively to promote associationism. Laws passed in 1884 (on profes-sional associations) and in 1901 (on other associations) established the official status of such clubs. As a result, the sports associative movement, building on the happy coincidence of Republican political ideology and social policy with the new aspirations of the lower classes, experienced its golden age between the end of the nineteenth century and World War I.[44]

Republicans believed associations (including sports clubs) would form resp-onsible citizens by providing members with an activity and an environment in which they would experience the workings of democracy actively, directly and voluntarily. The sports club functioned as a Republican microsociety complete with executive, legislative, and judiciary branches. Elections for club positions and deliberations about club-related issues were held, attendance at meetings was required as was the payment of membership dues, and all political and religious discussion was forbidden. The club was conceived as a school where tolerance, discipline, obedience, and civic values would be inculcated to all members, and where inappropriate behavior would be penalized. It provided a model of voluntary and orderly collective life, which in turn would contribute to the construction of a social and national consensus in a country coming off military defeat and civil war. Meanwhile, employers saw sport as a tool for strengthening workers' bodies, teaching them discipline, defusing their frustrations and potential rebelliousness, and inculcating them with one of the principal tenets of liberalism, that of individual merit as the foundation of the social order.[45]

Municipal governments, too, were interested in promoting the new sport among local workers. When the Rally-Cycle Rennais, a cycling club comprised of workers and shop employees, applied for a municipal subsidy in 1905, the Mayor of Rennes, perhaps haunted by the fear of unruly *vélocipédards*, supported its request: "This club brings together the young cycling workers of Rennes in such a way as to distance them from the boredom and idleness that lead young men to the cabaret." The Municipal Council agreed, wishing to "bear witness of our sympathy toward an excellent working-class sports club which deserves to be encouraged" and "whose goal is highly moral."[46] A decade earlier, there had been disagreement within the Rennes Municipal Council over the attribution of city subsidies to a bourgeois cycling club. One councilor had argued against granting the latter a subsidy as its members were "young men all of a certain social status which permits them to face up to all the expenses of the club to which they belong."[47] Although the bourgeois club ultimately received its subsidy, such debates suggest that cycling clubs were often financially supported by local authorities to the extent they were believed to contribute to the moral edification of working-class youth and thus to social stability.

The organizing committee of La Pédale Lorraine in Neuves-Maison, founded in 1902, reflected this attempt at social control from above: the president and vice-president were landowners (*propriétaires*); the secretary/treasurer, the road captain, and one of the club advisors were accountants at the local ironworks; the assistant secretary/road lieutenant was a saddler; and the other club advisor was a factory worker.[48] The committee thus reflected the social and professional hierarchy of the community itself: factory workers who answered to middle management at work would find that relationship of subordination reproduced in their chosen leisure activity, notwithstanding the presence of one of their peers on the club's committee.

As important as such considerations were to economic elites and the Republican political class, the clubs themselves, although often chaperoned by local notables, were generally founded by members of the petty bourgeoisie and working class intent on providing activities and an opportunity for male sociability in their town, neighborhood or profession. Most cycling clubs held their meetings in local cafés and their goals, as defined in their official statutes, invariably included the desire to "establish and maintain friendly relations among the cyclists of the region" and "develop appreciation for and the use of the bicycle by organizing rides, trips, [and] races."[49] The latter included *brevet militaire* races, which were often accompanied by or included marksmanship competitions, foot races, and recon-naissance events. In return for their patriotic commitment to military preparation, cycling clubs could count on government subsidies.

Clubs also wished to participate in local *fêtes de bienfaisance* (charitable festivals).[50] The efforts of La Pédale Lorraine, for example, were well received, especially given the presumed time constraints of its working-class members: "We were surprised to note such a successful organizing effort by young men whose only free moments fall between their work schedules" was *L'Est Républicain*'s favorable assessment of the club's *fête de bienfaisance*, which included a parade, a concert, foot races, bicycling acrobatics, a hot air balloon ride, a dance and liquid refreshments, and which culminated in a fireworks' display.[51] The role of the Union Cycliste de Longwy-Bas in providing a wholesome activity for its members and sports spectacles for the local population was appreciated by the municipal government which granted the club a subsidy.[52] Such involvement by cycling clubs was the rule: cyclists all over France clearly wished their clubs to be actively integrated into their community's social and festive life.

An important function of cycling clubs during this period was the organization of excursions. On Sunday, May 25, 1902, the Véloce-Club de Tours organized a memorable ride from Tours to the town of Ouchamps through the valleys of the Loire, Bièvre, and Beuvron rivers, and numerous villages along the way.[53] The pretext for the excursion was to honor *père* Galloux, an 89-year-old inhabitant of Ouchamps, believed to be the oldest cyclist in France. In 1837 Galloux, at the time an apprentice artisan and a Compagnon du Devoir, accomplished his journeyman's Tour de France traveling from town to town on a "wooden horse" he had built: two wheels connected by a wooden seat plank, without pedals but with a steering mechanism upon which was mounted a carved horse's head.

Upon their arrival in Ouchamps, the club members were greeted by artillery salvos as well as by the mayors of Ouchamps and Les Montils, the assistant of the former, the entire Ouchamps municipal council, including one councilor who was also a member of the Union Vélocipédique de France (the French cycling federation), and the local schoolteacher. The town had been decorated in the club's honor with a triumphal arch, flags, garlands, Venetian lanterns and flowers, as if for a national holiday. Once the cyclotourists had been presented with flowers to welcome their "handsome and patriotic club," a procession was formed with *père* Galloux at its head, perched upon a primitive bicycle he had built in 1838. As the band played, the procession made its way to the town hall where the municipal government had organized a reception. There, both the mayor and the president of the Véloce-Club de Tours made speeches and Galloux was awarded a medal and a diploma by the club. The visit was crowned by a banquet for two hundred guests held in the town marketplace (an opportunity for all those in the food and drink business to turn a handsome profit).

In his speech the president of the Véloce-Club de Tours extolled the values promoted by the sport of cycling and personified by the old artisan Galloux: "We shall always be happy to have brought, with our respectful friendship, the homage that was due, first to the family man, to the worker and especially to the persevering worker, full of endurance and tenacity, whom we saw earlier astride his respectable wooden horse." The club president stressed qualities and values that buttressed the social order: endurance, tenacity, respectability, and family. *Père* Galloux, hard-working family man, was clearly a safe example for younger workers, a counter-model to the disorderly, disrespectful *vélocipédard*, to the dissipated, excessively paid working-class cycling champion, and to the militant working-class activist, all of whom seemed more or less consciously bent on destroying the political and social status quo. In his conclusion the president reminded his audience that, beyond their value as a leisure activity, beyond their educational and moralizing potential, cycling clubs like his had "their noble and useful side," a higher, patriotic end, "the preparation of soldiers for the defense of the fatherland!"

The outing had achieved much. It had offered club members an opportunity for exercise in the great outdoors among congenial companions, and had reinforced patriotic sentiment and appreciation for French history (including that of the bicycle). Perhaps most important, the day-trip had provided its participants with a sense of belonging to a number of communities: first, their own club; second, the larger cycling brotherhood which they celebrated in the person of Galloux and which was officially represented by the UVF delegate; third, a mythical national community of traditional, unthreatening, and idealized workers, whose tenacity, perseverance, hard work, and family values were also personified by the old artisan; fourth, the regional community of neighboring villages and towns that had cheered the cyclists on during their ride; and fifth, the nation itself, whose army would soon swell with young, healthy soldiers formed in France's cycling clubs. That such excursions might foster and reinforce a number of different but compatible collective identities was of consequence to French elites seeking to build social cohesion and national unity.

Conclusion

Such excursions, like the clubs that organized them, were a novel form of leisure and festivity made possible by the increasing accessibility of the bicycle to petty-bourgeois and working-class pocketbooks. Organized leisure was no longer the exclusive preserve of the French middle and upper classes: the visible, public assertion by lower-class male cyclists of their right to leisure was part of a larger transformation underway in fin-de-siècle France. This transformation, facilitated by the bicycle, created a social dynamic in which attempts at emancipation from below were met with strategies of control from above.

It is difficult to measure how successful local elites were in controlling lower-class men as they discovered cycling. In the case of those cycling clubs whose membership more or less reproduced the class hierarchy of local society, their objective may have met with some success. It is clear from their involvement in local festivities that many socially modest members of these clubs appreciated the opportunity to contribute to their communities, to exist as full-fledged citizens. No doubt they also enjoyed their contact with local notables, however hierarchical the context of such contact may have remained.

It is also important to note that if the previously cited figure of 150,000 for French cycling club membership in 1910 is even remotely accurate, it represents an insignificant percentage (about 5.5 percent) of the total number of bicycles in France that year, which was at least 2,724,467.[54] Thus, even if it is impossible to calculate precisely, the number of male working-class cyclists who were actually members of clubs and therefore came under supervision and scrutiny by state and local government officials is negligible when compared to the total number of working-class cyclists (and even less significant when compared to the total number of French workers) in the years preceding World War I. That the Third Republic and local elites nevertheless focused their attention on these clubs as potentially providing an integrating mechanism for members of the French lower classes illustrates how much of a priority resolving – or at the very least defusing – the social question remained during the Belle Epoque.

As much as some members may have enjoyed the opportunities club member-ship provided to participate in their community's social life and rub shoulders with local elites, it is plausible that many petty-bourgeois and working-class members of such clubs tolerated the ideological agenda of Republican officials and local notables in return for municipal subsidies from the former and gifts from the latter, which in turn provided them with leisure opportunities they might not otherwise have been able to afford.[55] Furthermore, the bourgeois obsession with the *vélocipédard* suggests that despite efforts by bourgeois moralists and Republican officials, lower-class men found ways to express and celebrate a public and autonomous social identity through the bicycle.

This obsession also reveals the extent to which the French middle classes felt vulnerable to encroachment – and thus debasement – from below. In the Third Republic, formal political equality among adult men was guaranteed by universal male suffrage and complemented by an implicit democratic commitment to merit (as opposed to birth) as the source of social distinction. The determination of bourgeois cycling enthusiasts to formulate and maintain a cycling etiquette in the face of the popularization of the bicycle was a cultural strategy aimed at preserving social distinctions no longer enforced by the privileges that had characterized, with the exception of the early months of the short-lived Second Republic, the political regimes and social order of nineteenth-century France prior to 1870.

Ultimately, whether successful or not, these turn-of-the century initiatives to protect the social order and political regime from the laboring masses and their bicycles enjoyed a relatively brief window of opportunity. The growing militancy of French workers, their ideological opposition to the bourgeois order many of them believed the Republic served, the ongoing shift from traditional manufacturing to large-scale factory production and the resulting social and geographic dislocation, all contributed to the explicit politicization of sport along class and ideological lines: 1905 saw the founding of both the SFIO (the unified French Socialist Party) and the first militantly working-class French sports clubs; in 1908, the French Socialist Sports Federation, the Fédération Sportive Athlétique Socialiste, was created, to be renamed the Fédération Sportive du Travail in 1914.[56] After the war and in the wake of the 1920 Tours Congress of the French Socialist Party, the French working-class sports movement would suffer from the same divided and divisive fate as its political parties: Socialist and Communist sports clubs and federations, tied to international organizations and claiming that they alone embodied the purity of working-class sport, competed against each other and against established secular and Catholic sports clubs for working-class members. This explicitly class-based, ideological polarization of the French sports scene would make the coexistence of several collective identities, such as those celebrated in the speeches at Ouchamps in 1902, problematic for working-class cyclists and create new challenges for French governments and elites in the interwar period.

Acknowledgments

I am grateful to Janet Horne, Shanny Peer, Charles Rearick, and Robert Hall for their comments on earlier versions of this chapter.

Notes

1. Dr Just Lucas-Championnière, *La Bicyclette* (Paris: Léon Chailly, 1894), p. 46.
2. Ibid., pp. 46–7.

3. See my article, "Un troisième sexe? Les bourgeoises et la bicyclette dans la France fin de siècle," *Le Mouvement Social* 192 (July–September 2000), pp. 9–39.

4. Garsonnin, *Conférence sur la vélocipédie faite à Tours le 31 mars 1888* (Rouen: Imprimerie Julien Lecerf, 1888), p. 12.

5. Preface by Maurice Martin in Louis Baudry de Saunier, *L'Art de bien monter la bicyclette*, 3rd edn (Paris, 1894), pp. 10–11.

6. *Rennes-Vélo* (November 1, 1897).

7. A. Berruyer, *Manuel du véloceman ou notice, système, nomenclature, pratique, art et avenir des vélocipèdes* (Grenoble: Typographie de F. Allier Père et Fils, 1869), p. 21.

8. For the technological history of the bicycle see Jacques Seray, *Deux roues: La véritable histoire du vélo* (Rodez: Editions du Rouergue, 1988) and Jean Durry, *Le Vélo* (Paris: Editions Denoel, 1976).

9. Baudry de Saunier, *L'art de bien monter la bicyclette*, pp. 45–6; Louis Baudry de Saunier, *Le Cyclisme théorique et pratique* (Paris: Librairie Illustrée, 1892), pp. 161–219.

10. Preface by Martin in Baudry de Saunier, *L'Art de bien monter la bicyclette*, pp. 10–11.

11. Garsonnin, *Conférence sur la vélocipédie*, p. 24.

12. Baudry de Saunier, *L'Art de bien monter la bicylette*, pp. 26, 149, 150.

13. Ibid., p. 18.

14. M.D. Bellencontre, *Hygiène du vélocipède* (Paris: L. Richard, Libraire-Editeur, 1869), p. 8.

15. Médecin-Major de 1ère classe Salle, *La Reine de la route: Eléments de physiologie et notions d'hygiène pratique à l'usage des officiers-cyclistes* (Paris: Henri Charles-Lavauzelle, Editeur militaire, 1899), p. 51. To this day, the word for saddle, "*la selle,*" is used in French for "bicycle seat."

16. Berruyer, *Manuel du véloceman*, pp. 64–5.

17. Baudry de Saunier, *L'Art de bien monter la bicyclette*, p. 79.

18. Ibid., pp. 80–1; Dr Philippe Tissié, *L'Education physique* (Paris: Librairie Larousse, 1901), p. 56.

19. Tissié, *L'Education physique*, p. 55.

20. Salle, *La reine de la route*, pp. 51–2.

21. Ibid., p. 50.

22. For a more detailed discussion of medical debates about the bicycle in fin-de-siècle France see my article, "Regeneration, *Dégénérescence*, and Medical Debates about the Bicycle in Fin-de-Siècle France," in Thierry Terret (ed.), *Sport and Health in History* (Sankt Augustin: Academia, 1999), pp. 339–45.

23. See Jack D. Ellis, *The Physician-Legislators of France: Medicine and Politics in the Early Third Republic* (Cambridge: Cambridge University Press, 1990).

24. For the development of bourgeois cyclo-tourism in France, see Catherine Bertho-Lavenir, *La Roue et le stylo: Comment nous sommes devenus touristes* (Paris: Editions Odile Jacob, 1999), chs 4–6.

25. Berruyer, *Manuel du véloceman*, p. 54.

26. Lucas-Championnière, *La Bicyclette*, p. 40.

27. Eugen Weber, "Gymnastics and Sports in Fin-de-siècle France: Opium of the Classes?" *American Historical Review* 76, 1 (1971), pp. 80–2; *L'Echo de Longwy* (January 17, 1909); *Le Longovicien* (January 21, 1909).

28. Louis Baudry de Saunier, *Recettes utiles et procédés vélocipédiques* (Paris, 1893), p. 25.

29. Salle, *La Reine de la route*, p. 16. For similar criticisms, see *Le Parisien de Paris* (November 28, 1897), cited in Seray, *Deux roues*, p. 163, and Garsonnin, *Conférence sur la vélocipédie*, p. 16.

30. For French fears of degeneration at this time see Daniel Pick, *Faces of Degeneration: A European Disorder, c. 1848–c.1918* (Cambridge: Cambridge University Press, 1989), chs 2–4; Robert A. Nye, *Crime, Madness and Politics in Modern France: The Medical Concept of National Decline* (Princeton, NJ: Princeton University Press, 1984).

31. Bellencontre, *Hygiène du vélocipède*, pp. 35–8; Garsonnin, *Conférence sur la vélocipédie*, p. 41; Baudry de Saunier, *Recettes utiles et procédés vélocipédiques*, p. 97; Dr J. Basset, *De l'influence de la bicyclette sur la diminution de la tuberculose à Toulouse* (Toulouse, 1905), pp. 7–8.

32. Garsonnin, *Conférence sur la vélocipédie*, p. 8.

33. Bellencontre, *Hygiène du vélocipède*, pp. 36–7. The emphasis is his.

34. Lucas-Championnière, *La Bicyclette*, pp. 41–2; Dr Raymond Martin, "Les avantages du sport vélocipédique," in *L'Echo Sportif* (Nancy), (January 7, 1905), p. 4; Baudry de Saunier, *Recettes utiles et procédés vélocipédiques*, p. 16.

35. Baudry de Saunier, *L'Art de bien monter la bicyclette*, p. 150.

36. Ronald Hubscher (ed.), *L'Histoire en mouvements: Le sport dans la société française (XIXe–XXe siècle)* (Paris: Armand Colin, 1992), pp. 81, 141–2; Archives Municipales de Montbéliard-Service Educatif, *Sport et société dans la région de Montbéliard à la fin du 19e siècle* (Montbéliard: Archives Municipales de Montbéliard, 1980), p. 8.

37. Hubscher (ed.) *L'Histoire en mouvements*, pp. 77–8. For typical club memberships, see those of the Cyclistes Lunévillois (Lunéville), La Pédale de Baccarat (Baccarat) in the Departmental Archives of Meurthe-et-Moselle, series 4M85 ("Associations Vélocipédiques") and that of Le Touriste (Verdun) in the Departmental Archives of Meuse, series 251M1 ("Associations. Sociétés sportives. Autorisations. Dissolutions.").

38. Departmental Archives of Ille-et-Vilaine, series 4M221.

39. *L'Echo de Longwy* (August 7, 1910).

40. *Le Longovicien* (January 7, 1909).

41. Rennes Municipal Archives, series Rx103 ("Sociétés sportives. Cyclisme, motocyclisme, sports athlétiques").

42. Departmental Archives of Meurthe-et-Moselle, series 4M85 ("Associations Vélocipédiques").

43. Hubscher (ed.), *L'Histoire en mouvements*, pp. 101–2; C. Petiton, *Histoire du Véloce-Club Rouennais: Son origine, son but, ses présidents, ses courses, ses travaux* (Rouen: Imprimerie Administrative E. Cagniard, 1896), p. 29.

44. Hubscher (ed.), *L'Histoire en mouvements*, pp. 15, 93–4, 104. See Pierre Arnaud (ed.), *Les Athlètes de la République: Gymnastique, sport et idéologie républicaine, 1870–1914* (Toulouse: Bibliothèque Privat, 1981) and P. Arnaud and J. Camy (eds), *La Naissance du mouvement sportif associatif en France (1869–1889)* (Lyon: Presses Universitaires de Lyon, 1991).

45. Hubscher (ed.), *L'Histoire en mouvements*, pp. 15–16, 94–6, 123–6.

46. Rennes Municipal Council, Minutes (August 25, 1905), pp. 374–5.

47. Rennes Municipal Archives, Series Rx103, Extract from the Register of the Deliberations of the Rennes Municipal Council – Meeting of April 12, 1895.

48. Departmental Archives of Meurthe-et-Moselle, series 4M85 ("Associations Vélocipédiques").

49. Statutes of the Cyclistes Lunévillois and the Pédale de Baccarat, Departmental Archives of Meurthe-et-Moselle, series 4M85 ("Associations Vélocipédiques").

50. Departmental Archives of Meuse, series 251M1 ("Associations. Sociétés sportives. Autorisations. Dissolutions.").

51. *L'Est Républicain* (Nancy) (August 30, 1905).

52. *L'Echo de Longwy* (December 18, 1910).

53. The following summary is derived from Paul Sainmont, *Le Véloce-Club de Tours et le doyen des cyclistes de France* (Tours: Librairie Péricat, 1902).

54. Bruno Dumons, Gilles Pollet, and Muriel Berjat, *Naissance du sport moderne* (Lyon: La Manufacture, 1987), p. 31. The bicycle tax which was imposed during this period provides us with precise figures, but only for those machines that were taxed. They constitute therefore an absolute minimum given that there were undoubtedly bicycle owners who chose not to declare their machines throughout the period this tax was in effect.

55. Richard Holt makes a similar argument about the motivations of lower-class members of French gymnastics clubs at this time in Richard Holt, *Sport and Society in Modern France* (Hamden, CT: Archon, 1981), ch. 3.

56. See Pierre Arnaud (ed.), *Les Origines du sport ouvrier en Europe* (Paris: L'Harmattan, 1994), especially pp. 29–85, 111–27, 141–65.

8

'Every German visitor has a *völkisch* obligation he must fulfill': Nationalist Tourism in the Austrian Empire, 1880–1918

Pieter Judson

Recently, a German Provincial Association to Promote Tourism in Southern Austria was founded in Laibach [Slovene: Ljubljana] for the purpose of encouraging German Tourism. The Association hopes to convince at least some of the current wave of German tourists to visit the nature-rich beauties of Carniola. Naturally, the organization will take care that the economic advantages of this tourism only benefit the German or German friendly populace in Carniola. (Südmark, 1912)[1]

"The Bohemian Woods are glorious, the inhabitants robust and good-natured. Have you ever been there?" "No, I've heard about it, read about it, even admired panoramic pictures of places there." "Well, save the words of praise, and go visit this splendid land; if you can offer your national brethren any moral and material support in their struggle for national survival, you will have achieved a deed worthy of the highest thanks." (German School Association, 1904)[2]

When middle- and upper-class Austrians left the city for the clean air of the countryside, to wander alpine trails, swim in the Adriatic, or tour historic sites at the turn of the nineteenth century, did their vacation plans reflect a nationalist commitment? As the above quotations indicate, several nationalist organizations certainly hoped so. When traveling in an ethnically mixed region of the monarchy, the German nationalist Südmark urged that "No German on vacation should patronize an anti-German tavern!"[3] Nationalist organizations exhorted tourists to do their part to support their "nation" within Austria by spending money according to the nationality of the hotelier, restaurant owner, or innkeeper, and wherever possible, by convincing other tourists to do the same.

This chapter investigates how Austro-German nationalist associations around 1900 used tourism to constitute and promote their particular visions of national

147

identity in the Austrian empire.[4] What exactly did such groups hope to gain from their rhetorical invocations of tourism or from material investment in this developing new industry? How did ideas about tourism and its uses engage with the rest of the German nationalist agenda in Cisleithania? Finally, this chapter tries to consider the kinds of impact this nationalist preoccupation may actually have had both on the habits of tourists and on the local tourist industry. The nationalist associations examined here functioned at several levels of Austrian society, from the interregional to the provincial to the local village level. Did the decision by nationalist leaders in urban centers like Vienna, Prague, or Graz to promote tourism in the countryside actually reflect the desires or concerns of local village activists? Or did the promotion of tourism reflect an attempt by the nationalist "center" to nationalize an a-nationalist "periphery"?

An examination of the nationalist promotion of tourism may also provide some interesting new perspectives on more traditional questions in the historiography of the Habsburg Monarchy. Chief among them is the question of nationalism's transformative effect on Austrian political culture at the turn of the century. For decades historians of Austria have blamed the nationality conflict within the monarchy for its supposedly crippling effects on local, regional, and national political culture. Competing demands, particularly among Czech and German nationalists in Bohemia, polarized the political environment in Austria and prevented parliamentary institutions like the Bohemian Diet or the Austrian Reichsrat from functioning. Nationalists, it is claimed, held important social and economic legislation hostage to their radical sectarian demands, making it all but impossible for the monarchy's democratic institutions to function. The paralysis of political institutions at all levels of society produced a political culture of bureaucratic absolutism around 1900 that governed the monarchy from above in its final decades.

One aim of this chapter on tourism is to suggest a different understanding of nationalism's diverse effects on regional and local Austrian society.[5] Particularly in a local context nationalism could influence politics much differently than it did in the Reichsrat or in the provincial diets. The promotion of tourism – unlike other issues of interest to nationalists like education or administrative reform – required an activism that paid far greater attention to the most local of social concerns. Fostering a nationalist tourist industry required far too much initiative or cooperation from locals to allow the simple imposition of an urban and largely abstract nationalist vision on a clueless rural populace. Activists had to recast their nationalist agendas in terms meaningful to village inhabitants, by citing, for example, the locally specific economic and social benefits nationalist tourism might bring them. In doing so, nationalists may, however inadvertently, have pushed local political cultures to become more democratic and integrative in nature. In some village communities, harsh nationalist rhetoric became a tool to build the social consensus necessary for achieving local economic development, a greater degree of popular political participation, and a greater degree of social integration of the rural populace into interregional networks.

In the 1880s both tourism and organized German nationalism came of age in the Habsburg Monarchy, and by the 1890s, some nationalist organizations had begun to reconceive newly popular forms of tourism like mountain climbing or the *Sommerfrische* (summer vacation), in a fundamentally political light. Activists now urged their followers to remember the nation not simply when voting, but also when it came to regulating personal consumption and private leisure time. Always on the lookout for innovative strategies to use against their opponents, nationalist organizations quickly seized upon tourism as a potential means to reinforce the nationalist commitment of the individual consumer.[6]

The notion that tourism could somehow serve national interests assumed a far different form in Austria than elsewhere in Western and Central Europe. In France, Germany, or Italy at the turn of the century, tourism offered nationalists a symbolic means to define and unify the culturally diverse societies that made up their emerging nation-states. Tourist literature might emphasize the unique identity of a given region, but it also located that region in a larger narrative whose inexorable logic produced a united national culture.[7] This was in fact the approach promoted both by the anti-nationalist Habsburg State and by most of the growing number of tourist clubs in Austria.[8] This view avoided all nationalist rhetoric and promoted the monarchy as a culturally diverse yet institutionally united entity. By contrast, nationalist tourism in Austria reinforced particularistic loyalties, and undermined official attempts to create an inter-regional, unified public culture around dynastic patriotism. Nationalist tourism fed the already fierce political competition that pitted Czech, German, Italian, Polish, and Slovene nationalist politicians against each other for regional political hegemony and the distribution of financial resources.

It is important to situate this deployment of tourism to promote nationalist goals in a larger process that by the 1890s had radically changed the character of German nationalist ideologies in Austria. Earlier more elitist forms of German nationalism going back to 1848 had borrowed heavily from a liberal worldview, imagining that universal education and increased social mobility in the monarchy would, for example, inevitably transform Slavs into cultural Germans. By the 1880s, however, it had become clear that liberal educational reforms had only strengthened a Czech nationalist movement, and that Slav nationalists in general had little interest any more in "becoming" Germans. This reality was brought home to most German nationalists when the unthinkable occurred in 1879 and the German liberal government, in power since the dawn of the constitutional era, fell and was replaced by a coalition of anti-Liberal Slav and Conservative parties.

German nationalists in the 1880s quickly abandoned much of their socially elitist heritage and attempted to mobilize a broader constituency defined purely by national identity rather than education or property. They turned increasingly to a less flexible, populist definition of nation that was rooted in the specifics of language use and place. To strengthen their arguments they deployed newer kinds of statistical data (and even developments in cartography) both to justify their cultural claims and to lend them a greater aura of positivist objectivity. Increasingly, nationalists could be heard making new kinds of assertions about the character of populations and places, irrespective, of course, of how local Austrians actually viewed themselves.[9]

A crucial point to understanding the nature of nationalist politics in Austria is the predominant role activists gave to language use in defining identity. The liberal constitution of 1867 never recognized the existence of nationalities as such in Austria, but it did promise to establish linguistic equality in public life to the greatest extent possible. After 1867, nationalist politics in the monarchy focused almost exclusively on extending, or in the case of German nationalists, limiting the application of this constitutional promise as much as possible. Nationalist conflict revolved around language use in public life, particularly on the privileges the system accorded to the German language. Activists of all kinds therefore stressed the close correlation of language use to national identity.[10] Such concerns, however, appear to have been far more pressing to politicians in the Reichsrat or in the Diets than to the general population. Thus a key challenge to nationalist activists throughout Austria was to "awaken" the sense of national identity that lay dormant among all potential members of a nation, that is, those who spoke a given language, by making visible the boundaries that divided nations in daily life.

In what follows I outline three ways that German nationalists used tourism as a means to make their national identity meaningful to German-speaking Austrians. First, they made tourism a key part of their rhetorical attempts to anchor German identity more strongly in the consciousness of individual consumers. This effort produced little more than propaganda, but it added a popular theme to the rhetoric of economic self-help and nationalist boycotts.[11] Tourist literature may not have brought German-speakers in great numbers to visit the *Sprachgrenze* (language frontier), for example, but its aim was to make them more aware of the nationalist conflict by familiarizing them with the local sights and sounds of such regions. Second, nationalists used tourism to give the landscape a national character. This effort produced a great deal of aggressive propaganda and occasional violence. Third, and perhaps most important, some nationalists used tourism as a way to raise the economic viability of German-speaking populations in order to prevent further mixing among peoples. This effort produced less strident nationalist rhetoric and some real economic changes. After surveying these three categories I will examine the efforts of local activists in one rural region to see how tourism resonated in village society around 1900, and how tourists responded to nationalist appeals.

Long before Austro-German nationalists took up tourism, their publications had featured informative articles about particular places that, while part of the broader German cultural heritage, were unfamiliar to the average reader. Starting in the mid-1880s, almanacs, associational reports, journals, and nationalist newspapers encouraged their readers to learn more about German peoples and their physical environment without ever leaving home. These articles sought to define for their audience just what it meant to be German. But they also aimed to root the reader's abstract understanding of national identity more fully in a specific geography, suggesting that their common language use meant that their reader's shared an identity with other German speakers across the monarchy.[12]

Organizations like the *Deutscher Schulverein* or the *Südmark* increasingly sought to raise nationalist awareness by convincing the individual to apply nationalist principles to questions of personal consumption. Nationalists tried to break down the barriers separating public activism from personal life by making national identity a critical consideration in how consumers spent both their income and their leisure time. Associations soon offered inexpensive household items for sale, items whose purchase both supported the nationalist cause and marked the consumer as a nationalist. The *Deutscher Schulverein*, the *Südmark*, the *Nordmark*, the *Deutscher Böhmerwaldbund* (to name but a few such associations) produced and sold mountains of kitchen matches, soap, shoe polish, pipes, postcards, stationery, and stamps to advertise their members' nationalist loyalties.

A few organizations proceeded beyond small-scale consumption to suggest that tourism in one of the so-called *Sprachgrenze* regions might help to raise an individual's nationalist consciousness. The consumer, who visited the sites where it was imagined that nations fought a daily battle over the boundaries that separated them, would return home with a personal understanding of the importance of nationalist identity. The newly enlightened nationalist would then be more careful about other forms of daily consumption, such as where one shopped or whom one employed.

This issue was not a simple one. Nationalist literature frequently depicted Austrian Germans as people who sought only enjoyment in life, and whose easy-going ways had enabled the Slavs and Italians to make so many territorial, cultural, and legal gains at their expense. German speakers who lived in areas where there was little or no Slav presence were described as lazy or unthinking, since they could easily ignore the problem of nationalist conflict when it was not part of their daily existence.[13] As a form of leisure and enjoyment, tourism too might also be suspected of encouraging the worst traits among the Germans. Thus nationalists who promoted tourism linked it consciously to concepts of duty, labor, and personal virtue. A 1903 manifesto published by the German Tourist Association of Brünn (Czech: Brno), for example, stressed tourism's potentially moral and hygienic functions.[14] And yet, tourism was also meant to be enjoyable. So even as they couched their appeals in moralizing terms, nationalists maintained that work for the nation could also be personally fulfilling. "The summer resorts and spa towns, with their well-to-do visitors, offer a promising sphere of action for every kind of *völkisch* activity which for the truly German-minded vacationer involves no hard work but pleasure and enjoyment."[15]

Nationalists published guides to the *Sprachgrenze* for tourists, directing them to inns, hotels, and restaurants owned by reliable German or German-friendly natives. One guide to the South Tyrol explained that: "There are still great numbers of German tourists who have no idea, that every German visitor to this nationally imperiled region has a *völkisch* obligation he must fulfill."[16] The guides often warned tourists against the efforts of the enemy to mislead them. In one case it was reported of the Gasthaus Valentini in the South Tyrol that its owner, "Felix Valentini, is an agent of Italian nationalism; in order to fool German travelers he has attached an enormous metal Edelweiss to the wall of his inn." Appearances inside the hotel could be deceiving as well. According to Wilhelm Rohmeder, several restaurants run by closet Italian nationalists offered German-language newspapers and German-language menus in order to fool an unsuspecting German clientele into spending its money in enemy establishments.[17] Other such guides alerted travelers to unscrupulous Czech doctors in the Bohemian spa towns, or warned mountain climbers against patronizing Slovene-run Alpine huts in the Karawanken Mountains.[18]

Several nationalist organizations helped their members to make better consumer choices by listing the names of inexpensive German-owned inns or summer vacation rentals in their publications. The *Südmark* even asked local members to keep watch over these advertised establishments, to make certain they indeed remained in German-friendly hands.[19] Soon smaller local groups with fewer resources jumped on the bandwagon. Seeing economic opportunity in this development, they parroted the *Deutscher Schulverein* or *Südmark*, advertising their German identity as a way to lure tourists in search of inexpensive *Sommerfrische* rentals to their villages. Local German tourist clubs, beautifying associations, and hiking clubs worked both to improve local conditions for tourists and simultaneously to promote their regions. They published modest guides, stressing both the Germanness and natural beauty of their locales.[20]

Tourist literature became an important instrument as nationalists increasingly sought to give real places a national identity, using a mix of ethnographic and historical arguments. Tourism added the element of geography to a nationalist rhetorical arsenal that had previously relied on the issue of language usage alone to argue its positions. Earlier nationalist debates had often revolved around relatively abstract questions regarding the rules of language use in the civil service or in educational institutions. Now, however, popular guidebooks redescribed traditionally multiethnic regions in Bohemia as originally and therefore authentically German or Czech, providing a focus on the specifics of place.

Guidebooks, for example, redescribed traditionally multicultural regions as authentically German. They claimed a homogeneous German Bohemian Woods, South Tyrol, or South Styria, using an anti-historical argument that nevertheless looked to history for its justification. This argument located a region's authentic identity in the distant past, and then rendered all historical change since this original moment invalid. The imagined national past justified attempts to restore an original nationalist identity to a place in the present where Slav immigration or even Slav tourism posed a threat. Of course Czech, Slovene, and Italian nationalists deployed similar arguments to make the same kinds of claims for the same regions.

It is worth taking a moment to consider the ramifications of this curious development as it applied specifically to Bohemia. Was that "German Bohemia," so enthusiastically referred to by nationalists, an idea, or was it in fact a real place? German nationalists had promoted the rhetorical concept of German Bohemia as an economic and cultural entity ever since 1890, when negotiations for a political compromise between Czech and German nationalist leaders had failed. At that time German nationalists gave up hope that they would ever regain complete political control of Bohemia and they began to demand an administrative division of the province based on ethnic lines.[21] However, it was not until 1906, with the publication of the guidebook *Durch Deutschböhmen*, that this discursive phenomenon became embodied territorially.

Like many other publications of the period, this guidebook defined the place German Bohemia through its particular inclusions and exclusions. But *Durch Deutschböhmen* went well beyond other attempts to imagine German Bohemia in the way it reorganized and presented practical information for the traveler. Railway lines, bus lines, road systems, waterways, steamer trips were all reconceived in order to stress the coherence of travel within this area, and to avoid any contact with the "other" Bohemia. The traveler did not necessarily gain information about the fastest way to travel from one point to another, but rather, how to make the trip without leaving the confines of German Bohemia. This radical reinvention of the landscape had practical ramifications, as when activists used it to demand better railroad connections within German Bohemia from the state.[22]

Nationalists used tourism not simply to raise consumer consciousness, but also as a means to stake specific territorial claims. The physical presence of German tourists could itself be seen as a real conquest of the landscape for the nation. The tourists' presence transformed nationalist rhetoric about space into real action, and tourists often quite literally became terrorists. When a club planned a trip to a nationally disputed territory or when it set up a system of marked paths, its members physically asserted their ownership to that terrain. And whether or not individual Austrian tourists identified themselves as nationalists, activists nevertheless framed their actions in a highly partisan light. Nationalists, who already interpreted the Monarchy's non-nationalist censuses as a statistical picture of nationalist competition, now began to estimate the numbers of each nationality who visited their region as tourists.[23] Josef Taschek, chairman of the *Böhmer-waldbund*, repeatedly warned of a Czech invasion of German territory using such statistics. "The Czechs frequently organize trips to the Bohemian Woods and strive to promote Czechification of individual places through mass tourism. The only way to respond to this policy is through a mass immigration of as many German summer vacationers as possible."[24] While some retailers might have been happy to gain the income generated by tourists of any nationality, Taschek and other German nationalists could see the presence of the enemy only as a threat to national survival.

Over time activists constructed other kinds of alarming statistics, such as the numbers of local hotels and restaurants bought or sold by each nationality. Alarmist headlines like "The Czech Fiasco in the Riesengebirge Mountains" regularly warned against Czechs who were on the lookout to buy tourist properties in supposedly German resort areas. "As in other regions, the Czechs want to set down roots here in the German mountains and pursue a Czech linguistic and economic policy there. The recent leasing of the Hotel Austria in Spindelmühle to a Czech will prove useful to this goal."[25]

These warnings, along with the statistics that informed them, suggest just how strongly nationalists worked to reconfigure local reality in their own terms, increasingly describing multilingual regions as historically German, in order to justify their depiction of recent Czech, Slovene or Italian immigration as an illegitimate invasion.

In 1907, for example, the *Südmark* advertised a tour of the German–Slovene language border in South Styria and Carinthia. The ten-day trip was meant to give those nationalists who were interested in the subject a chance to meet people and experience first hand the hard life on the language frontier. In addition, the planners emphasized the feelings of solidarity the visit would awaken in the brave inhabitants of the border. The trip aimed not merely to teach visitors about the *Sprachgrenze*, but to act as a gesture of defiant ownership against the Slovene-speaking population. It presumed that the *Sprachgrenze* must somehow be won back from the invading Slovenes.[26]

Such trips often ended in violence as activists clashed over symbolic ownership of the land. When German gymnasts from Bergreichenstein (Czech: Kašperske Hory) made a typical Easter excursion on foot to nearby Eleonorenhain (Czech: Lenora) in 1908, they had to pass through the majority Czech village of Stachau (Czech: Stachy). Here, according to a local paper, Czech "fanatics" attacked the gymnasts. Whether the gymnasts' actual behavior provoked the confrontation is irrelevant, since the Czechs clearly understood this trip as a territorial violation.[27] When the Slovene School Association decided to hold a celebration in the town of Pettau (Slovene: Ptuij) in the same year, German nationalists mobilized residents and activists from neighboring towns to demonstrate at the train station and assert Pettau's authentic German identity against the Slovene intruders.[28]

Czech and German-speaking student groups frequently ventured into hostile rural territory for outings. They asserted their ownership of the territory by wearing nationalist colors and singing nationalist songs around bonfires. Frequently they incited physical attacks from their nationalist opponents, and what started with shouted insults often escalated into stone throwing or fist fights.[29] Perhaps the most notorious of these episodes involved a provocative trip to the Trentino region by German nationalist members of the Turnverein in the summer of 1907. Led by artist and Professor Edgar Meyer, a founder of the *Tiroler Volksbund*, the group of thirty-four men and seven women planned a walking tour of this predominantly Italian-speaking region in the South Tyrol. Italian nationalist activists resolved to prevent the tour from taking place. Hostile demonstrations in several villages greeted the travelers. When they arrived in the village of Calliano to board a train for the trip back home an angry mob physically attacked them. The five policemen present lost control of the situation and the ensuing bloody battle left several people badly wounded.[30]

Some German nationalist dreamers saw tourism in the Austrian Riviera as a means to create a German outlet to the Mediterranean by a program of cultural Germanization. This represented a far more grandiose form of the same kind of nationalist thinking about territory. Cultural Germanization, usually through language education, was hardly a realistic strategy in most areas of ethnic conflict, since by this time non-German speakers had organized themselves to oppose anything that faintly resembled such a policy. But many nationalists in the south hoped to create a "German outlet to the Mediterranean" in the newly developing tourist centers on the Adriatic – the so-called Austrian Riviera. Here, activists viewed tourism as a key factor, along with growing commerce and the *Südbahn* connection, to bringing German culture to a backward Slavic or Italian enclave. German national ownership of hotels, local shops, the founding of German schools, German leadership in cultural life all could bring modern urban culture to this developing region, helping to integrate it more fully into the supposedly German-dominated hinterlands of the monarchy.

The fact that national conflict in this region tended to pit an Italian elite against a Slovene or Croat majority allowed the Germans to imagine a role for themselves above local politics that might gain greater influence for their nation. Trieste, according to many of them, was in fact a German city, with a rich tradition of German culture and social life. The authors of *Die deutsche Mark am Südmeer* believed it was Austria's destiny to transform Trieste from a sleepy Italian port into a booming German commercial metropolis.[31] In 1908 one newspaper reported enthusiastically about a German cultural revival in Görz (Italian: Gorizia, Slovene: Gorica) created by increased tourism to the area:

Ever since the opening of the Karawanken railroad, that has brought Trieste closer to German territory, a new German spirit has begun to unfold in Görz. A new German school is developing admirably, and German nationalist associational life is picking up as well. They're now planning to build a gymnastics hall and a German Kindergarten, which will doubtless be a great support to the German schools here. May the Germans in this formerly German region of Friulia look forward to a successful future![32]

Contemporary observers liked to note that exactly this kind of transformation had occurred in Abbazia (Croatian: Opatija). Once an insignificant Croatian fishing village, Abbazia now flourished as the center of the Austrian Riviera, home to luxury hotels, German high culture, and most importantly, a rapid *Südbahn* connection to the cities of the North.[33] In 1911 a group of hoteliers, restaurant owners, and other entrepreneurs created the German League for Tourism in Southern Austria to promote German-friendly tourism to the region. The group worked to lobby the government for better transportation links that would bring Carniola, Istria, and Dalmatia closer to Vienna, and to raise the level of accommodations in the region.[34]

The easy equation of Germanization with civilization, along with the desire to populate endangered landscapes with German tourists if necessary, points to yet another type of problem embedded in the promotion of a nationalist tourism. What, after all, was to be the relationship between the urban tourist and the German peasant? Nationalist rhetoric, particularly in its most radical formulation, stressed the commonalties that united all members of the nation, across conceivable barriers of class or of educational difference. Yet the peasant on the *Sprachgrenze* who embodied the best Germanic virtues was as much the object of the nationalists' educational efforts as was his urban bourgeois counterpart. Peasants too needed to be taught their heroic identity. Those urban nationalist students who traveled to the countryside often focused their activities on bringing peasants into nationalist activities. Guides for students who hiked in such areas stressed the need for treating peasants with respect, thus betraying the assumption that in fact the opposite would more likely be the case.[35]

Tourism did indeed offer considerable potential for economic development as long as activists were willing to make a sustained investment. Unlike the approaches to tourism discussed above, which focused on intensive propaganda campaigns and leisure-time activism, this kind of vision for tourism demanded a strong commitment to research, publicity, and the development of local infrastructure. Only one major nationalist organization, the *Deutscher Böhmerwaldbund*, actually undertook such an ambitious effort. The others simply presumed that their rhetoric would somehow create a generally positive economic effect for local Germans.

Economic problems in the Bohemian Woods had generated a large-scale emigration to North America among German speakers there in the nineteenth century. Activists argued that tourism could help to revitalize the economy and sustain the local German-speaking population in the face of an increasing Czech migration to the region. When Josef Taschek and his colleagues founded the *Deutscher Böhmerwaldbund* in Budweis (Czech: Ceský Budĕovice) in 1884, they immediately made a priority of encouraging tourism to their region. At that time, with the exception of the Bohemian spa towns and some parts of the Tyrol, tourism in the monarchy had not yet been organized as an industry. Taschek firmly believed that the developing institution of the *Sommerfrische* offered a solution to the economic misery of the Germans in the Bohemian Woods. The leaders of the *Böhmerwaldbund* wagered that southern Bohemia's sumptuous landscapes, its meandering rivers, its small medieval towns, and its forested hills, high enough to offer dramatic views, but easily accessible to the average nature lover, not to mention its low cost of living, could attract summer vacationers from neighboring Bavaria or Austria. The problem was that the Bohemian Woods was virtually unknown to the outside world. The major commercial routes of the nineteenth century had bypassed the region; its glass factories, paper mills, and wood-processing plants had all languished due to their isolation from markets. Farmers and artisans in the region produced primarily for local markets, with few opportunities to make use of larger commercial networks. Seeking to make a virtue of this isolation, the *Böhmerwaldbund* published guidebooks and worked actively with local beautifying or tourist associations to generate grassroots excitement for tourism. It encouraged local groups to create well-marked systems of paths to lead tourists to unique natural attractions, and it encouraged village councils to undertake beautification, renovation and building projects, such as the creation of local swimming pools.

Ironically, the *Böhmerwaldbund* soon found it necessary to call on the anti-nationalist Austrian state for assistance. In order to compete with traditional tourist destinations, *Böhmerwaldler* needed public transportation links to make their region accessible to vacationers. They found themselves forced to lobby the state to build new railroad connections, roads, bus service, more telegraph and later telephone connections in the places they hoped to transform into centers of tourism. The need for state assistance in turn moderated the content and tone of the *Böhmerwaldbund*'s nationalist rhetoric. Unlike the more strident *Südmark*, for example, the *Böhmerwaldbund* promoted a positive vision of self-help within a loosely defined German national community. It did not define Germanness racially, and it only rarely demonized the Slav enemy.[36]

The need to lobby the state more effectively for improved transport and communications connections eventually led to the formation of a Provincial League for Tourism in German Bohemia. By 1910 almost every Austrian crown-land (including Galicia) had such an umbrella organization whose task it was to promote the interests of provincial tourist industries. In several crownlands (Styria,

Carinthia, the Tyrol) the dominant German nationalist position was politically so well normalized, that the League, in all essentials a German organization, never even had to name itself as such. To read the publications of the Styrian League, for example, one would never guess that more than one-third of the crownland's population was actually Slovene speaking. Yet so well organized were both Czech and German nationalists in Bohemia that this crownland sported two leagues. One, situated in Prague, represented so-called general Bohemian interests, and another located in Karlsbad (Czech: Karlový Vary) represented the interests of the region that styled itself German Bohemia.[37]

The *Böhmerwaldbund*'s success in lobbying the state for the modest Budweis–Salnau railway line in 1893 emboldened the organization to launch its most ambitious effort to bring tourists to the region. In that year it financed the production of a local Passion Play in Höritz (Czech: Hořice na Šumavě), a small rural village located just to the south of Krummau (Czech: Český Krumlov) on the new rail line. The Passion Play had been a tradition in Höritz since the time of the Napoleonic Wars. It had been presented at irregular intervals over the years by villagers dressed in their Sunday best, usually at a local inn and to a local rural audience. In 1890, a local Gymnasium teacher in Krummau, Peter Ammann, researching folk traditions, took note of the play and began investigating its origins. In conjunction with the *Böhmerwaldbund* he updated and published the play in 1892. In the same year the association built a modern festival theater on a hill overlooking Höritz.

The theater accommodated some 2,000 spectators under its roof and was the first fully electrified building in the region. The organizers imported two coal-burning locomotives to the nearby railroad station at an almost prohibitive cost, to generate enough power for each performance. Well-known theatrical artists designed sets and costumes, and in the 1890s the production was directed by the chief of Budweis's German theater. The *Böhmerwaldbund* made this financial investment in the expectation that Höritz would eventually rival Oberammergau for international attention and bring fame to the Bohemian Woods. Although the Passion play was controversial among anticlerical German nationalists, and the high cost of producing it meant that it rarely made a profit, it helped to draw far more tourists to the region. It was advertised across Europe and even attracted visitors (and in 1897 a motion picture crew) from the United States.[38]

So far I have focused on the ways that nationalist organizations used a form of leisure activity like tourism to transform a discursive national identity into a material reality for the average German speaker, and thereby lay claim to specific territory as well. I would like to conclude with a necessarily brief consideration of an altogether different question: how did this movement for a nationalist tourism influence social relations in the rural areas it targeted? Did it function as an imposition of an urbanized center on a rural periphery? Did it engage at all with the perceived needs of local activists? And did it actually create nationalist tourists?

The answers to these questions differed significantly depending on the region under discussion. In general, an effort like that of the *Böhmerwaldbund* to promote nationalist tourism for primarily economic purposes resulted in a high degree of engagement with the needs of local activists. The fact that the Bohemian Woods had no tourist industry to speak of made the efforts of the nationalists all that much more important. On the other hand, more ideologically radical propaganda, such as that directed by the nationalist boycott efforts at visitors to the South Tyrol (a region that boasted a well-developed tourism industry) could backfire. Local hoteliers of almost every political or nationalist persuasion viewed any effort to direct the flow of tourists to one set of establishments or another in the South Tyrol as dangerous meddling by outsiders. In 1907, for example, a local paper reported that in municipal elections in the region around Lake Garda, moderate Italian and German nationalists had banded together to oust radical nationalists from the town halls. Why? The paper reported that the tourist trade had clearly suffered (with hotel bankruptcies in both Arco and Trient) from the lamentable intrusion of nationalist activism into local society. Moderates on both sides wished to signal to tourists that the area was once again safe for vacationers.[39]

The success of activists in the Bohemian Woods in building a modest tourism industry did not necessarily imply that local activists who worked with the *Böhmerwaldbund* to promote tourism to their villages did so for transparently nationalist reasons. Rather, it seems that in many of those villages a nationalist agenda was often linked to a whole series of other local agendas that had little to do with nationalism as such. Nor did the promotion of a nationalist tourism mean that visitors to the region came away with a stronger sense of national identity, nor even that they made their decision to travel there on the basis of nationalist concern. The example of Höritz and its Passion Play is particularly instructive in this regard. The play certainly fulfilled the ambitions of local and regional nationalist activists by bringing more tourists to the region. And in their public statements, at least, both German and Czech nationalist leaders did treat the play's nationalist significance as self-evident. Yet whether tourists themselves actually returned home with a more distinct consciousness about the national struggle on the so-called *Sprachgrenze* is harder to evaluate.

The Passion Play may have brought more tourists to the Bohemian Woods, but nothing about it (including the international theatrical style in which it was performed) appears to have reinforced a German national identity among visitors or performers. Personal testimonies of visitors to Höritz instead emphasized the profoundly moving emotional quality of the experience rather than its particularly Germanic qualities (whatever those might have been). Visitors do not seem to have left believing they had witnessed something particularly German, but rather an example of folk art, impressive in its rural simplicity. Visitors rarely commented on the play as a national event until after the First World War when the area became part of the new Czechoslovak nation-state, and the play developed a new significance.

Did the institution of the Passion Play increase the nationalist consciousness of the Höritzers? Actually, the play seems rather to have strengthened the villagers' consciousness of themselves as Höritzers more than as anything else. Recollections and anecdotes confirm that their participation in the Passion Play was indeed of central importance to the villagers' lives. Already in the 1890s, for example, male Höritzers were known to wear extremely long hair and full beards in order to recall old testament scenes, especially in years when the play was not performed. The village did everything in its power to market itself as a kind of goal for cultural pilgrims, especially in those off years. Nor did the fact that the nationalist *Böhmerwaldbund* had contributed so much to Höritz's newly found fame create a stronger sense of nationalist identity there. Rather, as elsewhere in southern Bohemia, villagers seem to have considered the *Böhmerwaldbund* to be something of a local welfare organization, its German nationalist identity secondary to its important economic self-help functions.

The nationalist promotion of tourism also looks different when viewed from the perspective of the interaction between the urban groups promoting it and the village activists who took up the cause locally. In the first place, the tourism question seems to have caused several unanticipated problems for the urban nationalist organizations. In the second place, as we will see, the nationalist agenda when adopted at the local level served different functions than it did at the level of high politics.

Böhmerwaldbund leaders learned a surprising lesson early on: that villagers did not always appreciate the benefits tourism might bring them. Nationalist vacationers who visited their persecuted German brothers and sisters deep in the Bohemian Woods were often shocked by the low standard of accommodation the natives provided. Many complained about sanitary conditions both to the *Böhmerwaldbund* and to the Provincial League for Tourism in German Bohemia. In the winter, tourists complained that villagers reported temperatures and snow conditions so intermittently, as to make it impossible to plan winter sport vacations. And when surveyed about what their district could offer outside visitors, some local activists expressed a deep frustration with the unwillingness of their fellow villagers to comprehend the potential economic benefits tourism offered to them.[40]

The *Böhmerwaldbund* leadership walked a difficult line between defending the quality of village accommodations to the outside world, and urging local organizers to do a better job. In 1904, Taschek wrote optimistically of tourist accommodations in the twenty years since the founding of the *Böhmerwaldbund*: "Arrangements for lodging visitors to the Bohemian Woods have gradually improved; at least in the towns good accommodations can now be found. The inns have made real progress regarding overnight accommodations and food for tourists, although not as much as we would have liked to see in this period."[41] Nevertheless in another report a year later Taschek had to admit that "Most innkeepers are simply not prepared to make any kind of sacrifice in order to convince the public of the charms of a trip to the Bohemian Woods."[42]

The question of quality accommodations for visitors became more pressing once the Passion Play in Höritz received international attention. That attention was not always flattering. The 1910 Baedeker advised visitors to the Passion Play to avoid actually spending a night in Höritz if possible.[43] And in 1908, a feuilletonist for Vienna's *Neue Freie Presse*, Raoul Auernheimer, published a scathing account of his visit to Höritz. Although he praised the simple intensity of the play's performers, Auernheimer denounced the unacceptable level of accommodation and general boredom that he found characterized life in the surrounding region. Of the highly touted Krummau he wrote: "However, only in a small town like this does one learn the meaning of tedium, true tedium." Although this depiction of rural life drew angry protests from all kinds of *Böhmerwaldbund* supporters, including *Heimat* author Peter Rosegger, it nevertheless reflected an image that local promoters of tourism could not easily change.[44]

Those villagers who did embrace tourism as potentially beneficial to their community were themselves relatively recent arrivals to the rural world. The rapid growth, first of a uniform imperial school system, and later of transport, communications, commercial, and administrative networks, had brought a real invasion of teachers, civil servants, and generally lower-level white-collar employees to many formerly isolated rural regions. The presence of such people in small towns and villages often changed social relations substantially. These outsiders brought with them traditions of voluntary association as a way to gain economic, cultural, or political ends. Often themselves of rural background, they usually had acquired some schooling in a larger town or city, and had frequently already joined some professional or nationalist organizations when posted to rural districts. In general they tended to view the interests of the local village in a larger regional, provincial, or even nationalist context. In combination with local professionals and innkeepers, these invaders worked to expand local economic connections to regional and interregional commerce, often through the development of tourism. They also tended increasingly to provide leadership in local village branches of nationalist organizations.

Issues like the quality of accommodation became a field for such local activists, usually teachers, civil servants, innkeepers, small business people or railroad employees, to impose their specific nationalist vision on their fellow villagers. The invaders defined German nationalism by its very modernity. In Bergreichenstein, a town of 2,500 near the northern *Sprachgrenze* of the Bohemian Woods, those who promoted nationalist tourism consistently used nationalist arguments to justify a wide range of modernizing projects. Their rhetoric explicitly connected German identity to progress, and progress to tourism. Using reports in a local paper from the year 1908, we can trace the specific content of this nationalist message and the role tourism played in its construction. Local German activists expressed pride at local accomplishments and impatience with the lingering vestiges of backwardness. Progress and modernity were defined in both moral and nationalist terms; backwardness, however, derived either from ignorance or from local Czech politics.

In a 1908 New Year's editorial, activists listed a series of recent accomplishments of which Bergreichensteiner could be proud. The town had restored several historic houses, it had demolished unsightly deteriorating buildings, and it had built a system of streetlights. Of equal importance, however, to these physical improvements were the moral ones: revival of the town's Beautification Society, and the growing branches of its singing, gymnastics, charitable, and nationalist organizations. Yet another sign of accomplishment was the growth of two new schools. On the negative side the editorial deplored the fact that the unsympathetic Czech regional administration often stood in the way of progress (for example, road repair), wasted district funds on unnecessary bilingual signs, or fought against a railway connection for the town.[45]

During the year the paper repeatedly endorsed the continued efforts of the Beautification Society to make the town more attractive to tourists, particularly the projected renovation of some nearby castle ruins and a path leading to them. It related approvingly that the (German) mayor's office took the beautification of the town seriously, that the main square was kept clean, and that nearby trees and gardens were well taken care of.[46] In May, however, it prodded the town to advertise more. The paper claimed that "German summer vacationers pay far too little attention to our beautiful little corner [of the Bohemian Woods]," and added a nationalist slant, claiming that the Czechs did a much better job of bringing in tourists to the Bohemian Woods than did the Germans.[47] A month later, the paper raised the demand: "Give us a swimming pool!" In a fascinating rhetorical flourish, the paper connected the concepts of national progress to two of the town's important industries: education and tourism. Noting that Bergreichenstein was home to "a grammar school, a trade school and a high school," the paper complained that "in the 20th century [we] still have no swimming pool! Not from a lack of water, mind you – of that we have plenty – but from a lack of insight into the salutary effects of bathing." The newspaper then reinforced the rhetorical connection further, asking "How should our students stay fresh and healthy? How should Bergreichenstein become a summer resort, when it offers no opportunity for swimming! How much money is our town losing because of this?"[48]

A month later, the newspaper accused Czech nationalist administrators of actively working to thwart progress in the town. Not only was it claimed that administrative posts in Bohemia were increasingly closed to Germans and their children, but also Czech administrators apparently worked against progress for the town economy. Yet not every barrier to progress could be blamed on the Czechs. A July article linking nationalism to knowledge and progress chided the town's Germans for not yet having organized a reading club or library. The fact that the town's tiny Czech minority already sported such a reading group put the Germans to shame. "How many wasted hours could be rescued from numbing card games and foolish beer drinking? Therefore, off to the deed, whoever has a concern for Bergreichenstein's future!"[49] This suggests a lingering fear by local nationalists that the town's Germans might in fact culturally have more in common with Czech peasants than with themselves. Here we see the ambivalence of nationalists who would like to locate nationalist virtue in the hardy Germans of the *Sprachgrenze*, but who must in fact teach those virtues to the local German speakers.

In August the paper urged the town fathers to create more available rental rooms – too often there were not enough to accommodate all the visitors to the area.[50] The paper then reported with pride that the swimming pool was finally completed and that it proved the progressive spirit of Bergreichenstein's town council.[51] On September 13, however, the paper published a highly illuminating editorial about tourism in nearby Prachatitz that crystallized nationalist frustrations with local backwardness. Entitled "Examining our Conscience," the article stressed that tourism was critical to both the region's economic survival and to its German identity. The experience of the recently concluded summer season demonstrated that several problems remained to be addressed by local villagers. People had charged far too much, both for rooms and for meals, a shortsighted practice that would simply drive tourists away or into the arms of the Czechs. Furthermore, the editorial claimed that customers received far more polite service in Czech shops than in German shops. Wares also needed to be displayed more attractively and shopkeepers should watch out for cleanliness. This latter fact, noted the paper, often counted far more among tourist customers than price. To strengthen national identity, to improve the local economy, to achieve social progress, tourism must be promoted far more effectively.[52]

It seems clear from this brief discussion of Bergreichenstein that the forces promoting nationalist tourism there also fought internally to promote a kind of liberal modernity. They invoked a moral rhetoric of progress that linked national identity to education, hygiene, commerce, and historic preservation. The local tourist industry would benefit from an active policy of self-improvement, and the town's German population would gain a more solid economic basis for survival. This rhetoric certainly fostered local bitterness toward the nationalist foe, but it defined that foe in highly specific terms. It was not the Czech speakers who brought their goods to the monthly Bergreichenstein market who were the enemy, for example, but rather the Czech nationalists who had been appointed the district's administrators; those Czechs in the eyes of the German nationalists who used their official positions to change the traditional character of the town from German to bilingual. However, it must be stressed that these local German nationalists too wished to change the character of the town, and often in ways far more radical than anything the Czech administrators contemplated. The promotion of tourism became the great justification for all kinds of other radical modernizing changes that occasionally did elicit local opposition. By successfully linking tourism to the nationalist interest, the local nationalists were able to push through what might well have been an unpopular agenda.

Nationalist constructions may have shaped personal identities at the turn of the century, yet they produced widely different kinds of outcomes, depending on the context where they were performed. When it worked, nationalism gained its power largely from its ability to make sense of the world in very different regions of imperial Austria. The Habsburg state's necessary rejection of nationalism created all kinds of alternative contexts, spaces where nationalism could function in ways that would have been impossible in self-proclaimed nation-states like France, Germany, or Italy. Nationalism served as an effective organizing tool in Austrian civil society, a tool whose use was rejected by the state, and a tool whose character could therefore be defined more completely from below without having to compete for legitimacy against the state.

If nationalist activists used tourism as an instrument to transform their rhetoric into aggressive action, supporters of this same instrument at the local level used it to impose an orderly modernizing village agenda. While at one level of society in Austria nationalist discourse promoted urban street violence, thus limiting the ability of Reichsrat or Diet to function, at another level, nationalism might well promote economic modernization, social integration, and social mobility. In towns like Bergreichenstein nationalism encouraged the development of associational life, educational projects, greater participation in town politics, and, perhaps ironically, a greater appreciation for the opportunities brought by closer connections to the outside world.

In a larger sense, tourism represented only one of several aspects of daily life that nationalists in Austria worked to nationalize. In doing so they hoped to transform what until 1914 remained largely an elusive, discursive category of identity – Germanness or Czechness – into a material force, relevant to the daily existence of most Austrians. And just as individuals would assume a deeper nationalist identity through changed consumer habit, so contested geographic sites would be transformed into homogeneously German or Czech places as well. The guidebooks that denied Austria's rich multilingual, multicultural heritage posited in its place a new nationally authentic past to justify a brave new nationally homogeneous future. Against official efforts to depoliticize nationality and replace it with a kind of Austrian patriotism, the new tourist literature suggested that the places in Austrian public culture where such patriotism might be rooted were rapidly diminishing. It remained for the events of the First World War and its aftermath to convince many former Austrian German speakers – those who now found themselves minorities in hostile nation-states like Czechoslovakia, Italy, Poland, or Yugoslavia – to see themselves for the first time, in terms which earlier nationalists had created for them.

Notes

1. Südmark, *Mittheilungen des Vereines Südmark* (1912), p. 150.
2. German School Association, "Im Böhmerwald," in *Der getreue Eckart: Monatsschrift des Deutschen Schulvereins* (January 1904), p. 54.
3. Südmark, *Mittheilungen des Vereines Südmark* (1907–8), p. 255.
4. This chapter uses the terms Austria and Cisleithania interchangeably to refer to the state that constituted the non-Hungarian half of the Dual Monarchy, Austria-Hungary.
5. For rethinking of the "new absolutism" model that also suggests the relative strength of Austrian civil society, see Gary B. Cohen, "Neither Absolutism nor Anarchy: New Narratives on Society and Government in Late Imperial Austria," *Austrian History Yearbook* 29 (1998); Lothar Höbelt, *Kornblume und Kaiseradler: Die deutschfreiheitliche Parteien Altösterreichs 1882–1918* (Munich: Oldenbourg, 1993); Pieter M. Judson, *Exclusive Revolutionaries: Liberal Politics, Social Experience, and National Identity in the Austrian Empire, 1848–1914* (Ann Arbor, MI: University of Michigan Press, 1996).
6. According to the Finance Ministry, the annual number of tourists in Austria grew from 2.5 million in 1903 to over 4.5 million in 1910. Franz Bartsch, "Einfluss der Wanderbewegung und des Fremdenverkehrs auf die Zahlungsbilanz Österreich-Ungarns," in *Mitteilungen des k. k. Finanzministeriums* (1911), pp. 125–83. It is important to note that popular Czech nationalism in Bohemia had come of age far earlier in the 1870s, and that German nationalists often adopted or modified strategies that had already been tested by their Czech nationalist opponents. See, for example, Pavla Vosahlikova, "Bädertouristik: Ihre Bedingungen und ihre Form in Österreich-Ungarn bis zu dem ersten Weltkrieg," unpublished manuscript. I thank Dr Vosahlikova for sharing the results of her research on Czech nationalist efforts to establish spas that would compete with the traditionally German-dominated spa towns in Bohemia. On German nationalist efforts, see Rainer Amstädter, *Der Alpinismus: Kultur – Organisation – Politik* (Vienna: WUV-Universitätsverlag, 1996). There is now a growing literature on the institution of the *Sommerfrische* in Austria, but nothing yet that connects it explicitly to nationalist concerns. See, for example, Hanns Haas, "Die Sommerfrische – Ort der Bürgerlichkeit," in Hannes Stekl, Peter Urbanitsch, Ernst Bruckmüller, and Hans Heiss (eds), *"Durch Arbeit, Besitz, Wissen und Gerechtigkeit". Bürgertum in der Habsburgermonarchie* (Vienna: Böhlau, 1992), pp. 364–77.

7. On tourism and national identity see Rudy Koshar, "'What ought to be seen': Tourists' Guidebooks and National Identities in Modern Germany and Europe," *Journal of Contemporary History* 33, 1 (1998). For good examples of how the concept of *Heimat* tied a particular regional identity to a larger national one, see Alon Confino, *The Nation as Local Metaphor: Württemberg, Imperial Germany, and National Memory, 1871–1918* (Chapel Hill, NC: University of North Carolina Press, 1998).

8. See, for example, the publication *Reise und Sport*, originally the *Österreichische illustrierte Alpenzeitung*, whose lavish illustrations, frequent supplements, and international readership bespoke a far bigger budget and audience than any comparable German or Czech nationalist tourism journal. Although *Reise und Sport* occasionally praised German nationality cultural achievement and listed several German nationalist organizations among its sponsors, it clearly aimed to avoid conflict, and promoted a kind of generalized German pride that frequently lauded the accomplishments of the Czechs and other national groups in Austria.

9. Pieter M. Judson, "Frontiers, Islands, Forests, Stones: Mapping the Geography of a German Identity in the Habsburg Monarchy, 1848–1900," in Patricia Yaeger (ed.), *The Geography of Identity* (Ann Arbor, MI: University of Michigan Press, 1996).

10. Along with government statisticians, this preoccupation with language led nationalists to categorize several regional dialects in the monarchy (like "Moravian") in terms of larger national literary languages such as Czech or German, presuming that those who spoke these dialects must belong to a nation.

11. For an excellent consideration of the controversial rhetoric of economic boycotts within the Czech and German nationalist movements in Bohemia, see Catherine Albrecht, "The Rhetoric of Economic Nationalism in the Bohemian Boycott Campaigns of the Late Habsburg Monarchy," in *Austrian History Yearbook* 32 (2001).

12. Judson, "Frontiers, Islands, Forests, Stones." After 1900, organizations like the *Südmark* or the *Deutscher Schulverein* circulated traveling slide shows to their local branches to teach local German speakers about other German peoples and regions in Austria. See *Mitteilungen des Vereins Südmark* (1906–7), p. 24.

13. "Zwecks Vermehrung des deutschen Fremdenverkehrs," in *Mitteilungen des Vereins Südmark* (1912), pp. 150–1.

14. "An unsere Leser!" in *Mitteilungen des Vereines Deutscher Touristen, Brünn*, 1 (January 1903), p. 1.

15. *Mitteilungen des Vereines Südmark* (1909), p. 329.

16. Wilhelm Rohmeder, "Gasthäuser in den sprachlichen Grenzgebieten Südtirols, welche deutschen Reisenden zu empfehlen sind," in special reprint no. 25 from *Alldeutsche Blätter* (Berlin, n.d.), p. 2.

17. Ibid., p. 10.

18. *Deutsche Volkszeitung* (Reichenberg), (July 21, 1908), p. 3, "Alpenreisen in das gemischte Sprachgebiet," in *Mitteilungen des Vereins Südmark* (1906–07), p. 277.

19. *Mitteilungen des Vereines Südmark* (1906–7), p. 242.

20. Such guidebooks rarely stood up to the standards of Baedeker. Their publishers could rely on no consistent local sources and consequently they reported different types of information for each place. Some mentioned the size of a town's German population, others a town's elevation, still others praised air quality or described local accommodations. See, for example, *Sommerfrischen in Schlesien und Nordmähren. Unter Mitwirkung des Vereines Nordmark in Schlesien und des Bundes der Deutschen Nordmährens* (Vienna, 1904), pp. 17, 43.

21. Both economists and cultural critics (such as some who wrote for the Prague journal *Deutsche Arbeit*) actively promoted the concept of a Deutschböhmen starting in the 1890s. See for example, Heinrich Rauchberg, *Die nationale Besitzstand*, 3 vols. (Leipzig, 1905).

22. *Durch Deutschböhmen: Die Weltbäder, Sommerfrischen, Fremden- und Touristenorte Deutschböhmens* (Karlsbad, n.d.).

23. The Austrian government officially collected statistics on *Umgangssprache* (colloquial language) and not on nationality. Nationalist activists defined *Umgangssprache* as the primary indicator of nationalist identity and thus politicized the census. Emil Brix, *Die Umgangssprachen in Altösterreich zwischen Agitation und Assimilation* (Vienna: Böhlau, 1982).

24. "Hauptbericht über die Thätigkeit des Deutschen Böhmerwaldbundes für die XVIII. Hauptversammlung am 7. September 1902 in Neuern, verfasst und erstattet von Bundesobmann Josef Taschek," in *Mittheilungen des Deutschen Böhmerwaldbundes* 45 (1902), supplement, p. 10.

25. "Die tschechische Fiasko im Riesengebirge," in *Deutsche Volkszeitung* (Reichenberg), (January 2, 1908), p. 4.

26. "Die erste Südmarkreise," *Mitteilungen des Vereines Südmark* (1906–7), pp. 273–5. The trip also offered participants more conventional tourist activities from a swim in the Millstättersee to the opportunity to hike certain peaks.

27. *Deutsch Böhmerwald* (Prachatitz), (May 3, 1908), p. 3.

28. *Deutsche Volkszeitung* (Reichenberg), (September 16, 1908), p. 6.

29. See, for example, "Studentenbesuch an der Sprachgrenze," in *Deutsche Volkszeitung* (Reichenberg), (June 30, 1908), p. 3.

30. Hans Kramer, "Der 'Argonautenzug' der Deutschen nach Pergine oder die 'zweite Schlacht von Calliano' 1907," *Mitteilungen des Oberösterreichischen Landesarchiv* 8 (1964).

31. Ottokar Schubert-Schüttarschen, Paul Pogatschnig-Peinenbach, *Die deutsche Mark am Südmeer* (Trieste, 1904), p. 58.

32. "Neues Aufblühen des Deutschtums in Görz," in *Deutsche Volkszeitung* (Reichenberg), (July 5, 1908), p. 3.

33. Peter Jordan and Milena Persic (eds), *Österreich und der Tourismus von Opatija (Abbazia) vor dem Ersten Weltkrieg und zur Mitte der 1990er Jahre* (Frankfurt a/M, 1998).

34. *Satzungen des Deutschen Landesverbandes für Fremdenverkehr in Südösterreich* (Laibach, 1911).

35. "Wandervogel und Jugendwandern," in *Der Kampf ums Deutschtum* 2 (1913), p. 30.

36. In this the *Böhmerwaldbund* resembled the *Deutscher Schulverein* but differed markedly from the anti-Semitic *Südmark*, *Nordmark*, or the *Bund der Deutschen in Böhmen*.

37. Josef Taschek, Chairman of the *Böhmerwaldbund*, helped organize the *Landesverband für Fremdenverkehr in Deutschböhmen* and served as its vice-president.

38. For statistics on visitors to the Passion Play, see *Rückschau über die zwanzigjährige Tätigkeit des Deutschen Böhmerwaldbundes: Für die 20. Hauptversammlung berichtet vom Obmann Josef Taschek* (Budweis, 1904), p. 13. The play was performed in the interwar years until the Nazi occupation. After World War II the communist regime demolished the theater, but current Czech Catholic inhabitants of the village have recently revived the German nationalist tradition.

39. "Deutsche und Italiener in Südtirol," *Bozner Zeitung* (January 10, 1907), p. 3.

40. See, for example, the complaints of activists in the village of Kirchschlag who bemoaned their lack of a post office, a physician, and a population at all interested in taking

advantage of the opportunities of tourism or even participating in basic associational life: *Mittheilungen des Deutschen Böhmerwaldbundes* 10 (1887), p. 128, 11 (1887), p. 155. For complaints to the Landesverband, see for example *Fremdenverkehrs-Nachrichten des Landes-Verbandes für Fremdenverkehr in Deutschböhmen* 3 (1910), pp. 5–7.

41. *Rückschau über die zwanzigjährige Tätigkeit des Deutschen Böhmerwaldbundes. Für die 20. Hauptversammlung berichtet vom Obmann Josef Taschek* (Budweis, 1904), p. 12.

42. Bericht über die Hauptversammlung des Deutschen Böhmerwaldbundes am 27. August in Prachatitz, *Mittheilungen des Deutschen Böhmerwaldbundes* 48 (1905), p. 9.

43. Karl Baedeker, *Österreich (ohne Galizien, Dalmatien, Ungarn und Bosnien)* (Leipzig, 1910), p. 328.

44. Raoul Auernheimer: "Auf der Reise nach Höritz," in *Neue Freie Presse* (Vienna), (August 2, 1908), p. 2, *Böhmerwald-Zeitung* (Krummau), (August 21, 1908), p. 271.

45. Bergreichenstein. Neujahrsbetrachtungen, in *Deutsch Böhmerwald* (Prachatitz), (January 12, 1908), p. 6.

46. *Deutsch Böhmerwald* (Prachatitz), (May 31, 1908), p. 5.

47. *Deutsch Böhmerwald* (Prachatitz), (May 10, 1908), p. 5.

48. *Deutsch Böhmerwald* (Prachatitz), (June 7, 1908), p. 3.

49. *Deutsch Böhmerwald* (Prachatitz), (July 19, 1908), p. 6.

50. *Deutsch Böhmerwald* (Prachatitz), (August 23, 1908), p. 5.

51. Ibid., p. 5.

52. "Gewissensforschung," in *Deutsch Böhmerwald* (Prachatitz), (September 13, 1908), p. 5.

9

La Vieille France as Object of Bourgeois Desire: The Touring Club de France and the French Regions, 1890–1918

Patrick Young

Long a loosely connected – if nevertheless steadily expanding – group of thermal stations, beaches, and canonical attractions, tourism in France became in the years 1890–1914 a matter of greater interest to certain members of the French bourgeoisie, who organized themselves into associations with the intention of more systematically developing a national tourist network, and contributing to France's national revival. Informed by a mix of progressive solidarist-republican principle, amateurism and certain class-specific social imperatives, these associations spearheaded the very significant expansion of France's capacity for receiving tourists which occurred in these years. Tourism was now to have advocates, who sought a more systematic and directed development of leisure travel in keeping with the great commercial (and non-commercial) potential they saw in the international tourist trade. Indeed, this might be considered the most distinguishing feature of the tourism of this period, the leadership by private associations – rather than business or the state – in the more "rational" (to use the term preferred by the principals themselves) organizing of tourist structures and moulding of tourist practices.

Among the associations working on tourism in these years, it was the Touring Club de France (TCF) which most clearly articulated, and successfully acted upon, a coherent vision of a modern tourism and tourist development. Possessing the most developed organizational structure, and the greatest capacity to envision and effect improvements in the tourist infrastructure, the Touring Club led the way in developing French tourism after its founding in 1890.[1] The TCF worked in league with local syndicates d'initiative, the French railway companies, spa and beach resort entrepreneurs, organizations of hotel owners, and the automobile and Alpine clubs, to prompt improvements in infrastructure and publicity which might expand tourist traffic in France.[2] The work of this emerging "tourist industry," as it came to be called in this period, was essential in widening the appeal of tourism in France for both French and foreign tourists, and in developing France's capacity for receiving ever-larger numbers of those tourists. Equally important, though, and highly characteristic of this period, was its insistence upon the broader social and national potential of tourism to function as a progressive, recuperative activity, of deep value not only economically, but also morally, physically and even, in the final instance, politically. Consistent with its nationalist and solidarist convictions, the Touring Club in particular would strive to recast French tourism as a redempt-ive experience of the national available to middle-class consumers. The sense of "place" more commonly registered in the new tourism adduced both to the immed-iate agenda of republican nation-building, as well as to the broad need within the French and international bourgeoisie for always-updated markers of interior distinction.

Tourism as Regional Preservation

One of the defining ambitions of the new, professedly more modern tourism was to generate a new breadth of attractions, as opposed to the tried and true resort areas – the spas and beaches – which had come to define French tourism before 1890.[3] Doing so was consistent with the desire to have tourism represent more faithfully, and market more successfully, France and "Frenchness," a desire harboured most resolutely by the TCF. These aims led the club and its allies deep into the traditional regions of *la France profonde*, the lesser known areas of the country which, while possessing worthy historic, cultural or natural landmarks, were not yet fully "open" to tourist traffic. It was this "France inconnue" (unknown France), as they called it, which galvanized the imagination of tourist organizers, and gave tourist organizing its nationalist élan in these years. Indeed, the Touring Club rarely even mentioned Paris – perhaps the most important tourist attraction in the country – let alone devote itself to developing its attractions or capacity for tourist reception.[4] Nor did it promote the spas or beaches, referring to them only as attractions within the larger regions it was attempting to constitute. For the TCF as in tourist representation taken as a whole, the region would come to weigh more heavily in this period, as a privileged signifier of the authenticity tourism now offered.[5]

Like many in this period, tourist activists fretted over the growing distance they perceived to be separating an increasingly urban and factious society from the deepest sources of its national being. Tourism in the newly outfitted French regions might, they believed, connect individuals to their regions of origin, but stood also to connect the French more generally to the deeper rural, regional bases of their contemporary national being. This *oeuvre*, one leader in French publicity argued at the Fifth Congress of the syndicat d'initiative, was an "eminently French and patriotic one"; it was in

> bringing together, through more frequent voyages, the natives of our various *petit pays* [local areas] that one would teach them better to know and love one another, as well as better to appreciate the beauty of this so fecund and picturesque soil, and would realize the moral unity of this prodigiously active, intelligent and enlightened race to which we have the great fortune to belong.[6]

Of course, tourist organizers were hardly alone in their "turn" to the provinces in these years. "Régionalisme" as such was a neologism of the prewar Third Republic, encompassing a great variety of new efforts to know, promote, and defend the regions. Herman Lebovics has explained such efforts as part of the broader impulse in French politics and culture to locate a "True France."[7] As Lebovics demonstrates, the more extreme and expressly political regional advocacy – for example that of Charles Maurras and Maurice Barrès – tended to promote narrow and exclusionary visions of French nationhood, and rejection of the claims of the universal republic.[8] Yet, regionalism lent itself to a range of inflections, many informed by the desire consciously to avoid the charged polarities of French politics. The main organization of regional advocacy in these years, the Fédération Régionaliste Français (FRF), claimed like the Touring Club to be "above parties and doctrines" in its advocacy of regional development as a service of ultimately national ends.[9] The great growth of interest in things regional was broad and unmistakable in this period, be it in the amateur societies and emerging academic disciplines of geography, ethnography, and folklore,[10] in new schoolbooks and popular texts such as *Le Tour de la France par deux enfants* and *Bécassine*,[11] or in the universal and specialized exhibitions which commonly featured regional artefacts in their spectacular displays.[12]

The shared assumption of these efforts of regional advocacy and representation was that heightened awareness and appreciation of the regions ultimately supported preeminently national objectives, and tourist outfitting was no different on this score. Tourism was offered, by its advocates, as a means of preserving local landscapes, monuments, cultures, even populations, through making them part of a more clearly defined national *patrimoine* (patrimony). While many might lament the disappearing region, leaders of the Touring Club argued, a genuine regional preservation and even revival of the regions would depend upon the drumming up of public interest, and the spending of tourist money.[13] In opening up those regions to both French and international travelers, they believed, tourism provided the foundations for the potential economic revitalization of the provinces, guaranteeing them a continued place within a revived French nationhood. Regions whose traditional economic base was shrinking could, this thinking ran, develop a new viability through their incorporation into the tourist economy, as tourist commerce provided direction for improvements and lured greater investment from both within and without.[14] Tourism would bring them into line with the drift of modern development, but would do so not in coercive, top-down fashion; rather, as viewed attractions, the regions would be integrated in the modern national and international economy on terms respective of their essential distinctiveness. Further, the basic economic argument TCF leaders made for tourism in France as a whole was even more compelling when applied to the regions: tourists brought money into the area and spent it liberally, making tourism the ideal economic endeavor for an area preoccupied with self-preservation. "With the *industrie du voyageur* becoming a source of considerable riches," one speaker at the TCF's 1902 General Assembly urged, "let us keep it to ourselves, and let's not benevolently carry out money abroad when the *pays de France* have such need of it."[15] "The traveler, in time," one writer in *La Route* suggested, was becoming "as indispensable to the economic life of the *pays* as the client passing in the street was for the urban shop owner."[16]

The Regions as Viewed Objects of Desire

It was ultimately in being more readily and more widely viewed, tourist organizers believed, that the regions would truly be "preserved." The practical effort of tourist organization therefore now aimed at more clearly highlighting the regions, and making them figure more centrally in tourist representation overall. Improvements in roads, transport and hotels directed by the TCF (though most often effected by the Ministry of Public Works) had the aim of facilitating freer movement in all regions of France. The club hoped to constitute coherent regional units, which would then serve as *régions touristiques*, the foundation for tourism in France, and a grounding in the local deemed necessary to the overall enterprise. They identified certain major towns as *centres du tourisme*, to serve not only as attractions in and of themselves, but also as launching points for excursion into the less-traveled towns and villages surrounding them.[17] The train companies aided in this as well, partly in response to the complaints of the TCF that they had traditionally privileged the better known and more frequented spas and beaches of France in their publicity, their efforts of network expansion, and their ticket policies, at the expense of the *petits trous de province* (little provincial "holes").[18]

In their ticket policies, for example, they moved to accommodate the more comprehensive examination of a defined area, offering circular voyages with fixed itineraries, and special *cartes d'excursions* allowing unlimited travel within a given region, at a fixed cost. These made it possible for the tourist to move about freely and visit a greater variety of sites within a given zone, the better to discern the full "physiognomy" of a region, now commonly cited as the aim of tourism.[19] Even if still limited by lacunae in the network of transport and reception, this aim of offering up a more or less complete experience of region marked a significant departure from the narrower, *villégiature* of longer stay in a single station or resort.[20]

A similar shift is palpable in tourist literature and publicity, as guidebook series such as the Guides Joanne, Simons, and Baedeker, and the Manuel du Voyageur began to devote volumes to individual regions in France, beginning in the 1870s and 1880s. The Touring Club's "Sites and Monuments" collection, a comprehensive thirty-volume set profiling the natural, historic, and cultural attractions of the country, divided into regional volumes aiming at capturing what was most distinctive about each of France's traditional regions. The TCF also led the way in generating and diffusing maps both regional and national, tailored specifically to the needs of the tourist, including major routes, train lines and national and departmental roads, identified, as well as smaller paved roads, bike paths and often major attractions. Tourist maps were a significant means by which the regions were rendered more concrete, and the national territory imagined, at a time when public cartographic knowledge was still very limited.[21] One map of "La France touriste" offered for purchase from the Touring Club from 1905 onward portrayed the regional cities, or "capitals," more prominently than Paris, which is almost lost in the very decentered representation of the country. The great profusion of such maps in this period presented the regions as discrete and accessible geographic entities, and made of tourism a more conscious experience of regional and national territoriality.[22]

Within the regions themselves, the Touring Club and the syndicats labored to bring into relief the distinctive qualities of each region, the better to present, in the words of future TCF president Léon Auscher, "an image of being as geographically and ethnographically homogeneous as possible" and that "picturesque particularism" which defined each region.[23] To this end, the TCF worked with local cultural and tourist organizations to preserve and promote regional cultural manifestations. It agitated, for example, on behalf of regional museums of conservation, with each to be "a pious asylum for historic memories of the province . . . to safeguard what remains of its primitive originality, and to resuscitate what tends to disappear."[24] Having these museums, it was suggested, would force each region to make a more thorough inventory of its regional treasures, which might then serve as the basis for an expanded tourism. Similarly, the TCF supported efforts to preserve traditional costume and regional cuisine, as prime identifiers of regional specificity, holding contests for traditional dress, and encouraging provincial restaurants and hotels to serve traditional local dishes, and local wines, as against the increasingly standardized haute cuisine of the *grands hôtels*.[25] In its campaign to build and renovate provincial hotels, the TCF combined the objectives of hygiene and comfort with the need accurately to manifest locality in their design and operation.[26]

Regional Difference, National Unity, Class Distinction

Closer analysis of tourist representation of the regions suggests the degree to which tourism's commodifying and nationalizing tendencies were often inseparable in this period. This is evident, for starters, in tourist texts' insistence that it was the great range of landscapes, cultures, and possible experiences one encountered in the French countryside which made France French, and distinguished it as a potential destination for tourists. Tourist leaders' promotion of France as an attraction always proceeded from the assertion of its great variety – of landscapes, of cultures, of people – united in a "harmonious ensemble."[27] "One cannot say it often enough," a typical Touring Club article began, "no other country in the world offers, compressed into so small a space, as many architectural and natural beauties, as much variety and charm."[28] France, if more fully outfitted for tourism, stood to offer anything within its borders that tourists had previously sought elsewhere. Foreign tourists had traditionally followed established itineraries within the country, including Paris, the main thermal and beach resorts, and, for some, the Alps; now they were being invited more to experience "France."[29]

The assertion of a difference which testified ultimately to national unity was a common trope in representations of French locality and nationhood, stretching back at least as far as Michelet's *Tableau de la France* which emphasized difference in the genesis (and ultimate transcendence) of French nationhood.[30] The great profusion of geographic works appearing in the prewar Third Republic commonly proceeded from this assumption as well, most notably Paul Vidal de la Blache's *Tableau de la géographie de France,* which exhaustively dissected local physiognomies in its exploration of the (ultimately highly compatible) relationship between *pays* and *nation.*[31] One sees it at work in the regional advocacy of the FRF as well, in its encouragement of regional representation and identification as a means of "founding patriotism on tangible realities."[32] Thus the insistence of one tourist organizer that it was the "maintenance of local traditions which gives to our regions their character of originality" and could be replaced by no publicity text, as an argument for the distinctiveness of the country as a whole; depicting a more varied France was both good business and good politics.[33]

The Regional Picturesque

While tourist organizers would insist upon the seemingly limitless variety of France's regions as a defining feature of French national distinctiveness, individual representations of the regional in tourism tended to conform to certain dictates of the picturesque. What united the different regions in their representations was a shared invocation of "the old France," of a sort of local and traditional picturesque which could be readily embodied in specific cultural signifiers. In this formulaic image, the regional was defined by a "local color, its picturesque quality resulting from constructions unique to each region, varied costumes, fetes and games of the past, naively artistic furniture and utensils decorating the houses of the peasants of *la vieille France*" (the old France).[34] It was this easily identifiable quality that tourism had to deliver in its manifestations of the regional. Léon Auscher spoke, for example, of the need to "create" a local charm through efforts of tourist outfitting, a charm which could be easily conveyed to tourists.[35] Such charm lay nascent in every corner of the country: almost any village could be transformed into an attraction, one tourist writer argued, with the smallest effort of *embellissement*; the arranging of flowers throughout the town, for example, could change a banal village into something outsiders would have an interest in viewing.[36]

Thus, tourist organizers proceeded with a more or less clear sense of what regional life should look like, a sort of "regional picturesque," as they represented France for tourism. It was through the medium of this obligatory and familiar picturesque style that bourgeois consumers from without could gain ready access to the otherness of the provinces. A writer in the TCF's *Revue Mensuelle* invoked, for example, the essential features of the picturesque rural conglomeration:

> pretty villages huddled together at the bottom of a small valley or at the bend of a river, signalled only by the lovely point of their old steeple; or still more of these graceful little towns fanning out on a hillside with their old-fashioned houses, their monuments, built by the different centuries, the work of an entire history, of an entire civilization. We have vaunted them and stated repeatedly that one searches for charming places and marvels of art and nature which one can find here, right around oneself.[37]

This formula would be reproduced in postcard representations of rural villages, which usually depicted a set of houses surrounding a church, with trees, mountains, or cultivated fields providing the framing.[38] One sees it repeatedly in tourist posters, in the Sites and Monuments collection, and in guidebooks, a more or less standardized representation of French locality which could easily be called into service again and again. What is perhaps remarkable is that the Touring Club itself could so readily admit, in this passage, the formulaic quality of the scene; that it should do so suggests the degree to which representations of locality were often not very "local" after all. The clear assumption is that there was something identifiably French in such a scene, which had to, and did, come through, regardless of the locality represented.

If landscapes and villages conformed to this picturesque, so too did people. In their drive to capture local color, tourist organizers more commonly represented regional figures, themselves now picturesque, as components of the attraction.[39] Local traditions were dying out, and costumes becoming outmoded, one critic in *L'Estampe et l'Affiche* noted, but they were finding a new home in the tourist poster. Posters for Normandy and Bretagne, in particular, now more commonly represented "the *paysans* of the coast in the costumes of their *pays* and in the gay and festive finery which used to seem so appealing to them."[40] The critic was most taken with posters of Kowalski and Pal representing "the Breton, singing, dancing and playing on the bagpipes a round of the old Armorique, with the Bretonne, moving dreamily on the green land, guardian of her flock, humming a refrain, dreaming of love, her regard lost to the horizon where soon will arrive the mast of the boat carrying her father, her husband, or her fiancé."[41] What drew so many of the most important poster artists to doing work for the train companies and syndicates d'initiative, according to this journal, was precisely the opportunity to represent regional life, costumes, and people (if not always landscapes, which tended to be a bit more standardized). Representing these scenes of local life was a unique challenge for the artist, one charged with higher purpose, and more engaging of the artist's eye, talent and conviction.[42] Not all were enamoured of this tendency, certainly. Another critic, at the 1895 Salon, criticized the formulaic quality of such representations, positioning within an entirely predictable landscape "habitants who seem only to go about dressed in festive costume, the women all beautiful and pretty and showing only their most beautiful finery."[43]

These figures do, in fact, most often appear in the posters dressed in traditional costume, and are posed, as a sort of decor for the scene. Almost always women, they become themselves a part of an ensemble of attractions, offering an immediate point of entry into the otherness of the area. The gendering female of the French regions in tourist publicity is unmistakable in this period, as it would be for landscapes and the colonies as well. Women are often foregrounded in tourist publicity, consistent, on the most basic level, with the rendering of the represented areas as viewed objects of desire. Depicted as tourists, the women were cast as consummately modern, fashionably attired and passionately accessing the scenes open before them; made local, though, they became equally consummate markers of regional authenticity. It was assumed that the customs and the spirit of the areas represented resided more authentically and enduringly in women, made in these posters the archetypes of cultural constancy. The Touring Club would frequently deploy this strategy as well, in its more "documentary" representations of the regions, using posed female figures as the conduits for an access which could be very intimate indeed.[44]

While sometimes simply posed in the foreground, in welcoming aspect, the figures are at other times represented as occupied with specific activities which themselves register a distinct sense of place. For example, it became much more common in this period to represent work as itself something of an attraction, and a compelling signifier of provincial locality and tradition. Including images of work did not compromise the overarching need to present these places as above all places of leisure. For the work is presented in picturesque fashion, and at something of a remove, as a viewed reality. Usually performed by women, in regional costume, it is almost always work of a traditional sort, directly engaging of the terrain and the surrounding. Such images appeared most commonly in tourist representations of Bretagne and other coastal areas, which commonly positioned women doing maritime work front and center.[45] Religion too was now more commonly represented within tourism as an easily identifiable inducement to regionalist desire, whether in poster and brochure representations of religious ceremonies, or in the preservation and beautification of churches as national (rather than religious) monuments. Again, Bretagne was perhaps, more than other areas, constructed as a place where faith had not yet vanished. Rather than being simply a collection of beaches, or a magnet for a certain sort of bourgeois sociability – haute bourgeoise in the earlier part of the century, though more diversified by its close – Bretagne was now a conduit for connection to a vanishing world: *la vieille France* was passing already into memory, and into consumption, even as it still had a fair measure of reality to it.

Indeed, memory and consumption work together in these posters, effecting a sort of distance, while offering the tools for bridging it. The degree to which the imperatives of commodity could weigh on the provinces in tourist representation suggests itself most powerfully in a poster for Provence put out by its syndicat d'initiative. The distinct and immediately identifiable landscape of Provence – evoked here by the coast, the hills, and particularly, the twisted tree in the foreground – provides a backdrop for a set of loosely connected signifiers of alterity. The scene at the center does not, in any real sense, come close to adding up. Regional costumes, swarthy faces, music and popular festivity, and agricultural labor come together as a sort of hodgepodge, with locality reduced to gestures of suggestion. Is this work or is it fête? The only thing clear is that the scene is one of leisure, as the sailboats, panoramic view, and superimposed scenic attractions attest. It is only within the commodified cultural spaces of leisure – the newly constituted tourist regions, or even the space of the tourist poster itself – that this "sense of place" could become meaningful. In those spaces, "not adding up" was a boon, an invitation to an array possible experiences (and levels) of authenticity, none of which would be in itself entirely definitive. Tourism's projection of bourgeois desire onto the provinces would provide multiple avenues to an always incomplete appropriation of French locality.

Remoteness and Availability

Though this picturesque formula of representation rendered regional otherness more identifiable and available to bourgeois consumers, that availability was always a qualified one. This is evident even in the picturesque village motif described above: instantly recognizable as an iconic representation of rural France, and composed of certain obligatory visual features, the picturesque village also suggests a sort of inwardness and resistance. Whether in tourist posters, or in postcards from the period, these villages are usually represented as turned in upon themselves, the houses almost a "rampart" against the outside world.[46] The consumer appropriation of these images of locality was premised upon the guarantee of their (at least partial) remove, upon preserving some notion of unattainability or resistance to easy possession. This dynamic was essential to tourist representation of locality, and indeed to tourist representation as a whole; for insisting upon varying degrees of accessibility was necessary to maintaining hierarchies of tourist experience, and thus of cultural value and social distinction.

It is in the Touring Club's literary representations of the provinces, and of travel to them, that this dynamic expresses itself most clearly. After the Sites and Monuments collection, the Club's preferred medium for representing the provinces was the traveler's account, published in the pages of the *Revue Mensuelle*. From the early 1890s, the TCF published accounts of members' excursions – usually those performed on bicycle at the beginning, though later those on foot and in auto as well – detailing conditions encountered and attractions viewed, and dwelling on the technical details of roads, transport and hotels. By the turn of the century, these accounts were becoming more elaborate, appearing in series in the *Revue Mensuelle*, under the headings of "One Voyage a Month" and "La France Inconnue," and aiming at rendering a more or less systematic coverage of the lesser-known areas of the country, from the perspective of the informed tourist-viewer.

As such, they forged something of a middle course between an earlier tradition of literary travel writing grounded in reflection and personal response, and the rational-bureaucratic and consumerist orientation of the modern tourist guide-book.[47] The areas visited were often not yet fully, or even partially, outfitted for tourism, but were assumed to possess qualities which might potentially make them attractions for significant numbers of tourists. The narratives therefore unfold as explorations, as encounters with the unknown but ultimately very profoundly knowable. "La France inconnue" always offers a sort of resistance – whether it is a historic remoteness, a paucity of hotels or navigable roadways, inclement weather (though, interestingly, never a suspicion of outsiders) – but one which gradually breaks down before the dogged efforts of the TCF traveler. The honest accounting of local conditions was, of course, essential to the work of improvement, calling attention to necessary changes; but it also was offered as part of the appeal of traveling to these areas. One account of a voyage to the Eastern Pyrénées described the tramontane as the traveler's "constant companion," forcing early departure from certain areas because of its severity. While certainly presented as an inconvenience, the winds are also made a sort of décor for the courage and initiative of the Touring Club member, a testimony to the exploratory quality of his tourism.[48] Equipped with persistence, ingenuity, and often explicit patriotic and cultural conviction, the traveler comes slowly to penetrate the unknown, to, in effect, "discover" and report upon these regions of tourism.

The portraying of tourism as an experience of novelty, trial and discovery certainly suited the ethos of the Touring Club, bonding together its delegates in a shared identity and sense of nationalist mission. In this the Touring Club member served as a sort of model for other travelers; most, of course, did not, or could not travel in the same way, and with the same force of conviction. Nevertheless, this ethos of the traveler-discoverer did make its way into tourism as a whole, reconditioning tourist expectations and experiences of the regions. The thrill of discovering attractions "off the beaten track" was one which, with improvements in transport, was coming to be available to all tourists. Even if the routes around the Aude were well traveled, one TCF account suggested, the visitor to the area still had the chance to join "the avant-garde of tourists who will soon, in response to the appeal of the local syndicates d'initiative, hasten to the area to see marvels, which have not yet been rigged, prepared and transformed by the invasion of the crowd."[49] While the sites would always shift, and the population of tourists expand, tourism needed to preserve a sense of discovery at its core, and make it available to all tourists.

Travel in the countryside was simply impossible without the explorer's fortitude, the patriot's commitment, and the *amateur*'s taste and judgment. The author of one account of the Pyrénées in *Le Tour de France* complained that many people wanted too simple and immediate an access to tourist attractions, desiring, for example, a beauty which was "nice, welcoming, *mise au point* [arranged]":

> We are "feelers," not volunteers, *promeneurs* rather than mountaineers, artists and not conquerors. We seek to feel quickly, at first glance; the sublime is disconcerting to us; we need it tailor-made for us, adapted to our vision, reduced to pretty and gracious dimensions. What we want is what is ready at hand, immediate pleasure to satisfy our indolence, to calm the fleeting appetites of gourmets too quickly satisfied . . . For we have a great capacity to illusion, an unfathomable, incurable tendency to be dupes.[50]

These tendencies were opposed, by the author, to the taste for action and spirit of initiative which defined the new tourist, or at least the new tourist ideal propagated most insistently by the Touring Club. It was these qualities, he argued, which one needed to appreciate an area such as the Pyrénées, which did not so readily open itself up to every viewer:

> In the Pyrénées, the sublime is as yet scarcely appreciated. It is invisible, perched on high, timid. It doesn't disrobe, doesn't even show itself. It exists, all the more alive in that it hasn't been altered by human industry, vulgarised by storytellers, or by chronicles. Giving its exact reflection is an enterprise beyond our powers, one at which many of the better of us have failed.[51]

Constructed as, in effect, a high quality good, the region demanded of the tourist a certain disposition and preparation, if it was truly to be consumed and appreciated.

Not all tourists had these qualities, of course, and tourist writers recognized as much, attempting actively to school them in the categories of taste essential to the consumption of the provinces. The imperative for the tourist, overall, was now to open him or herself up to an area, rather than simply whiling away time at a single resort. The ideal was of a tourist who forged out, unafraid, preferably on bicycle, one who could penetrate, owing to transport and his or her disposition, beneath the veil of prejudice and ignorance to a discovery of the local area. Tourist literature from the period constantly bemoaned the influence of preconception as inhibiting response to a given local attraction. One account of a voyage in the Eastern Pyrénées, by a TCF delegate, regretted that it was for the most part only through regional products that most Parisians knew of the area, and that therefore the "general opinion" of the area held it to be little more than a bunch of vines and Castillet.[52] In his dissection of "the art of viewing," Alfred Danzat urged that effective viewing came only with the shedding of prejudices and *habitudes*: the true tourist observed, catalogued and responded emotionally, but did not judge. "Seeing a region, studying a people in a spirit of sympathy, is the best means of penetrating both . . . Sympathy is reciprocal: it loosens tongues, opens hearts and doors which remain closed to the grumpy."[53] As tourism continued to develop, Danzat argued, extending its reach and augmenting its facilities of reception, traveling to remote regions would come increasingly to resemble actually living in them. The easier travel became, "the more people will interest themselves in the *pays*, the better they will taste its charm and interest, and the more will the great number of facts and characters – which elude the first superficial viewing – strike our more open and attentive disposition."[54]

The Past as Consolation

In their dynamic of resistance and discovery, these accounts of the provinces made tourism into something of a search; and for many tourists, particularly those in the Touring Club, it was now France for which one searched in tourism. Pedalling off into the countryside, along dusty roads and through unknown territory, the Touring Club delegate represented him or herself as something of an explorer, searching for the deepest sources of French national identity.[55] In these terms, the voyage to the provinces was one which unfolded not simply in space, but in time as well, as an encounter with the full depth and enduring weight of the French past. If the tourist industry cast tourism in the provinces as a trip back in time, into *la vieille France*, it was nevertheless a trip in which one never lost one's bearings. For tourism presented a past which always existed in a relationship of continuity with the present. One tourist's account of a voyage in the north of France characterized the journey as an encounter with the past, albeit one which brought into relief France's modernity. The traveler is led, by his guide, to the essential regional attractions, through "a bunch of small towns, of villages, of tiny bourgs," stopping before "churches, occupied château, feudal ruins," and searching for the "originality" of what he was seeing.[56] As he moves about in the area, he is most struck by the juxtaposition of a rich local past and an industrial present, the two coexisting in a surprising harmony. A present of "magnificent constructions and immense factories" sat comfortably alongside old belfries, and the *histoire émotionante* of the old *pays*.[57]

The harmony this tourist finds "surprising" would have seemed less so to tourist organizers. For his description corroborates what was an essential French national myth, one which decisively informed the latter's representations of regional landscapes, cultures, and histories: the myth of a past which was uniquely present, of a *passé proche* (a close past), in a country in which tradition and modernity always existed in comfortable continuity. Even at its most "other," the regional past was always presented as essentially continuous with a modern, and always implicitly national present. One guide, for example, characterized the history of Picardy as one in which the region consistently "defended its invaded soil," served the glory of the great French monarchy, contributed to the formation of the French language and, finally, "proved [its] most ardent patriotism when patriotism absorbed all other sentiments, just as the nation absorbed all the old provinces . . . the bravery so characteristic of the Picardians has never served any cause other than the national one."[58] This is, to put it mildly, a rather stylised version of the past, though an exemplary one in its insistence that a more or less continuous French nationhood expressed itself even in regional difference. The characterization of these Picardians as a "race," and a fiercely proud one, always repelling outside incursions, could easily be conflated to a national feature, as could other regional depictions which made of regional distinctiveness a point of identification.

It was at their most different that these regions testified most compellingly to the strength of the French national principle. This is certainly one inflection of the myth of "la France éternelle," of the deep and ancient (indeed even prehistoric) roots of the French nation, and the inevitability of French nationhood irrespective of the workings of French political history.[59] As against a political nationhood which was relatively recent, and always conflictual, even fratricidal, tourism stroked the myth of an essential harmony which lay before and beyond French politics.[60] It was that harmony that tourist organizers of this period sought to conjure, or perhaps rediscover, and in this context, their dogged insistence upon "elevating" tourism above politics and political conflict takes on a new resonance. Tourism in this period becomes the pursuit of a national essence, an essence only incompletely and problematically arrived at in politics, but more readily available in conditioned encounter with regional difference.

The affinities between this characterization of the French provincial past and the earlier-cited geographic constructions of the French nation are striking. The insistence upon historical continuity mirrors the geographic privileging of metaphors of symmetry, proportionality, and regularity, and ultimately, I would argue, serves the same end. Eugen Weber has suggested as much in his brief discussion of the origins of the hexagon as a geographic metaphor for imagining French nationhood. He shows that people imagined France in all sorts of shapes in the fin-de-siècle, not simply the hexagon, but that all such attempts shared the assumption of a basic regularity. It was simply inconceivable that France would be anything other than somehow perfectly proportional, owing perhaps as much to the weight of shared national myth as to the actual contours of the country.[61] The connection was at its most seamless in the geography of Vidal de la Blache, who portrayed French nationhood as the product of an endless set of contrasts and interactions, a solidarity bred of the ultimately complementary nature of France's myriad differences. Those differences were, of course, above all regional differences, grounded in both geography and history, and Vidal de la Blache minutely detailed regional specificities, as a means ultimately of asserting France's unique capacity for absorbing diversity. In his geography, the life of the country people sat at the very core of national experience and identification.[62]

This imaginary of French nationhood as an essential symmetry suffused tourist representation, as almost anything within tourism – climate, geography, peoples, cultures, history – could be, and was spoken of in these terms. At the end of recounting an itinerary through Provence in the Touring Club de France's *Revue Mensuelle*, H Boland claimed the goal of the TCF and its allies was "to organize France for tourism, to have it be better loved in making better known the sweet land of varied landscapes, situated within an ensemble of marvellous harmony, *la Patrie, la mère*, alas, still ignored by her own children."[63] One is far removed, here, from the notion of modernity as disruption, as the agent of dislocation in both personal and collective life. Tourism instead forges a modernity of reconciliation, a uniquely French path toward the modern which others could, and should, view. Thus Charles-Brun's suggestion that development in the smaller towns and villages of the tourist countryside aim at providing "a minimum of cleanliness and comfort, of conveniences of access," but not so much as to menace the "charm" and "variation" which had to be preserved as their defining feature.[64] Whether or not this could be a realistic strategy for development, in either the short or long term, its importance lay far more in its insistence upon a certain vision of Frenchness and French modernity, one which exercised both in this period and beyond it a considerable appeal.

Conclusion

To flesh out fully the implications of tourism's constructions of regional and national identity in these years, it is necessary first to return to Lebovics's discussion of the "True France" ideology. For this essay has demonstrated how closely these constructions conformed to the broad outlines of this vision of a "True France," as Lebovics characterizes it, advancing promises of retrieving a lost, compromised or hidden national authenticity through informed travel in the French *terroirs*. Lebovics's argument obliges that one consider these codings critically, as he locates in them an implicit conservative and exclusionary political agenda. Though tourist organization proceeded as a work of political disinterestedness, at least according to its advocates, there is no severing of efforts of preservation and *mise en valeur* (tourist outfitting) from the political and social context of the Third Republic. Whereas the groups and individuals profiled by Lebovics manifested a "True France" in discourse mainly as a means of drawing clearer, and more absolute, lines of national membership, tourism aimed instead after realizing a sort of solidarity which was far more compatible with the republican project. Tourism did not place *nation* and *pays* in opposition: rather, the visualizing of the one always implied, and rendered more tangible, the other. Within its framework of commodified representation, tourism concealed the most glaring contradictions of modernity behind an ethic of reconciliation which was an article of faith for many in these years. The enthusiasm of tourist organizers was a genuine one: they thought they had found a way of making French national solidarity real, and visible.

But tourism's promises need further unpacking. What, for example, of the class dimensions of regional representation and consumption in tourism? For tourism was, above all, a form of middle-class consumption. As both consumption and "preservation," tourism assumed a national context for local cultures, with the latter consolidated as discrete and identifiable objects, viewable from without, from the modern, national perspective of the mobile middle-class tourist. The work on regional preservation and development was but one component of a larger effort to convert the regions into accessible commodities, available to circulating tourists. It institutionalized and spread the viewing position of metropolitan modernity, bringing more of France into the web. As a tourist encountered a regional attraction, he or she did so within a national frame of reference, from a perspective accommodating both a distance from, and possession of, the *terroirs*. When tourist posters represent work, regional identity, and religion, they do so from something of a distance, and assume a viewer who could, in fact, view such things from a distance. But, more importantly for the purposes at hand, they assume a national viewer, for whom such images would register as "differences" made more visible by the emergence of a more aggressive French nationhood in the prewar Third Republic. Indeed, these representations can make sense only from such a perspective. Thus, the tourist's viewing position confirmed his or her status as a national subject, even if politics would seem a rather remote matter when contemplating a landscape; and it scarcely requires mentioning that this position, and this status, were understood to be the exclusive province of the traveling bourgeoisie.

It is worth returning to the notion of a "France inconnue," in this context. For the phrase – which more than any encapsulates the way the Touring Club and its allies understood the French provinces – certainly begs the question of to whom, exactly, this France was "inconnue." Charles-Brun was certainly far from alone in believing that provincial dwellers were often incapable, or unwilling, to appreciate the beauty of their *pays*, either taking it for granted or even denigrating it in their hunger for the capital and its culture.[65] The regional picturesque implied, even required, an urban viewer, one, I would suggest, fully steeped in the viewing practices of an emergent consumer culture. It was in being viewed from without that the French provinces became known and, in a sense, "real," their locality salvaged for the project of nation-building and so made more universally fluent and evocative.

Unlike the proponents of the "True France," tourist organizers advanced a vision of the regional and traditional which fully buttressed the republican ideal. For the regional work of the TCF advanced the cause of both the republican nation, in its claim to represent the transcendence of difference and the logical culmination of the French past; and, more narrowly, of the French bourgeoisie, in its own claim to act as the stewards of French society, capable of identifying most convincingly with the deepest sources of French national identity, and so itself representing the sort of culmination of French social development, connected with equal vigor to both past and present. Just as the French republican nation, as now realized in tourism, could act as an effective container for regional difference, and for differentiated and formerly conflictual past, so too could the class tourism served in this period present itself as something of a telos, capable of existing in a peaceful relationship of identification and proprietorship *vis-à-vis* a past and present of great difference and conflict. The capacity for reconciling the great divisions of the French past was of course an essential part of the republican (or, for that matter, any) regime's claim to legitimacy, and tourist organizers no doubt realized as much in their insistence that developing tourism was one of the highest forms of national service and public-spiritedness. The version of France that they coordinated and presented back to France, and to the world, certainly adduced to this end.

Notes

1. The TCF was modelled on the English Cyclists' Touring Club, its membership growing rapidly from 1279 in 1892 to 90,000 in 1900 and 130,000 by 1912, and including many prominent political, business and professional figures of the Third Republic. Forming in the 1890s, touring clubs were active in all of the major countries of Europe. Léon Auscher, *Dix ans de Touring Club* (Paris, 1900) p. 199; 53/AS/163, letter of M Trappes to M Ballif, President of TCF.

2. The syndicates d'initiative were local and regional groupings of private individuals wishing to develop the appeal of their town or region, and its capacity to receive tourists. Members usually included notable local political-administrative and business figures, members of prominent local committees and societies and academics, united behind a sort of civic boosterism.

3. On thermal tourism, see Douglas Mackaman, *Leisure Spaces: Bourgeois Culture, Medicine and the Spa in Modern France* (Chicago: University of Chicago Press, 1998); Armand Wallon, *La Vie quotidienne dans les villes d'eaux, 1850–1914* (Paris: Hachette, 1981). On beach tourism, see Gabriel Desert, *La Vie quotidienne sur les plages normandes du Second Empire aux années folles* (Paris: Hachette, 1983): Alain Corbin, *The Lure of the Sea: The Discovery of the Seaside in the Western World, 1750–1840,* trans Jocelyn Phelps (Berkeley, CA: University of California Press, 1994).

4. The exception to this was the club's work surrounding the Great Exhibition, its development of the environs of Paris for weekend excursions, including those of Parisian petites bourgeois and workers.

5. Dean MacCannell was the first to suggest modern tourism's function of providing access to "the authentic"; Dean MacCannell, *The Tourist: A New Theory of the Leisure Class* (New York: Schocken, 1989). Perhaps the most striking index of the new prominence of the region in tourism is the degree to which even the more established spas and beaches had resort to these representational strategies drawing upon the regional identities of the areas within which they were situated, in their advertising. Whereas the better known beaches and spas had previously, in effect, sold themselves, on the basis of their *mondanité*, or their existing reputation, they too were now finding it wise to submit to an urban framework of representation, and to trade in local stereotypes, as a way of selling tourism as a broader experience of connection.

6. *La publicité des Syndicats d'Initiative de France. Conférence faite à Nancy par M. Vergné* (Paris, 1908).

7. Herman Lebovics, *True France: The Wars over Cultural Identity, 1900–1945* (Ithaca, NY: Cornell University Press, 1994).

8. On Maurras, this classic account is Eugen Weber, *Action Français: Royalism and Reaction in Twentieth Century France* (Stanford, CA: Stanford University Press, 1962), though it gives only passing attention to the regional question. See also Michael Sutton, *Nationalism, Positivism and Catholicism: The Politics of Charles Maurras and French Catholics, 1890–1914* (Cambridge: Cambridge University Press, 1982); on Barrès, see Maurice Barrès, *Les Déracinés: le roman de l'energie nationale* (Paris: Gallimard, 1988); Ze'ev Sternhell, *Maurice Barrès et le Nationalisme Française* (Paris: Editions Comlexes, 1985), pp. 322–36; see also Robert Soucy, *Fascism in France: The Case of Maurice Barrès* (Berkeley, CA: University of California Press, 1972); an older account, though one which nevertheless offers interesting points of comparison between Maurras, Barrès and Sorel, is in Michael Curtis, *Three Against the Republic: Sorel, Barrès and Maurras* (Princeton, NJ: Princeton University Press, 1959). Curtis discusses the protest against centralization on pp. 155–65.

9. Shanny Peer, *France on Display: Peasants, Provincials and Folklore in the 1937 World's Fair* (Albany, NY: SUNY Press, 1998), p. 62. The FRF directly supported the tourist organization of these years as "essentially provincialist," its leader, Jean Charles-Brun, explicitly lauding the work of the Touring Club and syndicates d'initiative in the TCF's *Revue Mensuelle* (September 1910) as well as in his 1911 *Le Régionalisme* (Paris: Bloud, 1911).

10. In all three cases, what had been a rather limited pursuit became, in the Third Republic, a much more serious and professional endeavor, taking the form of university chairs, and a wealth of new organizations and societies dedicated to exploring the local differences against which (or, more accurately, perhaps, upon which) an emerging republican national identity was being forged. A Société des traditions populaires was founded in France in 1886, and was followed by other organizations, such as the Société d'ethnographie nationale et d'art populaire in 1895, and the Renaissance provinciale in 1906, these too mounting exhibitions of popular folkloric artefacts for both specialized and general audiences. See Peer, *France on Display*; on the growth of geographic societies in France, see Dominique Lejeune, *Les sociétiés de géographie et l'expansion coloniale au XIX siècle (*Paris: Albin Michel, 1993).

11. See Mona and Jacques Ozuf, *"Le Tour de la France par deux enfants:* The Little Red Book of the Republic," in Pierre Nora (ed.), *Realms of Memory*, trans. Arthur Gold-hammer (New York: Columbia University Press, 1992), vol. 2, ch. 4.

12. The Musée d'Ethnographie was created in Paris immediately following the Expo-sition of 1878, permanently to house the Exposition's ethnographic displays, and a Salle de France was added in 1884, specializing in the regional cultures of France, particularly Brittany. Provincial cultural artefacts, particularly costumes, were an even more significant presence at the Exhibitions of 1889 and 1900 in Paris, often presented alongside advertise-ments for regional products and tourist attractions. Peer, *France on Display*, pp. 136–7, 139. On the development of a consumer gaze at the exhibitions, see Thomas Richard, *The Commodity Culture of Victorian England: Advertising and Spectacle, 1851–1914* (Stanford, CA: Stanford University Press, 1990), esp. ch. 2. On Brittany, which was the focus of a large share of the effort at folkloric and historic preservations in these years, see Olier Mordrel, *L'Essence de la Bretagne* (Guipanas: Kelenn, 1977), and Caroline Ford, *Creating the Nation in Provincial France: Religion and Political Identity in Brittany* (Princeton, NJ: Princeton University Press, 1993).

13. *Revue Mensuelle du Touring Club de France* (September 1910), p. 386.

14. For discussion of the economic bases of regionalism, see Charles-Brun, *Le Regional-isme;* William Brustein, *The Social Origins of Political Regionalism, France 1849–1981*

(Berkeley, CA: University of California Press, 1988). Such arguments were especially convincing when applied to the mountain areas of the country – the Alps, the Pyrénées, and the Massif Central – whose ample picturesque and athletic attractions seemed to offer a solution to depopulation and declining economic prospects.

15. TCF Procès-Verbaux, General Assembly (1902), p. 27.

16. *La Route* (February 21, 1909), p. 82.

17. This plan directly mirrored the outlines of the FRF's proposed administrative division of France into discrete regions, each with an urban regional center, serving as an administrative, economic and cultural pole of attraction for the surrounding area, and as a seat for vital local institutions, such as regional assemblies, and universities. The idea was hardly a farfetched one in this period: Auguste Comte, Frédéric Le Play and Georges Vidal de la Blache were only among the more prominent of those who advocated the scheme, seeing in it a better reflection of the "natural" divisions of the country. Peer, *France on Display*, p. 61.

18. While a more common refrain in the 1890s, this was an attitude still expressed in the later part of this period as well; *Revue Mensuelle du Touring Club de France* (March 1907), p. 116.

19. The term is used commonly in this period, but see, for example, *Le Pays de France* (1913), p. 15.

20. That Jules Arren would offer his discussion of railway advertising in his 1914 *Sa Majesté la publicité* under the chapter heading of "How One Launches a Region," suggests the change in the company's orientation. Jules Arren, *Sa Majesté la publicité* (Paris, 1914), p. 115.

21. Eugen Weber makes this point in his chapter "The Hexagon," in Weber, *My France: Politics, Culture, Myth* (Cambridge, MA: Belknap, 1991).

22. Consistent upon this more "territorial" disposition, the Touring Club and many other tourist and sporting advocates asserted the virtues of tourism on bicycle or on foot (as opposed to the train), as more engaging of the terrain, connecting hygienic renewal with the experience of more consciously traversing national territory. This point is made in greater detail in ch. 7 of my dissertation, "The Body Rested, A Class Revived: Tourism, Hygiene and Bourgeois Embodiment, 1890–1914"; *The Consumer as National Subject: Bourgeois Tourism in the French Third Republic, 1890–1914* (dissertation, Colombia University, 1999).

23. Léon Auscher, *Urbanisme et Tourisme* (Paris, 1919), p. 87.

24. *Revue Mensuelle du Touring Club de France* (October 1909), p. 455.

25. The Touring Club would begin referring to "tourisme gastronomique" in this period, though it would develop more fully in the interwar period, as part of the continuing interest in regional cuisine, and regional cultures more generally. See *Revue Mensuelle du Touring Club de France* (April 1910), p. 145, (June 1910), p. 255. Stephen Harp's forthcoming book on Michelin, *Marketing Michelin: A Cultural History of Twentieth Century France,* deals more extensively with interwar regional tourism and gastronomy. Priscilla Ferguson is also currently working on regional gastronomy, as part of a larger project on food, taste and class in modern France.

26. While the small, local *auberge* was often the target of withering critiques by tourist organizers – who lamented their failure to adhere to basic standards of hygiene and comfort, or to be run in line with efficient business practices – neither they nor hotel industry leaders ever wished fully to replace them. The *auberge* remained a potent symbol of regional traditionalism and distinctiveness, and for that reason was a staple of postcard representation in the fin-de-siècle. The tiny local inn was more grounded in local history, and the local

landscape, than the newer hotels, and had the added benefit of suggesting linkages to an earlier period and tradition of travel.

27. A constant refrain, but see, for example, TCF Procès-Verbaux, General Assembly (1903), p. 53.

28. *Revue Mensuelle du Touring Club de France* (April 1911), p. 165.

29. According to Harvey Levenstein's history of American travelers in France, this was still the case in the period under consideration. Foreign tourists would continue to fear voyaging too deeply into the French countryside. H. Levenstein, *Seductive Journeys: American Tourists in France from Jefferson to the Jazz Age* (Chicago: University of Chicago Press, 1998).

30. Jules Michelet, *Tableau de la France* (Paris: Société les Belles Lettres, 1934).

31. For a succinct explication of his "regionalist nationalism," see Vidal de la Blache, "Les Régions Françaises", in *Revue de Paris* (December 15, 1910); see also Jean-Yves Guiomar, "Vidal de la Blache's *Geography in France*," in Nora, *Realms of Memory*, vol. 2, ch. 6.

32. Peer, *France on Display*, p. 63.

33. Vergné, *Conférence faite à Nancy*, p. 16.

34. *Revue Mensuelle du Touring Club de France* (October 1909), p. 454.

35. Léon Auscher, *Des Moyens Propres à développer le Tourisme en France* (Paris, 1912), p. 38.

36. "Le Rôle du village Française dans le tourisme de demain," in *La Renaissance du Tourisme* (January 1918), pp. 3–4

37. *Revue Mensuelle du Touring Club de France* (March 1907), p. 116.

38. On the turn-of-the-century postcard, see J.P. Blazy and D. Guglielmetti, *Le Pays de France en 1900* (Paris Editions du Villemeil, 1992); Serge Zeyons, *La France Paysanne: les années 1900 par la carte postale* (Paris: Larousse, 1992).

39. Earlier representation of both mountains and sea had most often avoided or minimized the human presence, presenting these as places of pathos, desolation and other-worldly magnificence. On representation of the sea, see Corbin, *Lure of the Sea.*

40. *L'Estampe et l'Affiche* (1898), p. 157.

41. Ibid., p. 158.

42. Ibid., p. 160.

43. Ernst Maindron, quoted in *Cent Ans d'Affiches des Chemins de Fer* (Paris: Pierre Belvès, 1981), p. 4.

44. In its profiles of the attractions of rural areas "off the beaten track," the Touring Club often included photographs of local women, at times depicted in their domestic interiors.

45. Impressionist painting offers an interesting point of comparison. T.J. Clark and others have suggested that these paintings' allusions to the industrial world, or to work, in their depictions of scenes of leisure marked a sort of return of the repressed, an indictment of the city's tendency to hide its contradictions beneath the shimmering artificial facades of leisure and leisure space. T.J. Clark, *The Painting of Modern Life: Paris in the Art of Manet and his Followers* (Princeton, NJ: Princeton University Press, 1986); Robert Herbert, *Impressionism: Art, Leisure and Parisian Society* (New Haven, CT: Yale University Press, 1988).

46. J.P. Blazy and D. Guglielmetti, *Le Pays de France en 1900* (Paris: Editions du Villemeil, 1992).

47. These are the terms of the analysis in James Buzard, *The Beaten Track: European Tourism, Literature, and the Ways to Culture, 1800–1918* (Oxford: Clarendon, 1993).

48. *Revue Mensuelle du Touring Club de France* (May 1903), p. 217.

49. Ibid., p. 216.

50. *Le Tour de France, Guide de Touriste* (May 1904), p. 21

51. Ibid., p. 21.

52. *Revue Mensuelle du Touring Club de France* (May 1903), p. 216.

53. Albert Danzat, *Pour Qu'On Voyage: essai sur l'Art de Bien Voyager* (Paris, 1911), pp. 101–2.

54. Ibid., p. 70.

55. The club in fact embraced a military and colonial demeanour – as well as the military as an institution and colonialism as a project – in its quest to build membership and a distinctive *esprit de corps*. The Club had an insignia, and an official uniform as well, and it was customary for leaders and members to slip into military and colonial metaphors when describing themselves and their work.

56. A. Martin, *Les Etapes d'un Touriste en France* (1897), p. vi.

57. Ibid., p. viii.

58. Ibid., p. viii.

59. For discussion of the animating myths of French politics and national culture, see Weber, *My France;* Olier Mordrel, *Le Mythe de l'hexagon* (Paris: Editions Jean Picolles 1981); Raoul Girardet, *Mythes et mythologies politiques* (Paris, 1989); my interpretation draws upon all three.

60. Tourist landscapes, in particular, lent themselves to this type of national myth-making, conferring, in their presumed pre- or transhistoricity, an eternal and transcendent quality to the principle of French nationhood. As simultaneously eternal and national, French landscapes transcended the contestation which had traditionally accompanied all attempts at defining *la nation*, conferring upon the national principle a permanence which French institutions could only imperfectly embody.

61. Weber, "The Hexagon," in *My France.*

62. Guiomar, "Vidal de la Blache's *Geography in France*," in Nora, *Realms of Memory*, vol. 2, p. 204.

63. *Revue Mensuelle du Touring Club de France* (December 1902), p. 549.

64. *Revue Mensuelle du Touring Club de France* (September 1910), pp. 387–8. One of the main projects of the TCF and syndicates d'initiative was the hygienic renovation of the small towns and villages of the countryside, as well as of local hotels, with the aim of prompting local governments to undertake hygienic reforms which would make them more accessible to the modern tourist.

65. *Revue Mensuelle du Touring Club de France* (September 1910), p. 387

10

The Michelin Red Guides: Social Differentiation in Early-Twentieth-Century French Tourism

Stephen L. Harp

Leisure cannot be separated from the work presumed to be its opposite, or the society in which both work and leisure take place. Similarly, tourism, that oft-supposed escape from work, actually mirrors the social segmentation of who does what kind of work for whom. When some social groups work while others tour, the relationship between those working and those touring seems to reflect the broader social structure. In the early twentieth century, just as poor women washed sheets by hand and poor male servants drove carriages in the city for wealthy men and women, so too did early automobile tourism to the country often include a male chauffeur as well as a hotel where the sheets had been cleaned and food prepared by the maid or modest proprietress. Early tourism by car, like the leisure that made it possible, neither created nor erased social distinctions but instead reformulated them in a changing context.

In a cultural sense, the very technological changes that facilitated automobile tourism may well have necessitated a desire to reaffirm existing notions of class and gender, lest the automobile be seen as challenging the social status quo, as many early critics of the automobile charged.[1] Certainly, a new form of transport among tourists did have the potential for altering assumptions about the differences between the urban bourgeoisie and the rural peasantry, between men and women, and between the rich and the poor, but it also had at least as much potential for merely shoring up the status quo, defining that presumed status quo in the process. To the extent that early advocates for tourism articulated the continued existence of important social distinctions unchanged by automobile tourism, they served to make those distinctions into real ones. As work in cultural history has made clear for two decades now, the existence of "real" social differences in modern Europe resulted as much from people's perceptions of such differences as from any occupational or economic standard such as one's profession or relative wealth.[2]

This chapter, tied to a book-length study of how the Michelin company both reflected and defined cultural assumptions in twentieth-century France, traces the origin and development of the Michelin red guides in the early twentieth century with an eye for how Michelin expected tourists to see themselves.[3] Before the First World War, like the Touring Club de France, the large non-profit association that promoted tourism in France, Michelin affirmed both implicitly and explicitly that men who toured by automobile were a veritable club of brothers-in-arms, in control of their cars, their itineraries, and their families. Michelin managed to rearticulate the nineteenth-century notion of separate spheres for women and men to accommodate automobile tourism. On the one hand, Michelin's assumptions appeared inclusive and almost solidarist; upper-middle-class and aristocratic men were encouraged to see themselves as forming a large, interrelated family working together for the good of all, and even for the good of France.[4] On the other, it was exclusive; women and those who could not afford a car were subordinate. In the interwar years, as the company began to advocate mass ownership of automobiles and as the number of automobile tourists did slowly grow to include a greater swath of the French bourgeoisie, the red guide and the few advertisements for it lost the earlier explicit references to class and gender without necessarily losing the potential to reaffirm social distinctions. Gastronomy, so closely associated with the Michelin guide by the 1930s, allowed readers to put themselves into an exclusive group of fellow diners, excluding those who could only dream of meals in France's best restaurants. The distinctions among social groups were increasingly implicit, resulting from the structure of gastronomic tourism itself. This did not necessarily mean the erasure of culturally constructed social differences so much as it meant that the lines of social distinction became harder to see because they became embedded not in whether one got to travel, but where one could afford to eat while traveling.

In 1900, Michelin published its first *Guide Michelin* to France. Containing 399 thin pages with small print and a red cover, and measuring approximately 3¼ by 6 inches, the guide was designed to slip easily into a tourist's pocket. The preface noted that "this work desires to give all information that can be useful to a driver, traveling in France, to supply [the needs of] his automobile, to repair it, and to permit him to find a place to stay and eat, and to correspond by mail, telegraph, or telephone."[5] Although the guide itself focused on these simple facts, the company optimistically articulated its larger vision. "This work appears with the century; it will last as long. Automobiles have just been born; they will develop each year and the pneumatic tire will develop with them, because the tire is the essential organ without which the automobile cannot go."[6] Offering the guide free of charge, the company recognized that by encouraging automobile travel, it promoted the consumption of tires.

Michelin announced in this first guide that an updated version would be published each year, allowing the guide to evolve with the needs of motorists. In the first edition, the fueling and repairing of patently unreliable early automobiles were the most pressing needs, so the contents were overwhelmingly technical, more so than in any subsequent editions. The guide of 1900 included three parts. In the first section (pp. 17–50), the company described in excruciating detail how to use tires, how to inflate them, how to change the tire tube (*la chambre à air*), how to reinstall the tube, how to change the tire (*l'enveloppe*), how to request that Michelin do repairs at the factory, and how to do one's own repairs, both of automobile and of bicycle tires. Abundant drawings in black and white illustrated the various parts of the tire with the appropriate terminology. Early tires, and the valve stem apparatus in particular, were technically quite complicated, and the tubes and tires were fragile enough that mishandling was a serious concern. The first section also included a comprehensive list of all *stockistes*, the tire dealers that had contracted with Michelin to carry a full line of Michelin products (*les stocks*), divided into summer (May 1–October 1) and winter depots. In all, forty-eight French cities had *stockistes* in the summer, while there were only six that remained open all year, not including Michelin's plant in Clermont-Ferrand or its offices in Paris. Not surprisingly, the six open all year (Biarritz, Bordeaux, Lille, Marseille, Nice, and Pau), with the exception of Lille, were in the south, where a portion of the upper bourgeoisie and French aristocracy went for the winter social season.[7]

The second section (pp. 54–280) listed French cities and towns alphabetically. Here too the focus was mostly technical, with hotels reduced to one among many necessities while traveling, and restaurants separate from hotels received no mention at all. The only two criteria for a town's inclusion in the list was whether it possessed a mechanic or a place to buy gasoline.[8] In the early days of the automobile, before the installation of actual gasoline stations, gasoline was purchased in 2, 5, or 10 liter containers in small groceries (*épiceries*) and hardware stores (*quincailleries*) as frequently as in repair shops or bicycle dealers. Michelin listed such establishments as well as the brand of gasoline sold, be it Automobiline, Stelline, Motonaphta, or "other gasolines."[9] Above all, the list noted the address and phone number of the Michelin *stockistes* and of mechanics. For the thirteen provincial cities with rudimentary maps, the locations of hotels, mechanics, Michelin *stockistes*, the railroad station, and places to buy gas were all marked on the maps. The third section (pp. 281–344) included practical information about the rules of the road, taxes assessed on automobiles, information about maps, and a bibliography of tourist guides. This last section also included advertisements from various French automobile and auto part manufacturers with long descriptions of how to use and to install their products. At the end of the guide, the company also had a calendar, so that the motorist might keep track of days of the week and holidays, sunrises, sunsets, the moon, distances traveled, the consumption of gasoline and oil, as well as how much was spent on these.

Although historical accounts have focused on the vision and ingenuity of Michelin in producing the first guide,[10] the company's primary contribution was in building a better mousetrap (at least from the perspective of people traveling by automobile) and rebuilding an ever better one with each successive edition of the guide. Completely overlooked by everyone who has even briefly praised Michelin's first red guide is the extent to which Michelin borrowed both its format and much of its information from the *annuaires*, or directories, published by the Touring Club de France (TCF) in the 1890s. While Michelin did introduce the inclusion of its *stockistes*, of places to buy gas, and of city maps, the TCF pioneered the comprehensive list of mechanics. Lists of hotels had long been a mainstay of both Baedeker guides to France and Guides Joanne, and the TCF included them in its *annuaires*. Michelin's genius was in adapting the TCF's focus on information useful for motorists and in quickly altering the red guides to keep pace with the changing conditions of automobile travel.

The Touring Club published its first *annuaire* in 1891, listing its leaders and regular members with their addresses. The *annuaire* also included a short list of towns with hotels that had offered the TCF guaranteed prices for meals and a room in addition to a short list of towns with mechanics. As the membership grew, the TCF could not list all members, shifting its focus to practical tourist information for its members.[11] By 1899, that is the year before the first Michelin guide, the TCF's *annuaire* (gray in color, of approximately the same dimensions as the first red guide; the TCF's special *annuaire* for motorists sported a red cover) featured a list of French cities and towns with the number of inhabitants, the department in which each was located, whether it was the seat of a canton, subprefecture, or prefecture, whether it had a train station, a post office, a telegraph office, each of which was represented with a symbol to save space in the list. Both the items and the symbols were exactly duplicated in the first Michelin guide. Moreover, the Michelin guide used distinctions established by the TCF in evaluating mechanics. Claiming that Michelin's close relationship with mechanics, who often made decisions about what kind of tires to stock and to install on automobiles, precluded the firm's objectivity, the Michelin red guide merely listed whether a given mechanic had met the TCF's certification procedure for minor or major repair jobs.[12]

Initially, Michelin's listing of hotels differed markedly from that of the Touring Club. Although Michelin included essentially the same hotels as the Touring Club, Michelin did not – unlike the TCF – guarantee exact prices in 1900. Instead, Michelin had three categories of hotels, but the categories suggested price ranges; and they did not vouch for the quality of the accommodations. Hotels marked with three asterisks in the guide were those where an average room, candle (for lighting before widespread use of electricity), and three meals including wine cost 13 or more francs daily. Hotels with two asterisks offered the same items for 10–13 francs, and those with one asterisk charged less than 10 francs.[13] After a hotel's listing, the notation ACF indicated that it was a place recommended by the Automobile Club de France, whereas the notation TCF indicated that it was a hotel where TCF members received the 10 percent discount negotiated by the organization on behalf of its members.

Michelin's guide most resembled the work of the Touring Club in its appeal for readers to assist in correcting and improving the guide, making a plea reminiscent not only of such appeals in the Baedekers and Guides Joanne but especially of the Touring Club de France's constant calls for joining hands (*se serrer les coudes*) in order to work together. As Michelin put it, "The present edition . . . will inevitably be considered very imperfect, but the work will improve each year; it will be perfect as quickly as drivers respond carefully and in the largest number to the questionnaire we are asking them to fill out . . . Without them, we are capable of *nothing*; with them, we can do *anything* [emphases in the original]."[14] Like the TCF, Michelin also began to establish a certain control over mechanics and especially hotel owners. Already in 1899, the TCF had worked out an elaborate system for insuring that its members were not taken by mechanics and hotels. TCF mechanics accepted a price list of maximum prices for routine automobile and tire repair; those mechanics overcharging were then purged from the list. In return for a listing in the TCF *annuaire*, hotel owners made even more concessions. Hotel owners promised to offer a 10 percent discount to all TCF members. Moreover, the TCF made hotel owners guarantee the published price of room and board, including wine, for the duration of the year.

Michelin solicited readers' help in several domains, asking them to send comments to the company. First, readers were supposed to check Michelin's calculations of the distances between towns, which always appeared in the guides. Second, readers were to report any absences from the stock of Michelin products that *stockistes* had committed to carry. Third, any mechanics listed who were not good or who were good but not listed needed to be reported to the company. Fourth, readers were asked to report whether the sellers of gas actually carried gas. Fifth, Michelin wanted readers to write with any information about mechanics who could charge electric cars. Finally, Michelin wished to exercise oversight of hotel owners by ensuring that readers did not pay more than the averages reported by the hotel owners. Readers were asked to provide specific details, "particularly whether there are bedbugs," in a given hotel.[15] Michelin, like the TCF, assured readers that their corrections would be acted upon with rigor.

We promise to purge without pity any hotels that [drivers] report as having inadequate meals, rooms, toilets, or service; and poorly stocked gas dealers [Nous promettons de rayer impitoyablement de nos listes tous les hôtels dont ils nous signaleront comme défectueux la table, la chambre, les W.C., le service; les dépôts d'essence mal approvisionnés].[16]

Along with corrections, the company asked for drivers to supply information about themselves, their car, and their tire brand, allowing for early market research as well as improvements to the guide. The company then promised that people writing in with corrections would have the guidebook mailed directly to their homes in 1901, signaling the importance of driver participation in the improvement of the Michelin guides.

Drivers' assistance remained a constant theme. In 1901, Michelin told clients what would happen if they avoided sending in corrections for the guide. If no one reports back, "Monsieur" will find himself entrusting his car to a mechanic who damages it instead of fixing it. "Madame" will exit the hotel covered with "little brown marks as disagreeable in odor as cannibalistic [referring to bedbugs]."[17] Similarly, the 1902 guide reminded the reader that Michelin would remove mention in the guide of any poorly kept hotel, having bedbugs or making people with the Michelin guide pay to park their car, an equally serious sin for a company preoccupied with encouraging automobile tourism.[18] Michelin quite articulately appealed to drivers' sense of belonging to a larger, though exclusive, group that needed to stick together against predatory hotel owners. Urban tourists with cars could rely on each other, via Michelin, to protect themselves against provincials who might otherwise take advantage of them.

Michelin appealed entirely to men, whom it assumed planned the trip, drove the car, and used the guidebook, thus asserting turn-of-the-century gender roles while reinforcing them. Michelin exploited the image of the family and men's sense of patriarchy in this patriarchal society. "Yes, you like [the guide] very much . . . like those weak parents who do not correct their children because the sight of tears gives them an attack of nerves . . . *Drivers, the Michelin Guide must be your work. Please don't be easy on it [ne ménagez pas votre peine] for the sake of the Guide* [emphasis in the original]." Little distinguished the indulgence of parents from that of readers. More to the point, Michelin's prescribed parenting was gender specific.

> You are all part of the same big family. More than any other, [the family] needs its members to practice the motto *All for one and one for all*. In particular, you *fathers [pères de famille]* give [the guide] to *your sons* during your vacation. Have them go through the details. Let those young brains so taken with novelties come up with an original idea [for improvement of the guides]. *Thus you will have well served the cause of motoring.*[19] [emphases in the original]

The Michelin guide of 1905 included a postcard to make the process easier, so that the driver might "serve all of his *brothers in motoring [frères en automobile]* [italics in the original]."[20] The language was unmistakable; not only were men in control of their families as well as their cars, but also motoring itself was construed as a brotherhood, *une fraternité* of equals for which sons might be prepared. For wives and daughters the calculations of distance would presumably prove taxing and irrelevant given their designated stations in life.

   Over time, the Michelin guide gave increasing importance to accommodations over technical matters. In addition to more maps, more *stockistes*, more mechanics, and more information generally, hotels became a focal point for improvement. Beginning in 1902, the guide included a questionnaire that a hotel owner wishing to be listed needed to fill out and send back to Michelin in Paris. The questions reveal annals about the assumptions of early urban bourgeois tourists in the French countryside as well as about Michelin's efforts to control hotel owners, an effort that complemented the TCF's own rigorous work. The Michelin questionnaire reads:

1. Is your hotel open all year?
2. How much should an automobile tourist expect to spend daily at your hotel?
    –   for an average room including service and lighting?
    –   for breakfast in the morning?
    –   for lunch?
    –   for dinner?
        (Specify if wine is *compris*)
3. Do you offer TCF members a reduction of 10 percent?
4. Do you have hygienic rooms [*chambres hygiéniques*] in the TCF style?
5. Does your establishment have a bathroom?
6. Do you have advanced WCs [*des WCs perfectionnés*]? (We call advanced WCs those that are equipped with water flush mechanisms with mobile seat, and of which the walls are covered in tile or earthenware, kept in extreme cleanliness and always equipped with toilet paper).
7. Do you have a dark room for photography?
    –   Does it have a red light, basins, and water?
8. Do you have in the hotel itself a covered garage?
    –   Is it completely closed/locked [*fermé*]?
9. Do you make people pay for the garage? How much?
    –   Do you agree to let people with the Michelin guide park for free?
        (The only hotels listed in our guide agree to this condition)
10. Do you have a repair pit [*une fosse à réparations*] in the hotel?
11. Do you have a stock of gas *in the hotel*?
12. Do you have *in the hotel* a source of electric energy that would permit motorists to recharge an electric car? Or only batteries for lights [*accumulateurs d'allumage*]? Do you know of any in your town? What is the address? What are the prices?
13. Do you have an intercity telephone? What is the number?

14. Do you have a telegraph number? What is it?
15. What are the sights [*curiosités*] to be seen in your town? (attach a page)
16. What are the interesting excursions to make nearby? (attach a page)[21]

In order to assure the honesty of the hotel owner, two members of the Automobile Club de France, or if there were no local ACF members, two members of the TCF, needed to attest to the accuracy of the hotel's responses.

The questionnaire reveals the centrality of care of the automobile for early automobile tourists. Electric cars needed to be recharged and drivers of gasoline-powered cars needed to ensure the supply of gasoline. Before many automobiles were enclosed, a covered garage was useful, and given the value of cars, a locked garage a reassurance. Early cars were unreliable enough that a repair pit, a hole in the floor that allowed one to get underneath the car, might also prove handy.

The other most pressing questions concerned the level of accommodations. Michelin continued to list the average prices of a room until 1908 and needed to verify them. At a time when a bathtub was not taken for granted, the company needed a specific statement that one was present. Tourists' growing expectations for hotels centered, however, on the WC. Although specific information about the WCs in a hotel had not been part of the first Michelin guide or the early TCF *annuaires*, WCs were important enough to merit detailed questions by 1902. In this instance, the red guide reflects the preoccupations of an urban French bourgeoisie which was increasingly adopting new hygienic standards and bemoaning the lack of them among rural hotel owners.

Here too Michelin fit squarely within a larger tourist movement, picking up on the Touring Club's own obsession with toilets at the turn of the century. In the late 1890s, the regular articles in the *Revue mensuelle* of the TCF focused frequently on WCs. In 1896, an article complained that either the installation or the maintenance of WCs was inadequate, even when they were present. In 1897, Emile Gautier called for "a crusade" in the pages of the review. Implicitly equating provincials without WCs with natives in the colonies, Gautier claimed that "cleanliness is an indication of progress, a sign of civilization. All savages are dirty," whereas "all civilized people are clean." Europeans were supposed to know better. "How many individuals, how many cities [*cités*, which could imply a place where workers in particular lived], in the heart of our European societies, so proud of their prodigious flowering that have not yet picked themselves up from the apathy of barbarian races!" He was convinced that the English provided the model for improvement, "one knows that the English people, at least those of the cultivated elite, are the cleanest race in the world: it is noteworthy [*piquant*] to observe that it is also one of the most powerful, one whose influence is simultaneously the most widespread, the most profound, and the most solid." There was, however, cause for hope. The French could go beyond English standards of cleanliness; to do so, France required a "national league," and that league was the TCF, which would lead the crusade for WCs for the sake of the French nation. "It is a crusade to undertake. To succeed, one need only want it. The Touring-Club wants it. It will thus have deserved [praise not only] from the nation [*patrie*] but from humanity. So be it!"[22] Regularly thereafter, the TCF reported on the progress of equipping hotels with WCs. In 1899, it provided drawings of WCs that it offered for sale to hotel owners, according them a 25 percent reduction over the retail price with the difference covered by the TCF.[23] Toilet paper was similarly subsidized to encourage its adoption. The TCF even showed its model toilets at the Universal Exposition held in Paris in 1900 along with an entire "hygienic [hotel] room."[24]

In the pages of the TCF's *Revue*, the WC became identified with tourism generally and the attendant economic progress of France. In an era of growing nationalism, the TCF often deployed nationalist arguments in favor of its members' personal interests. In 1901, an article in the *Revue* entitled, "The Defense of National Interests," reminded readers that "France is both better gifted [in touristic treasures] and worse served than most of her neighbors."[25] WCs were key to the salvation of France because they helped to make French hotels competitive with those of other countries. As H. Berthe wrote in the *Revue*, "We should thus consider the hotel industry not as a private enterprise, but as an essentially national work, destined to raise up in large measure the intellectual level of diverse social classes [he does not indicate how] and to contribute powerfully to the financial prosperity of the country [*pays*]."[26] Thus, clean toilets in hotels could improve overall hygienic standards of lower classes while bringing in money that would enrich France as a whole. Nationalism was a convenient mental fig leaf to hide bourgeois self-interest in having hygienic accommodations, a much-vaunted hygiene that separated themselves not only from "natives" in the colonies but also from those in the provinces. Hotels, and the WCs in them, were supposedly crucial to the economic future of France. André Michelin, who ran the firm's advertising, was quite attuned to trends in the world of tourism and arguments for it; he no doubt realized the importance of WCs for rich French tourists in the first decade of the twentieth century, hence the preoccupation of the red guides.

Advertisements for the red guides further exploited the new focus on hygiene with the gendered notion that men, the providers, needed to supply a comfortable, hygienic place to stay for women, the presumed consumers. In one telling newspaper advertisement, Michelin recounted the story of newlyweds traveling without a red guide. After the chauffeur informed them that a mechanical break-down would leave them stranded overnight, the Viscount René de la Ribaudière (a name suggesting bawdiness) and Giselle, his new wife (the text notes that "she was not yet [really] the countess"), got a room in a hotel that was, according to the owner, "the best in the region." They then sat down to eat.

Although the newlyweds were more preoccupied with their first evening together rather than with dinner, they did however notice that the food was abominable. They could not even finish their dinner before retiring to their room . . . [After encountering a bat] it took a quarter of an hour and all of the eloquence that M. de la Ribaudière had in order to calm down Giselle. However the little viscount did not waste any time, and he quickly addressed his very imminent wife [*sa très prochaine femme*] the most legitimate compliments on the beauty of her legs and the finesse of her ankles, when suddenly he cried out in distress. "Ah! my God, what is the matter?" Giselle asked him. "Nothing, I . . . [elipses in original], but you my darling, where did you get this bit of red on your shoulder which was so white a moment ago?" The same exclamation came out of both of their mouths, "Bed bugs" . . . They killed 10, then 100, then 577; they could not have fought off the yellow invasion with more ardor. Finally, overtaken by sleep, Giselle resigned herself to stretching out on her uncomfortable and hard bed. And the viscount wanted to begin the conversation again. "Oh, no, my dear," she told him; "we are both way too ugly [nous sommes bien trop vilains tous les deux!]" . . . When the sun rose, Giselle was still not yet Madame de la Ribaudière, though she looked like cream with strawberries [that is, her cream-colored skin had red marks resembling strawberries].[27]

By playing on the notion of a legal consummation of the marriage, Michelin could politely make the point that the viscount, however desperately he may have tried, did not get to have sex with his new wife because he had not ordered a copy of the red guide, so he did not realize there was a fine hotel nearby. The idea, no more unfamiliar to an early-twentieth-century reader than to a late-twentieth-century adolescent one, that men wanted sex and delicate women were more reluctant, was thus confirmed. Having not fulfilled his role as good provider, the viscount could not fulfill his role as a man in the act of sex. Thus, the red guide – which began ostensibly as a list of mechanics and places to buy gas – could assert certain assumptions about the appropriate behavior of men and women in French society: men were supposed to take care of the practical details while traveling, by buying a red guide and handling the chauffeur, and women were to worry about their appearance.

In 1908, Michelin completely reorganized its presentation of hotels, eliminating some of the uncertainty of the earlier rating system. Rather than divide the hotels by the average price of daily room and board as had been done since 1900, the guide began to place hotels in one of five categories from "the most sumptuous palace to the good village inn," thus admitting that the better and cleaner hotels might cost less. Then, as the Touring Club had done since the late 1890s, Michelin engaged listed hotels to set a minimum price for each room and each meal, prices that anyone possessing the Michelin guide would be charged. Thus the tourist knew in advance how much room and board should cost in a given hotel and could ask Michelin to intervene should the hotel not honor the published prices. The move removed the uncertainty for the tourist, that urbanite alone in the provinces, and continued to provide free advertising for the hotel, while reinforcing tourists' collective control over the latter.[28]

In the years before the war, the Michelin red guides became a major marketing device for the company. Print runs climbed from 35,000 for the 1900 edition, to 52,815 in 1901, to 70,000 in 1911, and 86,000 in 1912.[29] The 1900 edition contained 400 pages with 13 city maps, the 1901 edition 600 pages with 80 city maps, the 1912 edition with 757 pages and approximately 600 city maps.[30] The guide received a hard cover, so that it would hold up better, and it took on a larger format, reaching by 1912 the rough dimensions of late-twentieth-century red guides. Although tourist sights, or *curiosités* as both the Touring Club and Michelin consistently called them, were listed as one-line entries under the nearest city, the red guides did not provide any significant details about those sights, leaving to the Joanne, Baedeker, and TCF tourist guides the determination of what needed to be seen in France and why. Michelin did, however, expand the approach of the red guides beyond France just as it had expanded its tire production and sales outside France. By 1912, Michelin published guides to the British Isles, the Alps, and Rhineland (northern Italy, Switzerland, Tyrol, Bavaria, southern Württemberg, the Rhineland, Belgium, the Netherlands, and Luxembourg), *Les pays du soleil* (Algeria, Tunisia, Egypt, southern Italy, Corsica, and the Riviera), Spain and Portugal, and Germany in several different languages. In 1912 Michelin boasted that the combined international and French distribution of guides had totaled 1,286,375 between 1900 and 1912. The staff had the responsibility for more than 1,300 city maps.[31]

After the First World War, as improved roads and better road signs made France increasingly accessible by car, there was a commensurate expansion in the number of hotels, inns, and restaurants catering to automobile tourists. In addition, tires themselves required less specialized knowledge on the part of the driver because the number of *stockistes* who could repair and replace tires increased, tires lasted longer, and they were easier to change. In 1912, the guide had over 600 pages, 62 of which concerned tires. By 1927, however, the first section of the guide devoted to changing tires included only 5 pages, out of 990 total. The prewar guide to hotels and *stockistes* quickly became a guide to hotels and especially restaurants. The company continued to claim that it was at the service of the client, but these elite clients' perceived needs changed considerably after the First World War. Gastronomy, often claimed to have undergone a renewal before and just after the war, soon became the veritable *raison d'être* of the Michelin guide. Gastronomy itself, once the preserve of royalty and the aristocracy, had become widely accessible to wealthy bourgeois eating in restaurants in the nineteenth century. As the notion of regional gastronomy, by definition in the provinces, grew in the interwar years, Michelin adapted the guide to meet tourists' perceived desires.[32] In the process, the company avoided overt references to class or wealth at a time when automobile use exploded in France, but the guide itself offered a new stratification. In one sense, access to fine eating establishments was rationalized and even democratized to the extent that good contacts or membership in an exclusive gastronomic club were no longer necessary to locate and dine in restaurants reputed to be the best in France. In another sense, the stratification took a new twist. Only the filthy rich could actually afford a three-star restaurant. For the less well-off, but nevertheless bourgeois in interwar France, the guide offered the spectacle of the rich and famous, revealing where they ate and what they ate there.

Despite the reduction of pages devoted to narrow, technical information, the overall size of the guides grew considerably. From 399 pages in 1900, to 774 in 1922, to 1,022 (not including maps) in 1929, and to 1,107 in 1939. The numbers of *stockistes* and garages grew. More towns received a listing, and more of those with listings had a map. The number of hotels and later restaurants grew as did prefatory information about how to use the complicated abbreviations of the guide, which were designed to save space. At the same time, advertising, except for Michelin tires, tire-changing equipment, guides to the battlefields, regional guidebooks, maps, and golfballs, disappeared entirely.

In the meantime, the company began charging 7 francs for the guides to France in 1920, a price that grew with interwar inflation to 10 francs in 1925 (about twice the price of a decent hotel room, equalling approximately five hours of work of a provincial worker earning the average wage),[33] 20 francs in 1928, 25 francs in 1933, and 30 francs in 1939. Although Alain Jemain has reported the company's version of the pricing strategy to be the result of André Michelin's trips to garages where he found Michelin guides used to prop up a work bench and André's assertion that people respect only what they pay for, the new pricing coincided with the guide's increased focus on hotels and restaurants, rather than information about Michelin tires.[34] Initially, people appear to have bought fewer guides than they had accepted gratis. Whereas Michelin had printed 75,000 in 1919 and 90,000 in 1920, the company printed only 60,000 in 1922 (no guide appeared in 1921 because of the firm's preoccupation with producing guides to the battlefields).[35] The number printed climbed in the late 1920s and 1930s. Between 1926 and 1939, Michelin sold approximately 1,340,000 guides to France, just under 100,000 yearly on average.[36] Although these numbers were quite high compared with the press runs of moderately popular novels, for which the average printing was about 15,000 copies in the early 1920s, they paled in comparison with those of Michelin's own interwar pamphlets, which ranged in several cases from 500,000 to 1 million copies, and with the sales of maps, which totalled 33,300,000 from 1926 to 1945.[37]

The major innovation of interwar guidebooks was their inclusion of restaurants. Before the war, the price of board (*pension*), as well as the room, was included for hotels, but in a period before there were many restaurants in provincial France, the guide had no category for restaurants per se. In 1923, the Michelin guide began to include restaurants. "In a certain number of important cities where the tourist might stop simply to have a meal, we have noted the restaurants that have been indicated as serving good food [nous avons indiqué des restaurants qui nous ont été signalés comme faisant de la bonne cuisine]." They were as follows:

***   Restaurants de premier ordre [First-class restaurants]
**   Restaurants moyens [Average restaurants]
*   Restaurants modestes [Modest restaurants][38]

Michelin thus began ranking restaurants at the same time that it began to list them, much as it already listed hotels by level of comfort and amenities. From the outset the company thus took for granted a notion widespread in interwar France; there was a clear hierarchy of restaurants in France and elsewhere, one that could be discerned and reported to the traveling public. It was not, however, clear in 1923 what the relative weights of the surroundings versus the quality of the food were in the determination of the rankings. As interesting, while soliciting information from guide users to perfect the list, Michelin distanced itself from these initial rankings with the passive construction, "qui nous ont été signalé," implying that Michelin was doing little more than repeating reports it had received.

The Michelin system evolved rapidly in the interwar years. In 1925, the company instituted five categories for restaurants, which corresponded closely with the gradations established for hotels. The introduction to the rankings was the same as in 1923, including that passive expression "qui nous ont été signalés comme faisant de la bonne cuisine":

...   Restaurants de tout premier ordre – grand luxe
         [First-class restaurants – real luxury]
..   Restaurants de très belle apparence – cuisine recherchée
         [Well-appointed restaurants – meticulous cuisine]
.   Restaurants renommés pour leur table [Restaurants renowned for their food]
**   Restaurants moyens [Average restaurants]
*   Restaurants simples, mais bien tenus [Simple but well-maintained restaurants].[39]

In the meantime, hotels "possédant une table renommée [possessing renowned cuisine]" received a single star or, in 1927, a diamond.[40] That is, hotels were ranked by their level of comfort, but then received an additional notation if their food was considered particularly good. In 1927, the stars with periods denoting restaurants were replaced with small diamonds, ranging from five diamonds to one, but the five categories remained the same.[41] By 1929, the tiny stars and periods had returned, and the five categories were also maintained.[42]

The 1930s brought even more changes, most notably distinctions among hotels and between the appearance of the restaurant and the food. In 1931, the guide abandoned its earlier distancing from its own rankings and noted that

> in our earlier editions a single sign (*) pointed out the hotels where the cuisine was particularly carefully prepared. Pushing that precision farther, we now distinguish:
>
> | * | hôtel ayant une cuisine de très bonne qualité |
> |---|---|
> | | [hotel having a cuisine of very good quality] |
> | ** | hôtel ayant une cuisine d'excellente qualité |
> | | [hotel having a cuisine of excellent quality] |
> | *** | hôtel ayant une cuisine fine et justement renommée |
> | | [hotel having a fine and justly well-renowned cuisine][43] |

The guide thus made a clear distinction between the comforts provided by a hotel and the quality of its food. Michelin also altered its earlier five categories of restaurants and offered a separate ranking of the quality of the restaurants' cuisine, thus instituting the company's famous system of stars. The references to cuisine disappeared from the five categories denoting a restaurant's comfort:

> Restaurants de tout premier ordre – grand luxe
> [First-class restaurants – real luxury]
> Restaurants de grand confort moderne [Very comfortable, modern restaurants]
> Restaurants très confortables [Very comfortable restaurants]
> Restaurants moyens [Average restaurants]
> Restaurants simples [Simple restaurants][44]

At the same time, restaurants, like hotels, would be ranked by the quality of their food:

> | * | Cuisine de très bonne qualité |
> |---|---|
> | ** | Cuisine d'excellente qualité |
> | *** | Cuisine fine et justement renommée.[45] |

Henceforth, the specialty of the restaurant or hotel, which sometimes coincided with the very regional specialties being inventoried by the Touring Club and Curnonsky, that interwar *prince des gastronomes*, would also be listed under the institution's entry in the guide.[46] A sign of the extent to which the Michelin guide was designed for Parisians visiting the provinces was the fact that it was only in 1933, after provincial establishments had been ranked, that the cuisine of Parisian institutions (and not just their level of creature comforts) was subjected to the Michelin stars.[47]

By 1933, Michelin's system of stars for restaurants and hotels serving food was in place. In the course of the 1930s, further changes established the broad contours of Michelin's rating system. The guide of 1939, the last before World War II, maintained the separate ratings for the comforts of hotels and restaurants and the assessment of the quality of their food. Moreover, the three stars remained, though the explanations stressed that the tourist was traveling for the sake of food, a fundamental part of seeing the regions of France by the interwar years:

> *** Une des meilleures tables de France; vaut le voyage
> [One of the best cuisines in France; worth the trip]
> ** Table excellente; mérite un détour
> [Excellent cuisine; worth a detour]
> * Une bonne table dans la localité
> [Good cuisine in the area].[48]

In the 1930s, the company vouched for its ratings, no longer attributing them to others' assessments. Michelin did, however, qualify the awarding of stars, pointing out the conditions under which the ratings should be used. For establishments with "* and **: We have first taken into account the **price of the meal** [bold in the original]." That is, the stars indicated a better meal for the price one would pay at another local restaurant. Accepting widespread early-twentieth-century French notions that some regions simply had "better" food than others, the guide noted that

> Certain regions . . . such as the Lyonnais, are traditionally regions of fine dining [régions de bonne chère]. Wherever the motorist stops, he is more or less sure of finding a good meal. The stars thus indicate "what is better among the good."

Other regions are less well provided for:

> a meal any old place [au petit bonheur] risks being mediocre. In an establishment with a star, one has a better chance of "eating better." One can even eat very well there. For the same price, **one must not then do a comparison except among establishments of the same region** [bold in the original].

Only the three-star restaurants escaped this relative assessment:

it is a matter of cuisine "without rival," [they are] the flower of French cuisine [Il s'agit de tables "hors classe," la fleur de la cuisine française]. Whatever the region, everything must be perfect: food, wine, service. There is no longer a question of price.[49]

Michelin clearly assumed and defined a hierarchy of cuisine both among restaurants and among French regions. By the late 1930s, several introductory pages in the guide were devoted to gastronomic maps of France in which towns with a three-star restaurant were in bold, capital letters, those with a two-star restaurant in large font, and those with a one-star restaurant in small font. The maps allowed a tourist to plan an itinerary, a veritable *tour de la France gastronomique*, around the meals that might be consumed. For the very well-heeled *gastronomes*, the longstanding importance of the gastronomic voyage on *routes nationales* 6 and 7 from Paris to the French Riviera was confirmed: in 1939, with the exception of Bordeaux and Annecy, every town or city with a three-star restaurant was on or near the axis from Paris to the French Riviera. Regions well represented with one- and two-star restaurants were many of the usual tourist destinations: Alsace, Brittany, Normandy, the Loire valley, the Lyonnais, the Pyrenees, and the French Riviera.[50] Large sections of northern and south-central France were apparently bereft of any fine French cuisine.

Under the individual restaurants and hotels, Michelin recommended the special dishes and wines at some restaurants receiving at least one star, and very frequently at those receiving three stars. At the pinnacle of French cuisine were those restaurants with three stars, which served traditional French, but not usually distinctive regional, dishes. While restaurants recommended for their regional dishes, such as those in Brittany and Alsace, could make it into the ranks of one-star restaurants, in 1939 not one had three stars and only a couple had two stars. That is, regional gastronomy was a fundamental part of French gastronomy more generally, but it had little hope of reaching the top, where the restaurants of Paris, and to a lesser extent Lyon, largely served the classic dishes from the early nineteenth century and before. In the provinces, the one- and sometimes two-star restaurants usually served the regional specialties inventoried by the Touring Club and Curnonsky in the interwar years. In 1939, all but three of the twelve one-star restaurants (none received two or three stars) in Nice were noted for their bouillabaisse, and two were listed for their raviolis à la niçoise.[51] In Strasbourg that same year, only five restaurants received one star (none received two or three stars), and in all but one case the establishments were noted for their choucroute garnie or their choucroute à l'alsacienne (sauerkraut).[52] Whereas it is true that such regional fare was recognized with a single star, it is equally true that the hierarchy of gastronomy remained dominated by Paris, where six of the fourteen three-star restaurants could be found in 1939. To use the guidebook's own language, the so-called "flower of French cuisine" clearly grew best in Ile-de-France. Despite the growth of provincial tourism by automobile, Paris, and to a lesser extent Lyon, set the culinary standard. Urban, bourgeois desire for variety came to include provincial fare, but that food, even though altered for the urban palate, could not surpass that of the Parisians.

Consistent with the general association of French cuisine with French national identity in early-twentieth-century France, the Michelin guides largely ignored foreign food. The foreign restaurants of Paris did not receive any stars. In the guide to Belgium, Luxembourg, and the southern Netherlands, the city of Brussels, that French-speaking enclave dominated by French culinary norms, did have a three-star restaurant, and the seaside city of Ostende as well as Anvers and Bruges had two-star restaurants. But only a handful of other cities and towns in Flemish-speaking Belgium had even one-star restaurants, whereas Wallonia, or French-speaking Belgium, had a concentration that matched several tourist regions within France. Within Belgium, more telling is the utter absence of regional specialties besides Waterzoie. The fine beers of Belgium receive no similar attention, nor do chocolates. No restaurant in the Netherlands received a ranking of any kind.[53] The guidebook to Switzerland, the Tyrol, and northern Italy similarly ignored regional specialties. There was nothing special to be found in Geneva, Milan, Neuchâtel, Salzburg, Zürich, or even Venice; the sole regional specialties noted are the unspecified "wines" of Maienfeld and the "biscuits 'Ours de Berne'" in Bern.[54]

In France's own empire, it was assumed that the French ate French food. In 1930, Michelin issued a new guide to Morocco, Algeria, and Tunisia to celebrate the hundredth anniversary of French intervention in Algeria. It replaced the older Pays du Soleil guide that grouped the Riviera, Italy, Greece, Egypt, Algeria, and the Mediterranean. In the new guide, Michelin advised French tourists to avoid local water in favor of bottled mineral water. They were instructed to avoid raw vegetables and any fruits that could not be peeled.[55] More telling because it was less related to health concerns resulting from bacteria in the water, the company took for granted that French tourists to the empire would be looking at sights rather than experiencing the cuisine, a marked contrast to interwar norms of touring in the metropole. The guide assumed that French tourists would not be seeking couscous or other north African specialties, so it offered no such lists of local cuisine. Recommended restaurants and hotels clearly served European, and especially French, food. As was the case in Indochina at the time, French colonists themselves ate French food, which symbolized French civilization and marked the French as superior to the *indigènes*.[56] Tourists were hardly supposed to be different. The exceptions to this norm are rare: whereas there are no regional specialties listed for Algiers, Casablanca, or Tangiers, Fez is unique in receiving the short notation, "gâteaux arabes (kaabrezel)."[57]

Without question, Michelin reflected preexisting French and often European notions of gastronomy while at the same time further defining them. In creating a hierarchy of restaurants the firm revealed one of the ironies of its own and the TCF's efforts to encourage the development of hotels and restaurants to serve tourists. Just as many elite tourists since the nineteenth century have attempted to make a distinction between themselves as "travelers" and the less well heeled as "tourists," self-proclaimed *gastronomes* viewed the expansion of the number of restaurants in the 1920s with alarm. As more and more middle-class people went to restaurants while touring, those diners who saw themselves as preserving the tradition of fine dining set themselves apart from the new hordes by founding exclusive gastronomic clubs. These organizations, which rarely admitted women, met periodically at restaurants in Paris and the provinces in order to sample what they considered to be the finest cuisine in France. In 1939, R. Bodet estimated that there were some 1,200 such clubs in France.[58] They included Curnonsky's own "Académie des gastronomes," modeled on the Académie Française with forty members and founded in 1928, as well as one that played on the title of famed gastronomic theorist Brillat-Savarin's *Physiologie du goût.*[59]

One of the oldest and best known of such clubs was the "Club des Cent," founded in 1912 by Louis Forest, a journalist at *Le Matin*. The exclusive Club des Cent was expected to include one hundred *gastronomes* who met together at leading restaurants. Forest wrote in 1912 that the "mission" of the group was

> to defend in France the taste of our old national cuisine, threatened by chemical formulas imported from countries where they have never even known how to prepare chicken stew [défendre, en France, le goût de notre vieille cuisine nationale, menacée par les formules chimiques, importées de pays où l'on n'a jamais su préparer même une poule au pot].

Members of the group traveled frequently to the provinces and then reported in detail on the fine meals they had eaten in the pages of the group's private public-ation, signing their membership numbers rather than their names. In 1921, Louis Forest and Emile Lamberjack sponsored André Michelin's entry into the Cent. Michelin soon began to supply a *carte gastronomique* to members of the Cent along with a special edition of the Michelin guide.[60] In return, Michelin had access to members' recommendations to restaurants across France. Both the notion of a hierarchy of French cuisine as well as specific details about individual restaurants were obviously well established before the Michelin guide introduced its system of stars rating restaurants in the early 1930s. Michelin could, without comment, play on the exclusivity that gastronomy had already symbolized among the wealthy.

The obvious hierarchy built into the stars themselves allowed Michelin to use existing assumptions about tourists' accommodations. Although Michelin may today be the single organization most associated with a system of stars, the firm was not, as noted earlier, the first to use stars or asterisks to rank either tourist attractions or hotels. John Murray's guides, which began to appear in 1836, had used stars. Since the middle of the nineteenth century, Baedeker guides, including those to France, included an asterisk next to a hotel that was particularly recommended and eventually one or two asterisks for a noteworthy tourist sight.[61] When Hachette launched, under the direction of Marcel Monmarché, the new Guides Bleus (blue guides) to provincial France after World War I, one asterisk noted an especially good hotel, one or two noted a tourist sight.[62] The Touring Club's *annuaire* had also used asterisks to denote the price ranges of hotels.[63] Michelin's innovation was not in using stars or asterisks but in doing so systematically to recommend places for fine dining. To a greater extent than any interwar guidebook or any interwar writer on gastronomy, Michelin provided an inventory of French hotels and restaurants ranking their fare. In essence, the company took the Touring Club's "concours de la bonne cuisine [good cooking competition]," which focused on the restaurants and inns of a few departments, to include the entirety of France.[64] By 1930s, Michelin had managed to represent the best in French gastronomy, at the same time that gastronomy itself was becoming an important part of French tourism.

Michelin ratings were further distinguished by their brevity. The stars became the sole indicator of relative quality of restaurants. The long descriptions of meals that were so important in the writings of Curnonsky, Touring Club members, and various *gastronomes*, had no counterpart chez Michelin. In gastronomic circles, writing, reading, and talking about meals was as much a part of the process as eating itself, hence the irony that Michelin, as identified with gastronomy as any French institution in the late twentieth century, provided no commentary whatsoever with its rating. Restaurants received no more detail in the guide than did the *stockistes*. The very brevity of Michelin entries added over time to the mystery surrounding the Michelin rankings. Although the company has made periodic references to its inspectors, their absolute anonymity, their procedures, and even at times their number,[65] Michelin has carefully cultivated a secrecy that garners yet more attention than outspoken clarity of criteria could ever offer.

Michelin managed a considerable feat in interwar France. Although "service to the client" had been a preoccupation of prewar business people, such as champagne makers, after the First World War markets were becoming bigger and more anonymous. Michelin maintained the myth of service to the individual client, such a fundamental part of its marketing in the prewar years, while obviously profiting from the growth in the number of tourists in the interwar years and doing everything in its power to foster that expansion.[66] Clearly, Bibendum's ratings were meant to replace the word-of-mouth recommendations of restaurants' clients to each other; Bibendum himself became a friend in the know. James Buzard has asserted that part of the success of Thomas Cook and Karl Baedeker in the nineteenth century resulted from the ways that companies used the men themselves, even after their deaths, as images of personal service for tourists in unfamiliar environs. Cook and Baedeker symbolically guaranteed their information, serving as knowledgeable personal contacts.[67] Michelin, represented by Bibendum, provided a similar service for early-twentieth-century motorists.

The fact that most people, even a good many wealthy interwar tourists, could not afford three-star restaurants did not keep the guides from working as a marketing device. For the well off, Michelin offered the ratings of the restaurants and hotels. For the less fortunate, Michelin offered a reminder of the glories of French cuisine that was not less pervasive among the French bourgeoisie for being hierarchical. By providing the list, Michelin made clear that the exclusive nectar of the "flower of French cuisine" was open to all, allowing those who could afford it to distinguish themselves from others and those who wished they could afford it to dream of the possibilities if only they had the cash. It was not unlike the strategy deployed by interwar American advertisers (that they have since continued) who consistently associated their products with social groups higher on the economic ladder than the average buyers of the products as revealed in market surveys;[68] one could get the guide, buy Michelin tires, and get a vicarious pleasure out of knowledge of where one could eat one day. Even a one-star restaurant could set some people apart, just as clients in three-star restaurants utterly unconcerned about price were different from the one- and two-star diners.

In the end, the Michelin guide is an important reminder of how intertwined the history of business and the history of tourism can be. Of course, unlike the other major guidebooks, the Michelin guide was not a product in itself so much as it was an inducement to get tourists to buy Michelin tires. The guide was a "service to the client," an attempt to offer a supposedly personal service, that was in fact impersonal, at a time when the expanding market for tires was already making such personal contact between producer and buyer increasingly impossible. In short, the Michelin guide was a sophisticated attempt at advertising. Its rearticulation of existing social distinctions, both blatant and latent, was meant to appeal to the likely buyers of tires. Like the automotive and tourist industries, Michelin had a great deal to gain from increased tourism in early-twentieth-century France; that much is obvious. Yet for all of the company's focus on sales, that does not mean its assertion of proper social roles for women and men, Parisians and provincials, *gastronomes* and mere eaters, was any less important. In fact, a guidebook with such a high rate of circulation (which has since grown to some 600,000 copies each year) requires attention for what it took for granted about the construction of French society as well as for its overall effort to advertise Michelin's product. As recent work on the history of the United States has made clear, advertising did a great deal – all too frequently overlooked by "serious" history in the past – to reformulate social norms in nineteenth- and twentieth-century America.[69] The same may well have been true in twentieth-century France, but that assertion has not yet been proven by scholarship.

Like advertisements, guidebooks have only recently been subjected to the rigorous analysis with an attention for historical context that used to be reserved for more traditional sources. Despite the obvious importance of guidebooks in both nineteenth- and twentieth-century Europe, they have received comparatively little serious consideration as historical sources. Although the Baedeker guides have garnered some attention and are now receiving their due,[70] there is but one rather limited essay on the nineteenth-century French Guides Joanne.[71] Their successors, the Guides Bleus, have also faced neglect. The lower-brow and apparently more widely distributed Guides Thiolier seem to have been entirely forgotten.[72] Michelin guides, because of their obvious importance in defining French and European tourism since World War II, have received a sort of journalistic coverage of their development that has obscured their use as potential historical sources. The issue of reception of the guidebooks and other tourist literature remains a potential stumbling block, but the necessity for guidebook editors to meet the changing demand of tourists made the guidebooks at least as responsive to their clientele as newspapers were. Moreover, cultural historians have for some time used novels, not as transparent sources of "what happened" but as sources for how ideas were juxtaposed and presented.[73] Guidebooks deserve comparable treatment. I hope that this chapter has provided an example by showing how the Michelin guide, one among many such sources, offers an angle for considering not just the history of tourism but also the social construction of class, gender, and other attempts at social differentiation in twentieth-century France.

Notes

1. Among interwar French critics of life in the United States, the predominance of the automobile in American society was a frequent target. See the best known of these commentators: Georges Duhamel, *America the Menace: Scenes from the Life of the Future*, trans. Charles Miner Thompson (Boston, MA: Houghton Mifflin, 1931, reprinted 1974). For an international survey of the automobile and some of the images associated with it, see Jean-Pierre Bardou *et al.*, *The Automobile Revolution: The Impact of an Industry*, trans. James M. Laux (Chapel Hill, NC: University of North Carolina Press, 1982).

2. Lynn Hunt (ed.), *The New Cultural History* (Berkeley, CA: University of California Press, 1989); Victoria E. Bonnell and Lynn Hunt (eds), *Beyond the Cultural Turn: New Directions in the Study of Society and Culture* (Berkeley, CA: University of California Press, 1999).

3. Stephen L. Harp, *Marketing Michelin: Advertising and Cultural Identity in Twentieth-Century France* (Baltimore: The Johns Hopkins University Press, 2001). The book considers the wide array of Michelin initiatives including not only the red guides but also the regional guides, maps, road signs, guides to World War I battlefields, the advent of Bibendum as well as the company's advocacy of aviation and pronatalism.

4. On the solidarism of the Touring Club itself, see Catherine Bertho Lavenir, *La roue et le stylo: Comment nous sommes devenus touristes* (Paris: Editions Odile Jacob, 1999), pp. 98–100.

5. *Guide Michelin* (1900), p. 5.

6. Ibid., p. 5.

7. Ibid., pp. 11–13.

8. Ibid., p. 54.

9. Ibid., p. 56; Marc Francon, "Le guide vert Michelin: L'invention du tourisme culturel populaire" (thèse, Université de Paris VII, 1998), p. 15.

10. For the latest such retellings of the launching of the red guides with little regard for the historical context, see Jean-François Mesplède, *Trois étoiles au Michelin: Une histoire de la haute gastronomie française* (Paris: Gründ, 1998), pp. 9–10; Herbert Lottman, *Michelin, 100 ans d'aventure* (Paris: Flammarion, 1998), pp. 67–9.

11. Touring Club de France, *Annuaire* (1891).

12. *Guide Michelin* (1900), p. 56.

13. Ibid., pp. 54–5.

14. Ibid., p. 5.

15. Ibid., pp. 57–8.

16. Ibid., p. 5.

17. "Le Lundi de Michelin," *L'Auto-Vélo* (August 26, 1901), p. 2.

18. *Guide Michelin* (1902), p. 78.

19. "Le Lundi de Michelin," *L'Auto* (August 17, 1903), p. 7.

20. "Lundi de Michelin," *L'Auto* (February 5, 1905), p. 7.

21. *Guide Michelin* (1902), p. 618; *Guide Michelin* (1906), n.p.

22. Emile Gautier, "Une croisade," *Revue mensuelle du Touring Club de France* (February 1897), pp. 43–4.

23. "Note," *Revue mensuelle du Touring Club de France* (April 1899), pp. 142–3; "W-C," *Revue mensuelle du Touring Club de France* (June 1899), p. 229.

24. Dr Léon-Petit, "Hôtel recommandé," *Revue mensuelle du Touring Club de France* (December 1899), pp. 507–8.

25. "La défense des intérêts nationaux," *Revue mensuelle du Touring Club de France* (May 1901), p. 197.

26. H. Berthe, "Patriotisme et profits," *Revue mensuelle du Touring Club de France* (August 1903), pp. 390–1.

27. "Lundi de Michelin," *Le Journal* (July 6, 1908), p. 5.

28. *Guide Michelin*, (1908); "Lundi de Michelin," *Le Journal* (April 20, 1908), p. 5.

29. "Le Lundi de Michelin," *L'Auto-Vélo* (May 19, 1902), p. 5; *Guide Michelin* (1911); *Guide Michelin* (1912).

30. "Le Lundi de Michelin," *L'Auto-Vélo* (May 19, 1902), p. 5; *Guide Michelin*, (1913).

31. "Ce que Michelin a fait pour le tourisme," (1912), Conservatoire Michelin.

32. For a more detailed account of gastronomy and tourism in the interwar years, see Harp, *Marketing Michelin*, ch. 6.

33. Jean Fourastié with Jacqueline Fourastié, *Pouvoir d'achat, prix et salaires* (Paris: Gallimard, 1977), p. 65.

34. Alain Jemain, *Michelin: un Siècle de secrets* (Paris: Calmann-Lévy, 1982), p. 107; Georges Ribeill, "Du pneumatique à la logistique routière: André Michelin, promoteur de la "révolution automobile," *Culture technique* 19 (1989), p. 202.

35. Ribeill, "Du pneumatique à la logistique routière," p. 202; Herbert Lottman, *Michelin: 100 ans d'aventure* (Paris: Flammarion, 1998), p. 177; *Guide Michelin France* (1922), p. 772.

36. "Les guides et les cartes Michelin," *Bulletin Intérieur Michelin* (June 20, 1946), pp. 1–2.

37. On the *tirage* of popular novels, Mary Louise Roberts, *Civilization without Sexes: Reconstructing Gender in Postwar France, 1917–1927* (Chicago: University of Chicago Press, 1994), p. 47; on Michelin pamphlets, "Les guides et les cartes Michelin," *Bulletin Intérieur Michelin* (June 20, 1946), p. 2.

38. *Guide Michelin France* (1923), p. 9.

39. *Guide Michelin France* (1925), p. 9.

40. *Guide Michelin France* (1927), p. 8.

41. Ibid., p. 9.

42. *Guide Michelin France* (1929), p. 9.

43. *Guide Michelin France* (1931), front matter.

44. *Guide Michelin France* (1932), p. 1.

45. Ibid., p. 1.

46. On the Touring Club's inventory and Curnonsky, see Bertho Lavenir, *La Roue et le stylo*, pp. 233–9; Harp, *Marketing Michelin*, ch. 6.

47. *Guide Michelin France* (1933).

48. *Guide Michelin France* (1939), p. 11.

49. Ibid., p. 11.

50. Ibid., pp. 29–35.

51. For one of the twelve, nothing at all was listed: *Guide Michelin France* (1939), pp. 712–13.

52. Ibid., pp. 994–5.

53. *Guide du pneu Michelin: Belgique, Luxembourg, Hollande* (1936–7), p. 8.

54. *Guide Michelin: Suisse, Lacs Italiens, Dolomites, Tyrol* (1931–2).

55. *Guide Michelin: Maroc, Algérie, Tunisie* (1930), p. 25.

56. Erica Peters, "National Preferences and Colonial Cuisine: Seeking the Familiar in French Vietnam," paper presented at the Western Society for French History, Monterey, CA, November 2, 1999.

57. *Guide Michelin: Maroc, Algérie, Tunisie* (1930), p. 168

58. R. Bodet, *Toques blanches et habits noirs: L'hôtellerie et la restauration d'autrefois et aujourd'hui, recettes nouvelles, le service de table, les vins, gastronomie, tourisme* (Paris: Dorbon, 1939), pp. 79–87.

59. Pierre Béarn, *Paris gourmand: Ce que doit savoir un gourmand pour devenir gastronome*, 6th edn (Paris: Gallimard, 1929), pp. 135–7.

60. Jean-François Mesplède, *Les Trois étoiles au Michelin: Une histoire de la haute gastronomie française* (Paris: Gründ, 1998), pp. 19–21; Bodet, *Toques blanches*, p. 135.

61. Karl Baedeker, *Les Bords du Rhin depuis Bâle jusqu'à la frontière de Hollande: Manuel du voyageur* (Coblenz: Baedeker, 1862), p. v; Baedeker, *Paris et ses environs: Manuel du voyageur* (Paris: Paul Ollendorff, 1900), p. v.

62. Marcel Monmarché, *Normandie* (Paris: Hachette, 1926), front matter; Marcel Monmarché, *Provence* (Paris: Hachette, 1925).

63. Touring Club de France, *Annuaire générale* (Paris, 1921).

64. The *concours* solicited individual restaurants and inns to commit to a set price for a fine meal including wine to be served during the summer tourist season. The establishments

would then be ranked by judges: the first place entry received 5,000 francs, the second 3,000 francs, the third 1,000 francs. "Concours de la bonne cuisine," *Revue du Touring Club* (May 1930), p. 145; "Concours de la bonne cuisine," *Revue du Touring Club* (July 1930), p. 212; "Résultats du concours de la bonne cuisine," *Revue du Touring Club* (January 1931), p. 25.

65. Michelin's reputation for secrecy, particularly in the realm of the red guides, is of course legion. For recent popular portrayals of the mystery of Michelin rankings, see Mesplède, *Les trois étoiles*; Lottman, *Michelin*.

66. On marketing in the Champagne industry, see Kolleen M. Guy, "'Oiling the Wheels of Social Life': Myths and Marketing in Champagne during the Belle Epoque," *French Historical Studies* 22, 2 (1999), pp. 211–39.

67. James Buzard, *The Beaten Track: European Tourism, Literature, and the Ways to Culture, 1800–1918* (New York: Oxford University Press, 1993), pp. 49–77. On Cook, see also E. Swinglehurst, *Cook's Tours: The Story of Popular Travel* (Poole, Dorset: Blandford Press, 1982); Lynne Withey, *Grand Tours and Cook's Tours: A History of Leisure Travel, 1750-1915* (New York: Morrow, 1997); Piers Brendon, *Thomas Cook: 150 Years of Popular Tourism* (London: Secker and Warburg, 1991).

68. See, in particular, Roland Marchand, *Advertising the American Dream: Making Way for Modernity, 1920–1940* (Berkeley, CA: University of California Press, 1985).

69. See, among others, Marchand, *Advertising the American Dream*; Jackson Lears, *Fables of Abundance: A Cultural History of Advertising in America* (New York: Basic Books, 1994); Pamela Walker Laird, *Advertising Progress: American Business and the Rise of Consumer Marketing* (Baltimore, MD: Johns Hopkins University Press, 1998).

70. Rudy Koshar, *German Travel Cultures* (Oxford and New York: Berg, 2000). Burkhart Lauterbach, "Baedeker und andere Reiseführer: Eine Problemskizze," *Zeitschrift für Volkskunde* 85 (1989), pp. 206–34. See also Edward Mendelson, "Baedeker's Universe," *Yale Review* 74, 3 (April 1985), pp. 386–403.

71. Daniel Nordman, "Les Guides-Joanne," in Pierre Nora (ed.), *Lieux de mémoire*, (Paris: Gallimard, 1997), vol. 2, pp. 1035–72.

72. I am basing this comment on circulation figures touted in the Guides Thiolier themselves, which, if they are correct, far surpassed those of the Michelin guides and other guides. Thus far, I have found no more than a rare mention of the Guides Thiolier or other low-cost guides, so my tentative suggestions result entirely from my perusal of these guides at the Bibliothèque Nationale de France.

73. On the use of novels in cultural history, see in particular Mary Louise Roberts, *Civilization without Sexes: Reconstructing Gender in Postwar France, 1917–1927* (Chicago: University of Chicago Press, 1994).

Germans at the Wheel: Cars and Leisure Travel in Interwar Germany

Rudy Koshar

Serious historical analysis of the automobile has been dominated by an emphasis on production and design rather than on daily usage, leisure practices, or consumption.[1] One could make the same point about many areas of cultural history, about economic and business history, or about the history of technology. But this imbalance is particularly notable in automotive history, where the analysis of producers (manufacturers, engineers, or workers), transportation networks (both structures and builders), and designers (the darlings of art history) have shaped scholarly discussion almost from the beginning of the automotive age. When scholars *have* turned to the history (or philosophy) of the everyday consumption of the car, they have dealt in themes of destruction and excess. Paul Virilio's sweeping theory of the "dromocratic revolution," which defines modernity by an ever-more violent acceleration of speed and circulation even more profound than advances in production, is only the most dramatic example.[2] Many other recent works discuss the exploitation of workers, the dissimulation of the advertising industry (matched only by the gullibility of consumers hooked on "auto opium"),[3] the misguided policies of the auto manufacturers, and the environmental ruin brought on by the automobile.[4] Scholarship aiming for a more complex understanding of both the positive and negative effects and uses of the car is the exception that proves the rule – and it originates largely in the United States, not Europe.[5] In German historiography, both tendencies, the stress on production and everything associated with it, as well as the focus on the negative "externalities" of increased automobility, are pronounced.[6] Much scholarship on the car in German history does not deal with the automobile per se, much less with the history of leisure travel, but rather with the automobile's military-political-economic functions within the Nazi regime. The machine itself – along with its drivers, passengers, mechanics, salespeople, and all the others associated with its everyday existence – becomes lost in the narrative of political evil. Some of the best recent examples include studies on slave laborers at the Volkswagen plant; the Mercedes workforce in peace and war; Daimler-Benz's policies under Nazism;

the links between automobility, roads, and German economic recovery in the 1930s; and the racist-political functions of the Autobahns.[7] An article on the East German Trabant continues the trend for the historiography of the post-World War II era, putting more emphasis on the the former German Democratic Republic (GDR) regime's political instrumentalization of the car than on its design or the actual uses to which it was put.[8]

My point of departure is that such research is incomplete at best – and misleading at worst – without a greater understanding of the meanings (political, cultural, social, and economic) of the automobile in everyday life. Wolfgang Sachs' study of desire for the automobile, the exception that proves the rule to most historiography on the German car, is a good starting point here. In an analysis that is more evocative than analytical, he argues that many embraced the automobile by the 1920s in Germany even though per capita automobile ownership there was far behind what it was in the United States, Britain, or France.[9] Many Germans began to assume that ownership of an automobile was possible in their lifetime, that a new age of individual mobility was just around the corner, and above all, that contemporary leisure culture would not deserve the name "modern" without the presence of the motor car. Millions of Germans were already behind the wheel: there were around 3.3 million vehicles in Germany in the summer of 1938, thanks to two major spurts in car production in 1924–9 and 1933–8, both doubling the number of automobiles. Car ownership was still very much an upper- and middle-class phenomenon in German-speaking Europe, but between the world wars the car had begun to make the turn from luxury item for the few to object of more general use, including that of middle-class touring. The German auto industry produced more than a quarter of a million cars in 1938 alone. The total number of vehicles on the roads included cars, trucks and delivery vehicles, buses, and three-wheeled mini-cars (like the bravely named Goliath Pioneer) as well as over 1.5 million motorcycles.[10] The building of the Autobahn was expected to bring about even more dramatic increases in the number of cars and trucks, drivers, and tourists. The annual Berlin automobile show was not only an important event for manufacturers, advertisers, and prospective buyers, but also for the general public and tourists. Experiences of driving and representations of driving were already integral elements of everyday culture – in film and literature, for example[11] – even if the majority of Germans had still not driven a car or did not own one. For all these reasons, the interwar era may be seen as a turning point in the history of the culture of automobility even when the period of actual mass consumption of the car would not come about until as late as the 1960s.[12]

Roland Barthes once remarked famously that cars were like the Gothic cathedrals of earlier ages, "the supreme creation of an era, conceived with passion by unknown artists, and consumed in image if not in usage by a whole population, which appropriates them as a purely magical object."[13] It may be added that like

Gothic cathedrals, automobiles were also part of the political imaginary, in the broadest sense of the term. But unlike cathedrals, cars are mobile, and they are adapted to modern democratic civil societies in which participation and "voice" are predicated on movement and circulation. The argument here is that a great deal may be learned about the newly mobile German political culture of the interwar era by focusing on the quotidian itinerary of the car, and above all on a central element of the car's public use and imagery: the experience and representation of driving for pleasure.

Stated in this manner, the argument puts leisure culture at the center of an understanding of political and social identities rather than treating it as an effect or function of other forces associated more directly with the state or economic production. Despite its many practical uses in business and urban transport systems, in the period between the world wars the automobile was still a vehicle of pleasure, of weekend outings, and of motoring vacations. This was true throughout industrialized Europe, and it reflected one of the major differences with the United States, where the car was already embedded in the rhythms of public transport and business, and where it was already well deployed for the daily commute from burgeoning suburbs into sprawling cities. But it was even truer in Germany, with its relatively low rates of auto ownership. Significantly, when Adolf Hitler made his famous speech at the 1934 Berlin Motor Show declaring the need for a "people's car," he emphasized that the private automobile would be an important instrument of the working-class family's recreation, not a vehicle for commuting and the daily grind. He thereby linked the automobile not with "pledged," or work-related time, not with "compulsive" time spent on everyday transport or official formalities, but with "free" time, or leisure.[14] To drive for pleasure, to experience the freedom and mobility of motorized leisure, was in this sense an important prerequisite of citizenship, and of the mastery of a whole set of social competencies associated with it. That citizenship in Nazi Germany was woven around a language of "race" and "blood" – rather than one of civic or political belonging – should not lead one to overlook this constitutive relationship between leisure and societal engagement in all its permutations. That the interwar leisure culture – and the car as its central symbol – could be rearticulated with a program of democratic politics and neo-liberal prosperity in the Federal Republic of Germany after 1949 is evidence of the malleability of leisure's political connectivities.

Historians of the automobile have mined car magazines for many years, but cultural and social historians of Germany have done relatively little to exploit this source, especially for the period between the wars. Dozens of such magazines existed, including the *Allgemeine Automobil Zeitung* (*AAZ*), published by the Allgemeine Deutsche Automobil Club and appealing to a general audience; the contentious *Motor-Kritik*, whose editors vociferously touted the advantages of small, fast cars for a sportier and more technically inclined readership; the glossy *Motor*, which appealed to upper-class drivers with expensive tastes; and the gear head's bible, the *Automobiltechnische Zeitschrift*.[15] That this literature could appeal to audiences beyond the circle of automobile enthusiasts was revealed in a 1920s English commentator's claim that German car magazines amounted to nothing more than "women's literature" because of their emphasis on entertainment rather than hard-core technical discussion.[16] Whereas the obvious implications of this comment for gender history must be left aside in this chapter, there is little doubt that German car magazines offered information on the whole panorama of car culture. Readers could find tips on driving, racing accessories, service and maintenance, tourist routes, insurance, traffic regulations and "speed traps," coverage of racing events and automobile shows, automotive clothing and cosmetics, and vacation gear such as tents, canteens, and sleeping bags. The *AAZ* and other publications – like their fascinating counterpart in Britain, *Autocar* magazine – also kept up a busy correspondence with readers, who submitted hundreds of letters to the editors on every possible aspect of automobile usage. For many, reading such publications was an important part of contemporary leisure culture and did not entail ownership of an automobile, at least not at first; the English automotive writer Owen John noted that he was an avid reader of car magazines before he bought his first automobile.[17]

In the 1930s, no subject riveted the attention of German automotive writers and their readers more than driving on the Autobahns. Although planning for a limited-access German superhighway devoted exclusively to automotive travel dated back to before World War I, it was only under Hitler that planning became reality. After 1933, Germans built almost 4,000 kilometers of new highway, including some 9,000 bridges. Impressive though this accomplishment was, it fell short of Hitler's goal of 7,000 kilometers. Recent scholarship discusses the propagandistic success of the Autobahn project, the unthinking "passivity" with which drivers experienced the Autobahn's many natural landscapes and exciting banked turns, and the eventual exclusion of Jews and other minorities from "the Führer's roads."[18] One can hardly gainsay the last of these perspectives, particularly in the light of the publication of Viktor Klemperer's important memoir of life under Hitler's rule. A professor of Romance languages, a secular Jew, and the husband of a non-Jewish German woman, Klemperer was spared the worst consequences of Hitler's politics. But he lived an anxiety-ridden existence shaped not only by the loss of his profession but also by the innumerable small insults and persecutions that Nazi racial policy imposed on Jews and others. In 1939, all Jews were prohibited from operating motor vehicles. But for the preceding three years, after nervous driving lessons and the purchase of a used Opel, Klemperer drove a car when and where he could – for trips to the doctor or the store, to be sure, but above all for weekend outings, visits to relatives, and short vacations. His impressions of the Autobahn were not unlike those of many Germans, as can be seen from his comment on a newly opened stretch of superhighway near Dresden in October 1936: "This straight road, consisting of four broad lanes, each direction separated by a strip of grass, is magnificent." Even so, Klemperer noted that while the Nazis spent extraordinary amounts of money and labor building the new highways, German roads generally were inadequate if not poorly maintained and dangerous. Autobahn driving was for Klemperer only part of a larger obsession: "Car, car over all, it has taken a terrible hold of us, *d'une passion dévorante*," he wrote. But Klemperer would soon be excluded from the automotive nation and from the extended leisure culture on which it was increasingly built.[19]

The exclusionary nature of "Hitler's roads" must be recognized, but the argument of Nazi propaganda and the passivity it allegedly engineered – the idea that Germans allowed themselves to be swept away not only by the slipstream of Autobahn driving but also by the Nazi regime's exterminationist policies – overlooks other motivations and perspectives held by Germans as they got behind the wheel. Klemperer himself was not merely a passive consumer. He overcame numerous personal anxieties in order to learn to drive, and he was thrilled at the prospect of participating in the new automotive culture, albeit with a mixture of skepticism and fear not unlike that which one finds in African American representations of driving experiences in the United States.[20]

It is illuminating in this context to focus on the work of Heinrich Hauser, a well-known journalist, novelist, and travel writer whose published works included a primer on technology;[21] a history of the Opel firm;[22] a novel, *Brackwasser*, that won the Gerhard Hauptmann Prize in 1929; and a controversial commentary on the American Occupation of Germany after World War II.[23] Hauser's cultural politics were eclectic. He blended a Prussian, upper-class humanism with a love of engineering; cultural pessimism with an emphasis on controlled modernization, much as the famed industrialist Walter Rathenau or sociologist Max Weber did; and an aversion to the signs of social disintegration in the United States with a desire to rationalize German industry along American lines. Having angered the Nazi authorities over two articles he wrote (and with a Jewish wife) he emigrated to the United States in 1938, returning to Germany ten years later to become chief editor of the popular *Stern* magazine.[24] In a 1936 article published in *Die Straße*, a magazine produced by the General Inspectorate of German Roads, Hauser discussed the subject of "automobile wandering," or *Autowandern*, which he characterized as a "growing movement" of the 1930s.[25] Because he not only laid out an agenda for a new kind of driving experience but also pointed out, directly and indirectly, how Germans had driven their cars up to that moment, his article is a good reflection of everyday leisure driving practices as they existed in the mid-1930s.

Unlike some German and foreign commentators, who worried about the boredom that would occur when driving long, uninterrupted stretches of steely-gray concrete on the new superhighways,[26] Hauser maintained that driving on the Autobahn was an "uncanny experience."[27] The driver relaxed, the car seemed to move effortlessly, and the feeling was almost as if one was flying.[28] What is more, the driver was able to appreciate the landscape's beauty in unexpected ways. "In short," wrote Hauser, "the fast Autobahns bring us, as unusual as it may sound, a more thoughtful driving experience, they help us to develop a social skill [*Lebenskunst*], which up until only a few drivers really mastered, the art of automobile wandering."[29] To develop his point, Hauser made the distinction between "automobile travel" (*Autoreisen*) and "automobile wandering," and he used North America as the positive referent. In the United States, drivers understood the art of driving with only a more general or far-away goal in mind. This enabled them to experience "a happy sense of timelessness and a pleasant willingness to be steered by the landscape, the sun, and nature."[30] Automobile wandering thus represented a kind of "nonfunctional" driving that was hardly aimless but that allowed for a degree of flexibility between "home" and "away" that more rigidly defined itineraries overlooked or excluded. Implicitly, this form of driving also foregrounded the pleasurable sensations of the motoring experience itself, the sights, sounds, smells, and kinesthetic sensations emphasized among others by the American writer-driver George R. Stewart. Having undertaken a continental trip on the legendary US 40, Stewart wrote that "the continuous joggling from the springs, doubtless good for the digestion and the nerves and the general well-being" was "reminiscent perhaps even of the joggling of the child within the womb."[31]

Hauser was convinced that leisure driving of this kind was something entirely new for Germany. Of course, he also remarked that the practice of automobile wandering was already known to a few drivers, and he later referred to it as a "lost art," which is to say that it had been available to Germans before this time. One of the first major accounts of a German road trip, by the novelist Otto Julius Bierbaum, promoted the idea that the car driver should "travel, not race."[32] Bierbaum advocated a more settled and responsible approach to leisure driving that not only avoided excessive speed, sine qua non of the devil-may-care "automobilist" of pre-World War I Europe,[33] but also allowed car passengers to gain a better appreciation of nature and culture than the train passenger could get. The automotive press was using the term *Autowandern* in a generic sense, often with reference to the early camping movement, for which America was once again the model, but also with reference to the Autobahn experience.[34] More broadly, the term *Wandern* may have reminded Germans of the long tradition of artisan travel, and like English "rambling," it had populist connotations for everyone from bourgeois youth groups to working-class travelers.

Even so, Hauser insisted on the novelty of the *Autowanderer*, arguing that her appearance could be attributed not solely to the Autobahn but also to an important political transformation. "There could be no real automobile wandering here in Germany before," he stated, "because there was no real national community [*Volksgemeinschaft*]. This is also part of the concept: a personally felt sense of social opening, the wanderer's feeling of resonance not only with the landscape but also with its people."[35]

By emphasizing automotive travel's broader cultural resonances, Hauser implied that a new kind of socially engaged tourism was on the horizon. This idea, too, was not completely unprecedented, but Hauser's original view gave the point a unique twist. When Social Democrats or other left-wing writers advocated collectivized tourism in the Weimar Republic, they called for working-class travelers who would look beyond normal tourist sites to focus on labor conditions, technology, and political history. The politically inflected gaze was to be the workingman's answer to bourgeois tourism's alleged superficialities; it was an attempt to infuse leisure travel with critical energies rather than only with consumerist fantasies and "distraction." It necessitated its own unique set of markers, symbols, and guidebooks as well as its specific accounts of the relationship between leisure and power.[36] Hauser did not advocate such critical engagement, but he was in effect applying the idea of a more focused and socially aware tourism to automobile travel. In doing so, he reflected on how the automobile could insert itself into the culture, and how it could be used to realize new connectivities. But just as nationalist ideology rather than socialist revolution determined his view, it was the image of individualized automobile travel rather than mass leisure, as represented by the Nazi cultural organization Strength through Joy (*Kraft durch Freude*),[37] that was at the heart of Hauser's perspective. For Hauser, the Volksgemeinschaft enabled but also demanded new, more individualized driving practices, which is to say that the new driving experience went to the heart of both the state's claims on its inhabitants as well as the individual's claims on the state. Leisure driving was a deeply political issue, filled with nationalist meanings but also social reciprocities, and it is to this central feature of Hauser's commentary that we now turn.

Hauser averred that changes in the design of the car itself had played a constitutive role in bringing about the new relevance of automobile wandering. Until recently, the German auto was "incomprehensible to the ordinary person and had a bad reputation"; it created a "dividing wall between people." Lacking maneuverability and speed, ponderous in both body design and engineering, the German automobile of just a few years ago was "much more bound to the road than it is today, above all in the minds of the driver."[38] Hauser's observation must be viewed against the backdrop of a larger conversation already going on in German culture regarding popular desires for smaller, lighter, more maneuverable cars that fitted the demands of contemporary leisure. What may be called the "Volkswagen discourse" appeared early in the post-World War I era, if not already before 1914. It had become quite widespread by the late 1920s, when engineers, automotive writers, and many others clamored for a new small car that was more than a scaled-down version of bigger cars, economical, oriented to everyday needs, and also fun to drive.[39] Indeed, the "Volkswagen," as it would come to be known after World War II, had been designed by the time Hauser wrote – and not by the man usually credited with the accomplishment, Ferdinand Porsche, but in the 1920s by the young engineer and later automotive safety innovator, Béla Bérenyi.[40] Several auto manufacturers had already produced reliable small cars, including Opel (with the two-tone green *Laubfrosch*, or "Tree Frog"), Hanomag, and DKW (part of the Auto-Union group), though none had gained the kind of attention the "Strength-through-Joy Car" would generate in the second half of the 1930s.[41] The building of the Autobahn generated debates in German automotive magazines as to whether German cars were up to the new roads. Significantly, magazine readers often gave German motor vehicle manufacturers failing marks, maintaining that Italian or English sports cars were far more adapted to Autobahn driving than most German vehicles were. Others worried aloud that German automobiles, allegedly incapable of maintaining Autobahn speeds for lengthy periods of time, were prone to numerous engine difficulties, premature wearing of tires and brakes, and costly repairs.[42] Test reports of new models reflected changing expectations: not only were cars judged for their roominess or practicality but also for their durability on long trips, their ability to accelerate quickly, and their steadiness on curves at relatively high speeds.[43] Smaller, more flexible cars suggested not only a greater ease of movement for drivers and passengers but also the possibility for more integral relations between consumers and their cars, and between consumers on the roads. Like the other participants in this conversation, Hauser was aware that there were intimate connections among automotive design, driving practices, and social interaction in the broadest sense of the term.

Hauser maintained that theory and practice were still far apart when it came to learning a new way to drive. "We are still only beginning to rediscover the art of wandering by auto," he remarked.[44] A Sunday drive in Germany reflected the abysmal state of motoring in that country, according to the journalist. People still parked on curves, threw trash on the roadside, and undertook their motoring tours with too much equipment – everything from tents and canoes to gramophones. They should be learning from the Indian or the soldier, who knew how to make the most out of just a little equipment. Motorists were also taking too much food with them. To pack food for a longer journey was economical, observed Hauser, but this practice also robbed one of experiencing local cuisine and customs. "Eat and drink everywhere what the farmer eats and drinks," he counseled.[45]

In stressing the need for lightweight travel oriented to local cultures, Hauser anticipated his argument from the post-World War II era that Germany should reject both the attractions of American mass consumption and the totalitarian seductions of Soviet collectivism in favor of Prussian "austerity."[46] But this argument was still not fully worked out; it would take the massive destruction of the war and the abysmal state of German society under the early years of the Occupation to sharpen Hauser's perspective on this score. In the 1930s, his ideas about lightweight travel were deployed for another purpose: to make a point about speed. It has been noted that rapid travel by car was the explicit counterpoint to the idea of auto wandering, but it is necessary to consider the issue from another angle to understand what was at stake. It was easy, wrote Hauser, to become seduced by the "hypnotic force of attraction" one felt looking over the hood of a fast car, an experience only increased by Autobahn cruising.[47] But one has to be cautious as to how one interprets this seductive effect. It is worth remembering that historiography's emphasis on the "passivity" of the Autobahn driving experience – which doubles as the passivity of the German populace in the face of genocide – regards speed as the primary force of manipulation. From the side of theory, there is Virilio's work, of course, which as noted above identifies speed as the constitutive moment of modernity. But there is also Ross, who writes that "going fast . . . has the effect of propelling the driver off the calendar, out of one's own personal and affective history, and out of time itself."[48] In this approach, the absence of historicity, of being able to situate oneself with reference to known temporal (and spatial) coordinates, is one of the inevitable functions of motorized speed, which creates a culture of disjointedness, a sense of constant displacement. Yet it is precisely the opposite effect one notices when reading travel accounts of the period. English tourists in Germany were quite specific as to the time and place in which they thrilled to speeding along on the Autobahn, and they were quite aware of the unique – which is to say: German – nature of the roads they traversed.[49] As for German drivers, they were by no means immediately drawn to the pleasures of high-speed driving. Automotive writers referred again and again to German drivers' lack of preparedness for traveling at fast speeds and the slowness with which they learned to use the fast lanes only for overtaking other cars.[50]

Eventually, German drivers did learn how to drive very fast, and it was the alarming rise in Autobahn accidents, to say nothing of the waste of human and material resources needed for the impending war effort, that prompted authorities, at Hitler's insistence, to impose speed limits. In a February 1939 speech that was extraordinary for its violent imagery, Hitler declared that those who killed 7,000 people annually and injured another 30,000–40,000 people on German roads were "parasites on the Volk." Furthermore: "They act irresponsibly. They shall be punished as a matter of course, provided they do not escape the

Volksgemeinschaft's wrath by dying themselves."[51] For Hitler, speeding went to the very heart of the question of how Germans were to conduct themselves in modern leisure culture. To endanger others when at the wheel was an act of political aggression against which the state would defend itself – with breathtaking brutality if necessary. But whether one considers the history of driving practices or such rhetoric, it is clear that speeding was neither an automatic element of the new leisure culture nor something that proceeded inevitably from the nature of modernity. Rather, it was a learned practice over which different drivers, under historically specific conditions and experiences, gained a mastery that was both contingent and open to much conflict at its point of origin.

To return to Hauser's point of view, automobile wandering required not speed but patience and moderation, the ability to take one's time exploring the old peasant farm one sees on an incline, or the old mill one finds off the beaten track. Hauser made a point of noting that a growing palette of campgrounds also presented the auto traveler with new possibilities and new choices. [52] Mentioning country scenes and campgrounds meant that motorized wandering could not be confined to the Autobahn, but must include the older state and rural roads, the *Landstraßen*, which, according to a contemporary travel guide, were home to a variety of landscapes that could not be viewed from the new highways.[53] It was in such instances that the emphasis on moderation and variety had a connection to older discursive traditions that represented leisure walking as a more humane alternative to the "industrialization" of time and space caused by railway travel.[54] This tradition had an elitist connotation, to be sure. Train travel was "mass" travel, with all the negative resonances this term carried with it, whereas walking presupposed the possibility of "pure, pointless expenditure" and "expending . . . valuable time to no purpose," to use Pierre Bourdieu's analysis of elitist forms of cultural consumption.[55] Slow-paced car travel shared walking's potential for social distinction – but not only that. Unlike Hitler's vicious approach to disciplining German drivers, Hauser's view was based partly on the idea of the Volksgemein-schaft as a motorized nation in which balance and moderation, the ability to enjoy the variety of German landscapes, indeed, the educative nature of automobile travel, were foremost. Driving thereby became an ennobling leisure-time practice, a kind of stately, motorized promenade with the potential to raise the cultural level of all involved.

Whether one drove on the Autobahn or the country roads, the newer cars of the 1930s were better equipped to make detours or to pull back on to the road without too much effort or disruption of traffic. Here, too, the smaller, lighter cars of the era would facilitate a new kind of flexible travel that maximized the driver's choices. Whether such a consumerist approach was expressed in the desire for a German people's car, or in preferences for a more Italianate automotive design attuned to Autobahn requirements, the stress on flexibility and choice was

unmistakable. The differences between this individualizing vision and the collect-
ivist imagery (if not the reality) associated with both socialist and Nazi mass travel
cultures must once again be noted.

This difference is reinforced if it is pointed out that Hauser, after emigrating to
the United States, criticized Nazi state plans to reduce the number of car models
available to the public. National Socialist policy was based in part on vociferous
criticism of allegedly outmoded "liberal" approaches to automotive leisure by
which consumers would have the choice of many models and makes adapted to
the variety of everyday needs.[56] Formulated in 1938 as part of the Four-Year Plan
adopted two years previously, the National Socialist scheme anticipated large-scale
military requisitioning and the technical difficulties involved in army maintenance
of a large variety of car models. Hauser argued that standardization would only
hurt the German automotive industry, which would be unable to compete with
foreign auto firms that not only made technical progress through yearly model
changes but also were able to gain new consumers by marketing many automobile
brands. Consumer choice obviously mattered in Hauser's scheme of things. Hauser
also criticized the KdF-Wagen, inspired at least in part by Fordist images of a
standardized product for the masses, arguing that it was no "People's Car" at all
because it would remain too expensive for most Germans – a doubt shared, not
insignificantly, by many of the manufacturers and engineers opposed to the
project.[57] Whether its *design* suited Hauser's vision of more flexible and individualized leisure travel is impossible to say on the basis of the sources available for
the present study.

Hauser's critical remarks toward German drivers in the 1936 article were counter-
balanced by his praise for the collectivity, and especially by adoration for the
National Socialist regime.

> We now have at our disposal vacation areas and leisure time pleasures so great and varied
> that hardly any other country in the world can match them [he wrote triumphantly]. If
> German drivers now begin to live their existence more strongly and with greater pleasure,
> we know that our thanks must go to just one man, who has put the automobile in its
> rightful place, and who has forged the way for it: the Führer.[58]

Yet it is worth emphasizing that such adoration contained unspoken assumptions.
It was noted before that the Volksgemeinschaft both enabled and prescribed new
forms of driving, which is to say that it made innovative demands on its people,
who were expected to drive according to new rules and travel technologies. At the
same time, however, drivers might make new demands on other drivers and the
state. If Hauser expected German motorists to be more courteous, to avoid

excessive speeding, to be wary of overconsumption, to favor nimble automobiles rather than the ponderous barges of the past, and above all to practice the art of automobile wandering in their leisure-time pursuits – then those drivers could expect similar adaptations from others as well.

To speak of the demands of the Volksgemeinschaft is to touch on the issue of sovereignty, the state's right to exercise authority over its population; to speak of popular demands on the state is to touch on the matter of citizenship. If Hauser championed a kind of consumer sovereignty, or a more individualized consumer citizenship, there were significant limits to his point of view. It is not only that ideas of consumer sovereignty in Europe emphasized social participation more than individualized, American-style market choice even when they included a stronger individuating moment than could be found in the socialist or fascist traditions.[59] It is also impossible to argue that anything like a public sphere with origins in the free choice of individual citizen-consumers existed in Nazi Germany. Hauser credited one man, not the public actions or market choices of the German people, with the political transformation that ushered in a new era of driving experiences and that put the car in its "rightful place." Political parties, trade unions, voluntary associations, and all the other institutions that negotiate claims of sovereignty and citizenship with the state were violently dismantled and put under the authoritarian embrace of the Nazi state. Consumer society developed more fully under the Nazis than under Weimar, but it was heavily regulated and ultimately frustrated through the drive for autarky and military preparation. Yet in many areas of Nazi society, as recent scholarship has demonstrated, a process of negotiation and compromise, a multileveled adjudication between coercion and consent, was played out.[60]

It has been my argument that the road was central to this process because, more than other areas, it facilitated and embodied the mobility and circulation required of public spheres in motorized consumer societies. (That most concepts of the public sphere are rooted in more static visions of society based on eighteenth- or nineteenth-century urban models can be mentioned only in passing here.)[61] Sitting at the wheel of their cars, or imagining sitting at the wheel, Germans participated in the range of moving social adjustments that constituted everyday life in the Third Reich. Driving demanded sociopolitical *reciprocity*, even when the pleasures of motoring were associated on the one extreme with the regime's genocidal policies and on the other with individualistic escape and "getting away from it all." Hauser's endorsement of automobile wandering presupposed an educated public aware of its responsibilities and rights as it traversed the Third Reich's roads and learned of its changing relationship to the nation as a whole. Hitler himself saw the automobile as an index of the state's ability both to make claims on its people and to satisfy their wishes. But to focus on Nazi imagery of the automobile, particularly the Volkswagen, is also to narrow one's view, and to overlook claims

226

and visions emanating from the broader automotive culture for which Hauser (and even Victor Klemperer) wrote. Such claims and visions did little openly to challenge the Nazi state, but they nonetheless implied a degree of give and take over "the rules of the road." It is significant not only that these rules were still very contingent and unformed in Germany and most of Europe before the era of mass automobility, but also that they were being shaped directly by what was still primarily a leisure practice. Such facts make the history of driving a central subject for further investigation into the relationships between leisure culture and political community in the broadest sense.

Notes

1. For the argument of this paragraph, see Rudy Koshar, "On the History of the Automobile in Everyday Life," *Contemporary European History* 10, 1 (2001), pp. 143–54.

2. Paul Virilio, *Speed and Politics: An Essay on Dromology* (New York: Semiotexte, 1986); see also the discussion on Virilio by Christoph Maria Merki, "Plädoyer für eine Tachostoria," *Historische Anthropologie* 5, 2 (1997), pp. 288–92.

3. David Gartman, *Auto Opium: A Social History of American Automobile Design* (London and New York: Routledge, 1994).

4. Jane Holtz Kay, *Asphalt Nation: How the Automobile Took Over America and How We Can Take it Back* (Berkeley and Los Angeles: University of California Press, 1997).

5. A more balanced view of automotive history is taken by Virginia Scharff, *Taking the Wheel: Women and the Coming of the Motor Age* (Albuquerque, NM: University of New Mexico Press, 1991), which deals only with the United States, and Michael L. Berger, *The Devil Wagon in God's Country: The Automobile and Social Change in Rural America, 1893–1929* (Hamden, CT: Archon, 1979). But see also Sean O'Connell, *The Car in British Society: Class, Gender, and Motoring, 1896–1939* (Manchester: Manchester University Press, 1996). A more balanced perspective can also be derived from analyses of the vast "road trip literature" that, again, is much more ubiquitous in US than in European culture. See for example Kris Lackey, *RoadFrames: The American Highway Narrative* (Lincoln, NB: University of Nebraska Press, 1997); Ronald Primeau, *Romance of the Road: The Literature of the American Highway* (Bowling Green, OH: Bowling Green State University Popular Press, 1996); Roger N. Casey, *Textual Vehicles: The Automobile in American Literature* (New York: Garland, 1997). One might have expected more in this context from Kristin Ross's *Fast Cars, Clean Bodies: Decolonization and the Reordering of French Culture* (Cambridge, MA: MIT Press, 1995), but its view of the car's embeddedness in modern culture is still one-sidedly negative, and it has little to say about the daily uses of the automobile.

6. See Thomas Kühne, "Massenmotorisierung und Verkehrspolitik im 20. Jahrhundert: Technikgeschichte als politische Sozial- und Kulturgeschichte," *Neue Politische Literatur* 41, 2 (1996), pp. 196–229; Barbara Schmucki, "Automobilisierung. Neuere Forschungen

zur Motorisierung," *Archiv für Sozialgeschichte* 35 (1995), pp. 582–97. For a character-istically pessimistic account of the car's effects: Richard Birkefeld and Martina Jung, *Die Stadt, der Lärm, und das Licht: Die Veränderung des öffentlichen Raumes durch Motorisierung und Elektrifizierung* (Seelze/Velber: Kallmeyer, 1994). A useful exception is Christoph Maria Merki's comparative book project on Germany, Switzerland, and France, which nonetheless puts the emphasis on the motorization of transportation rather than on everyday usage, and also covers only the period up to 1930. For an example see his "Die 'Auto-Wildlinge' und das Recht: Verkehrs(un)sicherheit in der Frühzeit des Automobilismus," in Harry Niemann and Armin Hermann (eds), *Geschichte der Straßenverkehrssicherheit im Wechselspiel zwischen Fahrzeug, Fahrbahn, und Mensch* (Bielefeld: Delius and Klasing, 1999).

7. Hans Mommsen (with Manfred Grieger), *Das Volkswagenwerk und seine Arbeiter im Dritten Reich* (Düsseldorf: ECON, 1996); Bernard P. Bellon, *Mercedes in Peace and War: German Automobile Workers, 1903–1945* (New York: Columbia University Press, 1990); Neil Gregor, *Daimler-Benz in the Third Reich* (New Haven, CT and London: Yale University Press, 1998); R.J. Overy, "Cars, Roads, and Economic Recovery in Germany, 1932–1938," in Overy, *War and Economy in the Third Reich* (Oxford: Clarendon, 1994); Erhard Schütz and Eckhard Gruber, *Mythos Reichsautobahn: Bau und Inszenierung der 'Straßen des Führers' 1933–1941* (Berlin: Ch. Links Verlag, 1996).

8. See Jonathan R. Zatlin, "The Vehicle of Desire: The Trabant, the Wartburg, and the End of the GDR," *German History* 15, 3 (1997), pp. 358–80.

9. Wolfgang Sachs, *For Love of the Automobile: Looking Back into the History of our Desires*, trans. Don Reneau (Berkeley and Los Angeles: University of California Press, 1992; published in German, 1984). Barbara Haubner, *Nervenkitzel und Freizeitvergnügen: Automobilismus in Deutschland 1886–1914* (Göttingen: Vandenhoeck and Ruprecht, 1998) discusses the pre-World War I roots of automobility in Germany, whereas the effects of World War I are sketched by Kurt Möser, "World War I and the Creation of Desire for Automobiles in Germany," in Susan Strasser, Charles McGovern, and Matthias Judt (eds) *Getting and Spending: European and American Consumer Societies in the Twentieth Century* (Cambridge: Cambridge University Press, 1998), pp. 195–222.

10. Heidrun Edelmann, *Vom Luxusgut zum Gebrauchsgegenstand. Die Geschichte der Verbreitung von Personenkraftwagen in Deutschland* (Frankfurt a/M: Verband der Automobilindustrie, 1989); Reichsverband der Automobilindustrie, *Tatsachen und Zahlen aus der Kraftverkehrswirtschaft* (Berlin: Union Deutsche Verlagsgesellschaft, 1939), p. 5; Werner Ostwald, *Deutsche Autos 1920–1945. Alle deutschen Personenwagen der damaligen Zeit*, 10th edn (Stuttgart: Motorbuch Verlag, 1996), pp. 150, 530; "Automobile and Motorcycle," *Weekly Report of the German Institute for Business Research* 12, 17/18 (May 1939), p. 47.

11. One of the popular musicals of the 1930s was *Drei vor der Tankstelle*, which told the story of three young men, partners in a filling station, who vied for the affection of a beautiful woman. In literature, Ilya Ehrenburg's *The Life of the Automobile* (London and Sydney: Pluto, 1985), written in Russian in 1929, then translated immediately into German, took the car as its centerpiece in an evocative critique of capitalist society.

12. Arne Andersen, *Der Traum vom guten Leben: Alltags- und Konsumgeschichte vom Wirtschaftswunder bis heute* (Frankfurt and New York: Campus, 1997).

13. Roland Barthes, *Mythologies*, trans. Annette Lavers (New York: Hill and Wang, 1972), p. 88.

14. This tripartite definition of temporal modes comes from Henri Lefebvre, *Everyday Life in the Modern World* (New Brunswick, NJ: Transaction, 1984), p. 53.

15. See Ulrich Kubisch, *Das Automobil als Lesestoff: Zur Geschichte der deutschen Motorpresse, 1898–1998* (Berlin: Staatsbibliothek zu Berlin, Preußischer Kulturbesitz, 1998).

16. The criticism is recounted in Louis Betz, *Automobilia: Zeitgemäß-unzeitgemäße Betrachtungen über den Automobilismus* (Berlin: Verlag Ernst E. Rulf, 1928), p. 3.

17. Owen John, *Autocarbiography* (London: Iliffe and Sons, 1927), p. 8.

18. Schütz and Gruber, *Mythos Reichsautobahn*, pp. 145–58; Erhard Schütz, "'eine glückliche Zeitlosigkeit . . .': Zeitreise zu den 'Straßen des Führers'," in Peter J. Brenner (ed.), *Reisekultur in Deutschland: Von der Weimarer Republik zum 'Dritten Reich'* (Tübingen: Max Niemeyer-Verlag, 1997), pp. 73–99.

19. Victor Klemperer, *I Will Bear Witness: A Diary of the Nazi Years 1933–1941* (New York: Random House, 1998), pp. 165, 193.

20. See Lackey, *RoadFrames*, ch. 4.

21. Heinrich Hauser, *Friede mit Maschinen* (Leipzig: Verlag von Philipp Reclam jun., 1928).

22. Heinrich Hauser, *Opel: Ein deutsches Tor zur Welt* (Frankfurt a/M: Verlag Hauser-presse, 1937).

23. Heinrich Hauser, *The German Talks Back* (New York: Henry Holt, 1945).

24. See Michael Ermarth, "*The German Talks Back*: Heinrich Hauser and German Attitudes toward Americanization after World War II," in Michael Ermarth (ed.), *America and the Shaping of German Society, 1945–1955* (Providence, RI: Berg, 1993), pp. 107–9.

25. Heinrich Hauser, "Autowandern, eine wachsende Bewegung," *Die Straße* 3, 14 (1936), pp. 455–7.

26. See the unsigned article, "Gedanken auf Reichsautobahn," *Allgemeine Automobil Zeitung* 37, 21 (1937), p. 652; Stephen Spender, *European Witness* (New York: Reynal and Hitchcock, 1946), p. 145.

27. Hauser, "Autowandern," p. 455.

28. References to flying and airplanes were frequent among automotive writers, suggesting close linkages to the culture of "airmindedness" in the 1930s, as discussed in Peter Fritzsche, *A Nation of Flyers: German Aviation and the Popular Imagination* (Cambridge, MA: Harvard University Press, 1992), ch. 5.

29. Hauser, "Autowandern."

30. Ibid.

31. George R. Stewart, *U.S. 40: Cross Section of the United States of America* (Boston, MA: Houghton Mifflin, 1953), p. 29.

32. Otto Julius Bierbaum, *Reisegeschichten* (Munich and Leipzig: Georg Müller, 1906), pp. 244–5.

33. See Merki, "Die 'Auto-Wildlinge'," for numerous examples.

34. Schütz, "'eine glückliche Zeitlosigkeit'," pp. 81, 84–5; on the American camping movement, see Warren James Belasco, *Americans on the Road: From Autocamp to Motel, 1910–1945* (Cambridge, MA: MIT Press, 1979); Roger B. White, *Home on the Road: The Motor Home in America* (Washington, DC: Smithsonian Institution Press, 2000).

35. Hauser, "Autowandern," p. 455.

36. See Rudy Koshar, *German Travel Cultures* (Oxford: Berg, 2000), pp. 65–6, 97–113.

37. On Kraft durch Freude: Hasso Spode, "Arbeiterurlaub im Dritten Reich." in Carola Sachse, Tilla Siegel, Hasso Spode, and Wolfgang Spohn (eds) *Angst, Belohnung, Zucht und Ordnung: Herrschaftsmechanismen im Nationalsozialismus* (Opladen: Westdeutscher Verlag, 1982); Shelly Baranowski, "Strength through Joy: Tourism and National Integration in the Third Reich," in Shelly Baranowski and Ellen Furlough (eds), *Being Elsewhere:*

Tourism, Consumer Culture, and Identity in Modern Europe and North America (Ann Arbor, MI: University of Michigan Press, 2001); Christine Keitz, *Reisen als Leitbild: Die Entstehung des modernen Massentourismus in Deutschland* (Munich: Deutscher Taschenbuch Verlag, 1997), pp. 209–57.

38. Hauser, "Autowandern," p. 455.

39. Heidrun Edelmann, "Der Traum vom 'Volkswagen'," in *Geschichte der Zukunft des Verkehrs: Verkehrskonzepte von der Frühen Neuzeit bis zum 21. Jahrhundert* (Frankfurt a/ M: Campus, 1997), pp. 280–8.

40. Harry Niemann, *Béla Barényi: The Father of Passive Safety. A Biographical and Technical Documentation of the Development of Safety in Motor Vehicle Design* (Stuttgart: Mercedes-Benz AG, n.d.), pp. 89–106.

41. The name derived from the car's sponsorship by Kraft durch Freude, or Strength through Joy.

42. 'Der Sportwagen – wie unsere Leser ihn sehen,' *Allgemeine Automobil Zeitung* 37, 1 (1936), pp. 11–14; Hans Bahr, 'Mein Kraftwagen auf der Reichsautobahn,' *Die Strasse* 3, 13 (1936), pp. 415–16.

43. One of numerous examples: "Auto-Union Wanderer, Typ 'W24' im Anhängerbetrieb," *Der kraftfahrende Fleischer und deutsche Auto-Post* 11, 8 (1937).

44. Hauser, "Autowandern," p. 455.

45. Ibid.

46. See Ermarth, "*The German Talks Back*," esp. pp. 111–28.

47. Hauser, "Autowandern," p. 456

48. Ross, *Fast Cars, Clean Bodies*, p. 21.

49. See for example, Harold Nockolds, "Cross-Channel Holiday," *The Autocar* 77, 2130 (1936), pp. 390–2.

50. "Gedanken auf Reichsautobahn," p. 652.

51. Max Domarus, *Hitler: Speeches and Proclamations 1932–1945*, vol. 3: *The Years 1939 to 1940* (Wauconda, IL: Bolchazy-Carducci, 1997), p. 1478.

52. Hauser, "Autowandern," p. 456.

53. Fritz Kirchhofer, *Über schöne Landstrassen* (Berlin: Rudolf Mosse Buchverlag, 1933).

54. Wolfgang Schivelbusch, *The Railway Journey: The Industrialization of Time and Space in the 19th Century* (Berkeley, CA: University of California Press, 1986).

55. Pierre Bourdieu, *Distinction: A Social Critique of the Judgement of Taste* (Cambridge, MA: Harvard University Press, 1984), pp. 281–2; on the touristic "cult" of walking, see Orvar Löfgren, *On Holiday: A History of Vacationing* (Berkeley, CA: University of California Press, 1999), pp. 48–56.

56. See Wolfgang B. von Lengercke, *Kraftfahrzeug und Staat: Ein Versuch* (Heidelberg/ Berlin/Magdeburg: Kurt Vowinckel Verlag, 1941), pp. 95–6.

57. Heinrich Hauser, *Battle Against Time: A Survey of the Germany of 1939 from the Inside* (New York: Charles Schribner's Sons, 1939), chs 9 and 10.

58. Hauser, "Autowandern," p. 457.

59. Victoria de Grazia, "Changing Consumption Regimes in Europe, 1930–1970: Comparative Perspectives on the Distribution Problem," in *Getting and Spending*, 77.

60. For a recent example, see Michael Burleigh, *The Third Reich: A New History* (New York: Hill and Wang, 2000), pp. 239–51.

61. For this argument, see John Urry, *Sociology beyond Societies: Mobilities for the Twenty-First Century* (London and New York: Routledge, 2000).

Part III

Consuming

12

Confessional Drinking: Catholic Workingmen's Clubs and Alcohol Consumption in Wilhelmine Germany[1]

Robert Goodrich

Reflecting on his Catholic working-class childhood, Peter Fröhlich remembered a baptism in the Cologne Old Town shortly before the First World War:

> The *Pittermännchen*, a 25-liter keg of beer, and a few bottles of schnapps stood in the bedroom . . . Around ten o'clock they all went with the infant to the church. Mother was worried about the numerous pubs along the way . . . Before leaving, she made Aunt Anna promise not to let the small ones out of her sight and under no circumstances to tolerate that the group would stop [at a pub] anywhere on the way to the church. Up until the church all went well. Then came the first breakdown. When the pastor asked, "Do you denounce the devil?" the godfather, standing in for the infant, was supposed to say, "I denounce him." Instead, the no longer sober godfather said, "I'll tell him when I see him." The pastor accepted that. He was already used to it with the people on our street.
>
> After the baptism the uncles and aunts went to the bar across from the church to recover from all the stress. Even Aunt Anna had no objections. Mother had only spoken about the way to the church, not the way back. Strengthened by a few glasses of beer and some schnapps they all made their way back . . . The celebration lasted into the night. If the keg was empty, another was tapped. The entire street took part in the celebration . . . where Uncle Jupp sang:
>
> > Invite me to a baptism, you know,
> > I am sure to go; Yes, I'll be there,
> > 'Cause then I can leave the hectic behind.
> > There's lots of laughing and fun in the air.
> > What a noble fest, in th' quarter that's best,
> > The whole night long we'll all sing Trallala.[2]

Communal instead of familial consumption and the popular/profane reinterpretation of religious ritual were certainly not unknown in Wilhelmine Germany. But the Fröhlich baptism occurred in a society where elites and the middle classes opposed excessive alcohol consumption by urban workers. Indeed, observers interpreted the communal, popular, and public nature of working-class drinking as familial decay, irreverence, and public indecency.[3] This attitude went beyond observers during Germany's industrialization. Many historians into the 1970s also equated heavy drinking with alcohol(ism), which they recognized as a social pathology, addiction, or vice.[4] The presumed rise in alcohol consumption accompanying industrialization, above-average consumption among workers, and links between drinking and poverty were axiomatic to all commentators, whether middle-class, religious, or socialist, though here the cause-and-effect relationship could be reversed. One need only compare the descriptions in Friedrich Engels' *Condition of the Working Class in England* to those of non-socialist social critics to see the continuity. Alcohol consumption among workers became a social, moral, and medical reform issue as critics, embracing temperance as social reform, routinely condemned the perceived excessive drinking habits of the working classes. Indeed, the embeddedness of temperance rhetoric in a gendered, religious, reformist middle-class ideology reflected cultural class boundaries and, contrary to its unifying intention, often fostered class-based antagonisms.[5]

Everyone but the male worker, it seems, perceived his drinking as a problem. State officials and patriotic societies blamed proletarian drinking for declining birth rates and military unpreparedness. Municipal officials regulated it. Fröhlich's Cologne, for example, established thirty-four drinking kiosks in the late 1890s as non-alcoholic venues where workers "could afford a cheap refreshment without being forced to go into a pub," though financial failure led the city to grant them alcohol licenses.[6] Religious organizations moralized it as contributory to public immorality and broken families. Middle-class reformists viewed it as the cause of poverty. Professionals and doctors medicalized it through an alcohol-specific discourse of disease, hygiene, nutrition, and addiction. As alcohol reform quickly politicized, the medicalized discourse merged with nationalist interests in the racial hygiene movement. Anti-socialists were convinced alcohol fostered revolution, leading French temperance advocates after the Paris Commune to use alcohol as a metaphor for proletarian irrationality—a metaphor popular inside bourgeois Germany. Occasionally, even socialists saw alcohol as a new opiate of the masses undermining revolutionary politics.

Fröhlich's Cologne harbored all of these temperance tendencies, yet alcohol consumption remained a fixed part of workers' everyday leisure culture. German workers accepted and expected alcohol. The local *Kölsch* beer and a bottle of schnapps accompanied every celebration, and masculine leisure activity focused on a trip to the pub. Alcohol's ubiquitous presence merged the private with the public and the secular with the profane. Even religious rites of passage required public generosity in the form of alcohol as religious-liturgical practices intertwined with an alcohol-centered everyday leisure culture, reinforced by the pub visit following Sunday mass. Further, organizations dedicated to the improvement of workers' lives often fostered a drinking culture while simultaneously advocating temperance. This contradiction is best observed in the Catholic labor movement (KAB). The KAB centered on church-organized, confessionally segregated, and clerically led Catholic workingmen's clubs committed to creating a self-contained social-religious milieu by organizing and controlling leisure consumption. Although KAB leaders believed that "ennobling" the Catholic worker required a radical alteration in his relationship to alcohol, drinking habits remained deeply etched into the everyday leisure, associational, and festival culture of the Cologne working classes. As a result, alcohol consumption patterns within the clubs became culturally contested terrain between clerical temperance initiatives and a drinking working-class membership.

Several theories have explained the popularization of alcohol consumption among the lower classes in the nineteenth century. Unfortunately, all share a reductionist view of alcohol consumption as an economic derivative void of cultural considerations. Whether a psychological survival reflex to the dislocations of industrialization, a type of Foucauldian cultural resistance through noncon-formity to work discipline and rejection of the bourgeoisie's universalization of particular norms, a French *Annales*-style interpretation of alcohol consumption as a basic physical survival imperative based on nutritional needs, or the result of increased disposable incomes, leisure time and emerging mass markets and consumer outlets, the underlying assumptions contain an inherent distortion. To wit, statistical approaches to consumption ignore cultural contexts and presume a particular proclivity of the lower classes to consume more alcohol than other classes during industrialization – an assertion problematized by contradictory patterns.[7] Although alcohol consumption increased throughout the nineteenth century in Europe, considerations other than class including marital status, age, gender, region, religion, and occupation crosscut working-class drinking patterns.

Even along class lines, differentiation of habits was as much a perception as reality. The "drinking question" remained fixed on the working classes for subjective reasons based on a legacy from the early modern era of an urban proletarian drinking problem. Beginning as early as the sixteenth century, new forms of alcohol, mostly industrial spirits, entered the markets as the drink of choice for lower classes. The new drinking patterns of the lower classes thus clashed with those of the established classes, fostering a disjunction in attitudes between traditional alcoholic forms and the new.[8] In England, gin became synonymous with lower-class poverty and sloth by the eighteenth century. In France, the villain was absinthe. Also, public binge drinking, usually by peasants at festivals and workers on payday weekends, occasioned censure even if the overall level of consumption between bingers and more discreet drinkers did not differ.[9] Within the urban environment, workers, often recent rural immigrants, continued pre-industrial patterns and drank in public, consumed more than average, and drank despite poverty, leading observers to mistake concurrency of alcohol consumption and poverty for causality.

Yet other social groups consumed more alcohol than workers but generally escaped public censure. Alcohol consumption remained highest in rural areas, led by the East Elbian provinces.[10] Rural immigrants easily transformed their patterns of drinking to Cologne's pub-centered social life. In any case, the presumptive link between alcoholism and urbanization has not been established historically although contemporary reports lumped alcoholism and the living conditions of the urban working classes into one pot. Meanwhile, aristocratic circles, especially in the officer corps, ritualized excessive drinking. Certain middle-class sub-communities, most notoriously students, made it a central socializing experience, and the middle classes in general drank heavily, though in private. Clearly, if attitudes towards drinking were context dependent, the central issue to alcohol consumption is not *what* was consumed but *how* it was consumed.[11]

But if alcohol consumption is historically and contextually structured, quantitative data fail to illuminate the meanings of this consumption, especially relevant in the radically different context of the nineteenth century.[12] Alcohol played a central role in most social groups, not just the working classes, and emphasizing quantity of consumption falsely presumes conclusions related to the social role of alcohol, most significantly the presumptive link between consumption levels and alcoholism and poverty. In short, while the socioeconomic conditions of the working classes surely influenced proletarian drinking patterns, other highly variable factors such as political restrictions, commercialization, and pre-industrial drinking habits based on gender, work, and festival patterns shaped the contours of leisure consumption of alcohol. For example, workers did not necessarily see their leisure time, especially Sundays, as an excuse for drunkenness but for recovery. Alcohol abuse would have undermined the restorative intent, though its acceptable moderate use was regarded as a source of nutrition and socialization. Indeed, in one union survey from 1910, the overwhelming majority of respondents listed walks outdoors as their favorite leisure activity, not drunken revelry.[13]

A central component of virtually every society, alcohol exists as a medium of cultural exchange. As such, alcohol consumption alters in meaning and occasionally in form as cultures and values change. Since industrialization altered drinking customs, alcohol consumption belongs in the category of culturally variable mediated experience along with all leisure consumption. One such change brought by industrialization was the reification by reformists of drunkenness as a social problem. Yet, alcohol as popular culture contained meanings rooted in social practices and contexts independent from the middle classes. Reducing alcohol to its inebriating effects ignores three fundamental points: alcohol served a ritual and thus social function; it was widely considered an important nutritional supplement and safe alternative to drinking water; and it acted as a cultural buffer to social dislocation.

But how to approach this cultural construct theoretically? Here, we can draw upon the concepts of Raymond Williams and Pierre Bourdieu. Williams's notion of culture as "a whole way of life," informed by Gramscian concepts of enabling and restraining elements, expands definitions of the cultural to include mundane, seemingly unritualized everyday experiences into the pattern of meaning conveyance.[14] Bourdieu's notion of *habitus* augments this concept by including the notion of "structure improvisation."[15] Personal trajectories, cultural orientations, and the compromise inherent in social interaction structured the drinking practices of workers, and these practices as *habitus* inhabited contested terrain that emphasized the inherent possibilities of development rather than limits.[16] Although no homogeneity existed in working-class drinking patterns, drink cultures nonetheless were disposed towards stability based on "an ensemble of values, gestures and rituals, prohibitions and obligations."[17] Thus, we can account for the resistance of workers to attempts to alter leisure consumption not in an object/subject dichotomy, but as a dynamic intersection between worker and society. Rather than reducing the worker to the product of rational choice assessments, we allow for the element of the irrational as lived. Further, though rules obviously informed the parameters of actions, by recognizing that workers also could and did move outside these borders we can analyze multiple behavioral variation potentialities, which were situation dependent but nonetheless followed a social logic. The essence of a viable theory of social interaction centered on leisure consumption, therefore, is mediation rather than determinacy.[18]

Returning to Cologne, the KAB confronted an ingrained culture of alcohol consumption that, while expressing regional contours, typified a pub-centered leisure culture. Club leaders remonstrated that even simple tasks required a drink to seal the event or decision. After "something serious, a rehearsal, a consultation," the KAB press complained, the men had "to sit and to drink yet another glass."[19] Like the German working classes in general, the male Catholic worker sought everyday recreation in alcohol at the local pub. Numerous rituals, such as *Trinkzwang* (expected buying of rounds), ensured consumption as a common ritual of identity. Drinking, like pub visitation or club membership, was a sign of inclusion in a unique masculine social space that blurred public and private. By the 1880s when the clubs were first forming, the pub was the only social and public space available around which to organize workers, and the clubs appropriated the distinctively masculine ethos of the neighborhood working-class pub to facilitate recruitment.

Both club and pub formed an alternative masculine working-class micro-culture separate from home, factory, or church.[20] Club and pub inevitably blurred since most clubs met at local pubs in their early years. Public meeting halls were unaffordable on a regular basis. Men refused to gather in the feminine space of the church, and the clergy wished to avoid the appearance of dictating to the clubs by meeting in church venues. Private space was also unavailable in the worker's home, both to the family head and the ubiquitous lodger. The urge for extra-familial sociability, heightened by suffocating housing conditions, could thus only be expressed in the pub or associational life. Since only a few KAB clubs (Kalk, Ehrenfeld, Cologne-South) possessed the capital to maintain private clubhouses, they met instead in the only public space readily available—the pub.

Though the meeting places of many Cologne clubs remain unknown, those available almost uniformly listed pubs and restaurants as their meeting locales. Cologne-Bickendorf met in the pub In der Lier. Cologne-Zollstock held its monthly meetings in the restaurant Ettelt. The rural Cologne-Hohlweide held its organizing meeting at the pub of Adolf Groß on Schweinheimer Straße. Club Deutz met for its founding assembly in the pub Schwippert; Cologne-North in the brewery pub of Herr Vogel on Ursulaplatz; Cologne-South in the brewery pub of Herr Eschweiler; Cologne-Middle in the pub Zur Krone on Großer Griechenmarkt. Nippes initially gathered in a brewery bar in Wißdrof on Neußer Straße. Not surprisingly, pub-drinking rituals, rules of socializing, and patterns of interaction easily transferred to the clubs. Indeed, in 1887, the middle-class Catholic daily *Kölnische Volkszeitung* favorably commented on the joint Founder's Day cele-brations of Cologne-South and Cologne-North, "The owner of the Victoria Room . . . kindly accommodated the meeting by allowing as an exception the serving of beer, the quality of which earned everyone's recognition."[21] The clubs, it seems, demanded beer even from normally alcohol-free establishments, imposing the pub culture on non-pub venues.

The pub as meeting locale inevitably featured in every activity of club life. Founding assemblies gathered in pubs – the promise of alcoholic socialization always succeeded in bringing in men even if the agenda did not. Once established, clubs found no reason to withdraw their regular business meetings from the established venue. The festival life of clubs correspondingly centered on the pub-meeting hall. When the club in Ostheim, a rural annex on the right bank, consecrated its flag in 1910, the festivities included an early morning joint Holy Communion followed by breakfast in the pub of Gottfried Schmitz. The members of twenty-one fraternal clubs were greeted "in one of the three local pubs." A parade through town once again gathered the attendees at the Schmitz hall where they convened "until the early morning hours." For Ostheim, the celebration's links to the local pubs were natural. The monthly business meeting convened in one of the pubs, and annual festivals were held "in the same place at Gottfr. Schmitz."[22] All of these Ostheim events were held in drinking establishments, and we can safely assume that alcohol was consumed since the publicans relied on alcohol sales for profit.

Yet the intimate bonds to the pub-centered alcohol culture of German workers troubled the KAB's clerical leadership. Despite no indication that the semi-private and often heavy drinking of the clubs translated into public drunkenness, KAB leaders feared that it prevented cultural and material edification, encouraged so-called *Vergnügungssucht* (literally an "addiction to pleasure"), undermined personal morality and family integrity, was physically deleterious, and hindered organizing efforts by blurring "estate honor."[23] Temperance propaganda informed the worker of alcohol's dangers without distinguishing between alcoholism, alcohol abuse, and acceptable levels of alcohol consumption. Indeed, the temperance movement rarely attempted to quantify the problem of alcoholism, begging the question of its extent. Using a reformist medicalized language, the Popular Association for Catholic Germany even equated alcohol abuse with tuberculosis, the great health bane of the era.[24] The equation typified the KAB's support for Church and middle-class temperance initiatives as complements to its program of creating an ideal Christian culture. Catholics, however, joined temperance movements for different reasons, and often organized in different associations based on class and gender. Even within a single family, alcohol consumption could serve as a dividing line just as many men wandered back and forth between temperance advocacy and personal drinking. And of course, temperance had multiple meanings – not just abstinence.

If we reject the lurid tales of reform-minded abstainers as inherently skewed, we could turn to the autobiographies of the workers themselves for alcohol's contextual meaning. Alcohol appears frequently in their narratives of daily life. (I found no autobiography written by a self-proclaimed Catholic working-class alcoholic—not surprising given the manner in which most working-class biographies were solicited as moral tales meant to encourage members of a particular political inclination.) However, autobiographical descriptions generally presented tales of alcohol abuse with a great deal of sympathy for the alcoholic. The autobiographer viewed the alcohol (ab)user as a victim of an inhumane industrial work schedule.[25] As a corollary, this identification of alcohol and work relegated drinking to a male concern. The gendering of alcohol consumption required a temperance rhetoric suited to this reality and the KAB's domestic agenda.

Consequently, concerns for the Catholic family motivated the KAB's tailoring of a middle-class anti-alcohol critique to the Catholic working classes. As confessional associations dedicated to promoting a specifically Roman Catholic lifestyle, the workingmen's clubs moralized social problems. On the basis of individual responsibility, the KAB embraced the resolution of the "drink question" as a precondition to solving the broader "social question." The People's Association for Catholic Germany urged clubs to combat alcohol abuse through "enlightenment on the effects of alcohol," "elimination of *Trinkzwang*," "strengthening of the will," and unspecified "social reforms."[26] However, unlike socialist temperance advocates, who portrayed alcohol abuse as a product of the social misery imposed on the working classes by capitalism, the KAB judged a decent standard of living insufficient in and of itself to combat alcohol abuse. Indeed, prosperity was part of the problem since alcohol was a "luxury article." For the KAB, individual morality and self-discipline dictated alcohol consumption, not social conditions. A 1906 flyer entitled "The Struggle Against Alcohol Abuse" declared, "The simple economic improvement of one's position does not suffice since this allows for greater expenditures and therewith offers opportunity to extensive consumption of alcohol . . . Instead, a greater steadfastness of character, a greater sense of responsibility must accompany an economic improvement of one's position."[27] Reiterating an anti-materialist understanding of alcohol abuse, the KAB argued elsewhere, "The alcohol question will not be resolved through the destruction of the capitalist economic order."[28] Instead, alcohol fell into the moral-religious categories of the KAB's cultural edification program.

The economic analysis related directly to the KAB's understanding of the financial consequences of alcohol consumption on the family. Otto Müller, KAB secretary-general, cited the extra costs and male exclusivity of alcohol consumption as the reason for its removal from People's Educational Nights. "Many a visitor," he argued, "will be pleased to be able to save the costs of alcoholic beverages, especially if he would like to let his family members also participate in the evening's events."[29] Without the added costs of alcohol, the working-class father could afford to bring his family, turning the events into family excursions. "With regards to the family," the clubs claimed, "a completely alcohol-free life is a duty," and the ideal father considered his family's well-being rather than his carnal appetites and exercised "manly self-control and strength of character by abstaining from alcohol."[30] To emphasize the point, *Die Arbeiterfamilie*, the KAB's family supplement, portrayed the worker who squandered his money on drink as "a horse or a child."[31]

The domestic temperance rhetoric proved a double-edged sword, however. On the one hand, temperance shifted concerns for material improvement onto family life and lifestyle choices. On the other, temperance provided women, generally seen as the objects rather than subjects of KAB policies, with a legitimized discourse to criticize male drinking and by extension the KAB and patriarchy. The extra costs of club life related to drinking stretched the thin household budget, and Catholic working-class women used temperance to complain about alcohol consumption within the clubs. They already went to the factory gate on payday to prevent the disappearance of their husbands' wages in a round of drinking. Many autobiographies remarked on this practice as necessary to ensure the family's survival, as Peter Fröhlich attested: "On pay day the wives always stood by the factory gate and construction sites and waited for their husbands. For their colleagues, such men were henpecked and were not taken seriously. Other wives went looking for their husbands in the pubs if they did not return from work on time." [32] The alcohol-related gender tension weakened the KAB since husbands, for the sake of domestic tranquillity, often conceded to their wives' wishes not to spend the family budget on club life, leading Otto Müller to ask rhetorically, "How often has a woman's influence kept a husband away from the necessary clubs (workingmen's clubs, unions) because of her complaints about unnecessary 'club money'," primarily money for social drinking.[33]

Despite the KAB's explicit patriarchy, temperance activities thus provided women a platform for shaping the public arena politically and culturally. The political avenues afforded women, otherwise restricted, in part explain the influential role women played in the temperance movement internationally, though female temperance advocacy could also reinforce gendered presumptions about feminine familial nurturing.[34] In an unexpected twist, male KAB members justified their drinking with the KAB's domestic rhetoric. A flyer on domestic training for working-class daughters held the untrained housewife responsible for a husband's flight to the pub in asking, "How many [husbands] flee from the domestic hearth and vainly seek 'energy' in alcoholic beverages and the satisfaction of their appetites?"[35] Alcohol as male refuge appeared repeatedly in KAB literature that blamed women's insufficient domestic skills for alcoholism.[36] Franz Hitze, a sociologically trained priest and KAB and People's Association leader, argued that "visits to the pub" and "domestic quarrels" were the "inevitable consequences" of modern working-class domestic life – here, the strategic emphasis on domestic not industrial causality.[37] Otto Müller similarly traced "visitation of the pub by the husband" and "frequent discord between the couple" to the consequences of "an uninviting home."[38] Even advice for women, such as the pages of the wildly popular self-help manual for Catholic working-class housewives *Domestic Bliss*, recommended that women acknowledge alcohol in men's life and that they "not accuse him" of this fault; rather, they should "try to make the home more pleasant so that he wants to stay."[39] Though the KAB linked alcohol to the family question, from its male perspective, alcohol was just as often a symptom of familial dysfunction rather than its cause. Engaging in a palliative self-justification that shifted blame onto the worker's wife rationalized and effectively exonerated male working-class drinking within the KAB.

Nonetheless, Catholic temperance did confront drinking and suggest alternatives. Rather than drinking, the KAB proposed "ennobling leisure" consisting of "inexpensive and healthful sociability and entertainment that refresh the body and mind."[40] To counter nutritional arguments, mass-produced flyers listed excessive alcohol as a "major cause of malnutrition . . . and physical deformity";[41] it was "not a useful source of nutrition and fortification, only a luxury article that can have highly dangerous consequences for the person, for the family and the children of the alcohol consumer."[42] Where such direct appeals failed, the KAB attempted – usually disastrously – to regulate alcohol consumption in the clubs. Along those lines, Otto Müller forbade alcohol at any People's Educational Nights:

> The fears that have been expressed here and there that the number of visitors would be reduced if nothing were drunk have not been realized to our knowledge. Why should our people not learn to relax and have fun without beer or even schnapps! In the theater, in high-class concerts, etc., alcohol is always excluded and no one misses it; why do we then want to make an exception for the People's Educational Nights?[43]

Müller compared the drinking habits of the Catholic working classes to the middle classes where sobriety and self-improvement through the cultivation of the fine arts had replaced alcohol consumption and the associated "dirty jokes and insipid way of speaking of the beer bench." Müller and other leaders hoped that People's Educational Nights would counter the temptation "to visit the pub" and "excessive alcohol consumption," by "accustoming the individual to noble recreation and pleasures."[44] Clearly, the KAB was modeling its prescriptions on middle-class expectations. The *Arbeiterfamilie* argued that in public, "they [the bourgeoisie] drink nothing since they consider spirits as something serious that does not fit in well with the 'cozy' pub."[45] The KAB thus encouraged workers to emulate middle-class drinking specifically and middle-class cultural consumption generally.

Although moral-cultural imperatives drove much of the anti-alcohol agenda, KAB leaders also had direct political and organizational reasons for their opposition to drinking. They often viewed pubs and alcohol consumption as avenues towards socialism. Police officials tended to agree, as one report referred to private drinking clubs as "breeding halls for social democratic efforts and incitements."[46] As confirmation, no less a figure than Karl Kautsky referred to pubs as the "sole bulwark of political freedom for the proletariat."[47] Additionally, the KAB feared that drinking hindered organizing. A Cologne archdiocesan report complained, "Alcohol abuse among broad circles is a strong hindrance for the advancement of the laboring estate [because] it encourages a degrading lack of interest in material and intellectual cultural assets . . . and under its dominance there can be no talk of solidarity and self-education."[48] The "drink question" thus became entangled with the need for organizational growth and solidarity, an entanglement that produced competing imperatives and reflected similar developments in the socialist labor movements.[49]

Yet a public goal of the KAB remained temperance. To underscore this goal, in 1909 the annual report from the Cologne clubs concluded, "The Delegate's Congress considers it necessary to promote the fight against alcoholism in every way through educational lectures in club meetings and where possible through the formation of local branches of the Catholic *Kreuzbündnis*." The resolution called

242

for an abstinence pledge "as an example to those endangered and as a support for those susceptible to alcoholism."[50] The Cologne archdiocese encouraged all clubs to join the anti-alcohol Men's Association for the Struggle Against Public Immorality and the *Kreuzbündnis*.[51] The 1913 congress discussed "The Working-men's Clubs and the Anti-Alcohol Movement" with the following conclusion:

> The workingmen's clubs were requested to instruct their members over the consequences of alcohol abuse in the laboring estate and in the worker's family, whereby it was not just a matter of pointing out the economic causes of excessive alcohol use, but also, through individual education and education of family members, of pointing out the duty to overcome the dangers and opportunities for alcohol abuse. Lectures to this purpose have been held in a large number of clubs, especially in the Aachen, Essen, and Krefeld districts.[52]

The congress report referred to the 1912–13 winter program, which included a meeting on "Our Workingmen's Clubs in the Fight against Alcoholism," as a positive step on the local level.[53]

Through temperance, the clubs sought to mold proletarian leisure consumption to an ideal Christian lifestyle. Indeed, cultural and moral uplifting and sobriety remained firmly intertwined.[54] Within the clubs, the German Catholic Church thus participated in a broad Christian anti-alcohol crusade epiphenomenal to industrialization in all societies.[55] At the same time, the factors that created such noticeable variations in drinking patterns also contoured the meaning of temperance. German temperance, most closely associated with the German Association for the Prevention of Alcohol Abuse founded in 1883, eschewed teetotalism and prohibitionism, and women played a minor role, at best. Britain and North America, in contrast, embraced an evangelically derived abstinence program largely led by women that culminated in American prohibition. The origins of this distinction rest in the respective social, cultural, and political systems and in the groups that advanced temperance. Ideationally, Catholic and evangelical orientations differed fundamentally on a world-affirming versus world-denying attitudinal aesthetic. While evangelicals primarily carried temperance in the Anglo-American world, in Germany, although containing an undeniable religious element, temperance grew from a combination of progressive-liberal traditions and Catholic initiatives that prioritized moderation rather than abstinence. Further, even in Germany the movement fractured along political/cultural/religious fault lines as both the Catholic and socialist labor movements revealed deep ambiguities within their temperance initiatives, most clearly revealed in the failure of the socialist schnapps boycott of 1909 not only to convince the SPD of its program but also to collaborate with non-socialist temperance initiatives.

In a broader perspective, differing confessional and ethnic communities often diverged precisely on the point of alcohol. American and Canadian scholars have long noticed the closer ties of Protestantism to temperance. But even among the allegedly pro-alcohol Catholic immigrants in the United States, German Catholics and Irish Catholics differed on the issue as urban Irish Catholics often embraced teetotalism while more Midwestern German immigrants remained aloof.[56] At the same time, in religiously derived temperance initiatives, religion motivated worker as well as bourgeois and served as a bridge between classes and even confessions in religiously divided nations such Canada, the United States, Britain, and Germany.[57] Considering these variations, we must challenge the notion that alcohol reform was motivated exclusively or primarily by the needs for social control of the middle classes over workers, or in the case of North America over immigrants, during the upheavals of industrialization. Though German historiography, with notable exceptions, remains situated in Weberian models of rationalization and Norbert Elias's theories of the "civilizing process," authors as diverse as Detlev Peukert and Michael Foucault have demonstrated that direct social disciplining has limits. Working-class alcohol consumers resisted and adapted not only attempts at political supervision – be that from state, church, party, or middle-class reformers – but also commercializing rationalization. The relationship of Catholic workers in Wilhelmine Germany to alcohol consumption challenges a grand narrative of modernization as inexorably imposing the logic of commercialization on leisure consumption. The present-day density (and, a beer connoisseur might add, quality) of German breweries reflects the ability of German workers to preserve local drinking habits in the face of centralizing industrial pressures as well as temperance. That beer drinking in the United States evolved in a radically different manner attests to the importance of cultural variables at determining economic conditions. In the KAB, workers integrated traditional practices of alcohol consumption—its communal consumption, use in festivals, relaxation, and shirking—into modern forms that defied a market model of culture and the reduction of consumption to a supply-and-demand curve. At the same time, however, changes in drinking patterns reflected gradual shifts in working-class leisure attitudes that evolved over generations as conditions changed, including experience with the newer industrial spirits of the nineteenth century. Further, workers were not unaffected by the constant inculcation of middle-class values, including drinking behavior. Again, the key is to accept drinking cultures as inherently flexible within their stability.

Ultimately, temperance initiatives in the clubs faltered despite support from the Church and middle classes. In the face of workers' refusal to conform to clerical expectations, the KAB, led by its chaplain-presidents, confronted the choice of pushing an unpopular agenda or adapting that agenda. Efforts to advance temperance, especially abstinence, repeatedly led to membership dissatisfaction, negatively impacting the membership roster. Since the KAB's primary imperative was the maintenance of working-class loyalty to the Church, the chaplain-presidents, as the movement's lieutenants, decided that organizational needs outweighed a cultural ideal. Their socialist counterparts faced a similar dilemma, for despite the active lobbying of the German Abstinent Workers' League, formed in 1903 out of frustration at the SPD's refusal to advance temperance, when the socialist labor movement faced a choice between advancing temperance or respecting the membership's clear preference for drink, it too chose membership over principle.[58] Such a compromise was possible in each case since alcohol, unlike other vices or platforms, did not threaten the underlying morality of either the SPD or the Wilhelmine Catholic Church.

Even steps calculated to combat the pub culture often backfired. Some clubs, for example, built or purchased their own clubhouses to free the meetings from the publican noose. Most notably, Cologne-South consecrated the Anno House in 1898.[59] Yet by 1911, the forty-four clubs of the left-Rhenish Cologne-Mülheim district could still count only three clubs with their own house and twenty-one with a regular meeting place.[60] Though the KAB initially hoped that building or buying into private clubhouses would liberate the clubs from pub culture, owning a house brought an unexpected conundrum – the clubhouse relied on alcohol sales for profit. Club Cologne-Ehrenfeld typified the relationship between clubhouses and drinking. After years of meeting in local pubs, in 1891 Cologne-Ehrenfeld listed its meetinghouse as the KAB's privately owned Leo Building, which financed itself through hall rentals and a restaurant-pub.[61] Far from eliminating drinking, however, the clubhouses immediately began serving alcohol as the only way to finance operations. But the club turned pub could not count on the patronage of club members outside meeting nights, provoking the chaplain-president to complain, "It was truly not asking too much that you take a few extra steps to drink in our club house that glass of beer that you intend to drink."[62] Apparently members were wont to "drink their glass of beer in other pubs rather than in the club premises" due to social pressure from non-club acquaintances.[63] The chaplain-president of Cologne-Ehrenfeld scolded his members for their choice of venue, not their drinking. The drinking culture remained even if the publican as middle-man disappeared. In effect, the KAB became the publican!

On another level, the chaplain-presidents, as theologically trained priests, generally proved reluctant to lecture members on non-religious themes. They believed that moral-religious topics were the natural purview of the clubs, and they also feared exploring topics on which they were not clearly competent. The annual report from 1913 referred to this reluctance when it complained, "The religious lectures of the Winter Program have been held in almost all clubs . . . [but] the other lectures have not found the consideration they deserve." The "other lectures" included anti-alcohol topics. The report chastised right-Rhenish Cologne for showing "negligence" while left-Rhenish Cologne brought only "low consideration" to the alcohol issue. A disinterest and distance from temperance initiatives emerged even in the admonishments of reports calling for greater anti-alcohol agitation:

> Since other organizations already engage satisfactorily in the promotion of the temperance movement, the workingmen's clubs can generally restrict themselves to supporting these efforts through occasional enlightenment and encouragement of members, when appropriate by joining the *Kreuzbündnis*. The development of a corresponding drive for legislative measures by the Cartel Association of Catholic Workingmen's Clubs in West-, South-, and East Germany has not yet occurred due to more pressing concerns.[64]

The call to join the *Kreuzbündnis*, with this caveat, was no longer a goal but merely a suggestion "when appropriate." The KAB leaders granted the clubs tacit permission to "restrict themselves" on this front. Even the clubs' national leadership relegated the topic to the back burner as it pursued "more pressing concerns." Indeed, the report a year earlier in 1912, which had first adopted the anti-alcohol resolution of 1909, disclosed that, aside from "several clubs" joining the Men's Association for the Struggle Against Public Immorality and the *Kreuzbündnis*, "no special events or measures" related to drinking or moral issues in general had been taken in the year prior to the congress.[65] The temperance rhetoric was empty in practice.

The reluctance to confront alcohol as an "enemy of the worker," despite Church and KAB admonitions, lay in the unwillingness to alienate the working-class membership.[66] The chaplain-presidents recognized that the leisure consumption of alcohol by workers, for all the attempts to direct and control it, remained defiantly immune to quick changes. As a minority religion without full state support, German Catholicism by the turn of the century no longer was willing to participate in a test of wills between Church and workers. Alcohol was the social lubricant of KAB club life which otherwise faced mass defection. Despite a public stance against alcohol, the leadership had to confront the workers' willingness selectively to reject aspects of the movement—in this case, the anti-alcohol message. Quite simply, socializing required alcohol, and the members demanded socializing. To deny them their drink pushed them out the door and into a conceivably worse alternative. Additionally, privileging familial goals over men's cultural prerogatives by attacking alcohol consumption risked associating the clubs with femininity. As a result, the clubs mostly tolerated alcohol consumption in practice while agreeing with temperance platforms in theory. And the members continued to drink and insist on alcohol's presence at virtually every event. The chaplain-presidents in particular conceded since their personal popularity as well as the success of their local club required accommodation. Far from the KAB serving as a one-way transmission belt for Church cultural and ideological values, workers repeatedly asserted their independent identity. Provided fundamental theological questions were not involved when such conflicts occurred, the KAB accommodated and adapted rather than risk workers' alienation from the Church.

The conflict within the clubs reinforces scholarship on alcohol consumption as a social boundary, with boundaries serving as points of conflict and definition.[67] Important here is the contrast of alcohol's normalized and normalizing practice with its image as illegitimate. In Germany, this contrast served as a key social boundary between classes, genders, and religions. Indeed, in the process of temperance's mass mobilization, the control or directing intention of elites often collapsed as the mobilized lower classes asserted agency through these new social movements to shape the institutions and values of socially superior classes.[68] KAB members imposed a reinterpreted meaning of temperance on the temperance movement rather than accept the imposition of outside values. The KAB provided Catholic workers with an organizational-institutional basis from which they could successfully defend cultural consumption patterns despite the intention of these institutions to dictate social norms.

Though Catholic workers operated in a sometimes rigid social-religious context, they nonetheless had mastery over this context in so far as they made choices about their drinking habits.[69] Since the struggle over alcohol consumption did not occur solely in the pubs or in the meetings and activities of temperance activists but in the community, workers could rely on non-institutional domains to maintain their identities. Like most forms of leisure, whether public or private, alcohol consumption can only be understood in the everyday life of family, neighborhood, and workplace. Here, *Alltagsgeschichte,* the history of everyday life, has paved a clear path for considering these non-institutional domains of social and political life.[70] The outrage of middle-class reformers over perceived alcoholic excesses amongst workers does not serve as credible evidence for the reality of working-class drinking. Indeed, their repetition of critical tropes based on misleading presumptions and classist prejudices served more to estrange than convince. While the Church and clubs attempted objectively to coordinate and regularize workers' lives with the aid of the unseen forces of habit and disposition that the Church and clubs also helped structure, workers could reject efforts to alter their drinking patterns by relying on the strengths of other habits and traditions.

The Catholic workingmen's clubs sought to redefine proletarian Catholic patterns of leisure consumption to conform to an ideal Christian lifestyle based primarily on middle-class values. This transformation meant exposing the workers to "high" culture while simultaneously replacing older leisure practices with new patterns. Working-class alcohol consumption, however, was too deeply ingrained to be rooted out. Workers revealed a variegated understanding of drinking that differentiated between social drinking, private drinking, workplace drinking, and even medicinal drinking. All attempts to impose abstinence failed miserably because they did not account for clearly understood but evolving meanings of drink to workers. As a result, temperance initiatives in the KAB only alienated members. Over time, the KAB accommodated the drinking requirements of its members, even making excuses for their drinking.

Notes

1. This chapter comes from broader themes developed in my dissertation, "The Selective Appropriation of Modernity: Leisure, Gender and the Catholic Workingmen's Clubs of Cologne, 1885–1914" (dissertation, University of Wisconsin-Madison, 2000).

2. Peter Fröhlich, *Es war ein langer Weg: Erinnerungen eines alten Kölners* (Cologne: Willi Glomb, 1976), pp. 28–30.

3. For a discussion of alcohol reform discourses in Germany, especially in the relationship of workers to the "drink question," see James S. Roberts, *Drink, Temperance and the Working Class in Nineteenth-Century Germany* (Winchester, MA.: Allen & Unwin, 1984).

4. For a critical review of this literature in France see Michael Marrus, "Social Drinking in the Belle Epoque," *Journal of Social History* 7 (1974), pp. 115–41. For criticism of Marrus's disinterest in popular attitudes see Susanna Barrows, "After the Commune: Alcoholism, Temperance and Literature in the Early Third Republic," in John M. Merriman (ed.), *Consciousness and Class Experience in Nineteenth-Century Europe* (New York: Holmes and Meier, 1979), pp. 205–18.

5. See Paul E. Reckner and Stephen A. Brighton, "'Free from all vicious habits': Archaeological Perspectives on Class Conflict and the Rhetoric of Temperance," *Historical Archaeology* 33, 1 (1999), pp. 63–86. For a formative debate on class-based assumptions to alcohol consumption see the exchanges between James S. Roberts and Irmgard Vogt: James S. Roberts, "Der Alkoholkonsum deutscher Arbeiter im 19. Jahrhundert," *Geschichte und Gesellschaft* 6 (1980), pp. 220–42; James S. Roberts, "Drink and Working Class Living Standards": Irmgard Vogt, "Einige Fragen zum Alkoholkonsum der Arbeiter," *Geschichte und Gesellschaft* 8 (1982), pp. 134–40; Irmgard Vogt, "Alkoholkonsum, Industrialisierung und Klassenkonflikt," in Gisela Vögler and Karin von Welck (eds), *Rausch und Realität: Drogen im Kulturvergleich*, vol. 1 (Reinbek, 1982), pp. 202–11.

6. F. Gerlach, "Trinkhallen," in Eduard Lent (ed.), *Köln in hygienischer Beziehung: Festschrift für die Teilnehmer an der XXIII. Versammlung des Deutschen Vereins für Öffentliche Gesundheitspflege zur Feier des XXV jährigen Bestehens des Vereins. Im Auftrag der Verwaltung und Vertretung der Stadt Köln und des Niederrheinischen Vereins für Öffentliche Gesundheitspflege* (Cologne: M. Dumont Schauberg, 1898), pp. 90–1.

7. See Michael Grüttner, "Alkoholkonsum in der Arbeiterschaft, 1871-1939," in Toni Pierenkemper (ed.) *Haushalt und Verbrauch in historisches Perspektive: zum Wandel des privaten Verbrauchs in Deutschland im 19. und 20. Jahrhundert* (St. Katharinen: Scripta, 1987), pp. 229–73. For a review of quantitative alcohol consumption in Germany during the nineteenth century, including a review of Grüttner's data, see Gerhard A. Ritter and Klaus Tenfelde, *Arbeiter im Deutschen Kaiserreich* (Bonn: Dietz, 1992), pp. 510–16. For France see Sally Ledermann, *Alcool, alcoolisme, alcoolisation*, 2 vols (Paris, 1956–64).

8. For an argument of how this discourse was found even in the early modern era see B. Ann Tlusty, "Water of Life, Water of Death: The Controversy over Brandy and Gin in Early Modern Augsburg," *Central European History* 31, 1–2 (1998), pp. 1–30.

9. For perceptions of binging in Brittany, see Thierry Fillaut, *L'Alcoolisme dans l'ouest de la France pendant la seconde moitié du XIXe siècle* (Paris: La Documentation française, 1983), pp. 74–85.

10. Grüttner, "Alkoholkonsum," p. 237.

11. See Thomas Brennan, "Towards the Cultural History of Alcohol in France," *Journal of Social History* 23, 1 (1989), p. 71. See also David Goodman Mandelbaum, "Alcohol and Culture," *Current Anthropology* 6 (1965). Brennan drew upon several cultural histories of alcohol from the 1980s for his synthesis including: Wolfgang Schivelbusch, *Tastes of Paradise: A Social History of Spices, Stimulants, and Intoxicants*, trans. David Jacobson (*Das Paradies, der Geschmack und die Vernunft: Eine Geschichte der Genußmittel*, 1980) (New York: Vintage, 1993); Roman Sandgruber, *Bittersüße Genüsse: Eine Kulturgeschichte der Genußmittel* (Vienna, 1986); M. Hubner, *Zwischen Alkohol und Abstinenz: Trinksitten und Alkoholfrage im deutschen Proletariat bis 1914* (Berlin: Dietz, 1988); Alfred Heggen, *Alkohol und bürgerliche Gesellschaft im 19. Jahrhundert: Eine Studie zur deutschen Sozialgeschichte*, Einzelveröffentlichungen der historischen Kommission zu Berlin, no. 64 (Berlin: Colloquium Verlag, 1988).

12. For criticism of the quantitative Ledermann model see Gary H. Miller and Neil Agnew, "The Ledermann Model of Alcohol Consumption," *Quarterly Journal of the Study of Alcohol* 35 (1974), pp. 877–98. Cultural historians have always tended to reject the quantitative approach, which equated alcohol's social impact with physiological effects based on quantity of consumption. See Craig MacAndrew and Robert B. Edgerton, *Drunken Comportment: A Social Explanation* (Chicago: Aldine, 1969).

13. See *Schriften des Vereins für Socialpolitik*, 133–5/1–4 (1910), pp. 136–7.

14. Raymond Williams, *Culture and Society, 1780-1950* (New York: Columbia University Press, 1983).

15. For an introduction of Bourdieu's concepts see Richard Harker, Cheleen Mahar, and Chris Wilkes (eds), *An Introduction to the Work of Pierre Bourdieu: The Practice of Theory* (New York: St Martin's Press, 1990); Craig Calhoun, Edward LiPuma and Moishe Postone (eds), *Bourdieu: Critical Perspectives* (Chicago: University of Chicago Press, 1993).

16. For a discussion of the distinction between enabling and restraining elements see Raymond Williams, *Marxism and Literature* (Oxford: Oxford University Press, 1977).

17. Ulrich Wyrwa, *Branntwein und "echtes" Bier: Die Trinkkultur der Hamburger Arbeiter im 19. Jahrhundert*, Sozialgeschichtliche Bibliothek bei Junius, no. 7 (Hamburg: Junius Verlag, 1990), p. 22.

18. Drawing on these ideas, social movement theorists argue that the specifics of social identities, which include gender, religion, race and ethnicity, class, and nationality, created a culturally "embedded" individual. See Carol McClurg Mueller, "Building Social Movement Theory," in Aldon Morris and Carol McClurg Mueller (eds), *Frontiers in Social Movement Theory* (New Haven, CT: Yale University Press, 1992), p. 7.

19. "In der Stille: Pünktlichkeit und Heranwachsende," *Arbeiterfamilie: Beilage zur Westdeutschen Arbeiterzeitung* 10 (1912).

20. In the American context of the masculine space of the bar, see Roy Rosenzweig, *Eight Hours for What We Will: Workers and Leisure in an Industrial City, 1870-1920* (Cambridge: Cambridge University Press, 1983).

21. "Verbandsfest der katholischen Arbeitervereine von Köln und Umgegend," *Kölnische Volkszeitung* 231, 2 (August 22 1887).

22. Archiv des katholischen Pfarrgemeinde St. Servatius in Köln-Ostheim: *Protokoll-buch des Katholischen Arbeitervereins Ostheim, 1907 bis 1935*, in *Archiv des katholischen Pfarrgemeinde St. Servatius in Köln-Ostheim* (July 24 1910), pp. 23–5, 25, 9, 37.

23. See Franz Hitze, *Die Arbeiterfrage und die Bestrebungen zur ihren Lösung: Nebst Anlage: Die Arbeiterfrage im Lichte der Statistik*, 4th edn (Mönchengladbach: Verlag der Zentralstelle des Volksvereins, 1900), p. 198.

24. "Der Kampf gegen den Alkoholmißbrauch," *Gemeinnütziges Flugblatt*, no. 8 (Mönchengladbach: Zentralstelle des Volksvereins für das katholische Deutschland, 1906).

25. Alfred Kelly (ed.), *The German Worker: Working-Class Autobiographies from the Age of Industrialization* (Berkeley, CA: University of California Press, 1987), p. 32. For direct reference to alcohol see pp. 57–8, 263, 335–7, 364, 365, 376, 385–6, 390–2, 409, 410, 413, 416–7, 419.

26. See "Der Kampf gegen den Alkoholmißbrauch," *Gemeinnütziges Flugblatt*, no. 8.

27. Ibid.

28. "Zur Förderung der Sittlichkeit," *Jahresbericht des Verbandes der katholischen Arbeiter- und Knappenvereine der Erzdiözese Cöln für das Jahr 1909, erstattet für den Diözesandelegiertentag am 7. und 8. August 1910*, ed. Otto Müller, in *Mitteilungen an die Präsides der katholischen Arbeitervereine der Erzdiözese Cöln* 36 (1910), p. 349.

29. Otto Müller (ed.), "Die Veranstaltung der Volksbildungsabende," in *Volksbildung-sabende*, 2nd edn, Soziale Tagesfragen 27 (Mönchengladbach: Zentralstelle des Volksvereins, 1906), p. 32.

30. "Zur Förderung der Sittlichkeit," p. 349.

31. "In der Stille: Schaffensfreude," *Arbeiterfamilie* 14 (1912).

32. Fröhlich, *Es war ein langer Weg*, pp. 34–5. See also Kelly, *German Worker*, pp. 278, 364.

33. Otto Müller, *Katholische Arbeiterinnenvereine*, in *Soziale Tagesfragen* 32 (Mönchengladbach: Zentralstelle des Volksvereins für das katholische Deutschland, 1905), pp. 32–3.

34. The importance of women in North American temperance has led to several important studies. For a study of where such impulses led to conflict see Rachel E. Bohlman, "'Our House is Beautiful': The Women's Temple and the WCTU Effort to Establish Place and Identity in Downtown Chicago, 1887–1898," *Journal of Women's History* 11, 2 (1999), pp. 110–34.

35. "Wo sollen unsere Töchter haushalten lernen?" *Gemeinnütziges Flugblatt* no. 10 (Mönchengladbach: Verlag des Volksvereins, 1907).

36. See Dr Blumberger, "Haushaltungs-Unterricht," in *Köln in hygienischer Beziehung*, p. 412.

37. Hitze, *Die Arbeiterfrage und die Bestrebungen zur ihren Lösung*, p. 99.

38. Müller, *Katholische Arbeiterinnenvereine*, p. 28.

39. "Mahnwort eines Seelsorgers an junge Hausfrauen," in *Das häusliche Glück: Vollständiger Haushaltungsunterricht nebst Anleitung zum Kochen für Arbeiterfrauen: Zugleich ein nützliches Hilfsbuch für all Frauen und Mädchen, die "billig und gut" haushalten lernen wollen: Mit Interviews aus Arbeiterfamilien neu herausgegeben von Richard Blank* (Munich: Rogner & Bernhard, 1975), pp. 8–9.

40. Hitze, *Die Arbeiterfrage und die Bestrebungen zur ihren Lösung*, p. 198.

41. "Der Kampf gegen den Alkoholmißbrauch," *Gemeinnütziges Flugblatt*, no. 8. The flyer assiduously used the term "alcohol misuse" to navigate between abstinence advocates and an alcohol drinking working-class membership.

42. "Zur Förderung der Sittlichkeit," p. 349.

43. Otto Müller (ed.), "Die Veranstaltung der Volksbildungsabende," in *Volksbildung-sabende*, 2nd edn, *Soziale Tagesfragen* 27 (Mönchengladbach: Zentralstelle des Volksvereins, 1906), p. 32.

44. Otto Müller (ed.), "Zwecke und Nutzen der Volksbildungsabende," in *Volksbildung-sabende*, pp. 11, 8.

45. See "In der Stille: Pünktlichkeit und Heranwachsende," *Arbeiterfamilie* 10 (1912).

46. Staatsarchiv Münster, Oberbergamt 1834: Oberbergamt Dortmund an die Regierung Düsseldorf, Münster und Arnsberg 6.8.94.

47. Karl Kautsky, "Der Alkoholismus und seine Bekämpfung," *Die Neue Zeit* (1891), p. 107.

48. "Zur Förderung der Sittlichkeit," p. 349.

49. See Roberts, *Drink, Temperance, and the Working Class*, ch. 5.

50. "Zur Förderung der Sittlichkeit," p. 349.

51. "Bekämpfung glaubensfeindlicher und unsittlicher Bestrebungen im öffentlichen Leben," *Verband der katholischen Arbeiter- und Knappenvereine der Erzdiözese Cöln: Bericht über das Geschäftsjahr 1. Juli 1911 bis 30. Juni 1912*, ed. Otto Müller (Mönchengladbach: Volksvereinsverlag, 1912), pp. 30–1.

52. "Die Arbeitervereine und die Anti-Alkoholbewegung," *Verband der katholischen Arbeiter- und Knappenvereine der Erzdiözese Cöln: Bericht über die Tätigkeit vom 1. Juli 1912 bis 30. Juni 1913*, ed. Otto Müller (Mönchengladbach: Volksvereinsverlag, 1913), p. 15.

53. "Die Arbeitervereine und die Anti-Alkoholbewegung," p. 18.

54. See for an American examination of this link, Alison M. Packer, "'Hearts Uplifted and Minds Refreshed': The Women's Christian Temperance Union and the Production of Pure Culture in the United States, 1880–1930," *Journal of Women's History* 11, 2 (1999), 135–58. WCTU activists believed that sobriety alone would not transform youth into model Christians. Instead, the WCTU's Department for the Promotion of Purity in Literature and Art enacted a program of providing morally unobjectionable and edifying wholesome culture through movies, reproductions of famous paintings, and a children's magazine.

55. For the relationship of modernization to abstinence in Ireland see Colm Kerrigan, *Father Matthew and the Irish Temperance Movement, 1838–1849* (Cork: Cork University Press, 1992). For American society see Thomas R. Pegram, *Battling Demon Rum: The Struggle for a Dry America, 1800–1933* (Chicago: Ivan R. Dee, 1998).

56. See John F. Quinn, "Father Matthew's Disciples: American Catholic Support for Temperance, 1840–1920," *Church History* 65 (December 1996), pp. 624–40.

57. For Canada see Jan Noel, *Canada Dry: Temperance Crusades before Confederation* (Buffalo: University of Toronto Press, 1995).

58. See Hartmann Wunderer, *Arbeitervereine und Arbeiterparteien: Kultur- und Massenorganisationen der Arbeiterbewegung, 1890–1933* (Frankfurt a/M: Campus, 1980), pp. 48–51.

59. "Katholischer Arbeiterverein Köln-Süd," *Christlicher Arbeiterfreund* 41 (October 7 1898).

60. See "Sonstiges aus den Vereinen," *Jahresbericht 1911 des Bezirksverbandes der katholischen Arbeitervereine Köln-Mülheim linksrheinisch* (Cologne: Heinrich Houbois, 1911), p. 16.

61. *Festschrift zur Goldenen Jubelfeier, Sonntag, den 6. Oktober 1957, Katholische Arbeiterbewegung St. Peter - St. Barbara, Köln Ehrenfeld* (Cologne: Druckerei Wienand,

1957). See also "Katholischer Arbeiterverein Ehrenfeld," *Christlicher Arbeiterfreund* 46 (November 15 1896).

62. "Katholischer Arbeiterverein Köln-Ehrenfeld," *Christlicher Arbeiterfreund* 31 (August 4 1895).

63. See "Katholischer Arbeiterverein Köln-Ehrenfeld," *Christlicher Arbeiterfreund* 46 (November 15, 1896).

64. "Die Arbeitervereine und die Anti-Alkoholbewegung," pp. 18, 19, 15.

65. "Bekämpfung glaubensfeindlicher und unsittlicher Bestrebungen im öffentlichen Leben," pp. 30–1.

66. "Zur Förderung der Sittlichkeit," p. 349.

67. Such boundary studies research in the United States has drawn heavily on Fredrik Barth's anthropological discourse: Fredrik Barth, "Introduction," in Barth (ed.), *Ethnic Groups and Boundaries: The Social Organization of Cultural Difference* (Boston, MA: Little, Brown, 1969), pp. 9–38.

68. In the case of the temperance movement and the relationship of the Anglican Church of England to workers see Gerald Wayne Olsen, "From Parish to Palace: Working-Class Influences on Anglican Temperance Movements in Great Britain, 1835–1914," *Journal of Ecclesiastical History* 40 (April 1989), 239–52.

69. Susanna Barrows and Robin Room (eds), *Drinking: Behavior and Belief in Modern History* (Berkeley, CA: University of California Press, 1991).

70. See the programmatic collection, Alf Lüdtke (ed.), *The History of Everyday Life: Reconstructing Historical Experience and Ways of Life*, trans. William Templer (Princeton, NJ: Princeton University Press, 1995).

13

'As I walked along the Bois de Boulogne': Subversive Performances and Masculine Pleasures in Fin-de-Siècle London

Christopher Breward

A feature of London street life that was peculiar to the nineteenth and early twentieth centuries was the oafish custom of crying purposeless catchphrases. The phrases had no special application and were seldom used in any apposite sense. They were parrot cries from one dull mind to another. One finds no record of them in earlier times; they seem to coincide with the coming of the music hall. One of the earliest, current in the 'forties was "Wal-ker!" intended to convey incredulity. Others of later date were "I'll have your hat" "Fancy meeting you" . . . "Does your mother know you're out?" In the later years of the century they were chiefly used as an introduction between boys and girls at those now vanished institutions, Monkey's Parades. In a grosser, rather Silenian vein, but also of the 'eighties and 'nineties, were those parading groups of young men in Inverness capes and Gibus hats, who threw their sovereigns about, and were celebrated in such songs as . . . "The Rowdy Dowdy Boys" . . . "Hi-tiddley-hi-ti" . . . They were the last phase of that spirit. Getting drunk, sitting on the roofs of hansoms and singing choruses, staying out all night . . . The present century does not know the type . . . it really died with Mafeking Night and Victoria.[1]

In his description of urban street noise and its perpetrators in late Victoria London, popular journalist Thomas Burke recalled a "vulgarization" of the fashionable bachelor model which dominated commercial representations of masculine fashion in the period. Burke identified the activities of disruptive working-class youths who parodied the significant characteristics of such metropolitan idols. The exchange of popular catch phrases, culled from the latest music hall hit, drew attention to the physical shortcomings or idiosyncratic dress code of their targets, here labeled as effeminate mother's boys or unworthy possessors of overly spectacular headgear. At the other extreme, the disposable income and smart attire of bachelor role-models found a distorted reflection in the antisocial carousing of middle-class adolescents, followers of the very stage artistes whose songs lampooned their own misadventures and sartorial pretensions and provided ammunition for the less genteel hecklers of the monkey parades. What Burke's memoir infers is that the bachelor model found a broader circulation beyond the confines of West End culture. Far from passively representing the possibilities inherent in the goods of city-center sartorial entrepreneurs, the symbolic figure of the fashionable young man also preempted the contesting of masculine identities across the social and spatial gradations of the metropolis. This chapter aims to test the reproduction of such identities in the broader social life of London. It will argue that suburban middle- and lower middle-class men, alongside the gangs and "clicks" of the industrial inner city constituted a massive market for the fashionable commodity and its imagery, whether appropriating it into the rhythms of local fashion systems and assumptions regarding manly style, or refuting its expensive connotations for more subversive ends. Both strategies found a platform in the culture of music hall, whose role as a mediator and archive for modern fashionable masculinities deserves further examination.

For and Against Respectability: Suburban Savvy

When I arrived cabs and motors were forming a queue. Each cab "vomited" some dainty arrangement in lace or black cloth. Everybody was "dressed" (I think I said that it was Surbiton) . . . Everybody, you felt sure, could be trusted to do the decent thing, their features were clean and firm; they were well tended . . . Altogether a nice set, as insipid people mostly are: What are known in certain circles as Gentlemen. On one point I found myself in sympathy with them: they were a pleasure loving lot. They were indeed almost hedonists. [2]

The social rhythms of suburban life were often represented as a pale and anodyne reflection of inner-city energies by contemporary commentators. The suburbans themselves portrayed as a small-mindedly respectable rebuke to the excessive follies of fashionable modernity. Accordingly, much recent scholarship has attempted to track an objective history of suburbia or account for the prejudices directed at its inhabitants in a manner that rejects contemporary sentiment or hyperbole as unreliable.[3] However, there is scope within the primary literature for illuminating both the material culture of those who found themselves labeled as conservative, old fashioned or reactionary, and the attitudes of those who condemned them.[4] I would argue that within the rhetoric which both attacked and sometimes validated a suburban existence lay valuable coordinates for the structuring of social identities. For at the precise moment when more and more of the population were choosing to identify themselves with an untested life outside of the city center, authors and publishers were expending a great deal of print and energy in ensuring the provision of a literature which set such lives under unprecedented scrutiny.

In ironic tones of mock concern, Thomas Burke portrayed a Surbiton whist drive as the place where the spontaneous wickedness of West End gambling was watered down to an overstructured opportunity for the testing of local rivalries, hosted under the weak pretence of a little organized decadence. In a more direct appraisal of the suburban condition, C.F.G. Masterman echoed the sentiment when he stated in 1909 that

> no one . . . fears the suburbans, and perhaps for that reason no one respects them. They only appear articulate in comedy, to be made the butt of a more nimble witted company outside: like . . . the queer people who dispute – in another recent London play – concerning the respective social advantages of Clapham and Herne Hill. Strong in numbers and in possession of a vigorous and even tyrannical convention of manners, they lack organization, energy and ideas. [5]

Masterman overlooked the contradiction lurking in his assessment, for far from lacking any coherent sense of social direction, suburban tastes and cultural inclinations so far as they existed in the prejudiced opinions of professional observers, were underpinned and defined by a ferocious attention to propriety and good form, and by extension an attention to the nature of fashion itself. While this resulted in an undeniable conformity to rigid social rules concerning display and behavior, it also placed the material culture of life on the peripheries of metropolitan experience in a direct relationship to that enjoyed by those at the center. Its forms were as reliant on the inner city as a focus for both disapproval and emulation, as those sophisticates who defined the meaning of fashion at its supposed core were reliant on the "dull" censure or adherence of suburbia to set off their "brilliance" all the more brightly. These permeable boundaries and a sense of mutual existence underscored Masterman's more dismissive assumptions:

> They are the creations not of the industrial, but of the commercial and business activities of London. They form a homogenous civilization – detached, self centred, unostentatious – covering the hills along the northern and southern boundaries of the city . . . It is a life of security; a life of sedentary occupation, a life of respectability . . . Its male population is engaged in all its working hours in small, crowded offices, under artificial light, doing immense sums, adding up other men's accounts, writing other men's letters. It is sucked into the city at daybreak and scattered again as darkness falls. It finds itself towards evening in its own territory in the miles and miles of little red houses in little silent streets, in number defying imagination. Each boasts its pleasant drawing room, its high sounding title – "Acacia Villa" or "Camperdown Lodge" – attesting unconquered human aspiration.

There are many interests beyond the working hours . . . a greenhouse filled with chrysanthemums . . . a bicycle shed, a tennis lawn. The women, with their single domestic servants . . . find time hangs rather heavy on their hands. But there are excursions to shopping centres in the West End, and pious sociabilities. [6]

Conformity and aspiration, it was claimed, informed a life that otherwise found meaning through an adherence to the hollowness of commodity culture. Leisure and gossip filled the void once occupied, supposedly, by the moral energies of industrial production. The implications for the forging of suburban masculine identities, given the weight that such negative rhetoric carried, were profound:

Listen to the conversation in the second class carriages of a suburban railway train, or examine the literature and journalism specially constructed for the suburban mind; you will often find endless chatter about the King, the Court, and the doings of a designated "Society"; personal paragraphs, descriptions of clothes . . . a vision of life in which the trivial and heroic things are alike exhibited, but in which there is no adequate test or judgement . . . This is the explanation of the so called snobbery of the suburbs. Here is curiosity, but curiosity about lesser occupation . . . so . . . a feud with a neighbour . . . a bustling church . . . entertainment, or a criticism of manners and fashion . . . will be thrown force and determination which might have been directed to effort of permanent worth. [7]

Added to this, opportunities for the comparison of appearances and attitudes were legion in a culture that devoted greater energy and time to socially inclusive activities. For all the criticism of the introverted nature of suburban living, the practicalities of traveling to and from work every day and the intense engagement with street life enforced by city-center occupations that annexed a more homogenous experience of home and work, actually encouraged a tendency to observation, speculation, and competition; a tendency allied by some early sociologists to the degeneracy of crowd behavior and the feminizing pull of metropolitan social activity.[8] The popular journal *The Modern Man* is littered with examples of the attention paid by men to the appearance and behavior of others in such situations. In an article titled "My Fellow Passengers," William Thomson noted that:

The pawnbroker's assistant . . . gets into my carriage every morning. His suit has obviously been dry cleaned, and the cut does not quite seem to have been suggested by the figure of the present wearer; but what he lacks in the matter of tailoring he makes up for in jewellery. Sleeve links, watch chain, tie pin are all crudely visible, and his diamond ring is the more noticeable because the finger which adorns it is not very clean, and is actually in mourning at the tip . . . The callow youth is another unbearable. I have several in mind, but one in particular . . . is appropriately addressed as "Baby" . . . Fairly well dressed, he has every confidence in himself, and chatters inanely throughout the journey . . . his favourite subjects being allusions to going out to dinner, sly references to well known but perfectly respectable actresses, and complaints about the trouble it is to get into evening dress every night.[9]

A further column "Judging a Man by His Buttonhole" adapted the popular and sentimental language of flowers to an observational code that sorted the discredited "green carnation brigade" from the passion flower wearing collier, the orchid sporting "young dog about town" and the rosebud bedecked "ladies man."[10] Light hearted though such articles may have been, their jokey pseudosociological tone endorsed a lively masculine attention to the social detail of everyday appearances and encouraged the circulation and discussion of fashionable stereotypes in suburban life. Contemporary critics like Masterman failed entirely, of course, to see the joke:

No one can seriously diagnose the condition of the "suburbans" today without seriously considering also the influences of [their] chosen literature. There is nothing obscene about it, and little that is morally reprehensible. But it is mean and tawdry and debased . . . The reader passes . . . from one frivolity to another. Now it is a woman adventurer on the music hall stage, now the principal characters in some "sensational" divorce case, now a serial story in which the "bounder" expands himself . . . At the end this newspaper world becomes – to is victim – an epitome and mirror of the whole world. Divorced from the ancient sanities of manual or skilful labour, of exercise in the open air, absorbed for the bulk of his day in crowded offices . . . each a unit in a crowd which has drifted away from the realities of life in a complex, artificial city civilization, he comes to see no other universe than this – the rejoicing over hired sportsmen . . . the ingenuities of sedentary guessing competitions, the huge frivolity and ignorance of the world of music hall and the yellow newspaper. Having attained so dolorous a consummation, perhaps the best that can be hoped for him is the advent of that friendly bullet which will terminate his inglorious life.[11]

While this celebration of the ephemerality and endless variety of the fashionable world earned suburban men a condemnation that labeled them as emasculated, the development of more internalized identities, which drew their influences from the enclosed domestic world of the suburban home rather than the bright lights and bachelor stereotypes of the public stage, further aided a characterization of suburban masculinity and its appearances as effeminate. A renewed pleasure in the rhythms and material culture of domestic life has been identified by several recent histories as a defining trait of modern constructions of manliness from the turn of the century to the outbreak of World War II, though a reaction to the horrors of trench warfare after 1914 is more generally citied as the cause of the change.

Margaret Marsh urges a rereading of the cliché of the frustrated office worker that allows more space for the consideration of the satisfaction derived by men from marital and paternal relationships in the social context of the suburb. Her focus and material are American, but the thrust of her argument and the insights it provides for a reconsideration of chronologies and priorities are equally instructive for the British situation. She states that

> When historians think about . . . men at the turn of the twentieth century, among the images they usually conjure up are that of a bored clerk or middle manager in some impersonal office . . . counting the company's money, longing nostalgically for a time when a man could find adventure and get rich . . . conquering new frontiers . . . We owe the association of the corporate drone with the flamboyant Rough Rider to an influential essay by John Higham who argued that one of the most significant American cultural constructs at the turn of the century was a growing cult of masculinity . . . He cited the growing popularity of boxing and football, a disaffection from genteel fiction, and, not least, the rise in the level of national bellicosity, as important indicators of a new public mood . . . Those anxieties . . . undoubtedly existed, but in the course of my research on suburban families, I have discovered a different manner of middle class man. There is evidence to suggest that historians will need to supplement the image of the dissatisfied clerk, with a picture of a contented suburban father, who enjoyed the security of a regular salary, a predictable rise through the company hierarchy, and greater leisure.[12]

Marsh's revisions find a resonance in the gentle tone of light domestic novels published for a middle- and lower-middle-class London market from the late 1880s onwards. Focusing on the routines of suburban life they provided reassurance for their readers that the markers of their lives, moving house, pursuing courtships, hiring servants, attending local functions, taking an annual holiday and occasionally visiting the glowing lights of the West End, carried emotional worth. Largely descriptive and lacking the reforming drive that informed social realist novels of East End life, their purpose was reflective, self-validating, and entertaining. The power of their humor relied on a close observation of, and sympathy for, the rhythms of suburban life by the author, and a recognition of the veracity of situations and character types by the reader. In this sense their overlooked narratives provide a useful source for the historians keen to uncover nuances lost in the hostile characterizations of the suburban by polemicists such as Masterman. The particular value of the novels for the design historian lies in the emphasis they place on the role of clothing and other commodities in establishing a sense of place, time, and suburban order.

Foremost among the exponents of the genre was the novelist William Pett Ridge whose obituary in *The Times* informed readers that in 1895 Pett Ridge published his first novel *A Clever Wife* but it was not until 1898 that he really found himself with *Mord Em'ly,* a vivid presentation of a girl of the Walworth Road. Thereafter he produced some 30 novels and collections of short stories which established him securely in the affections of a large and faithful public . . . His characters were nearly all people who have come down in the world or have bettered themselves, and his highly selective art was shown especially in little scenes of daily life depicted with a sureness of touch and a nice economy of words. He was also an admirable lecturer choosing subjects such as "The London Boy," "The Cockney in the Theatre" and "The London Accent" on which he was an expert.[13]

Further supportive elaborations on suburban mores were penned by the author Keble Howard, who in his series on the Smith family of Surbiton included an open letter to his fictional heroes:

You confided to me, when first you made your appearance, that you were pained because certain people insisted upon regarding you as satirical figures, and the comedy in which the unimaginative take it for granted that any work with the name of "Smith" or "Surbiton" in the title must necessarily depend for success upon the old fashioned treatment. In the same class . . . you must place those who protest that there is no scope for artistic work between Mayfair and Whitechapel. To write of the middle classes, in short, is a confession of mediocrity. They do not understand, you see, how much more difficult it is to get an effect without flying to extremes. They admit that the middle classes are the mainstay of England, but venture to write about them, save in the blessed spirit of satire, and artistically you are forthwith damned. But you and I, my friends, are not to be frightened off our little stage by such easy disparagement.[14]

The suburban novel also differed from bachelor literature, though both focused with differing degrees of sympathy on the significance of domestic detail and routine. Authors like Pett Ridge and Keble Howard were keen to stress the inclusive social nature of "life outside the radius," coterminous with Marsh's claims that "the suburb served as the spatial context for what its advocates hoped would be a new form of marriage. Husbands and wives would be companions, not rivals, and the spectre of individualist demands would retreat in the face of family togetherness."[15] The bachelor novel was more likely to stress the benefits of independence from any broader family economy, and the freedom this allowed for the more "selfish" and "fashionable" consumption of leisure, clothing, or food that marked the "individualist" gradations of metropolitan distinction. Occasionally, however, the two forms overlapped, with bachelor households portrayed as the happy though temporary twin of suburban matrimonial bliss. A short story by A.J. Lewis titled "Our Treasures: A Story of Bachelor Housekeeping" of 1887, tracked the move away in authorial emphasis from a dissolute city-center bachelor existence towards a more comfortable approximation of familial comfort, which anticipated the particular social style associated with the "suburban man":

> Tidd and I are both . . . confirmed bachelors. Tidd is an architect with a taste for music and dry sherry. I am a tea-broker, with an office in Mincing Lane. We had always lived in apartments; sometimes apart, but more often together. We had endured every possible variety of landlady, and every conceivable species of "cat" from the feline who would use my Rowland's Macassar and my favourite hairbrush, to the "tom" who borrowed my diamond shirt studs and smoked my best cigars. We had tried chambers but we found that Scylla the "laundress" was, if possible, worse than Charybidis the landlady – the last straw in that case, I remember was finding Mrs Glooge . . . wearing my dress boots . . . We were [then] fortunate to secure a house . . . which . . . possessed a variety of exceptional attractions: a conservatory, a bath room, hot water laid on everywhere, and last but not least, a peculiarly admirable kitchen range . . . known as the "Treasure" . . . Tidd and I rejoiced in anticipation over the recherché little dinners we should be able to give our bachelor friends – Toller of the Stock Exchange, and Tracy of the Probate Department. [16]

The dual identifying features of "domestic" or suburban masculine style alluded to by Lewis found even bolder description in the context of the "proper" familial suburban setting where the appearance and social participation of men were contextualized rather than heightened. Here a man's occupation or role at work, together with his close involvement and enjoyment in the ceremonies and celebrations of a home-life, marked the two sides of his sartorial self. When Pett Ridge conveyed the material presence of men in his suburban tales they were either leaving for work en masse or returning to enjoy the freedom of evening or weekend. In both instances their characterization stood in relationship to a description of the office suit or its alternatives; the fashionable trappings of leisure providing the truer indication of taste and personality. Thus in *Outside the Radius: Stories of a London Suburb* of 1899, he described how:

> At about eight twenty every weekday morning The Crescent despatches its grown up male inhabitants in search of gold. The adventurers set out, each with a small brown bag, and, excepting on rainy mornings, are silk hatted, because there are many ways of getting on in the City, but none apparently in which a silk hat is not indispensable . . . Presently the detachment which went off in the morning to attack the City and to loot it, return, without perhaps any exuberant signs of triumph, but still preserving the small brown bags, and seemingly ready for the dinners whose perfumes stroll in The Crescent. The younger men come out in startling change of costume, having put aside the silk hat and frock coat which constitute the armour they wear in attacking the City, and appear in white flannels and straw hats, which straw hats are lifted as white shoed young women trip also in the direction of the tennis ground. [17]

Beyond an adherence to the structured organization of work and leisure, the suburban male wardrobe also played a part in marking weekly and seasonal evolutions, constituting a temporal fashion system as clearly differentiated as the pivotal commercial transitions from spring to summer, autumn to winter, that dictated change in women's fashionable dress. In *Sixty Nine Birnam Road* Pett Ridge's 1908 tale of lower-middle-class life in a Clapham house, the link between clothing and the passing of time was made explicit, with the fading of older traditions adding a piquancy to his description of the development of a young male suburban style that celebrated the sporty, leisured atmosphere of summer weekends. On Sundays

> as the morning advanced there came peals from a distance, reminding City men, who sat out on the lawn and smoked a pipe, of youthful days . . . when one had a suit kept for Sunday and one's hair was pomatumed and curled, and a handkerchief scented with lavender water . . . A considerable detachment of Birnam Road went to church . . . and this was made up principally of the aged and the young, who . . . gave a glance that might mean reproof or envy at young men and young women who started off for Epsom Downs on cycles . . . Smoke, at this hour, began to go straight up from chimney pots and in the roadway stood curls in the spring air . . . from cigarettes belonging to young blades who, always, slightly in advance of the times, strolled up and down in white flannel suits, appropriate to Henley and a few months later.[18]

The ending of the working week on a Saturday lunchtime offered a less contentious space for the pursuit of pleasure for

> it was the afternoon of the week when Birnam Road welcomed the presence of its men. Young fellows raced home and went out immediately afterwards, taking kicks at an imaginary football; their fathers came with more deliberation, and changing silk hat for Panama, entered upon the precise task of clipping hedges.[19]

The distinctive differences thrown up by a youthful adherence to informality, to light colors and textures, were influenced both by the ethics of sportsmanship that underpinned nineteenth-century constructs of respectable manliness and more directly by the importance lent to team sports and activities in the workings of suburban society, as well as the proximity of suburban developments to the open parks and fields necessary for the tennis, cricket, football, cycling, walking, and boating that Pett Ridge saw as superseding church attendance.[20] Their sartorial trappings marked young men out from the propriety of professional identities and the individualism of metropolitan dandyism. The resulting style, however, was no less commercial or mannered in its presentation. As summer turned to autumn in Birnam Road, Pett Ridge noted that

Brown leaves began to carpet the road at the side of the common ("Dash'em!" said City gentlemen as they slipped and slithered on the way to catch morning trains) . . . Cricket bats were oiled and put away, and white flannel suits sent to the wash ("They're never paid for" complained mothers. "Continual source of expense. You boys will have to make up your minds to bear the cost of washing another year!")[21]

The holiday season witnessed the apotheosis of a finely honed suburban identity in which white flannels and straw hat became synonymous with a respectable release from the daily round, while instituting recognizable modes, language, and demeanor which could signify a modern fashionability the whole year round. As Pett Ridge recalled, during the summer months

four wheeled cabs drew up of a morning in Birnam Road, taking pale faces away and returning them a fortnight later as Red Indians, with habits and customs gained from far off places lasting for several days; babies going out in burlesque costumes, with wooden spade and tin shovel, to pretend that the Frying Pan on the Common was the boundless ocean; girls strolling without hats or gloves, young men in white flannels, a straw hat set at the back of the head . . . and pianofortes in every house were badgered into efforts to recall the elusive airs learnt from Pierrots on the sands.[22]

Alongside the group photographs which recorded such fin-de-siècle excursions autobiographer Fred Willis provided the corroborative evidence of young men adopting "summer suitings . . . most popular of all in blue diagonal tweed cut in exaggerated double breasted formations, nautically accented with shaped waist, glass or metal buttons and peg-topped trousers with a permanent turn up, soft shirt collars and prodigious use of white handkerchiefs."[23]

Whatever the combination of the constituent parts, the overriding aesthetic stressed relaxation and a conscious paring down of formalities, replacing the archaic introversion of office or church decorum with the over-familiar heartiness of the playing field or promenade. Willis further recalled that

the young proletarian swells made certain concessions and modifications in their dress when they went on holiday – when for instance they took a trip by water to Margate or Ramsgate. The young man would discard his bowler for a . . . boater. His waistcoat, the joy of his life, would be packed away among the mothballs and replaced with a cummerbund . . . His patent leather boots would be replaced with brown shoes, and as a tribute to the nautical nature of his venture, his walking stick would be put out of commission.[24]

The extension of this irreverence for established sartorial etiquette beyond the beach could be felt in all those areas of suburban life where young men exerted their taste in the first decade of the twentieth century. MacQueen Pope credited the shift to the popularizing effects of theatre and the rise to prominence of the matinee idol, though he was probably simply witnessing the symptoms of sartorial trends that could trace their antecedents back to the establishment of a recognizable suburban culture in the 1870s:

> Sir George Alexander . . . was one of the leaders of male fashion, but he never went to extremes. He was always, of his time, the most perfectly and correctly dressed of men. So when he made a tentative start with a soft collar in "John Chilcote MP" there was a considerable flutter. And when he wore it again in "His House in Order" the deed was done! Men who might have been chary of this informal innovation hesitated no longer. What was good enough for Alexander was good enough for them. The double fold soft collar swamped the shops of 1906 and sold like wildfire. It was flannel when it first came in and striped . . . held together in front by the lower corners being linked by a gold safety pin . . . it made no pretence to match the shirt. It was, however, never worn in town. It was for home or country only.[25]

Pope's last line was telling. While perhaps the new informality of a look indebted to a suburban taste for pleasure was impermissible in the work environment, such indictments did nothing to curb its popularity. Suburban outfitters directed much of their energy to the promotion of soft collars and sportswear during the period, basing their advertisements on the style's suitability for leisure pursuits, allying their fashionability to the modernity of rowing, cycling, and flying. What was significant about the figure of the suburban masher was not the obvious affront his image offered to the desk-bound paterfamilias, but the roots of his wardrobe in a masculine celebration of the domestic sphere, its alliance with the sentimental and romantic features of the heterosexual suburban imagination and its concordance with the "wholesome" sporting atmosphere of an idealized suburban life. It was indeed a choice "for home . . . only," but "home" didn't necessarily imply a negation of modernity or fashionability, rather the opposite. In the end though, behind the negligent laid-back surface, the final point of reference for the fashionable young suburban still remained in the mocking guise of his cosmopolitan counterpoint. Keble Howard represented the two models with a savage wit. At the Surbiton Rowing Club Ball, where the hero Jack was attempting to impress his future wife, the example of the bachelor dandy and the suburban swell clashed with devastating results:

> As for the rival suitors . . . there was a disparity in their attire that made poor Jack feel sick at heart. For Harry, that cunning one, had taken every possible advantage of his superior means. His dress suit was new enough to be in the very latest fashion, yet not so new as to look uncomfortable. His pumps were of the shiniest, his socks in the most

exquisite taste, his shirt and collar of the finest, his gloves of superb quality and his tie so cleverly tied that the inexperienced might be readily pardoned for mistaking it for a made up one. And Jack? He was wearing a suit that his father had discarded and which had been altered, more or less skilfully, by a local tailor. His pumps were deadly dull in comparison with Harry's, his socks were of the ordinary woollen variety, his shirt was a wee bit frayed, his collar a size too small, his gloves had done duty more than once before, and his tie, alas! was obviously a made-up one.[26]

'Arryism and the Repudiation of Respectability

As suburban fashionability was mocked from above for its homely ties to domest-icity and pathetic attempts at modishness, the strata positioned directly below were also singled out for their lack of taste and presumptuous claims on style. Young working men had found their "selfish" spending habits the butt of social reformers' criticisms since the 1830s at least. The expansion of retailing outlets selling mass-produced clothing in working-class areas having increased the potential for wayward consumption:

It requires but a showy tailor's window, with offers of cheap ready made suits, to tickle a young man's fancy into wild extravagance. A boy earning twelve or fifteen shillings a week is always saving with an eye for a new suit for Sunday. He buys, not one, but two or more in the course of a year, for their smartness is short lived. They are too cheap to wear for very long. They are not kept with sufficient care at home; they are worn at the wrong times. Those tight green trousers, the waistcoat with fancy buttons, the coat which fits like a glove, are not to be wasted on only local eyes. They are taken for a day in the country and returned soaked and shapeless, with seams awry and far more than the fashionable number of creases . . . One good suit at nearly double their price, wisely worn and neatly folded would last a year or more, while for the weekday evening an old coat and grey flannel trousers, with a well tied scarf, would serve every purpose. On these points public opinion requires education, but with boys the process is comparatively easy, for they are of a highly imitative disposition.[27]

The rising profligacy of working-class consumption habits was condemned by Alexander Paterson in his 1911 report on the social life of southeast London. Young men as much as young women were targeted for their inappropriate spend-ing patterns, and the drive for fashionability discouraged in favor of encouraging a more concerted effort towards thrift. As Paterson continued:

it is more and more the custom of the working boy or man to spend a penny on being shaved, to spend a half penny on a tram . . . another half penny on an evening paper, another penny for having his boots blacked. All these little conveniences of civilization are pardonable as occasional extravagances, but as regular expenses they belong to a more prosperous type of life, where the struggle for daily bread is less acute.[28]

For all his insightful visual observations, however, the author failed to appreciate the wider returns on a new suit of clothing, its role as a symbol of belonging, of sharing tastes, and understanding the vagaries of style as a sociable practice. He read sartorial acquisition as a wasteful example of emulation without considering the meaning of fashionability in a personal context.

Paterson's descriptions of items bought do betray something of the vibrant idiosyncrasies of a popular working-class look at the turn of the century, but he dismissed their implications, preferring to support the adoption of the unthreatening overcoat and muffler which signified a more traditional proletarian compliance with the "proper" order of things. Tight green trousers, fancy buttoned waistcoats and a cut that fitted like a glove were features far removed from the loose flannels and easy masculinity of middle-class hearties, suggesting a sharper edge more akin to the tailored dandyism of the Piccadilly bachelor. But denuded of the social conventions and fitness for purpose accorded aristocratic or metropolitan models, Paterson merely viewed them as shoddy cash tailor copies, ruined by overwear and presumptuous in their pretence as modishness. Set in the context of the development of a recognizable working-class style that Paterson presumably neither knew nor cared for, the characteristics of the Bermondsey wardrobe actually announced a distinctiveness separate from both suburban sportiness and metropolitan flash models, and as well established. Indeed the subversive rhetoric of tight, bright clothing found its origins in popular representations of the London cockney seventy years before Paterson's comments, and offered its own attractions to retailers and consumers from both the East End and of more "respectable" provenance by the end of the 1870s at least.

In his study of the representation of working-class life in Victorian fiction, P.J. Keating isolates the figure of the cockney as a key symbol of London proletarian style, finding his most eloquent representatives in the characters of Sam Weller from Dickens's *Pickwick Papers* of 1837 and 'Arry from the satirist E. J. Milliken's popular *'Arry Ballads* of 1877. These two "gave their names to certain types of speech and attitude; both names were used as synonyms for cockney mannerisms; both inspired a host of imitators; and the personality projected was in each case a crystallisation of cockney characteristics current in popular literature of the time."[29]

Weller, as the prototype of urban "flash," is presented as the descendant of the devoted valet, a constant in eighteenth-century satirical literature. His wit and courage are reflected in the jauntiness of his carriage, his stylish clothing seeming to mock the vanity and priggishness of his superiors, while all the while containing a man confident of his position as a servant of beneficent middle-class paternalism.

As Keating infers, Weller epitomized a version of the urban picaresque that in the turbulent social context of the 1830s and 1840s provided comfortable imagery for a nervous bourgeois readership. 'Arry, by contrast, represented a later erosion of the boundaries that demarcated class stereotypes. He was not specifically working class, but symbolized a pervasive celebration of caddishness and vulgarity that were assumed to have lowly social origins. While his speech and dress trace a direct line back to the Weller type, his contemporary relevance reached out to all classes. As Milliken himself suggested: "My real subject indeed, is 'Arryism rather than 'Arry. And 'Arryism is not confined to the streets. Its spirit pervades only too plentifully the race course, the betting ring, the sporting club, the music hall, many spheres of fashion, and some sections of the press."[30]

Both Weller and 'Arry offered versions of working-class and thus inner-city masculinity to an audience safely removed from the source of such descriptions, and as such their relationship to the actual sartorial practices or attitudes of young cockney men is as problematic as that suggested by Patterson's subjective reports. All three, however, offer evidence of the circulation of knowledge about a satirical type whose influence infiltrated beyond its original target. The tailor' promotions, alongside the descriptions of elite bachelor carousing, all drew on its attractive power. Closer to home, the working-class or adventurously déclassé consumer found further cause for identification with a mode of dressing and behavior that intensified the veracity of the literary stereotype. Social historian Peter Bailey's important examination of the cartoon character Ally Sloper reveals an abandonment to pleasure anchored in working-class culture which found its clearest reflection in popular practice yet. Sloper, whose finest hour spanned his appearance in the weekly penny comic book *Ally Sloper's Half Holiday* between 1884 and 1888, when his mature image was fixed by the illustrator W.G. Baxter, had generally been depicted since his first appearance in the paper *Judy* in 1867, as a slovenly, inebriated lounger in battered top hat, tatty tailcoat, stiff collar, and tight trousers. Baxter's version, which remained the model after his death in 1888 until the demise of the *Half Holiday* in 1923, elaborated on the prototype, introducing the hero to many of the features which isolated Paterson's later Bermondsey boys as proletarian dandies. Loud checks, straw boater, coster costume and evening dress all found their way into Sloper's extravagant repertoire, hinting at the socially inclusive nature of his characterization, while still maintaining a sense of cultural specificity. [31] Bailey draws attention to the multiple readings to which his sartorial image gave rise:

> Sloper's dress may have been intended and read by some as a parody of the ineffable bad taste of the bookmaker, the publican and the stage army of vulgar swells, but there is nothing in his demeanour that suggests the conscious copyist or slave of fashion. What impresses is Sloper's unabashed sartorial confidence. His splendidly eclectic wardrobe

serves him admirably in whatever role he plays and he proves himself a master of the accessories – monocle, watchchain, hat and gloves, cigar and, most notably, the umbrella. For Sloper it is the umbrella, the symbolic insignia of the city clerk, that gives him additional powers, serving variously as a truncheon, cane, slap-stick, wand, hold-all and auxiliary phallus. In the manner of modern subcultures that make their own selection and combination from the dominant culture. Sloper creates his own style and conventions, and encourages others to do likewise.[32]

An encouragement to emulate was aided by the ubiquity of the Ally Sloper figure beyond the pages of the comic. The urban lounger could hardly miss his distinctive silhouette in his journeys round the city. Besides his reproduction on commodities ranging from buttons and socks through to pickle jars and firework displays, the consumption and replication of Sloper's adventures by a working-class audience, and their translation into behavior and attitude on the street, was viewed with some concern by more "discerning" contemporary commentators.[33] Richard Whiteing, never slow to incorporate local color and topical debate into his novels of London life, referred directly to the genre's appeal and its allegedly demoralizing effect in his discussion of working-class reading habits in *No 5 John Street,* crediting a thinly disguised *Half Holiday* with an insidious influence, as profound as that wielded in the suburbs by the romantic yellow back:

These weekly comics, as they are called, are nearly all illustrations. They have hundreds of cuts to the issue, and but a thin black line of legend to each. There is no vice in them in the sense of conscious depravation; it is but the bestiality of bad taste . . . Covey's . . . selection had failed to please him. "Swipey Loafer ain't up to much this week" he murmurs, as he lays it aside with a sigh of disappointment. In this elegant trifle, a typical family, and especially the typical head of it, lives before the public on a nutriment of winkles and gin. It gives us the humours of the beanfeast and of Margate sands, varied by glimpses into the backyards of Somers Town. All the men are drunk, and most of the women are in short skirts. It is 'Arry in 'Eaven, a heaven of plenty to eat and drink, plenty to wear, and a celestial choir for ever on the spree. Words cannot tell its vulgarity, its spiritual debasement. Better vice itself, if redeemed by a touch of mind. The police sheets detain him longer – the sheets in which the same scheme of social observation is more or less associated with crime. "That'll do to begin with" he says, laying aside one in which sprightly young women kick off the hats of maudlin young men in evening dress. As gin and shell fish are the principal ingredients of the first dish, so leg and chemisette are indispensable to the last. These in their innumerable varieties form the mirror of life for the slums. They should be carefully stored in our literary archives, for they will be priceless to the future student of manners . . . They represent the visible world as the incarnation, under an innumerable variety of forms, of the universal cad . . . The creative spirit moves upon the slime and we have organisms and institutions. In the first it is the cad as swell, as plutocrat, as strumpet, or as thief. In the other, it is the environment of the gin shop, the race course, the prize ring, and the police cell.[34]

267

The translation of Sloper's misadventures onto the streets of London was not straightforward, but many of the features discussed by the critics, especially the love of display and the promotion of consumption for its own sake, did find their parallels in leisure activities associated with inner suburban and working-class districts. It is in descriptions of institutions such as the weekly monkey parade that the features of 'Arry's "living" style can be discerned. In the Hackney monkey parade, a Saturday and Sunday night promenade down Mare Street in which gang rivalries, friendships, and courtships were subsumed into an excuse to parade in one's best clothing, young women attained an unusual prominence, and George Sims's description of the scene in *The Strand Magazine* during 1904 provides a useful context for considering the relationship of a masculine sartorial image to broader gender relationships. According to Sims, young women in Hackney set the tone for the evening and clearly led innovation in terms of adopting distinctive "coster" clothing styles. The emulative habits of the minority of young men, though equally theatrical in their own way, remained a foil to the brilliance of the street sellers and factory girls who made up the majority of the crowd:

> We have heard so much of the famous Monkey's Parade that we expect to see a bustling crowd directly we enter the thoroughfare. There are plenty of people on the pavement and in the roadway. Here and there are groups of typical London lads, cane, cap and cigarette, and we exclaim simultaneously "The Monkeys!" . . . And yet the scene was remarkable, and in one sense I should think unique. There were considerably more young women than young men . . . They were dressed in pairs like sisters, yet in many instances there was not the slightest family resemblance . . . The costumes were as gay and gorgeous as the costumes that grace the Heath of Hampstead on a Whit Monday. The favourite colors were petunia, violet, green and sky blue. Two young ladies, one dark and one fair, had adorned themselves in light green blouses, red hats and blue skirts, and waistbands of bright yellow . . . When the scene was at its busiest Mare Street was absolutely prismatic . . . Occasionally a weird effect was added . . . by a looping up of the skirt with the old fashioned dress suspender which fastens round the waist . . . As soon as the novelty of seeing a crowd of young women in pairs similarly attired had worn off, the feature of the crowd that leapt to the eyes was the complete absence of gloves and umbrellas.[35]

There is much here suggestive of the desire to both acknowledge and reject mainstream fashionable dictates and foster a "louder" appearance based on local networks of friendship, exchange, supply, and competition. A willingness and ability to consume underlies the extravagant clothing of the promenaders and the author indicated that young women in the district had greater access to disposable income than men of the same age, stating that there are a large number of industries in Hackney employing only women; there are a few in which men only are employed . . . the net result of this condition of affairs is that unmarried women are constantly attracted to Hackney and unmarried men are constantly compelled to leave it. This accounts for the magnificent display of finery in Mare Street on Sunday evenings, and for the fact that the Jills promenade together. Most of the Jacks are considerably their juniors – mere lads who have not yet come to the age when they must flit in search of work and the making of a home of their own.[36]

Attempting to read subcultural activity from the evidence of a monkey parade dominated by young women presents interpretative problems which are ultimately highly revealing, the field of writing on fashion and working-class youth culture having been largely dominated by discussion of the practices of young men, often directly contrasting with treatments of middle-class and aristocratic fashionable practices.[37] Indeed in the more recent texts on masculinity and consumption postwar male subcultures are usually credited with opening the gates to a wider masculine engagement with fashionable consumption in the final decades of the twentieth century.[38] Conversely in broader debates on the nature of modernity and mass culture, critics and historians have tended to link issues surrounding consumerism and femininity without recourse to considerations of class or masculinity, so the acknowledgment of a public engagement with various levels of fashionability by working-class girls is perhaps less surprising in this context.[39] Sally Alexander and Angela McRobbie have both provided more nuanced evidence of young working-class women's ability to read and reinterpret the messages of middle-class clothing retailers and advertisers, questioning the assumptions of explanations of consumption and gender that prioritize coercion, though much of this work has not been reflected in mainstream narratives of teenage style or the evolution of popular fashion.[40]

In fact, it is precisely the supposedly unprecedented emergence of young proletarian men as avid followers and decoders of fashion in the 1960s that historians of subcultures have isolated as an illustration of the uniqueness and revolutionary quality of the postwar experience.[41] However, by prioritizing new male consumers and male-oriented boutiques and subcultural groupings in the later period and accepting an overarching discourse of feminized consumption for earlier periods, such histories have missed a great deal. In the figure of 'Arry or the Mare Street girl promenader it is possible to discern the precursor of the former and an amendment to the latter propositions, which rather dilutes their significance. The unpacking of historical subcultural style thus presents a paradigm case of the manner in which constructions of gender and class, like notions of fashionability and modernity, are contingent on more immediate contexts and concerns.[42] The aggressive model of the sharply attired cockney needs to be read as part of the commercial, sexual, and social flux suggested by the forging of identities in Mare

Street and all those other turn-of-the-century monkey parades, not as a bit-player in some abstract subcultural grand narrative. Edwin Pugh, in his collection of journalistic vignettes *The Cockney at Home* of 1914, presented just such a male promenader, as sharp and self-aware as any Colin MacInnes character from fifty years later, though the subversive coding of his clothing and attitude have remained invisible to those who locate the emergence of such behavior after 1945:

> Said the cynical youth in the amazing collar: "There's a kind of young man who is merely background. I mean that without his clothes he wouldn't be noticed . . . There was Bertie Amplett for instance . . . I remember him as a perambulator . . . This Bertie you know . . . was a deuce of a fellow. He didn't 'work in the City somewhere', he drew, I believe, a quid a week, but I vow he never earned it. His wages went on clothes mostly, and Woodbines. His mother was a charwoman . . . Bertie was king of the local monkey parade. And if you don't know what a monkey parade is ask Anderson here. He's straight off one . . . It's a place where the elite of the beau monde of suburbia meet nightly for purposes of flirtation . . . the fellahs and the girls wink and smirk as they pass, and break hearts at two yards with deadly precision . . . The Kentish Town Road was his preserve, and he paraded it nightly, like a revolving sky sign. There wasn't any escaping him. You see he was a tall chap, and that isn't usual. He was good looking too, in the style of the novelette hero. And he really knew how to wear clothes. In fact it was in his blood, his father having been a shopwalker."[43]

Pugh's perambulator displayed all of the tensions that absolved his parading of the cosmopolitan image from becoming a straight emulation of more metropolitan or suburban modes. Aside from the question of his upbringing and occupation, his single-minded embracing of a "flash" façade for its own sake marked him out from the underplayed sentimentality of suburban masculine display or the nonchalant luxuriousness of the bachelor dandy. In all other respects his deceptive, parodic public persona mirrored the familiar respectable role models, though the ostentatious mention of a cigarette carried its own complex symbolism. MacQueen Pope nostalgically recalled that "a man could get gold-tipped cigarettes . . . if he wanted to be ostentatious. Some men even had their cigarettes specially made . . . with their name printed on the paper . . . there were cork tipped cigarettes then too, one brand known as 'the belted earl' having the cork surrounded by two little belts of silver paint."[44] In a similar vein Alexander Paterson referred to the practice whereby

> one commonly lights his fag, draws in the smoke twice, inhaling deeply, breathes it out, spits, says something, and then holding his cigarette in his right hand, extinguishes it with the thumb and first finger of his left, and replaces it in the bottom right pocket of his waistcoat. Ten minutes later the process will be repeated and by this means, though the boy will always seem to be smoking, he will only consume a penny packet a day.[45]

Thus clothing and gesture together produced a rakish mirage, subtly critical of the status quo and engineered to impress cronies or attract the opposite sex.

Echoing this strategy, the wearing of West End styles by female participants in the Mare Street parade was not in itself subversive. On the contrary, fashionable display and a concern with appearances were skills expected of young, respectable unmarried women in the 1890s. It was the deliberate choosing and mixing of colors and styles, and their massed display by promenaders more usually associated with the factory floor or the street market that constituted a challenge to accepted models. At their most extreme such practices blurred into criminality as a report in *The Times* of July 1914, quoted by Stephen Humphries in his oral history of working-class childhood, attested:

> At Marylebone yesterday Nellie Sheenan, 17, pattern matcher, was charged on remand for stealing a pair of shoes. She belonged to a gang of about twenty girls who went about the West End . . . taking advantage of the first opportunity to steal anything they could get hold of. One feature of the gang was that they dressed alike in check skirts and blue coats and all came from the neighbourhood of Harrow Road.[46]

Similarly Montague Williams noted of the clothing of match factory girls that "dress is a very important consideration with these young women. They have fashion of their own, they delight in a quantity of color, and they can no more live without their large hats and huge feathers than 'Arry can live without his bell bottomed trousers."[47] What is striking here is the complementarity between male and female modes of presentation. As suburban masculine style can be read as evidence of a domestic fashionability, a conscious distancing from the homosocial separatism of the metropolitan office or club, so working-class subcultural style could be said to have engineered a celebration of romantic friendship in the public sphere of the street. However, this was a celebration that often developed into a more disruptive lampooning of the rituals of courtship. Local historian W.J. Fishman places more emphasis on the violence inherent in the sexually provocative display of local fashionable taste, rather than the surface romance of its variegated image:

> The devil found work for idle hands long the Bow Road on Sundays. This was the infamous monkey parade when gangs of young lads, aged between 15 and 20, marched up and down the main highway between Grove Road and Bow Church molesting passers by, especially young women on their way to Sunday service. Early spring brought the lads out in force and their pranks were enumerated in court; such as "pushing respectable people off the pavement." Some of them had lamp black on their hands which they placed on young girls' faces, while others whitened their hands and clapped girls on their backs.[48]

271

This ambivalence went hand in hand with those constructions of aggressive heterosexuality that upheld notions of a female sphere concerned with conspicuous display, while simultaneously devaluing its worth by rejecting overt interest in sartorial matters as effeminate or antisocial, so that *any* major deviation from the standard conservative working wardrobe, 'Arry's bell bottoms excepted, signified a rebellious or even pathological act. Robert Roberts in *The Classic Slum* recalled the dangerous associations of particular modes of working-class dandyism in turn-of-the-century Salford when

> the proletariat knew and marked what they considered to be the sure signs of homo-sexuality, though the term was unknown. Any evidence of dandyism in the young was frowned upon. One "motherbound" youth among us strolled out on Sunday wearing of all things gloves, low quarters and carrying an umbrella! The virile damned him at once – an incipient nancy beyond all doubt.[49]

The subtleties of coding and detail that consequently surrounded "street dress" functioned subconsciously or associatively to produce forms of subcultural identification almost hidden to the gaze of the uninitiated contemporary observer, or else suggestive of a heightened violence that simply magnified masculine expectations. In his novel *To London Town* of 1899, Arthur Morrison alluded to the encoding of a bowler hat with connotations of workshop etiquette, and the observation of a hierarchical order that was easily fractured by inappropriate display, stating that "it was the etiquette of the shop among apprentices that any bowler hat brought in on the head of a new lad must be pinned to the wall with the tangs of many files; since a bowler hat, ere a lad had four years of service, was a pretension, a vainglory and an outrage."[50] This fine division between the proprieties of work and leisure clothing, and the contradictory codes pertaining to each, had a long-standing tradition and gave rise to frequent misinterpretation. Thomas Wright, writing under the pseudonym of "a journeyman engineer" in 1867, produced a very rich description of working-class habits that identified the various codings of weekday, Saturday, Sunday and holiday clothing among skilled laborers. The author acknowledged that

> in all phases of life there is I fancy a sort of inner life . . . that is known only to the initiated . . . there are traditions, customs and images interwoven with, and indeed in a great measure constituting the inner and social life of workshops, a knowledge of which is . . . essential to the comfort of those whose lot is cast among them.[51]

According to Wright the consequences of such intricate coding were a tight adherence to specific looks, policed by a merciless lampooning of the unfortunate who attempted to "rise above." He noted that the general body make one of their number unhappy by glancing meaningfully at a new coat that he has got on and telling him that "it fits him too much" that it is "like a ready made shirt, fits where it touches" and much more to the same disheartening effect.[52]

Saturday nights and Sundays, for Wright, presented the one opportunity for the display of more individual tastes without risk of censure, though his own preferences appeared to lie with the functional grace of work dress. The contrast between the two modes was significant. Thus

> When the workmen, with newly washed hands and their shop jackets or slops rolled up under their arms, stand in groups waiting for the ringing of the bell, it is a sight well worth seeing, and one in which the working man is, all things considered, perhaps seen at his best. He is in good humour with himself . . . in his working clothes, in which he feels and moves at ease, and not infrequently looks a nobler fellow than when "cleaned" . . . Some of the higher paid mechanics present a very different appearance when cleaned up . . . working class swelldom breaks out for the short time in which it is permitted to do so in all the butterfly brilliance of "fashionably" made clothes, with splendid accessories in collars, scarves and cheap jewellery. But neither the will or the means to "come the swell" are given to all men, and a favourite Saturday evening costume consists of the clean moleskin or cord trousers that are to be worn at work during the ensuing week, black coat and waistcoat, a cap of somewhat sporting character, and a muffler more or less gaudy.[53]

For Paterson, writing after the turn of the century, the ritual transformation from work to pleasure retained its drama when he observed that

> the programme of spare hours begins almost invariably with tea in the kitchen, a wash at the tap in the yard, and the putting on of a collar and another coat. The exact order of the preparation varies, but it is quite clear that the washing and dressing is not in honour of the tea . . . but a tribute to the publicity of the street . . . Percy's working clothes are old and worn, bespattered with mud and oil; hence the efflorescence of bright ties and new suits.[54]

Surviving images of working-class groups, assembled for a Whitsun outing, or even posing unawares on street corners, sporting bowlers and tight suits with a jaunty pride, gain a further resonance from their juxtaposition with documentary and literary evidence, which provide nuances that graphic or photographic representations themselves can no longer convey. From simple visual comparisons of middle-class and working-class clothing, the mechanic's "Sunday best" suggests only a clumsy emulation of bourgeois conservative respectability. Contemporary attitudes reveal a more studied and critical negotiation of gendered and occupational positions behind the frozen poses, producing a series of looks differentiated enough to earn subcultural labels. Both Geoffrey Pearson and Stephen Humphries in their investigations into late Victorian youth and criminality provide useful examples of hooligans adapting the usual coster uniform of flat cap, collarless shirt, reefer jacket, and flared trousers to communicate aggressive intentions and gang membership, creating a mannered appearance that avoided accusations of unmanly display by sending into higher relief the dandyism of monkey parade celebrants. Pearson quotes the *Daily Graphic* of November 1900, which stated that

> the boys affect a kind of uniform. No hat, collar or tie is to be seen. All of them have a peculiar muffler twisted around the neck, a cap set rakishly forward . . . and trousers set very tight at the knee and very loose at the foot. The most characteristic part of their uniform is the substantial leather belt heavily mounted with metal. It is not ornamental, but then it is not intended to ornament.[55]

Similarly, Humphries notes that the Napoo, a turn-of-the-century Manchester gang "were recognised by the distinctive pink neckerchief they wore and the razor blades that they displayed in waistcoat pockets or in slits in their cloth caps."[56]

Raphael Samuel's *East End Underworld*, an oral history of street life in the slum district of the Nichol, which straddled Whitechapel, Shoreditch, and South Hackney, and based on interviews with Arthur Harding, a "retired" petty criminal active from the years preceding World War I, is richly suggestive of those spatial and visual networks which informed and supplied local gangs with their influences and raw materials. Here was a smoky blend of public houses, shop windows, and music hall that underpinned the wider circulation of the street rough as glamorous anti-fashion stereotype. Harding remembered that

> the high heaven of everything in the Nichol was Church Street where all the shops were. The whole place was crooked, even those who kept shops . . . The White Horse Pub stands on one corner and on the other corner was a big men's and boy's tailor shop known as Lynn's. Turk Street was at the top of Brick Lane . . . there was an old clothes market on Sundays. The old girl, she had a shop in Turk Street, selling old clothes, next to the Duke of York . . . On the corner of the next street, Camlet Street, was a wardrobe dealer's shop which sold second hand clothing of all kinds . . . You could say that Shoreditch High Street was our Champs Elysees. It was a prosperous market place with stalls and shops . . . and pubs and also the London Music Hall which had performances six days a week.[57]

Descriptions of the varied dress codes adopted by East End youths prove the importance of those retail options suggested by Harding. The second-hand markets of Brick Lane offered the widest range of styles to those whose image was bricolaged together from the remnants of more respectable wardrobes. For the more solvent, the proliferation of tailors' shops in the district provided the sharper suits of gangs such as the Titanic Mob who Harding describes as "well dressed fellows" who concentrated on robbing men at race meetings, in theatres, and at boxing matches. Their "heroic" sartorial image must partly have been derived as a means to blend in with crowds composed of men whom Thomas Wright described thirty years before, though its threatening precision also positioned its adherents at the head of a local criminal hierarchy:

> They are great in slang, always speaking of the features of the human face in the technical phraseology of the day – according to which the nose is the beak or conk, the eyes ogles or peepers, the teeth ivories, and the mouth the kisser or tater-trap . . . Meantime they have their hair cut short, and when off work wear fancy caps and mufflers and suits of the latest sporting cut; in which they assume the swaggering walk of the minor sporting celebrities whom they are occasionally permitted to associate with and treat.[58]

George Ingram provided corroborative detail of the mob in his romantic recollection *Cockney Cavalcade* when he stated that

> most of them were dressed in the fashions of the day, with caps, jackets and waistcoats of lurid colorings and fantastic cut. The jacket was acutely waisted, had perpendicular pockets with buttons topping slits at the back, and well pressed pleats . . . Waistcoats had weird styles of their own, unknown outside the select circles and tailors who catered for them.[59]

Such distinctive garb would also have distinguished them from, and competed with the local Satini boys, an Italian rival gang who

> were flashily dressed in expensive suits, light colors predominating. No waistcoats seemed to be the rule, but touches of brilliant coloring were supplied by an expanse of silk handkerchief . . . Not a few possessed heavy gold . . . watch chains that flopped loosely from the button hole.[60]

Paterson's Bermondsey monkey paraders, the boys cited at the head of this section, who found it difficult to resist the "showy tailor's windows with offers of cheap ready made suits," were aiming for a similar loudness in their dress, though theirs was a choice much more reliant on the provisions of the local market. It was also closer to the blandishments of a consumer culture that encouraged young men to compare their image with that of sporting stars and vaudeville acts. The frisson of criminality merely added surface glitter to the finished effect. The main purpose of dressing up probably conformed more closely to Paterson's own opinion, however caricatured or sentimentalized its tone, and further undermines any literal notion of sartorial "renunciation." The opportunity to promenade provided a source of shared pleasure for its participants, affording space and time for the imaginative performance of the range of "modern" masculine identities, or at least their closest possible approximation. The social historian Michael Childs equates the freedom to explore such identities with the economic circumstances of Edwardian affluence and of "rapidly expanding cultural horizons" when "youths in general were . . . able to symbolise their outlook and their hopes by a selective and conscious use of distinctive clothes and practices."[61] Whether this positions 'Arry and his kind as "the original teddy boy"[62] is perhaps incidental to the fact that young men at the turn of the century from all social complexions were blessed with an unprecedented repertoire of fashionable models and choices, whose variety echoed the complex range of masculine subject positions opened up by the effects of a growing consumer culture. As Paterson suggested:

The pleasure to be derived from this haunting of the streets is the joy of wearing something a little brighter than working clothes. The variation may merely be a new tie of green and red and gold, or a straw hat with a brown ribbon, or a scarf pin, or a white silk scarf peeping from underneath the waistcoat like a nineteenth century slip. On Saturday evening and all through Sunday the change will probably be very thorough, and may include gloves, stick, bright waistcoat. These varieties add lustre to ten shillings a week, and make the Sunday promenade an active pleasure and no mere formality. Bill the conqueror has an athletic reputation and feels it incumbent on him to appear in something rather striking at these times, while Percy, with his good looks and wavy hair, never presents the same complete picture on two successive Sundays. Bert and Alf are mere hangers on, and feebly echo the taste of their leaders. Buster is rather reckless with his money and can only rise to a butterfly bow, and Fatty does his best by wearing clothes that are far too tight for him.[63]

The Mirror of Masculinity: Music Hall as Fashionable Space

My Life is like a music hall,
Where in the impotence of rage,
Chained by enchantment to my stall,
I see myself upon the stage
Dance to amuse a music hall.

'Tis I that smoke this cigarette
Lounge here and laugh for vacancy,
And watch the dancers turn; and yet
It is my very self I see
Across the cloudy cigarette.[64]

Arthur Symons, poet of the twilit London world of the 1890s, editor of its journal *The Savoy* and influential essayist on "The Decadent Movement in Literature," displayed an obsession common among the fin-de-siècle literati for the tawdry sexual glamour of music hall life. The verses quoted above from the prologue to his poem "London Nights" reflect on the hold that popular stage spectacle wielded over men of "bohemian" sensibilities, who reveled in the lowness of the form, finding in the tobacco haze and yellow limelight an authentication of their own mannered identities. A contemporary critic singled out Symons's adeptness at capturing the commonplace vulgarities of London life, which distinguished his work from the more profound resonances of Parisian symbolism. He claimed that

> Baudelaire and Verlaine generally ring true, and their horrors and squalors and miseries and audacities have the value and virtue of touching the reader to something of compassion or meditation. Symons no more does that than a teapot. "This girl met me in the Haymarket with a straw hat and a brown paper parcel, and the rest was a delirious delight: that girl I met outside a music hall, we had champagne and the rest was an ecstasy of shame!" that is Symons. And this sort of thing in cadences of remarkable cleverness and delicacy . . . A London fog, the blurred tawny lamplights, the red omnibus, the dreary rain, the depressing mud, the glaring gin shop, the slatternly shivering woman: three dextrous stanzas telling you that and nothing more.[65]

In his predilection for the licensed immorality of modern London, Symons succeeded in fixing its material features in a totemic and enduring manner. He also offered a reading of its culture which explored the formation of sexual identities through such fixings, and promoted the notion of a "glamorous" lifestyle that might be lived as much as performed, encouraging the blurring of boundaries between spectacle and self.

Peter Bailey has identified the notion of glamour as fulfilling an important role in controlling the performance and mediation of gender stereotypes from the mid-nineteenth century onwards. Through a study of the Victoria barmaid he has suggested that "the sexualisation of everyday life" sits at the center of debates regarding the gendering of modern power relations and the experience of material culture. He claims that "glamour and its stimulus to the sexual pleasure in looking that is scopophilia plainly gave a new emphasis to the visual element in the changing sexual economy."[66] The phenomenon of glamour, defined by Bailey as a visual property utilized in the management of arousal, positioned its subjects in an illusory realm, physically or emotionally distanced from the material world of the consumer, but its forms were engineered to encourage his engagement with the very real practice of consumption: "a dramatically enhanced yet distanced style of sexual representation, display or address, primarily visual in appeal."[67] The most familiar application of the device lay half a century in the future with the elevation of Hollywood screen actresses to the role of goddesses. But its effects can also be seen in the earlier alluring organization of shop windows, the sensual displays of the public bar which form Bailey's focus, and the paraphernalia of the popular theater which concerns us here. Glamour is also read as the visual code of a broader sexual ideology which Bailey identifies as "parasexuality." This he defines as "an inoculation in which a little sexuality is encouraged as an antidote to its subversive properties."[68] In other words, a strategy for managing the everyday circulation of sexualized codes and practices that constituted the exchanges of urban custom, which otherwise viewed sexuality as a dissonant force. This was a practice that was particularly pertinent in the "expanding apparatus of the service industries, and a commercialised popular culture" that typified the late-nineteenth-century urban scene. As Bailey continues:

> The barmaid and the pub were thus part of a larger nexus of people and institutions that stood athwart the public/private line and provided the social space within which a more democratised, heterosocial world of sex and sociability was being constituted, a world that is still inadequately mapped by historians. It is on this distinctive terrain that the less august branches of capitalism converted sexuality from anathema to resource, from resource to commodity, in the development of a modern sexualised consumerism. Parasexuality, with its safely sensational pattern of stimulation and containment, was a significant mode of cultural management in the construction of this new regime. It is plain from its operation . . . that it worked primarily to valorise male pleasure. Yet the making of this world was undertaken not just by a cadre of male managers – but by the members of this cultural complex at large, in a self-conscious and mutual working out of new modes of relationship between men and women.[69]

Taking into consideration the powerful "sexual" attraction of stereotypes including the bachelor dandy, the suburban hearty and the working-class masher discussed so far, I would argue for an application of the notion of parasexuality to the management of masculine sartorial figures. Where the glamorous fantasy of the barmaid smoothed the "determination of the informal rules and boundaries of sexual encounter . . . now pursued in a more fragmented and inchmeal manner, in the individual transactions of a continuously recomposing leisure crowd,"[70] so the popular communication of sartorial formulae attached to the varieties of urban masculinities present in the modern crowd, allowed young men to assess themselves visually and physically against other men in an increasingly competitive sexual marketplace. This led to a heightened awareness of their own sense of glamorous fashionability as well as placing them under the critical gaze of potential female suitors. Furthermore, the figure of the fashionable young gent, like that of the barmaid positioned in the public sphere of pleasure by "the mechanistic formula of parasexuality . . . dissolved in practice into a more popular discourse, the elasticity of whose rules was scrutinised in a vernacular know-ingness that informs music hall song and other popular idioms."[71] Arthur Symons's conception of himself as a reflection on the music hall stage was then particularly apt, for it was in the new sphere of variety performance that the drama of a glamorous masculine commodification was largely played out.

A large-scale elaboration of the plebeian singing salons of the 1840s and 1850s, themselves a formalization of the ad-hoc amateur singing contests that had punctuated public house activities since the late eighteenth century, the "classic" music halls of the fin-de-siècle incorporated the respectable comforts of middle-class supper rooms together with the democratized spectacle of the public entertainment familiar from pleasure gardens, circuses, and exhibitions. At the height of their popularity, from the 1880s to the 1910s, a night within their plush and gilt interiors promised a succession of "celebrity" turns who would make their performances carry over the general din of drinking and shouting through utilizing the inherited skills of street balladeers and minstrel troupes, while all the time suggesting the surface polish and drama of established opera and theater. This amalgamation of "high" and "low" cultural forms, its masterful manipulation under the promotional leadership of music hall caterers, and gradual appeal to a wider audience that no longer represented the original constituency for such forms of entertainment, has been variously interpreted by social historians as a betrayal of "authentic" working-class taste and creativity by the wiles of capitalism, a prime example of the late Victorian democratization and commodification of leisure, and a reflection or incorporation of shifting forms of popular identity. In the words of one historian the story of the music hall is the story of a shift "from class consciousness through emulative hedonism to domestication: or if you will, from a class culture to a mass culture."[72]

More recent analyses of the role played by music hall culture in wider public debates, marked by their deconstructions of the content of its performances and their attendant critiques, have emphasized the role played by the medium in a presumed crisis of morality, representation, and indeed masculinity, that defined the cultural complexion of the 1890s.[73] As literary historian John Stokes has claimed: "in the nineties, the music hall was a disorientating place. You could see society changing before your very eyes; but the longer you looked the less certain you became about where you were looking from. It was a vertiginous atmosphere that was to make the life of the halls an irresistible theme for artists and writers."[74] Thus artists including Joseph Pennel and later Walter Sickert, together with commentators from Max Beerbohm through to Arthur Symons, bequeathed an interpretation of music hall life that emphasized its immoral hollowness while celebrating its "entrancing iridescent surfaces."[75] The long-standing existence of a trade in female and (less famously) male bodies on the promenades of the more prestigious halls also underpinned the notion that what was being presented on the stage was of a nature not compatible with common standards of decency, and culminated in a vigorous moral debate that found its way into the pages of the broad sheets. In 1892 the renewal of the music and dancing licence of the Empire, Leicester Square, was opposed by Mrs Ormiston Chant and a committee of philanthropic society women on the grounds that the premises were given over to the pursuit of vice. The *Daily Telegraph* ran a celebrated series of articles under the title "Prudes on the Prowl," calling for deregulation of the theatre, while Ormiston Chant secured a compromise finding by the Theatres and Music Halls Committee of the London County Council that the promenade bar should be concealed from public view. The erection of a screen caused a near riot at a subsequent performance where "well dressed men," reported the *Evening Standard,* "some of them almost middle-aged, kicked at it from within, bursting the canvas . . . then went out into the street brandishing fragments . . . in all it was calculated that the crowd was swelled to the number of about twenty thousand."[76] While the argument carried with it the overblown features of farce, it was also indicative of the power played by music hall in fixing current attitudes and anxieties. Incorporating both the tendencies of decadent propaganda: "unique, individual, a little weird, often exotic, demanding the right to be" and the contrary appeal of the populist new journalism: "broad, general, the majority, the man in the street," the culture of music hall exemplified "the characteristic excitability and hunger for sensation" that typified both.[77] As such its forms were ideally positioned to mirror and construct the range of bewildering gender models on offer in the field.

The material culture of music hall was particularly well placed to effect an influence on the habits of an urban audience by the turn of the century. In 1898 *Little's London Pleasure Guide* listed fourteen venues within the central radius of London, each with its specialism and specific atmosphere, most of them advising that "Ladies generally wear high dresses" in a pitch at respectability, though others, including the Empire, and the Palace, Shaftesbury Avenue, retaining their soignée reputation with the notice "smoking permitted everywhere." The Guide, like many others, also provided information on Turkish baths, riding clubs, fancy dress balls, Royal levees, restaurants and regattas, so that the halls appear to have gained a comfortable place within the fashionable social round without jettisoning a mass audience composed of all ranks. The pricing policy at most halls, with tickets ranging from £3 3s. for a box to 6d. in the gallery, further ensured that a broad swathe of the population could afford to attend.[78] A handbill for the Canterbury music hall in Westminster Bridge Road of 1884 promised potential consumers an evening that easily fulfilled all the criteria of "variety" in its provision, and for all manner of tastes. The juxtaposition of comedians, singers, acrobats, melodramatic actors, classical pianists, and art gallery defied easy categorization, at least in class terms and rather backs up John Stokes's supposition that "the halls became too big a business not to carry a municipal significance and, like other kinds of popular diversion, they could be seen as the cause as well as the product of social instability."[79] The very instability of the presentation arguably aided the free circulation of fashionable stereotypes between performer and audience and back:

Canterbury Theatre of Varieties – "Westminster Bridge Road
Proprietors" – Messrs Crowder & Payne
The Sliding Roof opened when necessary, rendering this the coolest and best
ventilated theatre in London.
Monday May 26 1884 – Important Engagement for Six Nights Only.
Mr Frank Hall's Variety Company in his musical sketch entitled Robin Hood,
Supported by Mrs George Fredericks (specially engaged) Mr George English,
Mr Frank Hall and other artistes in addition to a numerous corps
of auxiliaries.
Medley – A.G. Vance (The Inimitable) Sisters Cassatti, Will Poluski and the
Black Eel.
TheWorld Renowned Paul Martinetti and Troupe in the successful
eccentricity entitled "A Duel
In the Snow" suggested by the celebrated picture of Jerome . . .
New Scenery – Original Music – Limelight Effects &c.
Charles Carlton & Maude Wentworth – Versatile Sketch Artistes
Frank Travis & Little Dori in Sketch "Out of the Ranks"
Lottie Collins
The Craggs – Unrivalled Acrobats
Jenny Hill – The Vital Spark
Pianoforte Recitals in the Grand Lounge every evening by Mr J.W. Speaight
LAM (Pupil of Sir Julius Benedict) at intervals from 8 till 11.45. Upright Iron
Grand Piano by John Brinsmead & Sons.
Canterbury Aquarium, A Fine Seal. Direct from the Arctic Regions, is on
view in one of the tanks and is fed nightly at 8.00 and 11.30, also a
Russian Water Rat – the largest specimen ever caught. Fed at 8.00 and
11.30 every evening.
The Grand Billiard Salon now open daily from 11am till 12 midnight. Also the
Grand Lounge and Refreshment Bar, with valuable collection of pictures by
Eminent Artists, open all day.[80]

In reminiscences of evenings spent at the halls it is the latter attractions announced by the Canterbury, the existence of comfortable lounges, promenades, bars and billiard saloons, that impressed the most upon the memory of variety habitués. The content of the performances paled a little besides the opportunities the halls offered for browsing, socializing, and enjoying the varied company of a diverse audience.

It was as though music hall offered two sites for performance, the stage being subservient to the action of the auditorium. J.B. Booth remembered of the Alhambra in Leicester Square that "the stalls, the most comfortable in London, rarely filled until after nine o'clock, in time for the principal ballet, while the promenade and the bars were in the nature of a club – a rendezvous for guardsmen, members of the House of Lords and of the Stock Exchange, barristers from the Temple, racing men and sportsmen of every description." Its crowds offered the ideal backdrop for fashionable displays and Booth recalled

a youth who acquired the nickname of "King of Diamonds" by reason of his unpleasant habit of wearing a dress tie, or rather a brooch in the shape of a dress tie, of these stones, his links and studs also being of huge diamonds; and a would-be sartorial reformer who affected black linen with his dress clothes, a funeral effect which obtained no followers.[81]

In contrast to the odd display of individuality, Percy Fitzgerald presented a rather cynical guide for "correct" sartorial behavior among the audience when he stated that

in places where there is a promenade we constantly see "gentlemen" moving in the crowd in pairs, who appear to have risen from some fashionable dinner table just to stroll into this scene of pleasure. There they are, imparting quite an air of refinement and high manners, as they lounge carelessly by, an Inverness cape lightly thrown over, but not concealing, the festive garments below: looking at the scenes about them with a blasé and haughty indifference, as though well accustomed to the West End . . . It is one of the social phenomena of the time to think of worthy shopmen and clerks taking all this trouble, night after night "making up" and dressing for the part; but there is no doubt an exquisite pleasure in the exhibition of the evening suit – transient dream though it be.[82]

The spatial context of the music hall further encouraged the practice of sartorial display by its male customers through significant strategies that have been isolated by Peter Bailey as central to contemporary perceptions of the culture of late-nineteenth-century mass entertainment. With respect to the competitive posturing of the promenade crowd he suggests that "it afforded proximity without prom-iscuity" and "reduced the open social mix of the city street to some kind of territorial order while retaining mutual audibility and visibility among its different social elements." Within the protected and carefully policed spaces of the theatre the social mix of the audience "was sufficient to generate a lively drama of individual and collective acts of display . . . a perfect setting for the aspirant swell, the young clerk decked out in the apparatus of the toff, graduating from the protective cluster of his own kind at the side bar to the public glory of a seat at the singer's table."[83] Gesture and dress, Bailey infers, were further heightened by the architectural setting itself, which in many halls employed the illusory effects of mirror glass. This clearly harked back to the fitting out of the gin palaces from which many halls had evolved, but besides increasing the sense of palatial grandeur, mirrors also intensified an atmosphere of critical surveillance, both of others and of the self. "All round the hall" remarked a review of the refurbished Middlesex in 1872, "handsome mirrors reflect the glittering lights, and offer abundant opportunities for self-admiration. As the lion comique paraded his fashionable self on stage, members of his audience could with a sidelong glance decide how their image matched up to that of their hero."[84]

Music Hall Performance and Conspicuous Consumption

Bailey stresses the way that social distinctions were maintained, albeit in a very fluid manner, in the organization and use of music hall space. Yet while it is true that pricing policies and the retaining of exclusive areas protected the elite from the touch, though not the gaze, of the hoi-polloi, an overriding rhetoric of leisured display in the decor, dress codes, and stage presentations, which often crossed social boundaries, also encouraged a more comprehensive mode of music hall fashionability that affected all classes of man. Dion Calthrop in his autobiographical *Music Hall Nights* attested that

> our music hall people love color, gold and crimson and marble with its glittering reflections. They like the red curtain with its big tassels; they like plenty of light, a big chandelier, brass in the orchestra, looking glasses everywhere and attendants in livery. If a singer wears a diamond stud they like it big enough to be seen from the gallery. They are hearty in their tastes and quite right too. They use words which make the middle classes squirm, but are interesting to the cultured man because he uses them too.[85]

This promotion of an inclusive, indeed "parasexual" masculine style associated with the glamorous escapism of the music hall promenade fed outwards in three directions, to the representations of masculine fashionability paraded on the stage, into the public world of commerce, and through to the life of the streets. As the department store and woman's magazine provided a complete template for fin-de-siècle versions of fashionable femininity, so the music hall fed the consuming desires of men in a manner which often prioritized their gender over their class in an open celebration of sybaritic pleasure. As Percy Fitzgerald noted:

The quiet airy reserve and nonchalance of the stage gentleman would seem at the music hall to be unintelligible, or uninteresting. But the East Ender has created his idea from a gentleman or "gent" of which he has had glimpses at the "bars" and finds it in perfection at his music hall. At the music hall everything is tinselled over, and we find a kind of racy, gin borne affection to the mode; everyone being "dear boy"or a "pall." There is a frank, cordial bearing, a familiarity which stands for candour and open heartedness, a suggestion of perpetual dress suit, with deep side packets, in which the hands are ever plunged . . . and we must ever recollect to strut and stride rather than walk.[86]

In its most concentrated form, the words and gestures of the music hall artiste provided the most fitting summation of popular masculine consumerism, largely through the projection of recognizable stage types. The swell song enacted by the lion comique had the most distinguished lineage in the repertoire, providing the basis for later explorations of fashionable masculinity after the turn of the century. Promoted at first during the 1860s and 1870s by performers including George Leybourne known as "Champagne Charlie," Arthur Lloyd, George MacDermott and Alfred Peck Stevens known as "The Great Vance," the swell bore a direct relationship to straight theatrical comedy and particularly to the celebrated figure of Lord Dundreary, the aristocratic fop of the 1861 play *Our American Cousin*.[87] Generally presented as an upper-class dandy addicted to the pleasures of club life, horse racing, and various forms of alcohol, the visual image of the swell conformed to established notions of how the upper ten dressed and behaved. Henry Chance Newton recalled how George Leybourne's "lithe splendid figure, handsome semi-Jewish visage and majestic sweep of his hand play [made him] quite an Apollo among men, and able to 'carry' the most distinguished apparel. He flaunted the broad check suits, the puce jackets, widely striped trousers and lurid vests of his so-called swells," and this despite his own origins as "a hammerman at Maudsley's, the marine engineers then in the Westminster Bridge Road" who was prone to display "flashes of illiteracy quite amazing to those who saw or who spoke to him for the first time."[88] Thus military bearing and a broad chest shown off through exquisite Savile Row tailoring, together with extravagant treatments in facial hair and an ostentatious use of the cane and top hat, arrived at a convincing approximation of Rotten Row style whose impact relied on the tension between illusory authenticity and the overblown talents of the performer. A late version of the type from the 1880s is illustrated in a song cover for T.W. Barrett's *He's Got 'Em On* in which the protagonist stands in tight morning coat with the requisite ivory handled cane, monocle, cigar, striped shirt, button hole, love heart tie pin, and gold fob chain.[89] The American investigative journalist Daniel Kirwan writing at the height of the lion comique's popularity in 1871 transcribed the lines of a song he had heard performed at the Alhambra which relied for its humour on just such a combination of gesture, pronunciation and visual attire:

The Beau of Wotton Wow

Now evewy sumwah's day
I always pass my time away
Awm in awm with fwiends I go
And stwoll awound sweet Wotten Wow;
Fow that's the place none can deny
To see blooming faces and laughing eye;
And if youw heawts with love would glow,
Why patwonise sweet Wotten Wow.

So come young gents and don't be slow
But stylish dwess and each day go
And view the beauties to and fwo,
Who dwive and wide wound Wotten Wow.

Dressed, according to Kirwan, "in the exaggerated costume of a Pall Mall lounger," the singer performed with "a very affected voice and lisp, keeping his body bent in a painful position the while". The audience responded to the cruel rendering of aristocratic idiosyncrasies "and relished all the local hits of the speech and the dress of the ideal do-nothing."[90] Later versions of the swell song shifted their focus away from social satire towards a direct celebration of the good life, and the benefits of prodigious consumption. This reflected the promotion of the singers themselves as "stars" who could afford to flaunt the prizes of their profession and were expected to extend their stage personas to their actions on the street by contracts that specified travel in a barouche between performing venues and the ostentatious adoption of fur coats, diamonds, and champagne bottles by the magnum.[91] The pointed promotion of champagne as a swell's beverage has been linked by Bailey with that particular commodity's entry into the drinking habits of the middle classes after a lowering of the tariff in 1861 and a broader myth of democratized consumption following the brief economic boom of the 1870s.[92] Its bubbling sparkle also provided a potent rhetoric for the unrestrained urge to consume in other areas of life, clothing included. James Greenwood, reporting on the performance of a lion comique in 1883, noted the recent concentration on issues of commodification, stating that

a star comique of such renown that he drives no fewer than three ponies in his carriage, led off with one of his latest and best approved melodies . . . It was quite in the new and highly relished style . . . The song with which the star comique flavoured the auditory was all about a hungry man, who, try what he might, could never lull his voracious appetite . . . clutching the forepart of his trousers with his hands and planting his hat well on the back of his head, the delineator of modern comic song changed – "I've tried

German sausages and sprats, boiled in ale, Linseed meal poultice and puppy dogs tail, Stewed gutta percha (which pained my old throttle), Sourkrout, ozokerit and soup brown and mottle."[93]

It was the visual appeal of the singer, though, that engaged most directly with the aspirations of the audience. Chance Newton remarked that

so strongly, always, did Vance's and Leybourne's many colored costumes for their "dude" ditties impress me, even in my callow youth, that whenever their respective names meet my eye . . . I at once think first of . . . gaily assorted rainbow lined coats, vests and "bags" and, especially of their yellow topped glistening boots. Vance's fascinating footwear indeed, filled me with awe.[94]

Albert Chevalier, one of the most celebrated of character turns from the turn of the century, who specialized in more "down to earth" representations of East End humanity, nevertheless acknowledged the powerful draw that the swell image held over those for whom its glamour represented an unattainable dream:

The "Great" may be a trifle conspicuous in the matter of attire. He may develop a weakness for diamond rings, elaborate scarf pins designed as an advertisement, and massive cable watch chains, but he has seen too much of the seamy side not to know that these articles have a value, apart from emphasising the "security" of his position as a popular favourite. I once met, at the seaside, a prosperous comic singer "got up regardless." He wore a frock coat, white vest with gilt buttons, flannel trousers, patent leather boots, a red tie and a straw hat. Strange to say everybody looked round – and stranger still he did not seem to mind. He knew his business! Oh! I forgot to mention, that for a scarf pin, he had his initials worked in diamonds, and it was almost large enough to conceal his neck tie.[95]

For Chevalier, as for the audience, the recounting of swell magnificence took on the currency of an urban mythology, full of anecdote and supposition. Though in the language of such descriptions, the pleasure with which sartorial value and outrage were considered and inevitably condoned, lay further opportunities for male spectators to evaluate their own position on luxury and its relevance to their lives. Paste tie-pins in the shape of skulls, horseshoes, and ballerinas, including some which sparkled by the aid of a concealed battery, were for example available from Gamages in tawdry emulation of music hall glamour. But Leybourne and Vance symbolized an attitude as much as they helped to focus the aspirational desires of a commodity-hungry audience. Furthermore their delight in fashionable consumption offered imaginative compensations for the drudgery of men's lives. In 1891 the illusory pursuit of the good life reached a destination of sorts with the popularity of Charles Coburn's song *The Man who Broke the Bank at Monte Carlo*. Here the promise of attaining the high life on the results of very little physical or mental effort was inspired by a financial scandal avidly reported by the popular press and induced by the activities of swindler Charles Wells,

> a man who has gained considerable notoriety of late . . . engineer and patent agent of London, he first came into note through his successful speculation at the gambling tables of Monte Carlo. The newspapers reported his immense gains from day to day, and many a sanguine individual drew his balance from the bank and wended his way to the fascinating principality of Grimaldi in the hope that he would be equally fortunate.[96]

The real protagonist formed an unlikely focus for music hall celebration, described as "a respectable looking man, of medium height, about forty five years of age, with a short black beard and a bald head, nobody would suspect that he was the biggest swindler living."[97] The translation of gambling notoriety onto the stage called for the ingenious use of stereotypical sartorial triggers that would identify character to the audience, and the song epitomized the late flowering of the swell genre. Coburn was adept at utilizing the visual codes of popular culture to inform his acts, and with respect to his preparations for another role, which lampooned Gallic pretensions, he noted:

> I got my first idea for it actually from a match-box. It was one of those little boxes in which we used to buy wax vestas years ago. When I took it to my tailor and showed him the picture of the Frenchman on the cover, and asked him to make me a similar suit of clothes he laughed at me: I must be joking of course . . . "You can do it" I replied . . . "All you've got to do is take your tape measure and see that you fit me. I want a collar just like that and the same comic trousers." Well, he did what I asked, and when the suit came I only had to add a little tuft of hair under the chin, a loose flowing tie and a glossy silk hat to complete the costume. It was a success from the first evening I wore it.[98]

Coburn's rendition of "Monte Carlo" was equally mannered: in a surviving recording the final syllables of every line are drawn out in a mockery of upper-class diction while the pace of the song increases to suggest the frenzied pursuit of material success.[99] The circumstances which the lyrics celebrated were far removed from the experiences of the majority of the audience. As the author of *All about Monte Carlo* suggested, the city was "not only the greatest gambling centre in the universe, it is also the most beautiful spot on earth. While we in London are having an old fashioned severe winter, there the palms, eucalyptus, lemon and orange trees, geraniums and aloes are growing luxuriantly."[100] Indeed Coburn had his reservations about their general appeal recalling that

Fred Gilbert wrote both the words and music shortly after . . . Charles Wells brought out a book entitled "How I broke the Bank at Monte Carlo" . . . I liked the tune very much, especially the chorus, but I was rather afraid that some of the phrasing was rather too highbrow for an average music hall audience. Such words as "Sunny Southern Shore," "Grand Triumphal Arch," "The Charms of Mad'moiselle," etc., seemed to me somewhat out of the reach of say Hoxton.[101]

The song's ensuing popularity attested strongly to the contrary, providing evidence of the capacity for men across the social spectrum to empathize with the appeal of conspicuous consumption. As the music hall historian Harold Scott affirmed:

In Coburn one sees how nearly the two aspects of the music hall approached one another. His adoption of the "swell" type in "The Man Who Broke the Bank" was not made without some misgivings and its success, outstanding though it was, did not eclipse the vogue of "Two Lovely Black Eyes" [a more proletarian "coster" song by Coburn], by which he discovered a common denominator for the audiences of the Mile End Road and Piccadilly Circus . . . [a] welding of flash life with the simple methods of the concert room.[102]

The distanced perfection of the swell was not the only model of fashionable style available to the music hall audience, though it was the most voluble. Dion Calthrop hinted at the competitive and envious tendencies which the swell's sartorial knowledge could engender when he recalled a companion's reaction to the polish of a swell performance: "I'll bet that man's got a fur overcoat . . . Look at him, he has been poured into his clothes and the only crease he has got is down his trousers; and look at his tie, it's tied just well enough to show it isn't ready made."[103] If such extremes threatened to exclude participation by their preciousness, other character roles, including that of the shabby genteel and the masher, elicited a more sympathetic, less awe-struck response; for these were individuals whose attitude to the fashionable world mirrored more precisely the surface realities of a suburban or working-class engagement with bon-ton, rather than their inner desires. The mode of shabby gentility addressed the nature of economic restraints which prevented the keeping up of fashionable appearances, and attributed a tragic pathos to those whose clothing betrayed a fall from material grace. In many ways the battered top hat and frayed frock coat of the genre represented an inverted version of the swell and referred to the ambivalence of clothing as a signifier of status and moral worth. Where the puffed-up self-regard of the swell's attire often concealed an emptiness within, the rags of the shabby genteel failed to distort the essential "breeding" of the wearer. Henry Chance Newton recalled Victor Liston "in his threadbare frock coat and shockingly bad top hat, as he sang in broken tones that reached the heart 'I'm too proud to beg, too honest to steal, I know what it is to be wanting a meal. My tatters and rags I try to conceal – I'm one of the shabby genteel'."[104] And Harry Clifton in a song of the same title averted that "We have heard it asserted a dozen times o'er, That a man may be happy in rags, That a prince is no more in his carriage and four, Than a pauper who tramps on the flags."[105] The image on the cover of the accompanying song sheet suggested just the opposite, with all the correct components of the wardrobe scrupulously correct though tragically creased and a decade out of date.

In order to ensure that the audience was able to converse with the social observations crucial to the construction of representations such as the shabby genteel, song writers and performers needed to ground their characters in a visual grammar that drew on what might be termed the tacit fashionable knowledge of the audience. The shabby genteel made sense only if the spectator realized that the pedigree of his frock coat belonged to 1870 rather than 1880, for it was in the detail that the affective depth of characterization lay. Calthrop suggested that some of the most popular turns in music hall were the patter comedians, who drew on the mundane and sentimental characteristics of daily life that constituted the basis for such satire:

> right down to the footlights they come, one neatly dressed in white flannels and the other in a very short Eton jacket, wide trousers of terrific checks and a doll's straw hat upon his head . . . this duet is a catalogue of low life . . . It contains allusions to the Walworth Road, beer, Scotch and soda, tripe and onions, little bits of fluff, swivel eyed blokes, the police by the name of rozzers, persons who are up the pole and mothers in law.[106]

In their litany of commodities, types, and locations, patter comedians came closest to affirming the priorities placed on things and images in the make-up of popular "modern" masculine identities. In his song *Second-hand Clothes* of the early 1890s, W.P. Dempsey was thereby able to incorporate allusions to the masher, the swindler, the pauper, and the politician through the use of old clothing as stage prop:

> I'm a bloke who's had some trouble, lots of ups and downs I've seen,
> I could almost write a novel about the different things I've seen.
> Now I deals in left off garments, here who'll buy this old dress coat?
> Once a masher used to wear it, when he used to act the goat.
> Once he was the pride of ladies, and their waists he used to squeeze,
> Often to some rich young heiress he would go down on his knees.
>
> Chorus: For he was a masher, a regular toff,
> A la-di-da as you'll suppose.
> A regular mash, who hadn't much cash,
> And that's what I found in his second hand clothes. (produces a pawn ticket)

Put that down then, nobody wants it, now then what do you say to this?
There's a lovely garment for you, that's a racing coat that is,
Once it mingled with the bookies at each popular resort,
And the cove who used to wear it dearly loved a bit of sport.
But my dear, once down at Epsom, someone overheard his name,
And that someone, a detective, went and bowled his little game.

For he was a welsher, a regular crook,
A wrong'un as you'll suppose.
The public he'd spoof, he'd collar their 'oof,
And that's what I found in his second hand clothes. (produces 3 card trick)

(produces workhouse jacket with medals pinned on breast)

'Ere's a coat that's got a history, I shan't offer it for sale,
I shall keep it for inspection, so that I may tell the tale.
Who do you imagine wore it? Don't think I'm telling lies,
Tis a fact my dear, tis really, though you'll hear it with surprise.
Once the man who used to wear it, fought hard by his colonel's side,
Tho' a Balaclava hero, in that pauper's coat he died.

For he was a veteran, a warrior bold,
A hero as you may suppose.
For his country he bled, yet he died wanting bread,
And that's what I found in his second hand clothes. (produces nothing)

Bet you know who this garment belongs to, him who buys this has a catch,
'Ere's a nobby garment for you, collar too as well, to match.
Once this frock coat ornamented one of England's greatest men,
Straight there isn't one to touch 'im, either with the tongue or pen.
Never mind how I came by it, at his house I often call,
And the goat who used to wear it, is well known to one and all.

For he is a statesman, a clever old man,
A grand old man as you'll suppose.
And in Ireland today, he'll have his own way,
And that's what I found in his second hand clothes.

(produces Home Rule Bill)[107]

Beyond the melodrama of the patter song, with its narrative that encapsulated the music hall standards of pathos and patriotism, other performances trading on the demotic currency of men's clothing and fashion presented a more bathetic interpretation of attempts by the "cove" or "bloke" to appropriate the language or looks of the swell. Here an emotional appeal to the charity of the audience was jettisoned for a gentle mocking of its pretensions. Thus in Harry Champion's *Any Old Iron* a dapper young man's boasts regarding his inheritance from "uncle Bill" are ridiculed when his gold watch and chain are found to be no better than base metal, fit only for the rag and bone collector: "You look neat, talk about a treat, / You look dapper from your napper to your feet, / Dressed in style, brand new tile [hat], / And your father's old green tie on, / But I wouldn't give you tuppence for your old watch chain, / Old Iron, Old Iron."[108] Similarly, Gus Elen's coster song *The Golden Dustman* drew its humor from the juxtaposition of everyday squalor and new-found wealth, in which malapropisms betrayed the aspirant dandy's social origins, and class allegiances threw the trappings of an idealized swell existence into sharper relief:

> And now I'm going to be a reg'lar toff,
> A-riding in me carriage and me pair,
> A top hat on me head,
> Fevvers in me bed
> And call meself the Dook of Barnet Fair.
> Asterrymakam round the bottom of me coat,
> A Piccadilly window in me eye –
> Fancy all the dustmen a-shouting in me ear,
> "Leave us in your will afore you die!"[109]

The masher song traded less on the disruptive potential of fashionable emulation, presenting its heroes as standard bearers for the liberating effects of commodity culture. Distanced from the rousing pomposity of the lion comique, whose version of heightened masculine beauty had dictated the characteristics of swelldom with the rhetoric borrowed from the 1860s, the masher encapsulated the commercial energy of the men's retail trade from the 1890s, and the propensity of broad swathes of young men to engage with its sartorial offerings. Occasionally the links between music hall representation and the marketplace converged completely, as in The Great Vance's late rendition of *The Chickaleary Cove* which functioned as an advertising coup for the tailoring firm of Edward Grove of Lower Marsh and Shoreditch. His marketing ploys engineered a street slang similar to that utilized by C. Greenburg and Harris of Whitechapel:

> I'm a checkaleary bloke with my one-two-three
> Vitechapel was the willage I was born in;
> To catch me on the hop,
> Or on my tibby drop,
> You must vake up wery early in the mornin'

I've got a rorty gal, also a knowing pal,
And merrily together we jog on.
And I doesn't care a flatch.
So long as I've a tach.
Some pahnum in my chest – and a tog on!

Chorus: I'm a chickaleary cove (repeat first four lines)

Now kool my downy kicksies – they're the style for me,
Built on a plan very naughty;
The stock around my squeeze is a guiver colour see,
And the vestat with the bins so rorty
My tailor serves yer well,
From a perjer to a swell,
At Groves you're safe to make a sure pitch.
For ready yenom down,
There ain't a shop in town,
Can lick Groves in the Cut as well as Shoreditch![110]

Groves supplied Vance with "a very shiny beaver topper, an extraordinary yellow-ish skirt coat, and a startling pair of light nankeen trousers,"[111] for the performance of this favor. But beyond the theatricality of Vance's stage wardrobe it was the accessibility of the masher image which generally cemented its popularity. T.W. Barrett in the role of *John the Masher* appeared in the bowler hat, horseshoe tie-pin and lounge suit that would have struck a cord with any monkey parader, crowning his act with the catch phrase "He's got 'em on."[112] The appropriation of the role by female male impersonators at the turn of the century further cemented its association with a new youthful audience, distancing it from the hirsute heartiness of the Champagne Charlies and their ilk. The modern masculine look celebrated on the stage now embraced a boyish agility with a bright, tightly cut wardrobe to match, echoing the blandishments of the outfitter's window from Bow to Burlington Arcade. In the newness of his clothing, its obvious espousal of novelty over lasting quality, the masher epitomized the brash modernity of turn-of-the-century urban life. His song lyrics concentrated accordingly on the easy bargain, the collapsing of social distinction and the ephemerality of style. Nellie Power, one of the earliest male impersonators, joked in the early 1880s that "He wears a penny flower in his coat, La di Da! And a penny paper collar round his throat, La di Da! In his hand a penny stick; in his tooth a penny pick, And a penny in his pocket, La di Da!" and Nellie Farren offered the question "How do you like London, how d'you like the town? How d'you like the Strand, now Temple Bar's pulled down? How d'you like the La di Da, the toothpick and the crutch? How did you get those trousers on, and did they hurt you much?"[113]

Moving beyond satire, several commentators credited the impersonator Vesta Tilley with the ability to inspire as well as critique fashionable pretensions. As Booth noted:

> not only did she wear the clothes of the youth about town, but she set his fashions, and with an art above mere mimicry, lived in her costume, whether it was that of an "Algy," a "Midnight Son" or a "Seaside Sultan." The Tilley commentary on the types of male youth and fashions of the day was cameo-like, clear cut, finished to the tiniest detail, and the old lion comique . . . faded before "The Piccadilly Johnnie with the little glass eye."[114]

Though Tilley claimed that her devoted following was made up largely of female admirers, and subsequent readings of her stage persona have stressed the actress's role in articulating fin-de-siècle worries concerning the public and professional role of women, the direct appeal her act made to the sartorial sensibilities of men in the audience is conveyed through Tilley's own reflections on the commercial impact of her dress and her art.[115] With respect to her American tour of the revue *Piccadilly Johnnie* she recalled that

> the dudes of Broadway were intrigued with my costume, a pearl grey frock coat suit and silk hat and a vest of delicately flowered silk – one of the dozens which I had bought at the sale of the effects of the late Marquis of Anglesey. Grey frock suits and fancy vests became very popular in New York; the dudes there loved to look English . . . All my male costumes were absolutely the latest in fashionable men's attire, and were made for me during many years by the well known West End firm Samuelson, Son and Linney of Maddox Street, Bond Street, London.[116]

A combination of authenticity and fantasy, heightened by Tilley's patronage of Bond Street tailors and her appropriation of clothing and a stylistic manner borrowed from the controversial, effeminate dandy the Marquis of Anglesey, lent her risqué characterizations a sense of controlled danger that was immediately marketable despite its perverse associations. So much so that when her dresser left her cufflinks out of one of her costumes, she "snatched a bit of black ribbon . . . and hastily tied the cuffs together with a bow. Shortly afterwards a leading firm of gentlemen's hosiers . . . were exhibiting cuff links in the form of a black ribbon bow."[117] Similarly after the success of her holiday song *The Sad Sea Waves* where she "wore a straw boater hat, made in England of course, with a band of white binding around the brim," a firm of outfitters "paid me a good sum to allow them to reproduce the hat under the name of the 'Vesta Tilley Boater' and it had quite a vogue. There was also a 'Vesta Tilley Waistcoat,' the 'Vesta Tilley Cigars,' the 'Vesta Tilley Cigarettes'."[118]

The fact of Tilley's gender cast the paradoxes of contemporary masculinity into high relief, for here was a woman aping the gestures, phrases, and appearance of a newly commodified and highly popular mode of public presentation for men, while appropriating the physical trappings of that mode in a manner that served to accentuate both its validity in the minds of the audience and the oppositional, invalidating power of her own femininity. It was an act that could only have succeeded at a moment of profound transition in the practice and representation of gender roles grounded in an expansion of the marketplace, revealing as it did the manner in which masculinity was a case of directed consumption and performance, as much as it was an accident of nature. The correspondence between Tilley's biological body and the social body that she lampooned on stage threw into sharp relief the deep shift in attitudes and behavior which some historians have claimed defined modern masculinity at the turn of the century, celebrating its more expressive surfaces while hinting at interior crisis.[119] That sense of crisis, embodied in the development of masculine appearance and leisure between 1860 and 1914, set a precedent for the problematic negotiation of fashionable life and consumer culture by men in the twentieth century.

Acknowledgments

A version of this chapter originally appeared in C. Breward, *The Hidden Consumer: Masculinities, Fashion and City Life 1860–1914* (Manchester: Manchester University Press, 1999), pp. 189–239. I am grateful to Manchester University Press for allowing its reproduction here.

Notes

1. T. Burke, *The Streets of London through the Centuries* (London: Batsford, 1940), pp. 134–5.
2. T. Burke, *Nights in Town: A London Autobiography* (London: George Allen and Unwin, 1915), pp. 183–4.
3. F.M.L. Thompson (ed.), *The Rise of Suburbia* (Leicester: Leicester University Press, 1982); J. Carey, *The Intellectuals and the Masses* (London: Faber, 1992); A. Jackson, *Semi Detached London* (Didcot: Wild Swan, 1991).

4. M. Marsh, *Suburban Lives* (New Brunswick, NJ: Rutgers University Press, 1990); A. Light, *Forever England: Femininity, Literature and Conservatism between the Wars* (London; Virago, 1991); D. Ryan, *The Ideal Home through the Twentieth Century* (London: Hazar, 1997).

5. C.F.G. Masterman, *The Condition of England* (London: Methuen, 1909), p. 68.

6. Ibid., pp. 69–70.

7. Ibid., p. 80.

8. G. le Bon, *Psychology of the Crowd* (1895), quoted in M. Boscagli, *Eye on the Flesh: Fashions of Masculinity in the Early Twentieth Century* (Oxford: Westview, 1996), p. 70.

9. *The Modern Man* (December 5, 1908), p. 8.

10. *The Modern Man* (January 1910).

11. Masterman, *Condition of England*, pp. 93–4.

12. M. Marsh, "Suburban Men and Masculine Domesticity 1870–1915," in M.C. Carnes and C. Griffen (eds), *Meanings for Manhood: Constructions of Masculinity in Victorian America* (Chicago: University of Chicago Press, 1990), pp. 111–12.

13. *The Times* (September 30, 1930).

14. K. Howard, *The Smiths of Valley View* (London: Cassell, 1909), foreword.

15. Marsh, *Suburban Men*, p. 127.

16. A.J. Lewis, "Our Treasures: A Story of Bachelor Housekeeping," in J. Strangewinter (ed.), *Wanted, A Wife: A Story of the 60th Dragoons etc.* (London: J. Hogg, 1887), pp. 104–6.

17. W. Pett Ridge, *Outside the Radius: Stories of a London Suburb* (London: Hodder and Stoughton, 1899), pp. 8–16.

18. W. Pett Ridge, *Sixty Nine Birnam Road* (London: Hodder and Stoughton, 1908), pp. 266–7.

19. Ibid., p. 299.

20. D. Birley, *Land of Sport and Glory: Sport and British Society 1887–1910* (Manchester: Manchester University Press, 1995).

21. Pett Ridge, *Sixty Nine*, p. 119.

22. Ibid., p. 77

23. F. Willis, *101 Jubilee Road: A Book of London Yesterdays* (London: Phoenix House, 1948), p. 127.

24. Ibid., p. 130.

25. W. MacQueen Pope, *Twenty Shillings in the Pound* (London: Hutchinson, 1948), pp. 182–3.

26. K Howard, *The Smiths of Surbiton: A Comedy Without a Plot* (London: Chapman and Hall, 1906), pp. 234–5.

27. A. Paterson, *Across the Bridges* (London: Edward Arnold, 1911), pp. 38–9.

28. Ibid., p. 44.

29. P.J. Keating, *The Working Classes in Victorian Fiction* (London: Routledge and Kegan Paul, 1979), p. 140.

30. Ibid., p. 141.

31. P. Bailey, "Ally Sloper's Half Holiday: Comic Art in the 1880s," *History Workshop Journal* 16 (1983), pp. 4–31.

32. Ibid., p. 20.

33. Ibid., p. 10.

34. R. Whiteing, *No 5 John Street* (London: Grant Richards, 1899), pp. 60–1.

35. G.W. Sims, "Off the Track in London: Around Hackney Wick," *Strand Magazine* (September 1904), p. 41.

36. Ibid.

37. A. Davies, *Leisure, Gender and Poverty: Working Class Culture in Salford and Manchester 1900–1939* (Buckingham: Open University Press, 1992).

38. J. Stratton, *The Desirable Body* (Manchester: Manchester University Press, 1996), pp. 179–80; F. Mort, *Cultures of Consumption* (London: Routledge, 1996); S. Nixon, H*ard Looks* (London: University College Press, 1997).

39. R. Felski, *The Gender of Modernity* (Cambridge, MA: Harvard University Press, 1995), pp. 61–90.

40. A. McRobbie, *Feminism and Youth Culture from Jackie to Just Seventeen* (London: Macmillan, 1991); S. Alexander, "Becoming a Woman in London in the 1920s and 30s," in D. Feldman and G. Stedman Jones (eds), *Metropolis London: Histories and Representations since 1800* (London: Routledge, 1989).

41. N. Cohn, *Today There are No Gentlemen* (London: Weidenfeld and Nicolson, 1971); D. Hebdige, *Subculture: The Meaning of Style* (London: Methuen, 1979).

42. C. Evans, "Street Style, Subculture and Subversion," *Costume* 31 (1997), p. 106.

43. E. Pugh, *The Cockney at Home: Stories and Studies of London Life and Character* (London: Chapman and Hall, 1914), pp. 15–16.

44. MacQueen Pope, *Twenty Shillings,* p. 277.

45. Paterson, *Across*, pp. 142–3.

46. S. Humphries, *Hooligans or Rebels: An Oral History of Working Class Childhood and Youth* (Oxford: Blackwell, 1981), p. 186.

47. M. Williams, *Round London* (London: Macmillan, 1892), p. 129.

48. W.J. Fishman, *East End 1888: A Year in a London Borough among the Labouring Poor* (London: Duckworth, 1988), p. 195.

49. R. Roberts, *The Classic Slum: Salford Life in the First Quarter of the Century* (Manchester: Manchester University Press, 1971), p. 36.

50. A. Morrison, *To London Town,* (London: Methuen, 1899), p. 129.

51. A Journeyman Engineer, *Some Habits and Customs of the Working Classes* (London: Tinsley Bros., 1867), pp. 83–4.

52. Ibid., p. 233.

53. Ibid., pp. 187–9.

54. Paterson, *Across,* p. 40.

55. G Pearson, *Hooligan: A History of Respectable Fears* (London: Macmillan, 1983), p. 94.

56. Humphries, *Hooligan*, p. 191.

57. R. Samuel, *East End Underworld: Chapters in the Life of Arthur Harding* (London: Routledge and Kegan Paul, 1981), pp. 8–10.

58. Journeyman Engineer, *Some Habits*, pp. 121–2.

59. G. Ingram, *Cockney Cavalcade* (London: Dennis Archer, 1935), p. 30.

60. Ibid., p. 14.

61. M. Childs, *Labour's Apprentices: Working class lads in late Victorian and Edwardian England* (London: Hambledon, 1992), pp. 15–17.

62. Ibid., p. 116.

63. Paterson, *Across*, pp. 143–4.

64. A. Symons, *Silhouettes 1896 and London Nights 1897* (Oxford: Woodstock, 1993), p. 3.

65. L. Johnson, "Notes on Symons prepared for Katherine Tynan 1895," in Symons, *Silhouettes*, Introduction.

66. P. Bailey, "Parasexuality and Glamour: The Victorian Barmaid as Cultural Proto-type," *Gender and History* 2 (1990), p. 168.

67. Ibid., p. 152.

68. Ibid., p. 148.

69. Ibid., p. 167.

70. Ibid., p. 167.

71. Ibid., p. 167.

72. P. Bailey, "Custom, Capital and Culture in the Victorian Music Hall," in R Storch (ed) *Popular Custom and Culture in Nineteenth Century England* (London: Croom Helm, 1982), p. 198.

73. K. Beckson, *London in the 1890's: A Cultural History* (London: Norton, 1992).

74. J. Stokes, *In the Nineties* (London: Harvester Wheatsheaf, 1989), p. 56.

75. Ibid., p. 63.

76. H. Scott, *The Early Doors: Origins of the Music Hall* (London: Nicholson and Watson, 1946), pp. 161–2.

77. Stokes, *Nineties*, p. 18.

78. C. Little, *Little's London Pleasure Guide* (London: Simpkin, Marshall, Hamilton, 1898).

79. Stokes, *Nineties*, p. 55.

80. London Handbills and Advertisements 1860–1880, Guildhall Library.

81. J.B. Booth, *A Pink Un Remembers* (London: T. Werner Laurie, 1937), p. 96.

82. P. Fitzgerald, *Music Hall Land: An Account of the Natives, Male and Female, Pastimes, Song, Antics and General Oddities of that Strange Country* (London: Ward and Downey, 1890), pp. 10–11.

83. Bailey, "Custom, Capital," pp. 199–200.

84. P. Bailey, "Champagne Charlie: Performance and Ideology in the Music Hall Swell Song," in J.S. Bratton (ed.), *Music Hall: Performance and Style* (Milton Keynes: Open University Press, 1986), p. 61.

85. D. Calthrop, *Music Hall Nights* (London: Bodley Head, 1925), p. 127.

86. Fitzgerald, *Music Hall Land*, p. 4.

87. Bailey, "Champagne Charlie," p. 54.

88. H. Chance Newton, *Idols of the Halls: Being my Music Hall Memories* (London: Heath Cranton, 1928), pp. 58–9.

89. John Johnson Collection of Printed Ephemera, Bodleian Library, Music Hall.

90. D. Kirwan, *Palace and Hovel or Phases of London Life* (Hartford, CT: Belknap and Bliss, 1871), pp. 469–70.

91. Bailey, "Champagne Charlie," p. 60.

92. Ibid., p. 58.

93. J. Greenwood, *In Strange Company: Being the Experiences of a Roving Correspondent* (London: Vizetelly, 1883), pp. 232–3.

94. Chance Newton, *Idols*, p. 21.

95. A. Chevalier, *Before I Forget: The Autobiography of a Chevalier d'industrie* (London: T. Fisher Unwin, 1901), pp. 227–8.

96. J. Pellie, *All about Monte Carlo: Extraordinary Career of Charles Wells, The Man who broke the Bank at Monte Carlo* (London: Comet, 1893), p. 2.

97. Ibid.

98. C. Coburn, *The Man who Broke the Bank: Memories of Stage and Music Hall* (London: Hutchinson, 1928), p. 110.

99. *The Golden Years of Music Hall* (Wootton-under-Edge: Saydisc, 1990).

100. Peddie, *Monte Carlo*, p. 2.

101. Coburn, *Man who Broke the Bank*, p. 227.

102. Scott, *Early Doors*, p. 164.

103. Calthrop, *Music Hall*, p. 51.

104. Chance Newton, *Idols*, pp. 173–4.

105. John Johnson Collection, Bodleian Library, Music Hall.

106. Calthrop, *Music Hall*, p. 29.

107. *The Music Hall Songster 1891–1893* (London: W.S. Fortey, 1893).

108. C MacInnes, *Sweet Saturday Night* (London: MacGibbon and Kee, 1967), pp. 55–6.

109. Booth, *A Pink 'Un Remembers*, p. 112.

110. Chance Newton, *Idols*, p. 25.

111. Ibid., p. 24.

112. J.B. Booth, *Pink Parade* (London: Thornton Butterworth, 1933), p. 145.

113. Ibid., pp. 44–5.

114. Ibid., p. 146.

115. S Maitland, *Vesta Tilley* (London: Virago, 1986).

116. V. De Frece, *Recollections of Vesta Tilley* (London: Hutchinson, 1934), p. 125.

117. Ibid., p. 126.

118. Ibid., p. 195.

119. Boscagli, *Eye on the Flesh*, p. 1.

14

"Jewish Taste?" Jews and the Aesthetics of Everyday Life in Paris and Berlin, 1920–1942

Leora Auslander

Human beings, always cognizant of our mortality, have a deeply ambivalent relationship with the potentially immortal objects among which we live. Across time and space people have given tremendous powers to those things, animating them, praying to them, making them the repository of memories of people and times long gone, and asking them to communicate to others what we fear to say aloud. I would like to suggest, however, that modernity – and more specifically representative polities and capitalist economies – has attributed specific powers to objects. As modern states created systems of representation and drew boundaries around something called "the nation," as mobility weakened or broke kinship ties, and labor commodified, the nature of "the self" changed and new notions of "identity" were created. Or, to put it in the eloquent words of the sociologist Zygmunt Bauman:

> Modernity makes all being *contingent*, and thus a "problem," a "project," a "task." Lifting identity to the level of awareness, making it into a task – an objective of self-reflexive activity, an object of, simultaneously, individual concern and specialized institutional service – is one of the most prominent characteristics of modern times.[1]

That contingency is a result of political and economic change.

Representative systems of government require criteria of likeness and difference in order to determine both access to the franchise and electoral units. For example, all republican systems excluded women from suffrage for periods varying from fifty to one hundred and fifty years following their founding, and all struggled to determine whether geography, wealth, religion, or race should be salient "identities" within the nation-state.[2] In a parallel move, modern nation-states systematized definitions of "native" and "foreigner," with the gradual establishment of freedom of movement within national boundaries and of the concept of appurtenance to the nation as a whole rather than to a locality.[3]

The industrializing economies synchronous with the making of modern polities created great unevenness of development – and therefore of employment – both within and across national boundaries. People responded by moving to where the work was, thereby loosening ties to kin and neighbors, and breaking the forms of recognition that were a part of geographic stability.[4] Finally, for many, the commodification of labor central to capitalist development gradually voided the workplace and work processes as a site of identification. As more occupations were deskilled and both subcontracting and factory production increased, fewer and fewer people controlled the conditions of their labor or had a connection with the final product of that labor. As systems of distribution became more complex, far fewer producers and consumers ever met. One result of this complex set of transformations was a shift in the meaning and use of goods in everyday life, a shift usually referred to in shorthand as the onset of "consumer society."

In consumer society, everyday aesthetic practices come not only to *reflect* the new "identities" of modernity, but also help to *form* people's sense of self, of likeness and difference. As the psychologist Mihaly Csikszentmihalyi puts it:

> men and women make order in their selves (i.e. "retrieve their identity") by first creating and then interacting with the material world. The nature of that transaction will determine, to a great extent, the kind of person that emerges. Thus the things that surround us are inseparable from who we are. The material objects we use are not just tools we can pick up and discard at our convenience; they constitute the framework of experience that gives order to our otherwise shapeless selves.[5]

The buildings, furnishings, paintings, food, cars, cutlery, rugs, music, odors, clothing with which people are in daily, bodily, contact – contact which is shared by others – shape the contexts in which people feel "at home." But while some furniture or clothing makes some "feel at home" by its appearance, those same goods make others suspicious of their capacity to identify with its owners. Taste, in other words, has come to play a particular role in the formation of self and social life.

People living in modern societies find themselves traversing a landscape burgeoning with offerings and exhortations to acquire goods of one style or another.[6] Billboards, shop windows, advertisements on the radio and in the cinema, popular fiction, etiquette books, and magazine and newspaper advertisements suggest goods and tastes for all occasions. Equally important are the consumption practices of peers; women study each other's dresses, guests note the tables at which they dine, children know the season's necessary toys. Despite, and in fact perhaps because of, this bombardment of injunctions to consume, and examples of consumption, people are not fully conscious of which influences on their taste are particularly salient. While people sometimes set out to buy a dining room set just like, or absolutely not like, that of their friend, or the one they had seen advertised or recommended, if asked why they had bought one style over another, most reply that they just "know what they like." Taste, in all things, but particularly in the things that furnish the everyday, is naturalized and thereby moved beyond question (or reason).

It is the very opacity of taste that makes it both intriguing and frustrating as an object of study. People say things about themselves through their goods, sometimes consciously, but often unknowingly. I would like to suggest that such choices are most often much less self-conscious than those of adherence to a political party, membership in a social organization, or even participating in the *production* rather than the *consumption* of an object of style. For example, the historian Herbert Strauss, writing his memoirs in his eighties, came to realize, or speculate concerning, the source of his sense of "at-homeness" in functionalist style:

> the only store specializing in modern art objects and fine reproductions for the young or the impecunious was Laredo's on Bahnhofstrasse, owned by probably the only Jew of Sephardic (Spanish North-African) origin in town. His son Günther went to school with me, they were our neighbors, and I spent quite a few happy hours in their house in Keesburgstrasse, the first flat-roof building in town and an object of wonderment to the conventionally roofed-over citizenry. Laredo's had the first fully Bauhaus interior I encountered. Beautiful, warm-hearted Mrs. Laredo . . . and her . . . husband, Oscar, the major, maybe the only, modernist in our neoromantic art world, may well have become unconsciously associated in my life with my feeling of being at home in New Functionalism ever since.[7]

It is only in reflecting back upon his life that the elderly Herbert Strauss can (perhaps) make conscious his unconscious associations. Implicit in this self-interpretation, is that had the young Herbert had a good friend whose beautiful and warm mother had been an advocate of historicism, he might well have "simply liked" and felt at home in historicism rather than functionalism ever after. And, presumably, he emerged from his experience not only with a sense of identification with the style of New Functionalism, but also with the Jews with whom it was so markedly (in this instance) associated.

In this new conjuncture, however, where identities are shaped by things, objects have not lost their older task of connecting the living to the dead. The capacity of goods to master time, to keep the dead present, is particularly striking in the case of narratives written by Jews who lived in Paris and Berlin in the 1930s and 1940s. These texts left behind – memoirs, diaries, novels – bear witness to the power of things to crystallize emotion and to facilitate communication. For example, the

French philosopher, Sarah Kofman, opened the memoir she wrote shortly before she committed suicide in 1994, with the following:

> Of him all I have left is the fountain pen. I took it one day from my mother's purse, where she kept it along with some other souvenirs of my father. It is a kind of pen no longer made, the kind you have to fill with ink. I used it all through school. It "failed" me before I could bring myself to give it up. I still have it, patched up with Scotch tape; it is right in front of me on my desk and makes me write, write.
>
> Maybe all my books have been the detours required to bring me to write about "that."[8]

This is the entirety of the first chapter. We enter the story of "that," of her father's deportation and death in 1942 and her life under the Occupation, and of her difficulty in coming to terms with it, through a banal object, a pen. Of the objects in her mother's purse, it is the pen, her father's instrument of communication, a tool he used daily, a tool in constant contact with his skin, that Kofman, the child who would become a philosopher, chose to take. The pen with which her rabbi father wrote his sermons became the pen with which his daughter wrote philosophy. Even when it, too, has submitted to time, it sits there, compelling her to write, exhorting her to face a past she seeks to avoid.

The capacity of goods to materialize human relations, including betrayal, is also vividly rendered in Lotte Strauss's memoir, as she recounts her return to her childhood home in Wolfenbüttel in 1958:

> Entering the caretaker's apartment, I realized immediately that some of our furniture stood in their entranceway. When we were asked into the living room, I became aware in a flash that most of their furniture had been ours: there was the couch with unmist- akable pattern (I could still describe it), the table on which I had done my homework, my father's leather chair, even the little print of Rubens's baby son. I could not walk one step further into that apartment: I felt nauseated, my stomach turned, words failed me: I had to leave, no matter what the others thought.[9]

Those few sentences economically convey the impossibility of a return "home" and reunion with those entrusted with the family's future. The tragedy is all the greater because she had brought her husband and adolescent daughter, hoping to show both of them the scene of her own childhood. In this case, it would have been better had the things been destroyed along with her parents, rather than faithlessly going on, serving other masters, participating in their betrayal.

In both Kofman's and Strauss's usages, the goods themselves carried memories and meanings, and in both cases the authors are very conscious that those memories and meanings will be fully apparent to their audience.[10] They write knowing that their readers, who may be incapable of identifying with much else that is described in the now distant world of World War II, will empathize with these reactions. That confidence in the communicative capacity of things comes from the shared modernity of Kofman and Stein and their readers. However distant the Holocaust now is, it and we are products of modernity, living with the conceptions of self and identity – and the understanding of things – shaped by our inhabiting polities based on representation and economies governed by capitalism.

The simultaneity of the seeming naturalness of taste and the reality of its constructedness make it a rich site from which to grasp how people conceived their place in the world. Through an investigation of the taste Parisian and Berlin Jews expressed in the things by which they chose to be surrounded in the intimacy of their homes, I hope to shed further light on what it meant to be a Jew in the third and fourth decades of the twentieth century. This question of Jewish identity, of how fully Jews were integrated into their national cultures, of the existence or not of a sense of Jewishness that transcended national boundaries, of assimilation and acculturation, has generated a vast literature. There have been three dominant directions in this investigation. Much of that research has focused on Jews' engagement in public life – in elected and appointed political office, in social movements and political parties, the civil service, the army, universities.[11] Other scholars have looked rather to what is more usually thought of as the domain of private life – conversion and intermarriage rates, patterns of charitable giving, where children were schooled, and what names they were given.[12] Still others have looked to Jews' role as the producers and patrons of the fine arts, particularly to their participation in modernist movements.[13] My work melds this research agenda with that of those concerned with private life.

Scholars have suggested that European Jews tended to express their Jewishness in the "private" rather more than the "public" sphere. Historian Marion Kaplan has argued, for example, that in the Imperial period (from 1871 to 1918), women in Jewish households in Germany created a distinctively Jewish mode of being German in everyday life.[14] The women Kaplan studied worked at inculcating bourgeois German norms in their children, but at the same were a force against complete assimilation. The work of Paula Hyman on France tells a similar story. But even Kaplan and Hyman, because of the scope of their projects, could not detail the small choices of everyday life. It is clear that bourgeois Jews in Paris and Berlin adhered to bourgeois norms of dress, decor, entertainment, cleanliness, and manners. But given that there was great variation in this period in those norms – particularly in styles of interior decoration and art, ranging from the most traditionally historicist to the most avant-garde – to know that bourgeois Jews lived in a bourgeois manner, is to grasp only part of the story. An analysis of taste, with a particular focus on domestic taste including its juxtaposition with an expression of taste necessarily very public – that of architecture – is therefore particularly productive in grasping who Jews understood themselves to be.

It is not, however, only the fact that people made choices that makes this terrain revealing, but the status of those choices. Choices of occupation, of conversion, even of marriage partner are directly subject to realities, or perceptions, of discrimination. People may hit the barriers of exclusion, or in their attempt to navigate around them (for themselves or their children) make different decisions than they might otherwise. Particular aesthetic choices about the appearance of one's own home often do not address perceptions of discrimination as consciously as do other choices.

This chapter, thus, seeks to tackle the question of Jewish identity through an analysis of the choices Jews made about their everyday habitat. Did Jews living in Berlin and Paris acquire furnishings and other everyday goods marked by a specific aesthetic? Did they tend to make the same choices among the various forms of domestic and foreign, historicist and modernist, new and antique, furniture, china, and silverware available to them? Did they tend to worship in synagogues and dwell in houses or apartments more in one style than another? And, when they had the means and desire to hang original artwork on their walls, which schools of painting did they favor? Finally, did French and Germans share a taste in these goods that furnished their everyday? Researching the everyday life practices of Jews living in two different countries should enable me to shed light on what may be attributed to particular national contexts and what was common to Jewish taste and/or processes of acculturation in this period.

The juxtaposition of the aesthetic practices of German and French Jews is particularly productive for an inquiry into the question of Jewish identity as a result of the complex configuration of likeness, difference, and interaction between the two communities. A series of parallels between French and German Jews seem, at least at first, to make it likely that similar dynamics of identification would exist in both groups. German and French Jews shared long histories from the medieval through the early modern period of oscillation between persecution and toleration, but were consistently excluded from full participation in social and political life. During the second half of the nineteenth century, by contrast, Jews on both side of the Rhine experienced increasing prosperity, accompanied by massive rural–urban migration, and the establishment of a substantial bourgeoisie. Both groups faced the common challenge of absorbing a considerable migration of poor Jews from Eastern Europe starting in the 1880s. In both France and Germany, Jews of longer standing were anxious about the impact that foreign, poor, and more often visibly religious Jews would have on how they themselves were perceived. Finally, both groups although tiny minorities nationally were relatively important presences in their nations' capital cities (although more so in Berlin than in Paris). I have reinforced the parallels between the two groups by choosing to focus on Berlin and Paris, rather than attempting a national-level study. Both Parisian and Berlin Jews shared the experience of living in, and shaping, thriving, growing capital cities, cities at the forefront of the transformations that characterized the fine and decorative arts in this period. Thus, by the 1920s and 1930s, Jews in Berlin and Paris shared some fundamental experiences of discrimination and acceptance, economic prosperity for a significant number, the challenge of understanding their Jewishness in the face of a foreign immigration, and the possibilities of life in their respective capital cities.

The differences, however, are equally striking. French Jews were emancipated in 1789, they were well integrated into the state and political and intellectual life (excluded neither from teaching in university nor from the practice of law), they were not deeply engaged in Zionism, had low conversion rates, created only relatively weak national collective organizations (although they did participate in the founding of an important international Jewish organization), and did not take the lead in the Reform or other religious-intellectual movements of the day. German Jews, by contrast, were emancipated almost a century later, in 1871, were generally excluded from state functions (political office, the judiciary, and civil service), and the professorate, were at the center of the Zionist movement, had relatively high rates of conversion, and united in powerful associations, including efforts to shape a version of Judaism appropriate to modern life. Furthermore, while Berlin and Paris both had Jewish populations that were highly diverse with respect to class, religiosity, and politics, the Parisian community was further split between those whose roots lay in Germany and Eastern Europe and whose habits and aesthetics had been shaped by the Ashkenaz tradition, and those whose roots lay in Spain and North Africa from whence they carried Sephardic cultural practices. Essentially all Berlin Jews were, by contrast, from the Ashkenazic tradition. Finally, it would appear that more Jews in Berlin than Paris responded to the model of Judaism provided by Eastern European Jews with attraction rather than fear, seeing there a vision of authenticity they perceived to be lacking in their own more acculturated lives.

Characterizations of likeness and difference are further complicated by the ties, sometimes as members of the same family, sometimes as business and friendship connections, sometimes the more abstract links forged by reading the same books, looking at the same paintings, seeing the same plays, that connected Parisian and Berlin Jews.[15] A simultaneous study of the aesthetic practices of these two communities characterized by such likenesses and differences in the experiences of inclusion, exclusion and social mobility, as well as of diversity and homogeneity among Jews, should enable us to think in a different way about the meanings of the terms assimilation and acculturation.

The history of the acquisition, use, and meaning of objects is a notoriously difficult one to research, however. Consumption, like other "leisure time" activities has most often been conceived of as falling within the private sphere, beyond the documentary grasp of the state. And, it has most often been considered trivial, unworthy of the attention of the statistician, sociologist, or archivist. A comparative study of consumption is further complicated by the different record-keeping habits of different nation-states. These caveats aside, however, there are more than adequate sources available. Some are the canonical sources for this kind of project memoirs, diaries, photographs, architectural drawings, and novels. Some are the more particular, and in some ways problematic, sources generated by the National Socialist regime in Germany and its ally, the Vichy regime in France. These sources are the reams of paper generated by the effort to expropriate and destroy French and German Jewry.

Three kinds of archives generated by the Nazi regime in Berlin have been of particular use here: inventories, correspondence, and documentation produced during the course of expropriation of real estate, and detailed auction records.[16] Those records include auctions of both "Aryan" and "non-Aryan" households, with those terms of course, being defined according to government, rather than self, definition. I have read through approximately half (250) of the extant auction records of the so-called non-Aryan households for which there are detailed listings. My research assistant and I have also worked through a parallel selection of the "Aryan" records.

The Vichy regime produced parallel, but different, documentation. In France, the end of the war saw the return of thousands of Parisian Jews to their homes, homes they usually found either empty or furnished with their new inhabitants' possessions. The administration quickly set up a claims process whereby people could attempt to repossess their goods.[17] To file a claim, one wrote a letter explaining one's circumstances and included as detailed an inventory as possible of the missing furniture, clothing, jewelry, toys, art work, books, and musical instruments. These inventories range from notes hand-written in pencil on the back of a torn paper-bag to twenty-page, typed, mimeographed lists accompanied by high-quality photographs. Some are accompanied by letters, others are not. I have read a sample of some 400 such letters and inventories in an attempt to establish what prewar Jewish Parisian households looked like, across differences of class, citizenship, neighborhood, and religiosity.

The records for both Berlin and Paris pose both technical and moral problems. The technical are more easily addressed. Both the French and the German government documentation poses the problem of determining who is, and who is not, a Jew. In both the Nazi and Vichy regimes, Jews were defined by the state along genetic rather than voluntarist principles, thus the records of many of those identified by the state to be Jewish, may have understood themselves to be Catholic, Protestant, or without any religious or "ethnic" identification at all.[18] And, even among Jews, of course, there were vast differences in what "Jewishness" meant. In a further stage of this project I will attempt to determine with greater precision who of those, defined by antisemitic regimes as Jewish, would have given themselves that identity. The auction records also pose problems of interpretation because people often sold off goods a bit at a time, so it can be difficult to reconstruct the entirety of a household. A further technical problem is generated by an unevenness of the source materials. The Parisian Jews who petitioned the government for restitution of their goods ranged from immigrant tailors living in one-room apartments in the poorest of neighborhoods to fifth-generation bankers living in twelve-room villas in the wealthiest of suburbs. By contrast, the vast majority of my documentation to date from Berlin is from those who were solidly within the middle class. That material is broader in kind, including more photographic evidence, but is more limited in its class scope. A complexity of interpretation is also created in the French records by the fact that people sometimes lied about what they had owned. A friend whose family's form I found in the archive was certain that her father had exaggerated the value of the family's prewar possessions.[19] Finally, the Berlin auction records will eventually allow me to make generalizations, at least among the wealthy, concerning likeness or difference between Jews and non-Jews. Finding evidence of non-Jewish consumption habits in Paris is more difficult. I have, of course, supplemented these sources with photographs, memoirs, and museum catalogues, but more research, both to determine my subjects' identification with Judaism and to obtain a broader distribution of sources will be necessary before the conclusions can be more definitive.

The moral problem – the legitimacy of using information generated in the interests of mass-destruction for any purpose other than that of analyzing that process of persecution – is more difficult. The story told here is that of life rather than death. It is the story of how people gave meaning to their lives, communicated their values and sense of self to others, and remembered their pasts, through the banal things of their everyday lives. The obligation to struggle to understand the deaths of European Jews in the 1940s, should not force us to forget their lives. It is an irony of history that the sources generated by the Nazi regime inadvertently provide a rich image of the *lives* of the people it was trying to kill. I see no reason to accept the Nazis' purpose and thereby leave these lives deeper in the shade than they need be. Jews in Paris and Berlin in the 1920s and 1930s, like non-Jews in the same period, created their senses of self, communicated with others, and fought mortality through the habitats they created for themselves. It is to the specifics of that story that we now turn.

The Aesthetic World of Parisian Jews

While Jews in Paris lived throughout the city, they tended, as in all other urban contexts, to group in certain neighborhoods, marked by class and other divisions.

Thus, the Marais in the center of Paris, the faubourg Saint Antoine to the east, and Belleville to the northeast were home to many immigrants from Eastern Europe, the ninth arrondissement had a large Sephardi population, the Latin quarter was the choice of many Jewish intellectuals, while bankers tended to live in the wealthy districts and suburbs to the west. Their dwellings ranged from the smallest and dingiest of rented rooms to the most splendid of family mansions. These homes were, of course, filled with an equally wide range of quality and quantity of furnishings, clothing, musical instruments, paintings, sculpture, china, silverware, and linen. There was, however, one striking similarity among these interiors.

The vast majority of Parisian Jews lived in emphatically *French* interiors. Whether the choice was historicist pastiche – Louis XIII, Henri II, Louis XIV, Louis XV, Louis XVI, or Empire – or real antiques, or modernist design, Parisian Jews most often bought, sat at, slept in, and ate at furniture both made in France and understood to represent their Frenchness. M. Roger Kahn, for example, who lived in the nineteenth arrondissement, described his dining room as having been furnished with a dining-room set in dark oak, in the Renaissance style, copied from some of the furniture in the Musée Cluny.[20] This very ornate, heavily carved, marble-surfaced set was given a firm location in the French past. The Musée Cluny was (and is) the French national museum of the Middle Ages, and holds any number of French national icons. Specifying that his dining-room set had been based on an object in the Cluny, helped ground M. Kahn firmly in the French past. Since the nineteenth arrondissement was a poor neighborhood heavily settled by Jewish immigrants from Eastern Europe, M. Kahn may have been all the more eager (whether consciously or not) to assert a connection to the French past in his everyday life. It would, however, be wrong to imply that it was only those who feared to be taken for an immigrant or who lived in a less-wealthy neighborhood who chose French historicist furnishings. It was the style of choice for the vast majority. For example, the wealthy household of M. and Mme Maurice Kron was furnished in a combination of antique and historicist furniture and *objets*. Along with a number of pieces identified as actually dating from the period of the transition from Louis XV to Louis XVI, they had owned a living-room set made in the appropriate style by the important Parisian manufacturer, Krieger.[21]

Some furniture was given a spatial rather than temporal location in French history. People who had migrated to Paris (or whose parents had migrated) from elsewhere in France would often bring a reminder or two of their provincial attachments with them. Furthermore, certain regions were known for cabinetwork and for certain pieces. Normandy was held to produce superior wardrobes, while Brittany was famous for sideboards. The late nineteenth and early twentieth centuries had, furthermore, seen a revival of regionalism and a new interest in "folk" craft, producing a new market for both new and old products of France's provinces. Parisian Jews shared this taste for sprinkling the occasional provincial piece among an interior generally identified with monarchical epochs. Thus, for example, Marcel Cain, who lived in a rather large apartment on 22 boulevard Saint Germain in the fifth arrondissement in Paris, had not only an impressive array of Directoire, Louis XIV and Louis XVI period furniture, but also an armoire from Bresse and another from the Lorraine, and two sideboards from Brittany.[22] All of these goods, whether linked to royal reigns or folk traditions had firmly French associations. In fact, there are almost no references to furniture of foreign origin, with rare exceptions to the norm in the form of the occasional small Italian Renaissance table, or furniture from the English exporter, Maple, which distributed in France.

This almost exclusive taste for French furniture by those identified as Jewish by the Vichy government was shared by their non-Jewish Parisian neighbors. I have argued elsewhere that French consumers' commitment to French objects in their everyday life may be linked to the French state's cultural policy.[23] From the time of the Revolution, successive French governments had invested considerable resources in the advancement of the French art industries and in promoting a certain vision of French taste both domestically and abroad. That effort was accelerated and intensified during the Third Republic and seems to have been generally successful. When it came to furniture – a major and symbolically weighty purchase – the vast majority of people living in France bought French.

Parisian consumers tended, furthermore, to overwhelmingly favor new versions of Old Regime style goods, over both regional and modern styles. Regional styles were less favored for the same reason a few acquired them – they were associated with provincial particularity and with ruralness, while monarchical style was associated with a shared, common French past, urbaneness, and elegance. Modernist styles – whether art nouveau or art deco – posed another set of possibilities and problems to consumers.

Art nouveau, the style made famous by the Guimard entrances to the Paris subway, was, when concretized in furniture, a luxury few could afford. It involved elaborate carving of expensive wood and extensive, time-consuming inlay. Because of its emphasis on the combination of carving (rather than turning) and inlay (rather than simpler veneers), little mechanization was possible so costs for both labor and materials were high. Art nouveau, although a significant aesthetic movement, therefore, never made its way into most French households. The other significant modern style, art deco, with its emphasis on linearity, mechanical production, painted surfaces, veneers, and use of artificial elements, had the potential to be within the reach of far more consumers, but was, in fact, adopted by relatively few.

The lack of popularity of modernist design can, I think, be explained by its suspect detachment from the French past. The inventories would indicate that these generalizations hold true across class boundaries, but that there are notable variations among some occupational groups. Consumers employed in the art, architecture, design, and fashion industries (broadly defined), for example, had a greater tendency than others to buy modernist design. Thus for example, while the widowed mother of the industrial designer, M. Khenkine, furnished her part of their shared apartment in Louis XVI, his studio was furnished with modern-style goods.[24] The attraction to modernism in this group, may, I think, be accounted for by their professional engagement with new aesthetic trends and a corresponding interest in the up-to-dateness of the aesthetic of their everyday life. For other consumers, art deco's internationalist, cosmopolitan, and ahistorical associations and aspirations clashed with their sense of their lives and their homes rooted in a French past and French traditions. It is not surprising therefore that in those dwellings in which the two styles were mixed, dining and living rooms tended to be historicist, while bedrooms and studies were more often modernist. Thus, the space in which the family's social life transpired was anchored in the French past, while the private space of the bedroom and the professional space of the study would be made forward-looking. Bedrooms were essentially never seen by those outside the family, and studies, as work spaces, had a foot outside of the domestic sphere. It would appear that the owners of such homes expressed their acceptance of conformity to bourgeois norms and the limits to that acceptance in these choices.

When it came to the smaller objects of interior decoration, however, Parisian Jews became somewhat more eclectic. Japanese and Chinese sculptures were relatively popular, as were "oriental" carpets, and some objects from North Africa and other French colonies. Mme Joseph Cohen, for example, had something she identified as a lamp from a mosque hanging in her front hall.[25] These non-French objects were usually finishing touches on otherwise quite domestic interiors. The living room of Mme Blitz is a case in point. It included:

> Two big smoking chairs upholstered in beige velvet, a sofa and four smaller chairs in the same fabric, an antique, Louis XV, chess table. A *bonheur de jour* in rosewood, a Lalik [*sic*] vase, two paintings and one engraving, one antique glass cabinet, one nesting table, two oriental carpets, two Chinese vases, and three pairs of curtains.[26]

I would suggest that while these households remained committed to things French for their capital-intensive acquisitions, intended to survive several generations, that ensemble could be leavened by less expensive and more moveable goods from other aesthetic traditions. More surprising, perhaps, is the almost complete absence of Jewish religious objects in these households.

Very few households listed Jewish or any other non-ethnographic or decorative religious signs, although there are interesting exceptions. Mme Omar, for example, listed among the things that had disappeared from her apartment, the "four tables of the law of the Israelites."[27] There is, however, a danger of over-reading this absence, as a separate inventory of libraries done by the German army makes clear. Of the eighty-six "Jewish" private libraries seized and inventoried, twenty were identified as having, among other things, either books on Jewish themes or books in Hebrew.[28]

Parisian Jews made use of the stylistic repertoire available to them to express the different pieces of themselves. Their furniture, with a few notable exceptions, rooted them firmly in the French past, even if they had, in fact, been transplanted. Their Japanese and Chinese *objets d'art* reflected the fascination they shared with their non-Jewish neighbors in things from the East. Sephardi Jews' ties to the Mediterranean world and Ashkenaz Jews ties to Eastern Europe were sometimes expressed in the smaller, more movable, less capital-intensive decorative objects adorning their homes. Their books, however, revealed many Parisian Jews' interest in things Jewish while the over-representation of violins reflected Jewish traditions of portable forms of music. Finally, the very modern interiors of some seem to have reflected a participation in the aesthetic transformations of their times, and perhaps enough of an ease with their French identity to not fear accusations of cosmopolitanism. The story from Berlin is quite different.

The Aesthetic World of Berlin Jews

Based on the evidence, from auction records, photographs, descriptions in memoirs, and two photographic collections, the most striking feature of the domestic aesthetic world of economically comfortable Jewish Berliners, was their attraction to modernism and the eclecticism and cosmopolitanism of their taste.[29] Of those households defined as "non-Aryan" in the auctions held from 1935 to 1942, and whose records are precise concerning the style of goods sold, more than a third combined modern and historicist style furnishings and tableware, while the remainder sat upon and slept in antique (and historicist pastiche) furniture from England, France, Italy, and Germany. Many of the homes photographed by Martha Huth in the 1920s, for example, reinforce this image. Her work reveals the homes of the banker Hans Fürstenberg and of the Goldschmidt-Rothschild family in the chic Tiergarten neighborhood to have been largely furnished with seventeenth- and eighteenth-century French and French-style furniture.[30] Furniture for living rooms, dining rooms, and bedrooms was most often acquired in matching sets, with as many as sixteen or seventeen pieces not being unusual. Among French styles, Louis XVI was the most popular followed by Empire and then the celebrated seventeenth-century *ébéniste* Boulle. Italy was represented through Renaissance furniture. German furniture was identified as Baroque or Biedermeier. Among English styles, Queen Anne and Chippendale were about equally present. E.A., for example, who was forced to auction off his goods in 1936, had a rather spectacular study furnished with an English Queen Anne style set in birds' eye maple, a sofa upholstered in green velour, a modern bronze light fixture, an oriental carpet, and four oil paintings.[31] Lotte Strauss's uncle echoed the fondness for English style having had built a country house in Kladow on the Wannsee following the model of an English country house, a style she remembered to have blended unobtrusively into the German landscape.[32] E.A.'s dining room was also in Queen Anne style (hazelnutwood), while the bedroom departed from both the English and historicizing impulse, being furnished in a white-lacquer modern style.[33] Bedrooms were the most likely to be left without a named style and they and men's studies were the most likely to be in the modern style in households that mixed historicist and modern design.

Moving from furniture to the arts of the table, Berlin Jews generally favored Meissen, Sèvres, KPM, and Rosenthal china, although they often had silver in Chippendale style. Both the china and silver collections attest to the conformity to bourgeois Berliner practice – many households had two or more "coffee and cake" services, and most had enough tableware (and chairs) so that a dinner for twelve would have posed no difficulties. The inventories attest as well to a taste for fine alcohol properly drunk, with many different shapes and sizes of crystal.

In the domain of decorative objects, by contrast, Berliners often left the European continent, preferring "oriental" carpets, and Japanese and Chinese objects, although French bronze and German and French statuettes were also popular. Collections of paintings and sculpture also included more objects from far distant places than did furniture. Like in France, furniture seemed often to be the last place where one took what were perceived to be aesthetic risks. The painter Max Liebermann, particularly known for his participation in the German Secession movement and his collection of French impressionism, for example, chose to furnish his home in furniture from a long-dead past at the same time as he advocated radical transformation in the fine arts.[34] Likewise, the apartment of one wealthy man who had his goods auctioned in 1935 included two rare and expensive seventeenth-century French chests made by Boulle, some Biedermeier furniture, Meißen, Berliner and Wiener vases, Barbedienne (fashionable nineteenth-century Parisian) bronzes, Chinese porcelain, Japanese ivory figures.[35] Another who sold his goods in the same year had chosen to furnish his apartment largely in Louis XVI and French first Empire style, but hung a mixture of Japanese woodcuts, and German naturalist paintings (as well as a Russian icon) on the walls, and scattered Chinese lacquered objects and lamps through his apartment.[36] Frederic Zeller recalled fondly the *objets* from far-off places that decorated his Aunt Cilly's apartment, on Krummerstrasse in Charlottenburg, "My upper kingdom . . . overflowed with incredible treasures . . . There were glass vitrines and drawers full of surprises: Japanese masks; silver spoons with miniature enameled pictures of towns; Indian chess figures of maharajahs on plump elephants; darkly glowing garnet jewelry; turquoise scarabs."[37] Occasionally the taste for the exotic would be present in more than just knick-knacks. The banker and businessman Herbert Gutmann included an entire "moorish" room in his villa in Potsdam. This elaborate room was decorated with inlaid walls, overlapping carpets, sculptures, and heavily upholstered furniture.[38]

Jewish middle-class interiors do not appear to have differed radically from their non-Jewish neighbors, with one exception. Bourgeois Berliners seem to have shared a taste for foreign and for antique furniture, and for "exotic" *objets d'art*. They all had large quantities of silver and china. But, while modernist furniture is far outnumbered by historicist furniture in all Berlin households, it was more present in the apparently Jewish households than in the others.

For example Paul Boroschek (1900–67) a leading stockbroker, who was an active Zionist as well as engaged with the Jewish Community of Berlin and his wife Edith Boroschek, a singer, moved in 1930 into a building on Xaantenerstraße, not far from the Kurfürstendamm, where they chose to live in an interior designed by Marcel Breuer. Extant photographs of these dwellings show the furnishings and decor reduced to the absolute minimum, although a few personal objects (a vase for example) were allowed to remain.[39] The Boroscheks were far from unique; the co-owner of a famous mosaic company, Gottfried Heinersdorff, for example, also shared this taste for the very modern.[40] It is important, of course, not to overstate this argument. The majority of Berlin Jews did not live in modernist interiors and the majority of consumers of modernism were not Jews, but it is nonetheless noteworthy both that Berlin Jews appear to have been more attracted to modernist style than their cousins in France, and than their non-Jewish neighbors in Berlin.

In the domain of religious objects there are noticeable presences *and* absences in the extant documentation. A surprisingly large number of those identified as "non-Aryans" by the Nazi regime had homes decorated with Christian religious icons. The Meinhardts, for example, appear to have slept under a very large painting of the Madonna and child. The Meinhardts were a wealthy family of industrialists who owned a large villa on Rauchstrasse at the corner of Drake-strasse.[41] Their choice of bedroom decor was not unusual. Mr H.G., for example, auctioned a small wooden angel as well as a wooden Madonna and child, a sculpture of Jesus and two holy paintings. Mr K.G. had an adoration and a Madonna, while Frau D.G. had a valuable antique Madonna and child in an apartment dominated by very elegant furniture and china and Frau B.G. had an extensive collection of religious objects including a wood bas-relief Madonna and child, a sculpted Madonna, a bas-relief Eremiten, and two old oil paintings, one of the Father, Son and Holy Ghost and the other of a holy scene. These were balanced by a few asiatic deities.[42]

The auction house records – which are admittedly biased towards the wealthy – would indicate that approximately 10 percent of the households identified as Jewish by the Nazi government had a significant number of Christian religious objects as part of their decor. Given that the conversion rate (to Christianity from Judaism) in Berlin was also approximately 10% of the Jewish population, it is possible that these were all people identified as Jews racially but who did not identify as such. It is also possible, however, that they did understand themselves as Jews but collected paintings and sculptures with Christian themes as they did art objects coming out of Buddhist or Confucian traditions, as did non-Jewish members of their class. The case of Victor Hahn would lend support to this hypothesis. Whether or not Hahn identified as a Jew is unclear, but his passion for collecting Christian art is not. His home on the Kurfürstendamm included at least two rooms devoted to Italian and German sculpture of the fifteenth and sixteenth centuries, largely, of course, religious figures.[43] Although more research is needed for a full explanation, my sense thus far is that some "Jews" furnished their everyday with Christian objects because they did not identify as Jews, others because they found them beautiful, and yet others in order to "pass."

Just as the strong presence of Christian objects is surprising at first glance, the essentially complete absence of any Jewish ritual object despite the importance of practice within the home in Judaism is equally striking. Research done in the context of exhibitions on Jewish life under the Third Reich as well as anecdotal information would imply simply that those menorahs, spice boxes, candlesticks, prayer books, shawls, and wine goblets were sufficiently precious to their owners that they were given into safe-keeping, buried, smuggled out, or possibly destroyed rather than sold. It would clearly be wrong to read their absence in these sources as an indication of either a massive lack of piety or lack of identification with Judaism on the part of Berlin's Jews.[44]

Conclusion

Jews living in Berlin and Paris appear to have participated in the taste of the nation and society of which they were a part. Wealthy Berlin Jews lived surrounded by what was considered the best in European and Asian design. They had Boulle furniture, Barbedienne bronzes, Chinese vases and lacquer furniture, Japanese woodcuts, Meissen, Rosenthal, and Sèvres porcelain, and English library furniture. They had objects from all periods from antiquity to the present. Among the distinctively German things they owned, many were defined by their regional origins – Meißen, Wien, Berlin, or Dresden china, for example. Parisian Jews, by contrast, lived surrounded by overwhelmingly French things. The goods came from all periods in French history (or were modern versions of historical styles), but were only occasionally linked to a particular regional location.

The differences between Jews in Berlin and Paris may perhaps be crystallized in their responses to the appearance of Ost-Juden in their midst. Jews in Paris appear to have reacted to these Jews whose Judaism was made visible – through their clothing and hair – to all, with systematic efforts to mark their difference, to claim their Frenchness. The response in Berlin, as the recent work of Michael Brenner most strongly emphasizes, was much more complicated.[45] While many Berliners reacted in ways analogous to the Parisians, for a significant number of Jews in Berlin, migrants from Eastern Europe and the shtetls they had left behind represented a possibility for recreating an authentic Judaism. While Parisian Jews seem to have been fearful of being marked as "other," as "alien," by association with these Jewish newcomers whose everyday practices were so different from French norms, many Berliners seem to have been less worried, perhaps more confident in their anchoring in German society, or perhaps, and I think this is more likely, sharing with their fellow Germans a sense that conformity in everyday practices was not necessarily required of them. A full explanation of how the relationship between Frenchness and Germanness, between national belonging in the two nation-states and everyday taste was different, must await another context, but for now the crucial point is that Jews in Paris and Berlin used the aesthetic repertoire available to them to express likeness and difference from the non-Jews with whom they identified (for reasons of class, national, professional, or political location) and to mark likenesses and differences with their fellow Jews. In the end, I would argue, the different tastes of Parisian and Berlin Jews speak to the power of the nation in shaping everyday taste. Deviations from dominant patterns are found at the level of individual experience rather than in something that could be called a "Jewish taste." Taste in everyday things is, therefore, revealing in how modern individuals live and negotiate among their multiple identities, within the very powerful framework of the nation.

Acknowledgments

I would like to thank Dr Heike Schroll and Gisela Erler at the Landesarchiv Berlin (LAB), who provided invaluable help negotiating the archive, Carla MacDougall for her research assistance, and Tom Holt for his most helpful reading of this chapter. Annette Timm and Carol Scherer provided great assistance in both academic and everyday life in Berlin. Joachim Schlör and Andreas Hansert were generous with suggestions of useful sources in Berlin for this project. The research could not have been done without the financial support of the University of

Chicago. This article has benefited from discussion in Gisela Bock's seminar at the FU in Berlin and the Modern European Workshop at the University of Chicago.

Notes

1. Zygmunt Bauman, "Soil, Blood and Identity," *The Sociological Review* 40, 4 (1992), p. 680.

2. On the question of the forging of a new concept of identity in modern democracies see: Craig Calhoun (ed.), *Social Theory and the Politics of Identity* (Cambridge, MA: Blackwell, 1994) and particularly his essay, "Social Theory and the Politics of Identity," pp. 9–16.

3. Gérard Noiriel, *La Tyrannie du national: le droit d'asile en Europe 1793–1993* (Paris: Calmann-Lévy, 1991).

4. On mobility, representation, and identity see Karen Halttunen, *Confidence Men and Painted Women: A Study of Middle-Class Culture in America, 1830–1870* (New Haven, CT and London: Yale University Press, 1982).

5. Mihaly Csikszentmihalyi and Eugene Rochberg-Halton, *The Meaning of Things: Domestic Symbols and the Self* (Cambridge: Cambridge University Press, 1981), p. 16.

6. For one of most succinct and useful theoretical accounts of consumer society, see: Jean Baudrillard, "The System of Objects," and "Consumer Society," from his *Selected Writings*, ed. Mark Poster (Stanford: Stanford University Press, 1988); Daniel Miller, *Material Culture and Mass Consumption* (Oxford: Basil Blackwell, 1987).

7. Herbert A. Strauss, *In the Eye of the Storm: Growing up Jewish in Germany 1918–1943. A Memoir* (New York: Fordham University Press, 1999), pp. 39–40.

8. Sarah Kofman, *Rue Ordener Rue Labat*, trans. with an introduction by Ann Smock (Lincoln, NE: University of Nebraska Press, 1996, originally Editions Galilée, 1994), p. 3.

9. Lotte Strauss, *Over the Green Hill: A German Jewish Memoir 1913–1943* (New York: Fordham University Press, 1999), p. 171.

10. On the issue of domestic objects and memory, see Csikszentmihalyi and Rochberg-Halton, *Meaning of Things*, p. 87.

11. For France see esp., Pierre Birnbaum, *Les Fous de la république: histoire des juifs d'Etat de Gambetta à Vichy* (Paris: Fayard, 1992) and for Germany, Ernest Hamburger, *Juden im öffentlichen Leben Deutschlands* (Tübingen: J.C.B. Mohr, 1968).

12. Marion A. Kaplan, *The Making of the Jewish Middle Class: Women, Family, and Identity in Imperial Germany* (New York: Oxford University Press, 1991); Paula E. Hyman, *Gender and Assimilation in Modern Jewish History: The Roles and Representation of Women* (Seattle: University of Washington Press, 1995); Antoine Halff, "Lieux d'assimilation, lieux d'identité: les communautés juives et léssor des stations thermales et balnéaires à la Belle Epqoue," *Pardès* 8 (1988), pp. 41–57.

13. Key texts for Germany remain Peter Gay, *Freud, Jews, and Other Germans: Masters and Victims in Modernist Culture* (New York: Oxford University Press, 1978) and replies including Dennis Klein, "Assimilation and Dissimilation: Peter Gay's Freud, Jews and Other Germans," *New German Critique* 19 (1980), pp. 252–65; Peter Paret, *The Berlin*

Secession: Modernism and its Enemies in Imperial Germany (Cambridge, MA: Harvard University Press, 1980). The contributions in Emily D. Bilski (ed.), *Berlin Metropolis: Jews and the New Culture, 1890–1918* (Berkeley, CA: University of California Press, 1999) bring this debate up to date. This theme has been less developed in the French literature, see, however: Kenneth E. Silver and Romy Golan (with contributions by Arthur A. Cohen, Billy Klüver, and Julie Martin), *The Circle of Montparnasse: Jewish Artists in Paris, 1905–1945.* Exhibition of the Jewish museum, (New York: The Jewish Museum, New York and Universe Books, 1985).

14. Kaplan, *Making of the Jewish Middle Class*; Hyman, *Gender and Assimilation*.

15. Pierre Birnbaum and Ira Katznelson, "Emanciption and the Liberal Offer," pp. 2–36 in their *Paths of Emancipation: Jews, States, and Citizenship* (Princeton, NJ: Princeton University Press, 1995); Paula E. Hyman, *The Jews of Modern France* (Berkeley, CA: University of California Press, 1998).

16. Both of these are held in the Landesarchiv Berlin. The auction records are in the series A. Rep. 243-04. The property lists (*Vermögenserklärungen*) are in: A Rep. 092 Der Oberfinanzpräsident Berlin. There are in addition property expropriation files in the same archive, some of which are very rich. See for example, Baupolizei, Bezirk Tiergarten/ Baupolizei und Straßenpolizei. 105 A Pr. Br. Rep. 030 Bln C Nr. 820 a. *Enteignungsakte Rauchstr. 11.*

17. AN 38 AJ 5909-5927. Lettres de spoliés addressés au Service de restitution au sujet de leurs biens (surtout inventaires de mobilier et de biens personnels), classées par ordre alphabétique, 1944–46.

18. This is supported by how people marked the "religious" as opposed to "ethnic" blanks on the inventories they filled out before being deported. All identified their ethnicity as Jewish, but a significant number claimed other religious affiliation (or none at all).

19. Communication from Jacqueline Feldman. Her family's claim is to be found in AN 38 AJ 591. But, of course, her perspective was that of a child at the time of the expropriation.

20. AN 38 AJ 5917.

21. Ibid.

22. AN 38 AJ 5912.

23. For the full elaboration of this argument, see Leora Auslander, *Taste and Power: Furnishing Modern France* (Berkeley, CA: University of California Press, 1996); for a more extensive discussion of conceptions of taste and citizenship in the 1920s and 1930s see L. Auslander, "The Everyday of Citizenship: Aesthetics, Affect and Law in France and Germany, 1890–1933," in Martin Daunton and Matthew Hilton (eds), *Material Politics: States, Consumers, and Political Cultures* (Oxford: Berg, 2001).

24. AN 38 AJ 1917.

25. AN 38 AJ 5912.

26. AN 38 AJ 5909.

27. Ibid.

28. AN 38 AJ 5937.

29. Enno Kaufhold, *Berliner Interieurs 1910–1930: Photographien von Waldemar Titzenthaler* (Berlin: Nicolai, 1999).

30. Jan T. Köhler et al., *Berliner Lebenswelten der zwaniger Jahre: Bilder einer untergegangene Kultur* (Frankfurt: Eichborn, 1996), pp. 50–3; 64–7.

31. Landesarchiv Berlin 243-04 46.

32. Strauss, *Over the Green Hill*, p. 41.

33. Landesarchiv Berlin 243-04 46.

34. Köhler et al., *Berliner Lebenswelten*, pp.104–7.

35. Landesarchiv Berlin 243-04 46. Please note: the regulations of the Landesarchiv Berlin prohibit the mention of names in these series of files. The files are arranged alphabetically with between one and two letters per file.

36. Ibid.

37. Frederic Zeller, *When Time Ran Out: Coming of Age in the Third Reich* (Sag Harbor, NY: Permanent Press, 1989), p. 42.

38. Köhler et al., *Berliner Lebenswelten*, p. 71.

39. Ibid., pp. 33–4.

40. Ibid., pp. 76–9.

41. Landesarchiv Berlin. Baupolizei, Bezirk Tiergarten/Baupolizei und Straßenpolizei. 105 A Pr. Br. Rep. 030 Bln C Nr. 820 a.

42. Landesarchiv Berlin, Rep A. 243-04 52.

43. Köhler et al., *Berliner Lebenswelten*, pp.72–5.

44. Beate Meyer and Hermann Simon (eds), *Juden in Berlin 1938–1945* (Berlin: Philo, 2000), particularly the article by Michael Schäbitz, "Flucht und Vertreibung der deutschen Juden 1933–1941," pp. 51–76 and the corresponding part of the exhibit. Stories like that of Craig Becker, whose mother smuggled their (rather large) menorah out of Berlin when she fled are also not rare.

45. Michael Brenner, *The Renaissance of Jewish Culture in Weimar Germany* (New Haven, CT: Yale University Press, 1996).

15

Leisure, Politics, and the Consumption of Tobacco in Britain since the Nineteenth Century

Matthew Hilton

Historians of leisure in Britain have traditionally been concerned with two major debates, both relating to power and control. First, there is the issue of control over time. In the early nineteenth century, industrialists' need for factory discipline ran counter to long established work and leisure patterns, a theme best illustrated by the persistence of St. Monday whereby workers extended their weekend leisure pursuits into the first working day.[1] By the early twentieth century, struggles over the control of time had taken a different turn, the rise of mass consumer society polarizing labor demands into either those for shorter working hours – and hence more time for leisure – or for more money with which to pay for the commodities of the expanding market.[2] The second major issue in the history of leisure has been over the control of minds. Various rational recreationists, evangelical organizations, temperance reformers, and moral leaders sought to direct and influence the content of working-class leisure. Traditional leisure pursuits – and especially those relating to festivals formed around the agricultural calendar – were discouraged, occasionally with the aid of legislation, and more uplifting, sober-minded and respectable activities were promoted in a typically crusading spirit.[3]

Much of this work on leisure has focused on those activities easily recognisable as non-work time: the pub, the wakes festival, sport, the music hall, the seaside holiday, and the cinema. Issues relating to the control of time and of minds has been central to the means by which their histories have been written. But what, perhaps, of the most popular leisure activity of all, an activity that by 1950 was indulged in by 80 percent of the adult male and 40 percent of the adult female population?[4] Tobacco smoking is hardly a leisure pursuit of the kind that was enjoyed and anticipated as a specific time and site separate from work in the same way as was the dance hall or the football stadium. Until the smoking and health controversy of the 1950s, it inspired nothing like the protests against drink that had occurred in the nineteenth century.[5] It had, of course, been the subject of enormous moral and political unease throughout Europe in the early modern period, but by the late nineteenth century, the only sustained opposition to adult smoking came from a radical wing of the temperance movement which at its peak in 1857 could raise no more than a few hundred pounds a year to fund its propaganda efforts.[6] If tobacco's content raised comparatively few objections, the time taken to enjoy it as a leisure pursuit raised even less; a pipe was often smoked through work or leisure and a cigarette took only a few minutes to consume.

Yet the importance of smoking as a leisure activity has not been lost on scholars outside of history. Contemporary social investigators and more recent feminist analyses of leisure have frequently referred to the "chameleon-like" quality of leisure, a cup of tea or a cigarette offering many women an important, if not the only, break from the routine of work in the home and outside.[7] Such detailed studies of leisure seem to raise a further set of questions relating not to the control, but to the experience of leisure. Indeed, we might turn around the original concerns of the historians of leisure and explore not only how leisure is controlled from without, but also how the internal forms of knowledge and role-playing produced through participation in a particular leisure activity are then taken on as wider cultural and even political identities. This is to ask how identity politics formed during time spent in leisure can affect the development of the marketplace and even the incremental expansion of the entire modern state apparatus. Here, histories of leisure can be intertwined with histories of consumption which demonstrate how detailed case studies of the use of specific goods can result in the formation of wider collective ideologies, attitudes, and social movements.[8]

Tobacco is ideally situated for such a case study, it being the one leisure commodity that came under the greatest contemporary scrutiny, whether through advertising, books celebrating its use, or through medical literature. The study of its history enables an analysis to be made of what it meant and signified to different sections of the community. In what follows I will trace the history of smoking among women and working-class men in the late nineteenth and early twentieth centuries, before outlining a particular culture or cult of smoking espoused by an expanding middle class in the cheap periodical press of *Chambers' Journal*, *Macmillan's Magazine, All the Year Round*, and *Once a Week*, as well as in numerous books and "odes" devoted to tobacco or "the divine weed." In these works, a gender specific "philosophy" of smoking emerged that emphasized the liberal values of independence and individuality. This masculine, largely bourgeois, understanding of smoking subsequently came to have much greater cultural resonance and, I will argue, was an important means by which smokers reacted to the revelations linking smoking to lung cancer in the 1950s and 1960s and also how governments have intervened in this individual act of consumption.[9]

For a leisure activity seemingly so ubiquitous, it is not surprising that smoking has meant many things to many people. The overwhelming Victorian attitude to smoking by women was that it was clearly unrespectable, despite the frequent allusions to aristocratic snuff takers persisting in what had been a common eighteenth-century practice and the anecdotal and archaeological evidence that points to the frequency of clay pipe smoking among older rural women.[10] Smoking was associated with actresses and prostitutes, an image fixed in popular imagination through the literary and artistic portrayals of Mérimée's and later Bizet's gypsy factory girl, Carmen, Ouida's androgynous Cigarette and the Zu-Zu's of various cavalry officers, the former model, Jacky, in E.M. Forster's *Howards End*, and the high number of scantily clad music hall actresses featured on the very first cigarette cards of the 1890s.[11] Against this cultural background, the "new women" of the 1890s smoked both in defiance of respectable codes of femininity and to assert their independence in a masculine controlled public sphere. "Girls of the period" and "wild women" caused much offence to commentators such as Eliza Lynn Linton, but others including Mark Twain and the society divorcee Lady Colin Campbell offered their support.[12] The tobacco trade was also not slow to respond, with London retailers offering small, expensive, and often gold-tipped cigarettes branded Two Roses, Dames, Miranda's Dream, Boudoir, Pour la Dame, Virginia, Gay Grissette, and Young Ladies.[13] Positive portrayals of female smokers also appeared in fiction, in H.G. Wells's *Ann Veronica* (1909), Grant Allen's *The Woman Who Did* (1895), and most persistently in Dorothy Richardson's autobiographical *Pilgrimage*, where Miriam marks each stage of her liberation and her entry into the public sphere through her skill and confidence in the rituals of smoking.[14]

The employment changes of the First World War enabled many working-class women to share in the liberatory aspects of smoking as they left domestic service to enter the munitions factories, the clerical and commercial offices of the city, and the transport industry.[15] Their smoking remained controversial, provoking something of a backlash in the 1920s, though by now it was associated with a host of other dangers of the modern Jazz Age – cocktails, Eton crops, and motor cars.[16] But what smoking connoted for the vast majority of women in the interwar years was glamour. Manufacturers were slow to pick up on this social trend and advertising directed specifically at women tended to follow rather than lead changing patterns in leisure. Instead, the cinema provided the strongest images of smoking, beginning with a series of infamous morally deviant leading stars, from Clara Bow's *It Girl* of 1927, Louise Brooks' fallen women in *Pandora's Box* (1929), the murderous Tallulah Bankhead in *My Sin* (1931), Mae West's carnival dancer in *I'm No Angel* (1933), and Marlene Dietrich's portrayals of the nightclub singer in *The Blue Angel* (1930) and the notorious Lily in *Shanghai Express* (1932).[17] Smoking glamour was rendered more respectable in the later 1930s and 1940s in the roles of Mary Astor, Ingrid Bergman, Rita Hayworth, Bette Davis, and most spectacularly by Lauren Bacall who in 1945 famously marked her screen debut in *To Have and Have Not* by standing in the doorway of Humphrey Bogart's hotel room asking, "Anybody got a light?" For the reality of everyday smoking behavior, though, the massive popularity among women of cheap brands such as Player's Weights and Will's Woodbines ("gaspers" as they were popularly known) suggests that smoking performed another role from that of social emulation.[18] This was no more apparent than during the stresses and strains of World War II when Mass-Observation noted that many women massively increased their cigarette consumption, especially during air raids, as a psychological prop to deal with the breaks from normality. Women respondents testified to smoking's ability to help them through emotional and intellectual difficulties, to help when tired, to alleviate boredom, to reduce nervousness and increase sociability.[19] Furthermore, the persistence of smoking among women after the links with lung cancer and other diseases were widely publicized has caused many investigators to conclude that the cigarette provides momentary escape when "life's a drag" and, as such, remains "a feminist issue."[20]

For working-class men, the great regional diversity in pipe smoking patterns in the nineteenth century is testament to the range of meanings attached to popular leisure. In a period when the larger part of tobacco consumed was sold loose in amounts of one ounce for 3d., tobacco preferences differed enormously across the British Isles. For instance, Welsh miners were known to prefer strong shag tobaccos (coarsely cut leaf) and rolls (tied tightly into a type of rope), dock laborers were associated with thick twists, cabmen for Irish roll, while the better paid and London workers preferred the lighter and more finely cut Virginian flake tobaccos, which were ready to smoke. Cavendish, which came in the form of a cake, required much manipulation before being ready for smoking and it gave way in popularity – especially in Ireland and the North of England – to more manageable rolls such as nailrod and twist, which had the dual advantage of being ready for chewing.[21] Briar pipe smokers of the later nineteenth century preferred mixtures where the lighter Virginian leaves were blended with the stronger flavors of Latakia, Perique, or Turkish, though the vast majority of smokers still used clay pipes, which included the short "cutty" of Scotland, the "dudeen" of Ireland, the "alderman" of rural England, and the much longer "churchwarden."[22] What united these many differences in smoking patterns was an older pre-industrial and communal form of smoking which meant that clays were usually given away free of charge in public houses and where tobacco could be passed around the group.[23] The offering of a clay pipe was a mark of hospitality, as Gabriel Betteridge found in Wilkie Collins' *The Moonstone*: "good Mrs Yolland performed a social ceremony strictly reserved for strangers of distinction. She put a bottle of Dutch gin and a couple of clean pipes on the table, and opened the conversation by saying, 'What news from London, Sir?'"[24] It is arguable that such collective forms of consumption continued into the twentieth century, as the proffering of cigarettes in the public house became an important means to define both the conviviality and exclusivity of the male group.[25]

But by far the most dominant and lasting culture of smoking was that found in the pages of the periodical press which brought the "art" of the connoisseur to a rapidly expanding pipe and cigar-smoking middle class. There is, of course, a rich literary tradition celebrating smoking stretching, most notably, from Robert Burton's "divine, rare, superexcellent tobacco" to Lord Byron's "Sublime tobacco!", and on through to Kipling's "a woman is only a woman but a good cigar is a smoke," Charles Kingsley's "lone man's companion" and Oscar Wilde's flippant quip: "A cigarette is the perfect type of a perfect pleasure. It is exquisite and it leaves one unsatisfied. What more can one want?"[26] But praise for tobacco reached a peak in the latter half of the nineteenth century as numerous hack journalists of the kind parodied in Gissing's *New Grub Street* churned out countless and highly derivative pieces which, importantly, enabled male consumers to escape the passive and feminine associations of consumption and the market place. Instead, their everyday, private, and self-indulgent purchasing acts were transformed into an activity in accord with the perceived male role in life. Men were taught how to appreciate a cigar, how to choose a pipe, how to develop their personal tastes and settle on their own personal tobacco mixture, all to ensure that they became the masters, not the victims, of commerce; not mere consumers, but "ardent votaries," worshippers, disciples, aficionados, and true friends of "the divine lady nicotine."

Specifically, the brief articles – or "whiffs" and "pipefuls" – taught male smokers first to rationalize their habit and, second, to celebrate its more irrational or ephemeral elements. To make consumption rational, smokers had to be informed of the intellectual, the skilful and the purposeful aspects of tobacco.[27] Articles thus summarized the various areas of expertise surrounding smoking, beginning with a general history stretching back to Columbus's discovery in 1492, outlining the plant's anthropology and pharmacology, as well as creating a compendium of easily digestible statistics. But in order to rid the act of consumption of any of its feminine connotations, readers would be taken on a tour of the more masculine sphere of production. Starting in the factories and wholesalers of Britain, the smoker was transported to the Cuban tobacco fields of the Vuelta Abajo and Veulta Arriba, before moving to the cigar *Fabricas* of Havana where native "sylph-like" female cigar rollers could be seen touching and caressing every part of the genuine article made for the lips of the Western male consumer. Once informed of the facts of tobacco, smokers were then taught the skills, as hierarchies of taste and appreciation were created for the aspiring connoisseur to climb. Here, professionalism, mechanistic production, commercialism, and adulteration were denounced by the ideals of amateurism and authenticity. Usually, only cigar and pipe smokers were let into this all-male club, cigarette smokers being dismissed as "less manly," foreign and passive, as well as suffering under the label of "false" "consumer" instead of "real" "smoker." With such knowledge and skill, smokers were then ready to serve their nation. Smoking always had a purpose, whether to support the economy through taxation, to aid the artist in his creativity, to support the soldier in his hunger and fatigue, or to comfort the sailor on his lonely voyage. Smokers became public collectors, of literary anecdotes, of pipes, tobacco boxes, cigars, ornamental snuff boxes, and later cigarette cards. Better still were the smokers who then wrote about their habit or who, as with William Bragge of Sheffield, Alderman William Ormerod of Todmorden, and George Arents of the United States, donated their huge collections of tobacco books to municipal libraries.[28] The usual trivializing accusations against consumption which had existed since the luxury debates of the eighteenth century, if not before, could not then be brought against informed smokers, who showed that they consumed for the benefit of all.

From this position of purposeful and independent confidence, smokers were then free to explore their individuality through what might at first appear the more irrational elements of their habit. Tobacco was raised to a level far higher than that of a mere object. It was frequently anthropomorphized into a trusty companion, feminized into a wife or a lover, and even deified into a god itself. J.M. Barrie opened his account of *My Lady Nicotine* by comparing smoking and matrimony, while an anonymous poet declared to "his lady," that a cigar, "'Tis but a type of thee."[29] Others spoke of a legend of the gift of tobacco from the gods, while some strode off in pursuit of the "Goddess in the clouds," singing praise to the "Diva Nicotina."[30] Tobacco was held to offer escape from the problems of the world as readers were encouraged to imagine their ideal smoking environment which, for many, was the smoking room of the gentleman's club.[31] As Ouida put it in 1867: "that chamber of liberty, that sanctuary of the persecuted, that temple of refuge, thrice blessed in all its forms throughout the land, that consecrated Mecca of every true believer in the divinity of the meerschaum, and the paradise of the narghilé – the smoking-room."[32] For those less financially fortunate smokers, the cigar and the pipe still offered temporal escape, aided by the "whiffs" of tobacco presented in the periodicals which, just as the smoke meandered across the room, so the mind was encouraged to wander, to reminisce, and to dream of perfect bliss, or a smoker's Arcadia, as Barrie put it. Ultimately, smokers had to satisfy themselves with more earthly pleasures, but they explored their individuality through their "paraphernalia of smokiana," from the tools of their habit (clay pipes, briar pipes, meerschaums, churchwardens, pipe cleaners, matches, cigar holders, cigar cases, ash trays, pipe-lights, spills, spittoons, tobacco pouches, storage jars, snuff boxes, pipe racks, and so on) to the more general objects that completed the smoking experience (favorite smoking armchairs, tables, slippers, jackets, hats, and smoking companions).

To inform oneself of the history and manufacture of cigars, tobaccos, and pipes, to build up a distinctive collection of smoking accoutrements, to stress a personal relationship with one's tobacconist and to reminisce about one's own smoking experiences – all this served to emphasize those classic tenets of Victorian political and economic liberalism: independence and individuality. Smokers were independent of the marketplace, they knew their own tastes, they were not directed by whim, fashion, or advertising, and through the knowledge acquired by these amateur gentlemen they avoided being "enslaved" to their habit. Through their experience of smoking they defined themselves against the supposed passivity of foreigners, women, and the masses. Smoking was central to identity, it signified character and personality. It was a phenomenon not lost on the Victorian novelist as Thackeray, Trollope, Dickens, Galsworthy, Collins, and most of all Conan Doyle used habits of smoking as shorthand signifiers of the individual characters of their heroes. The culture of smoking both reflected but in turn reinforced those political and social ideologies of self-help, Free Trade, independent parliamentary democracy and state–individual relations in which the British male was to be largely left to his own devices, as clearly he himself knew his own strengths, weakness, and individuality more so than any scientist, moralist, or apparently meddling government official.

This culture of individuality and independence was picked up and marketed back to smokers in the advertisements of Cope's, a famous Liverpool-based firm of tobacco manufacturers. Its advertisements segmented the market according to the supposed tastes of various sections of the community, yet they also brought all smokers together in the fraternal club united humorously against the dwindling band of "humbug philanthropists" of the anti-tobacco movement in its trade-cum-literary journal, *Cope's Tobacco Plant*, devoted to "Tobacco; all about Tobacco, and nothing but Tobacco."[33] Cope's contributed to the persistence of the Victorian smoking ideal well into the twentieth century when the rise of the mass produced, homogenous cigarette had the potential to destroy the emphasis on the individuality of taste. In the interwar period and beyond the literary tradition of Barrie, Kenneth Grahame, and the periodical press was continued in the books of Count Corti and Alfred Dunhill and in a host of literary articles, most notably by J.B. Priestley and Compton Mackenzie.[34] The demand for a diverse range of pipe tobaccos continued, being ever stimulated by the campaigns of the retail tobacconists who encouraged smokers to use a pipe, "the everyday sign of manhood."[35] The briar pipe assumed more egalitarian connotations, so that the "middle brow" Priestley was able to find his equivalent of Barrie's Arcadia mixture (Boynton's Benediction, as he called it, after his middle name), not through an exclusive tobacco dealer just off Regent Street, but in a shop "rather small and in no way to be distinguished from the ordinary" just off the Great North Road in Doncaster.[36] Stanley Baldwin and Harold Wilson were both well aware of the democracy of the briar and were eager to be seen with it clutched firmly between their teeth.

Significantly, however, the older culture of the differentiated pipe and cigar smoker was being used to establish the identities of the consumers of the standard-ized cigarette. Several investigations in the 1930s and 1910s by the social anthropologists of Mass-Observation demonstrated the increasing importance of cigarette smoking to notions of masculinity and femininity.[37] While the cigarette did not allow for the creation of such rigid hierarchies of taste as had been proposed in the Victorian periodicals, it did enable a mass standardized market to follow a culture of cigarette-smoking individualism promoted in popular literature and on the screen. In the adventures of Bulldog Drummond, the hero's pipe is replaced with a cigarette, smoked indiscriminately and with no obvious sense of aesthetic appreciation. Yet Drummond always smokes either defiantly or with indifference to his social surroundings, thereby heightening the independence of the go-it-alone individualist.[38] Similarly, in the James Bond adventures of Ian Fleming, the ultra-professional British secret agent lacks the idiosyncrasies of a Sherlock Holmes, but his chain smoking is often used by Fleming to demonstrate his aggressive individualism and refusal to conform to the behavioral demands of his superiors, his usually non-smoking adversaries and even his doctors, concerned as they are with the growing medical evidence against cigarettes.[39] When Bond was transferred to the screen, the nonchalant and manly smoking of Sean Connery merely followed an ethic of individualism that had run through the characters of Edward G. Robinson, James Cagney, Paul Henreid, Clark Gable, Spencer Tracey, Robert Donat, James Stewart, Gary Cooper and, most lastingly of all, Humphrey Bogart.

It is against such a cultural background that the evidence connecting cigarette smoking with lung cancer was first set in the 1950s. When the tentative conclusions of Doll and Hill were first reported in 1950, when the Medical Research Council (MRC) first announced a causal connection between smoking and cancer in 1957, and when the massively publicized Royal College of Physicians' report in 1962 marked the first in a series of authoritative summaries of an increasingly overwhelming professional medical consensus on the dangers of smoking, the knowledge they imparted was received in a popular culture geared towards letting smokers decide for themselves as to what was best for them.[40] Countless social investigations in the 1950s and 1960s reported on smokers' knowledge of the medical evidence but also their refusal to believe or accept that it had any bearing on their own lives, a feat of "logical acrobatics" as one newspaper put it.[41] Smokers of all social classes proposed alternative scientific theories to account for the increasing incidence of lung cancer, from petrol fumes to heredity factors. They argued of the existence of elderly relatives who had smoked all their lives, they looked instead for industry and science to produce a "safe" cigarette and, most stubbornly of all, they asserted, mantra-like, that "it never did me any harm."[42]

The persistence of smoking rates at a level that seemingly defies the scientific evidence can be accounted for by a number of factors. Physical addiction is certainly relevant, though it does not account for each new generation's adoption of the habit.[43] The refusals and rebuttals issued by the tobacco industry are also important, as they provided smokers with sustenance for fueling their own medical theories.[44] And the huge increases in promotional expenditure – in direct television and poster advertising as well as the more subtle forms of commercial sponsorship and product placement – which the tobacco companies embarked upon from the late 1950s, have ensured that cigarette brands have remained a common "sign" of commodity culture.[45] But a culture which locates smoking as central to individual identity has persisted – on film, radio, and television and in print. Moreover, throughout the smoking and health controversy, commentators harked back to that older liberal stress on individuality and independence: the *Daily Express* urged smokers to defy the "interfering" medics; a columnist in *The Times* announced that the "British don't scare easily"; in the *Daily Mirror*, Andy Capp puffed away on his habitual drooping cigarette; and the *Guardian*, while accepting the links between smoking and cancer, still found space to write of the "blissful tranquillity" of the cigar and the art of the briar pipe which was said to have become a "tribal badge" for the utilitarian Englishman.[46] Even the *Lancet* claimed that smokers were better people: they were "restless, energetic, impulsive, independent, interesting men, ardent in the pursuit of enterprises which appealed to them, and seeking service during the war with combat units." In contrast, non-smokers were "bland, steady, dependable, hard-working, rather uncommunicative family men who tended during the war to gravitate to specialised non-combat units."[47]

These beliefs influenced perceptions of the relationship between the individual and the state. When the government Health Minister, Iain McLeod, acknowledged a statistical association between smoking and lung cancer in 1954, most commentators argued that even though the link was "incontrovertible," there was no need whatsoever for government intervention in the matter, as smokers should be left free to make up their own minds on the issue.[48] The *Daily Express* was most vociferous in its opposition to meddling "paternalists" and scientists and their chief smoking correspondent, Chapman Pincher, provides in extreme form many of the attitudes that prevailed among the British press and public throughout the 1950s and 1960s. He vehemently opposed a national education campaign while doubts still remained about the "association" between smoking and health.[49] He continually attacked the medical establishment, mocking the attempts to induce cancer in mice and inventing ridiculous lies that doctors were turning their attention to smoked kippers as a possible cause of lung cancer.[50] His response to the Royal College of Physicians' report in 1962 proved equally skeptical as he urged "civilised" moderate smokers to continue their enjoyable habit.[51] He was ready to support alternative theories of the causes of lung cancer and was later quick to point out how one of the ten members of the US Surgeon-General's panel in 1964 intended to continue smoking. In 1965, he condemned the great "blow to freedom" and "outrageous interference" that was the TV advertising ban, instigated by the "usual muddle-headed" "socialists" in the Labour Party with all their "huffing and puffing."[52] Even in 1971, when all other British newspapers and radio programs had come largely to accept the findings of the Royal College in its second report, Chapman Pincher insisted on insinuating that the whole thing was a conspiracy to legitimize increased taxes.[53]

Pincher and others maintained a faith in the freedom of the rational individual operating independently within the marketplace, a socioeconomic ideology tied closely to the by now traditional culture of smoking. It was an attitude that came to influence many of the early anti-smoking health campaigns, beyond the more practical fiscal considerations which have also been shown to have curtailed government activity.[54] Until 1957, the Conservative government believed that the statement made in the House of Commons in 1954 was sufficient to enable smokers to assess the evidence for themselves. When it became obvious that further action was necessary following the MRC report in 1957, the government stuck to the policy of letting people "make up their own minds on the subject."[55] The posters initially produced by the government to be made available to local authorities to distribute at their own discretion reflected this policy of a broader liberal attitude to public health. The early posters featured no persuasive rhetoric and were entirely devoid of any visual imagery.[56] Propaganda directed at children did verbally and visually elaborate on the issues, though health workers early recognised their class specificity.[57]

Throughout the 1960s, government campaigns were limited both by finance and by ideology. Extensive campaigns might be focused on one particular town, when the sheer weight of publicity materials (in the form of advertisements in the local press and radio, loudspeakers, sandwich-boards, banners, lectures, meetings, film shows, and publicity caravans located in town centers) helped get the message across.[58] But the most prominent campaign of the 1960s consisted of two mobile anti-smoking vans, staffed by two male university graduates, which toured Britain giving talks and distributing rather factual material.[59] All of these efforts were minimal compared with what health campaigners now argue to be necessary to change public attitudes in the long term. Yet the limited efforts were in line with the liberal notions of the individual, which discouraged governments from getting too closely involved in personal consumption decisions. When alternative forms of health promotion were made available, in the anti-smoking clinics pioneered by the National Society of Non-Smokers and local medical officers of health, and which were shown to have a higher success rate in terms of the proportion of smokers quitting, the government decided against them because of cost, but also because they smacked too much of the nanny state.[60]

It seems logical that if government or state activity is said to be a product of a particular culture or experience of leisure, then that activity should impact only on certain sections of the population. Arguably, this has been the case in the history of smoking and health. Appeals to smokers in the early years of anti-smoking propaganda reflected the social and economic background of policy workers themselves and which therefore resonated most clearly with those bourgeois-liberal smokers who had always stressed the importance of independent and individual assessments of the smoking habit. That this has been the case is evidenced in the figures for smoking rates among different social classes. Whereas in 1945 smoking rates had been similar across different income groups, by 1994 it was found that among unskilled and manual workers, 42 percent of men and 35 percent of women smoked, but that these figures were as low as 15 percent of men and 13 percent of women of the professional classes.[61] Just as bourgeois smokers had the time and cultural capital to read about and cultivate their smoking habit in the nineteenth century, so too did their late-twentieth-century counterparts have the time and intellectual resources to weigh up the medical evidence against smoking. In recent decades, health campaigners have taken a more proactive line against the tobacco industry. In 1984 the British Medical Association labeled the smoker as victim rather than rational individual, and policy workers have stressed the importance of the differences in experience of the smoker, depending on region, age, gender, class, and ethnicity.[62] That it took until the 1980s to radically shift anti-smoking agendas attests to the strength and pervasive influence of a particular culture of smoking formulated in the latter half of the nineteenth century.

In concluding, I do not wish to deny the importance of taxation and revenue, industrial lobbying and advertising, physical addiction and dependency in the history of smoking and health. But the purpose of this chapter has been to demonstrate how a particular culture of leisure was translated into a set of political beliefs about the role of the state in individual consumption decisions. In an increasingly affluent society, this should, of course, be of no great surprise. Jean Baudrillard has argued that just as workers developed a politicized labor consciousness from their experience of the relations of production, so too will consumers develop a political consciousness out of their experience of the affluent society, in which leisure and consumption play an increasingly prominent role in our lives.[63] This has undoubtedly been the case: the consumer movements of the developed world have been perhaps one of the most significant social and political developments since the 1950s. As early as 1960, Michael Young warned that in Britain the Labour Party could well find itself under threat from a Consumer Party if it continued to reflect only the interests of workers and trade unionists.[64] Our experience of leisure has continued to shape our political development. In general, this has led to calls for greater consumer protection, but, in specific cases such as tobacco, the cultural identities formed through leisure have acted as important bulwarks against state intervention. Indeed, as consumption has formed an ever greater part of our leisure activities, our politics has consisted of a dual demand for both greater state involvement in issues of safety and protection and greater freedom for individual consumers to shape their leisure patterns in the manner of their own choosing. In an age of heightened concern for the health of oneself and those in one's surrounding area, the cigarette smoker appears as villain; but in an age also of expanding state authority in all spheres of life, the smoker remains, to many, a hero of the liberal ideal of individualism.

Notes

1. E.P. Thompson, "Time, Work Discipline and Industrial Capitalism," *Past and Present* 38 (1967), pp. 59–91; D. Reid, "The Decline of St. Monday," *Past and Present* 71 (1976), pp. 76–101; R.D. Storch (ed.), *Popular Culture and Custom in Nineteenth Century England* (London: Croom Helm, 1982).

2. G. Cross, *Time and Money: The Making of Consumer Culture* (London: Routledge, 1993).

3. P. Bailey, *Leisure and Class in Victorian England: Rational Recreation and the Contest for Control, 1830–1885* (London: Routledge and Kegan Paul, 1978); G. Stedman Jones, "Class Expression Versus Social Control? A Critique of Recent Trends in the Social History of Leisure," *History Workshop Journal* 4 (1977), pp. 460–508; H. Cunningham, *Leisure in the Industrial Revolution c.1780 – c.1880* (London: Croom Helm, 1980); J.M. Golby and A.W. Purdue, *The Civilisation of the Crowd: Popular Culture in England 1750–1900* (London: Batsford, 1984); J. Walvin, *Leisure and Society 1830–1950* (London: Longman, 1978).

4. P.N. Lee, *Statistics of Smoking in the United Kingdom*, 7th edn (London: Tobacco Research Council, 1976), pp. 21–3.

5. B. Harrison, *Drink and the Victorians: The Temperance Question in England, 1815–1872*, 2nd edn (Keele: Keele University Press, 1994). The exception is with regard to children: M. Hilton, "'Tabs,' 'Tags' and the 'Boy Labour Problem' in Late Victorian and Edwardian England," *Journal of Social History* 28 (1995), pp. 587–607. In the United States, opposition was stronger, but still of much less impact when compared to the campaigns against drink: C. Tate, *Cigarette Wars: The Triumph of the "Little White Slaver"* (Oxford: Oxford University Press, 1999).

6. J. Goodman, *Tobacco in History: The Cultures of Dependence* (London: Routledge, 1993); V.G. Kiernan, *Tobacco: A History* (London: Hutchinson, 1991); D. Harley, "The Beginnings of the Tobacco Controversy: Puritanism, James I, and the Royal Physicians," *Bulletin of the History of Medicine* 67, 1 (1967), pp. 28–50; R.B. Walker, "Medical Aspects of Tobacco Smoking and the Anti-tobacco Movement in Britain in the Nineteenth Century,"

Medical History 24 (1980), pp. 391–402; M. Hilton and S. Nightingale, "'A Microbe of the Devil's Own Make': Religion and Science in the British Anti-tobacco Movement, 1853–1908," in S. Lock, L.A. Reynolds, and E.M. Tansey (eds), *Ashes to Ashes: The History of Smoking and Health* (London: Rodopi, 1998), pp. 41–77.

7. M. Spring Rice, *Working-class Wives: Their Health and Conditions* (1939; London: Virago, 1981); E. Green, S. Hebron, and D. Woodward, *Women's Leisure, What Leisure?* (London: Macmillan, 1990); E. Wimbush and M. Talbot (eds), *Relative Freedoms: Women and Leisure* (Milton Keynes: Open University Press, 1988); R. Deem, *All Work and No Play? A Study of Women and Leisure* (Milton Keynes: Open University Press, 1986).

8. V. de Grazia and E. Furlough (eds), *The Sex of Things: Gender and Consumption in Historical Perspective* (London: University of California Press, 1996); S. Strasser, C. McGovern, and M. Judt (eds), *Getting and Spending: European and American Consumer Societies in the Twentieth Century* (Cambridge: Cambridge University Press, 1998); M. Hilton and M. Daunton (eds), *The Politics of Consumption: Material Culture and Citizenship in Europe and America* (Oxford: Berg, 2001).

9. For a fuller account of this argument see M. Hilton, *Smoking in British Popular Culture, 1800–2000* (Manchester: Manchester University Press, 2000).

10. M. Brickley, A. Miles, and H. Stainer, *The Cross Bones Burial Ground: Redcross Way, Southwark, London* (London: Museum of London, 1999), p. 66.

11. P. Mérimée, *Carmen* (London: Paul Elek, 1960); R. Klein, "The Devil in Carmen," *Differences: A Journal of Feminist Cultural Studies* 5, 1 (1993), pp. 51–72; Ouida, *Under Two Flags* (1867; Oxford: Oxford University Press, 1995); D. Mitchell, "The So Called 'New Woman' as Prometheus: Women Artists Depict Women Smoking," *Women's Art Journal* 12, 1 (1991), pp. 3–9; D. Mitchell, "Images of Exotic Women in Turn-of-the-century Tobacco Art," *Feminist Studies* 18, 2 (1992), pp. 327–30; E.M. Forster, *Howards End* (1910; Harmondsworth: Penguin, 1941); M. Koetzle and U. Scheid, *Feu d'Amour (Seductive Smoke)* (Cologne: Taschen, 1994); John Johnson Collection (hereafter J. J.), Bodleian Library, Oxford, *M.L. Horn and B.R. Lillington Cigarette Card Collections.*

12. L. Linton, "The Girl of the Period," from *The Girl of the Period and Other Essays, vol. I* (1883), reprinted in J. Gardner (ed.), *The New Woman: Women's Voices, 1880–1914* (London: Collins and Brown, 1993), pp. 55–60; L. Linton, "The Wild Women (Part I): As Politicians," *Nineteenth Century* 30 (July 1891), p. 80; L. Linton, "The Wild Women (Part II: Conclusion): As Social Insurgents," *Nineteenth Century* 30 (October 1891), pp. 596–605; article in *Girl's Own Paper*, reprinted in *Tobacco Trade Review* (hereafter *TTR*) 31, 370 (October 1898), p. 454; L. Linton, "The Partisans of the Wild Women," *Nineteenth Century* 31 (March 1892), p. 460; Mrs Ester, " 'Between Ourselves,' a Friendly Chat with the Girls," *The Young Woman* 3 (1895), p. 106; R. Pember Reeves, *The Ascent of Woman* (London: John Lane, 1896), p. 58; J.D. Hunting, "Women and Tobacco," *National Review* 14 (1889), pp. 218–28; *Daily Mail* (April 16, 1899), p. 11; C. Campbell, "A Plea for Tobacco," *English Illustrated Magazine* 11 (1894), pp. 81–4.

13. *TTR* 26, 301 (January 1893), pp. 2–3; *TTR* 31, 364 (April 1898), pp. 163–4; *Tit-Bits* 568 (September 3, 1892), p. ii; *TTR* 30, 353 (May 1897), p. 225; *TTR* 32, 374 (February 1899), p. 45; *TTR* 31, 363 (March 1898), p. 139; *Tobacco Weekly Journal* 1, 12 (November 1898), p. 177; *The Smoker* 1, 14 (April 1892), p. 209.

14. Gardner, *New Woman*; G. Cunningham, *The New Woman and the Victorian Novel* (London: Macmillan, 1978); D. Richardson, *Pilgrimage* (London: Dent, 1967).

15. E. Roberts, *Social Life in Barrow, Lancaster and Preston, 1870–1930* (oral transcripts held at Lancaster University Library), Mr. B.1.B, p. 76; Mr. H.1.L., p. 18; Mr.

J.1.L., p. 162; G. Braybon, *Women Workers in the First World War* (London: Routledge, 1981).

16. R. Graves and A. Hodge, *The Long Weekend: A Social History of Great Britain, 1918–1939* (London: Hutchinson, 1985), pp. 32–59; B. Melman, *Women and the Popular Imagination in the Twenties: Flappers and Nymphs* (London: Macmillan, 1988); D. Beddoe, *Back to Home and Duty: Women between the Wars 1918–1939* (London: Pandora, 1989); M. Kohn, *Dope Girls: The Birth of the British Drug Underground* (London: Lawrence and Wishart, 1992).

17. Beddoe, *Back to Home and Duty*; M. Haskell, *From Reverence to Rape: The Treatment of Women in the Movies* (Chicago: University of Chicago Press, 1987).

18. Mass-Observation Topic Collections, *Smoking Habits 1937–1965*, Box no. 4, File D: *Smoking Survey 1943*.

19. Mass-Observation, *First Year's Work, 1937–1938* (London: Lindsay Drummond, 1938), pp. 8–23; Tom Harrisson Mass-Observation Archive (hereafter M-O), File Report 520, *Women and Morale*, 1940; M-O, File Report 2192, *Man and his Cigarette*, p. 174.

20. A. Marsh and S. McKay, *Poor Smokers* (London: Policy Studies Institute, 1994); H. Graham, *When Life's a Drag: Women, Smoking and Disadvantage* (London: HMSO, 1993); I. Waldron, "Patterns and Causes of Gender Differences in Smoking," *Social Science and Medicine* 32 (1991), pp. 989–1005; L. Greaves, *Smoke Screen: Women's Smoking and Social Control* (London: Scarlet, 1996); B. Jacobson, *The Ladykillers: Why Smoking is a Feminist Issue* (London: Pluto, 1981).

21. "What to Smoke?" *TTR* 4, 41 (May 1871), p. 59; "On the Tobacco Trade," *TTR* 10, 115 (July 1877), pp. 79–80; B.W.E. Alford, *W. D. and H. O. Wills and the Development of the UK Tobacco Industry* (London: Methuen, 1973), pp. 97, 109; "Changes in the Loose Tobacco Trade," *TTR* 32, 373 (January 1899), p. 4; "Increase of the Irish Roll Trade," *TTR* 2, 13 (January 1869), pp. 8–9; "Decline of the Snuff Trade," *TTR* 2, 16 (April 1869), p. 56; "The Tobacco Trade of Scotland," *TTR* 19, 218 (February 1886), p. 42; "The Tobacco Trade of Scotland," *TTR* 20, 231 (March 1887), p. 78; "Irish Roll," *TTR* 23, 270 (June 1890), p. 158; "Trade Topics," *TTR* 24, 277 (January 1890), p. 24; "Trade Topics," *TTR* 24, 279 (March 1890), p. 68; "Chewing Tobacco: Points for the Retailer," *TTR* 27, 323 (November 1894), pp. 337–8.

22. [Anon], "All in the Clouds," *All the Year Round* 15, 369 (May 1866), p. 448; [Anon], "Old English Tobacco Pipes," *Chambers' Journal* 73 (August 1896), pp. 495–6; "Clay Pipes," *TTR* 6, 70 (October 1873), p. 123; R. Quick, "The Antiquity of the Tobacco Pipe," *Antiquary* 42 (1906), pp. 20–3. An extensive literature can be found in E. Umberger, *Tobacco and its Use* (New York: Rochester, 1996), pp. 146–69.

23. "On Smoking," *TTR* 2, 22 (October 1896), p. 158; "Novelties," *TTR* 8, 85 (January 1875), p. 6; [Anon], "Concerning Pipes," *All the Year Round* 10, 245 (September 1893), p. 247.

24. W. Collins, *The Moonstone* (1868; Ware: Wordsworth, 1993), p. 282.

25. M-O, *Man and his Cigarette*, pp. 121–7.

26. Robert Burton, "Democritus to the Reader," second partition, section 4, member 2, subsection 1, in *The Anatomy of Melancholy* (New York: Tudor, 1948), p. 577; Lord Byron, "The Island" (1823), Canto II, Verse xix: *The Poetical Works of Lord Byron* (London: John Murray, 1857), p. 268; R. Kipling, "The Betrothed," in *Rudyard Kipling's Verse: Definitive Edition* (London: Hodder and Stoughton, 1940), p. 49; O. Wilde, *The Picture of Dorian Gray*, in *The Works of Oscar Wilde* (London: Collins, n.d.), p. 96. The Kingsley quotations appeared on every packet of Westward Ho tobacco.

27. The remainder of this paragraph is based on the following articles: Anon., "Snuff-taking in England," *All the Year Round* 17, 409 (September 1876), pp. 62–7; Anon., "A Whiff from the Pipe," *All the Year Round* 64 (February 1889), pp. 160–4; Anon., "Tobacco," *The Penny Magazine* 1 (July 1832), pp. 148–9; Anon., "Illustrations of Tobacco-smoking," *The Penny Magazine* 4 (September 1835), pp. 349–51; Anon., "The Most Popular Plant in the World," *Chambers' Journal* 22, 50 (December 1854), pp. 393–5; Anon., "A Bird's-eye View of Tobacco," *Chambers' Journal* 7, 176 (May 1857), pp. 317–20; Anon., "Snuff-taking," *Chambers' Journal* 4, 172 (April 1867), pp. 238–40; Anon., "Nicotiana," *Chambers' Journal* 72 (March 1895), pp. 143–4; Anon., "On the Antiquity of Tobacco-smoking," *Macmillan's Magazine* 74 (1896), pp. 289–99; J. Bowie, "My Lady Nicotine," *Good Words* 45 (1904), pp. 51–4; Anon., "More about Tobacco" (Parts I and II), *Once a Week* 4, 103 (December 18, 1869), pp. 424–7; 4, 104 (December 25, 1869), pp. 455–8; Anon., "All Smoke," *London Society* 10 (1866), pp. 306–15; Anon., "The Divine Weed: In Two Parts," *All the Year Round* 69 (September 1891), pp. 271–8, 296–301; P. Kent, "A Whiff of Tobacco," *The Gentleman's Magazine* 45 (1890), pp. 575–82; Anon., "All Smoke," *Every Saturday* 2 (1866), pp. 495–500; Anon., "The Weed," *Chambers' Journal* 9, 449 (August 1872), pp. 484–8; Anon., "To Smoke or Not to Smoke?" *All the Year Round* 13 (1865), pp. 413–18; Anon., "A Cigar Scientifically Dissected," *Practical Magazine* 6 (1876), p. 334; M. Jules Rochard, "Tobacco and the Tobacco Habit," *Popular Science Monthly* 41 (1892), pp. 670–82; Anon., "Concerning Pipes," *All the Year Round* 10, 245 (September 1893), pp. 245–8; A. Vambery, "A Paper of Tobacco," *Every Saturday* 3 (1867), pp. 621–5; J. Hawkins, "The Ceremonial Use of Tobacco," *Popular Science Monthly*, 43 (1894), pp. 173–83; Anon., "Cigarettes and Cigarette-making," *Chambers' Journal* 2, 56 (December 1898), p. 56; N. Amarga, "My Cigar: A Memoir and an Appreciation," *Temple Bar* 114 (1897), pp. 589–97; Anon., "Cigars," *All the Year Round* 13 (February 1865), pp. 35–8; Anon., "Havana Cigars," *All the Year Round* 17 (January 1867), p. 112; Anon., "A Screw of Tobacco," *Chambers' Journal* 10, 239 (July 1858), p. 72; K. Grahame, *Pagan Papers* (London: Elkin Matthews and John Lane, 1893), "Of Smoking," p. 62; Anon., "Cigarettes," *Saturday Review* 67 (May 1889), pp. 528–9; Anon., "Cigarettes," *Chambers' Journal* 5, 248 (September 1868), pp. 617–18; Anon., "Confessions of a Cigarette-Smoker," *Chambers' Journal* 80, 6 (1902), p. 6; W.C. Flood, "How to Make a Cigarette: A Lesson for Smokers," *Harmsworth Magazine* 6 (1901), pp. 351–3; Anon., "Havana Cigarettes," *London Society* 21, (1872), pp. 505–10; Anon., "Costs, Joys and Woes of Smoking," *London Society* 15 (1869), p. 553; J.M. Barrie, "Wicked Cigar," *Illustrated London News* 98 (February 21, 1891), p. 255; Anon., "Literature and Tobacco," *Academy* 61 (September 14, 1901), pp. 225–6; H. How, "The Biggest Tobacco-box in the World," *Strand Magazine* 8 (1894), pp. 465–76; Anon., "Notes on Sales: Books on Tobacco," *Times Literary Supplement* (September 14, 1922), p. 588; J.E. Brooks, *Tobacco: Its History Illustrated by the Books, Manuscripts and Engravings in the Library of George Arents*, 4 vols (New York: Rosenbach, 1943).

28. On male collecting and female consuming see L. Auslander, "The Gendering of Consumer Practices in Nineteenth-century France," in De Grazia and Furlough, *Sex of Things*, pp. 79–112.

29. J.M. Barrie, *My Lady Nicotine* (1890; London: Hodder and Stoughton, 1902); Anon., "Defence of my Cigar," *Fraser's Magazine* 17 (1837), p. 155.

30. Anon., "All in the Clouds," *All the Year Round* 15, 369 (May 1866), pp. 448–50; Anon., "A Whiff from the Pipe," *All the Year Round* 1, 7 (February 1889), pp. 160–5; "An Old Smoker," "Apropos of Tobacco," *Bentley's Miscellany* 15 (1844), pp. 264–6; "The Weed."

31. "All in the Clouds," p. 448; Anon., "In a Traveller's Smoking Room," *All the Year Round* 71, 8 (November 1892), pp. 517–22; Anon., "The Smoking-room at the Club," *Cornhill Magazine* 6 (1862), p. 512.

32. Ouida, *Under Two Flags*, p. 18.

33. *Cope's Tobacco Plant* 1, 1 (March 1870), p. 12, in *The Papers of John Fraser*, University of Liverpool Special Collections, 665; A.V. Seaton, "Cope's and the Promotion of Tobacco in Victorian England," *Journal of Advertising History* 9, 2 (1986), pp. 5–26; R.D. Altick, "*Cope's Tobacco Plant*: An Episode in Victorian Journalism," *Papers of the Bibliographic Society of America* 45 (1951), pp. 333–50.

34. See, for example, Anon., "The Perfect Cigar," *Chambers' Journal* (December 1935), pp. 915–16; H. Warner Allen, "After Dinner," *The Saturday Review* 155 (January 28, 1933) p. 91; Anon., "Cigarette Pictures," *New Statesman* 20 (April 7, 1923), pp. 769–71; R. Lynd, "Smoking in the House," *New Statesman and Nation* 30 (February 11, 1928), pp. 556–7; J.D. Rolleston, "On Snuff Taking," *British Journal of Inebriety* 34 (July 1936), pp. 1–16; Sir D. Hunter-Blair, "Evolution of Smoking," *Empire Review* 69 (February 1939), pp. 83–9; Anon., "Books on Smoking," *Notes and Queries* 185 (July 31, 1943), pp. 84–5; A. Cruse, "The Charm of Cigarette Cards," *Strand Magazine* (March 1947), pp. 70–8; Count Corti, *A History of Smoking* (1931; London: Random House, 1996); A.H. Dunhill, *The Pipe Book* (London: A. and C. Black, 1924); A.H. Dunhill, *The Gentle Art of Smoking* (London: Max Reinhardt, 1954); C. Mackenzie, *Sublime Tobacco* (London: Chatto and Windus, 1957).

35. *TTR* 64, 758 (February 1931), p. 19; *TTR* 54, 762 (June 1931), p. 19.

36. J.B. Priestley, "A New Tobacco," *The Saturday Review* 144 (August 13, 1927), pp. 216–17; J.B. Priestley, *Delight* (London: Heinemann, 1949), pp. 26–7. On the democratic image of Priestley see D.L. LeMahieu, *A Culture for Democracy: Mass Communication and the Cultivated Mind in Britain between the Wars* (Oxford: Clarendon, 1988).

37. M-O, *First Year's Work*; M-O, *Man and his Cigarette*.

38. The first and four most important adventures are contained in H.C. McNeile (Sapper), *Bulldog Drummond: His Four Rounds with Carl Peterson* (London: Hodder and Stoughton, 1930).

39. For the best and most recent discussion of Bond's position within film culture and the literary tradition of the spy-detective thriller see J. Chapman, *Licence to Thrill: A Cultural History of the James Bond Films* (London: I.B. Tauris, 1999).

40. R. Doll and A.B. Hill, "Smoking and Carcinoma of the Lung: Preliminary Report," *British Medical Journal* (*BMJ*) ii (1950), p. 746; R. Doll and A.B. Hill, "A Study of the Aetiology of Carcinoma of the Lung," *BMJ* ii (1952), pp. 1271–86; Medical Research Council, *Tobacco Smoking and Cancer of the Lung* (London: HMSO, 1957); Royal College of Physicians, *Smoking and Health* (London: Pitman Medical, 1962).

41. *Guardian* (January 13, 1964), p. 8, (January 16, 1964,) p. 18; A. Cartwright, F.M. Martin, and J.G. Thomson, *Consequences of a Health Campaign* (1959), in Kew Public Record Office (hereafter PRO), MH 55 2225, *1958–1959: Smoking and Lung Cancer: Health Education Policy: Correspondence*; A. Cartwright, F.M. Martin, and J.G. Thomson, "Health Hazards of Smoking: Current Popular Beliefs," *British Journal of Preventive and Social Medicine* 14 (1960), pp. 160–6; A.C. McKennell, *Smoking and Health: A Preliminary Report on a Continuing Study of Public Attitudes to Smoking* (January 1964), in PRO, MH 151 27, *1964–1966: Smoking and Health: Social Surveys*.

42. *The Times* (July 20, 1957), pp. 8f; *Daily Mirror* (June 28, 1957), p. 10; *Daily Mirror* (March 3, 1962), p. 8; *Daily Mirror* (February 2, 1965), p. 6; *Guardian* (May 14, 1956), p. 6, *Guardian* (May 17, 1956), p. 8; BBC Written Archives, Caversham (hereafter BBC),

Radio Scripts, *Any Answers* April 5, 1956, March 15, 1962; PRO, MH 55 1012, *1953–1957: Cancer of the Lung: Investigation: Correspondence*; MH 55 2221, *1954–1957: Cancer of the Lung and Tobacco Smoking: Minister's Statement: Correspondence Arising*; G.W. Lynch, "Smoking Habits of Medical and Non-medical University Staff: Changes since RCP Report," *BMJ* i (1963), pp. 852–5; J.M. Bynner, *Medical Students' Attitudes towards Smoking: A Report on a Survey Carried Out for the Ministry of Health* (London: HMSO, 1967); C. Fletcher and R. Doll, "A Survey of Doctors' Attitudes to Smoking," *British Journal of Preventive and Social Medicine* 23 (1969), pp. 145–53; PRO, MH 151 26, *1962– 1964: Smoking and Health: Social Surveys*: A.C. McKennell, *Results of a Copy Test on Five Posters* (1963); A.C. McKennell, *Report of the Audience Reaction Test of the Film "Smoking and You"* (1964); Smith Warden Ltd, *Observations on the Smoking and Health Campaign Being Conducted by H. M. Government* (1962).

43. D.G. Gilbert, *Smoking: Individual Differences, Psychopathology, and Emotion* (Washington, DC: Taylor and Francis, 1995).

44. R.A. Fisher, *Smoking, the Cancer Controversy: Some Attempts to Assess the Evidence* (London: Oliver and Boyd, 1959); H.J. Eysenck, *Smoking, Health and Personality* (London: Weidenfeld and Nicolson, 1965), p. 15; PRO, MH 55 1011, *1946–1954*: *Cancer of the Lung: Investigation*; *Daily Mirror* (July 5, 1957), p. 5; G.F. Todd, *Comments on the Report on Smoking and Health by a Committee of the Royal College of Physicians*, in MH 55 2232, *1954–1962: Smoking and Lung Cancer: Reports and Memoranda*; *Lancet* i (1956), p. 748.

45. G. Parr, "Smoking," *Sight and Sound* (December 1997), pp. 30–3; Advertising Inquiry Council, *Advertising Tobacco: A Study of Expenditures and of Trends in Sales Promotion* (1962), in PRO, MH 55 2233: *March 8–28, 1962: Smoking and Lung Cancer: Action Following Report of Royal College of Physicians on Smoking and Health: Policy and Publicity. Correspondence*; E.S. Atkinson, "Cigarette Advertising: A History," *British Journal of Photography* 128 (1981), pp. 1190–1.

46. *Daily Express* (July 12, 1957), p. 6; *The Times* (April 7, 1958), pp. 7f; *Daily Mirror* (June 22, 1968), p. 20; *Guardian* (June 23, 1956), p. 5, (December 20, 1956), p. 6, (November 22, 1965), p. 7, (December 23, 1965), p. 6.

47. *Lancet* i (1958), pp. 680–1. Perhaps unsurprisingly, as medical journals became more committed to the anti-tobacco cause, smokers were instead found to be the more "neurotic" type of individual: N. Cherry and K. Kiernan, "Personality Scores and Smoking Behaviour: A Longitudinal Study," *British Journal of Preventive and Social Medicine* 30 (1976), pp. 123–31.

48. *Daily Express* (February 13, 1954), p. 1.

49. *Daily Express* (May 8, 1956), p. 1.

50. *Daily Express* (July 12, 1957), p. 6.

51. *Daily Express* (March 17, 1962), p. 6, (March 29, 1962), p. 14.

52. *Daily Express* (February 9, 1965), pp. 1, 8, (February 10, 1965), pp. 5, 8.

53. *Daily Express* (January 6, 1971), pp. 1, 8, 15.

54. On the history of the relationship between the tobacco industry and successive governments see P. Taylor, *Smoke Ring: The Politics of Tobacco* (London: Bodley Head, 1984); M. Read, *The Politics of Tobacco: Policy Networks and the Cigarette Industry* (Aldershot: Avebury, 1996).

55. PRO, MH 55 2204: *1961–1962: Public Health: Propaganda – Smoking and Cancer of the Lung: Publicity Policy*.

56. PRO, MH 55 960: *1953–1960: Public Health Propaganda – Cancer: Smoking and Lung Cancer – General Correspondence*.

57. McKennell, *Results of a Copy Test* and McKennell, *Report on the Audience Reaction Test.*

58. PRO, MH 151 19: *1965–1966: Smoking and Health: Campaign Policy*; A. Cartwright, F.M. Martin, and J.G. Thomson, *Consequences of a Health Education Campaign* (Edinburgh: Department of Public Health and Social Medicine, University of Edinburgh, 1959); F.M. Martin and G.R. Stanley, *The Dunfermline Anti-Smoking Campaign* (Edinburgh: Department of Public Health and Social Medicine, University of Edinburgh, 1964); F.M. Martin and G.R. Stanley, *Report on the Clydebank Anti-Smoking Campaign* (Edinburgh: Department of Social Medicine, University of Edinburgh, 1965).

59. PRO, MH 82 205: *March 15, 1962 – Sept 11, 1962: Organisation of Two Mobile Units: Programme and Financial Estimates*; MH 82 206: *12/7/1962 – 6/12/1962: Correspondence Regarding the Inaugural Ceremony of the Mobile Units*; MH 82 207: *19/7/1962 – 10/2/1965: Smoking and Health – Mobile Units: Miscellaneous Papers, Memoranda, Progress Reports, etc.*; MH 82 208: *13/10/1962 – 23/6/1964: Smoking and Health Mobile Units Progress Reports*; MH 154 177: *1963–1965: Smoking and Health: Health Education Co-ordinating Committee. Preparations for Meetings and Subsequent Action.*

60. PRO, MH 55 2236: *1962: Smoking and Health: Anti-Smoking Clinics*; MH 151 18: *1962–1965: Smoking and Health: Campaign Policy*; MH 154 178: *1962–1965: Smoking and Health: Health Education Co-ordinating Committee: Minutes and Papers*; MH 154 187: *1964: Smoking and Health: Anti-Smoking Clinics*; MH 154 189, *1964–1966: Smoking and Health: Medical Research Council*; MH 154 186, *1962–1963: Smoking and Health: Anti-Smoking Clinics*; MH 154 187, *1964: Smoking and Health: Anti-Smoking Clinics*; A. Cruickshank, "Smokers' Advisory Clinic – Ministry of Health: A Preliminary Report on an Experimental Project," *Monthly Bulletin of the Ministry of Health and the Public Health Laboratory Service* 22 (1963), pp. 110–16; E.G.W. Hoffstaedt, "Anti-smoking Campaign: Some General Observations on the Smoking Problem and the Place of 'Smokers' clinics'," *Medical Officer* (January 31, 1964), pp. 59–60; G. Edwards, "Hypnosis and Lobeline in an Anti-smoking Clinic," *Medical Officer* (April 24, 1964), pp. 239–43.

61. P. Hooper, *Smoking Issues: A Quick Guide* (Cambridge: Daniels, 1995), p. 3.

62. British Medical Association, *Smoking out the Barons: The Campaign Against the Tobacco Industry* (Chichester: Wiley Medical, 1986).

63. J. Baudrillard, "Consumer Society," in M. Poster (ed.), *Jean Baudrillard: Selected Writings* (Oxford: Polity, 1988), pp. 29–56.

64. M. Young, *The Chipped White Cups of Dover: A Discussion of the Possibility of a New Progressive Party* (London: Unit 2, 1960).

16

Hollywood Glamour and Mass Consumption in Postwar Italy

Stephen Gundle

After 1945 the United States indicated to war-torn European societies how to progress from recovery to modernization, achieving in the process greater prosperity for their populations and increased political stability. It is appropriate therefore that, in the study of Italy's transition to consumerism in the postwar period, much importance has been attributed to the impact of the American example and American techniques. However, while the history of this relationship has been extensively examined in terms of diplomacy, politics, and economics, very little by contrast has been said about the way in which mentalities were altered, new desires diffused and material dreams generated and managed. Sectoral studies of advertising, Marshall Plan propaganda, the impact of Hollywood, fashion, the popular press, and the star system all refer to the formation and diffusion of images of desirability, but do not underline the systematic nature or purpose of the development of a repertoire of images of wealth, beauty, elegance, style, and sex appeal.

It will be suggested here that the transformation of the Italian imaginary may be explained by reference to the concept of *glamour*. If properly employed, this under-theorized term can account for the particular seductive appeal which capitalism was able to take on in the early stages of mass consumption, and which enable it largely to bypass arguments about exploitation, imperialism, inequality, and alienation. Glamour, it will be argued, was part and parcel of the impact of the American model; but Italy did not merely absorb an externally generated allure, it also gave rise to forms of enchantment of its own. These were crucial both in privatizing and materializing dreams and in providing Italy with an imagery that could assist the export of goods and the promotion of services including tourism.

Glamour and Modernity

Despite the vagueness of its common usage, the etymology of glamour is reasonably clear. According to *The New Fowler's Modern English Usage* (1996) the word was originally Scottish. It was an alteration of the word grammar that retained the sense of the old word gramarye ("occult learning, magic, necromancy"). *The Oxford English Dictionary* (1989) also highlights the word's Scottish origins and derivation from grammar, although this is indicated to mean magic, enchantment, and spells rather than necromancy and the occult. According to *Fowler's*, glamour passed into standard English usage around the 1830s with the meaning of "a delusive or alluring charm." For *Websters Third New International Dictionary* (1961), glamour is "an elusive, mysteriously exciting and often illusory attractiveness that stirs the imagination and appeals to a taste for the unconventional, the unexpected, the colorful, or the exotic." In its secondary meanings glamour is said to be "a strangely alluring atmosphere of romantic enchantment; bewitching, intangible, irresistibly magnetic charm; . . . personal charm and poise combined with unusual physical and sexual attractiveness."

Some observers have suggested that glamour is a timeless quality. Camille Paglia, for example, has asserted that Nefertiti was the first public figure to turn herself into "a manufactured being" possessed of "radiant glamour" and that glamour's origins are to be found in ancient Egypt.[1] Undoubtedly, modern glamour has a complex and long prehistory that it is beyond the scope of this chapter to consider even briefly.[2] Here the concern is with the meanings and associations the term acquired in the 1930s, when it first entered everyday currency. From that time, the world of illusion, mystery, seduction and enchantment has been found largely in media representations. Glamour is also associated with commercial strategies of persuasion. Through consumer products, people are promised instant transformation and entry into a realm of desire. This effect is achieved by adding colorful, desirable, and satisfying ideas and images to mundane products thus enabling them to speak not merely to needs but to longings and dreams.

Glamour as it is understood today, as a structure of enchantment deployed by cultural industries, was first developed by Hollywood. In the 1930s, the major studios, having consolidated their domination of the industry, developed a star system in which dozens of young men and women were groomed and molded into glittering ideal-types whose fortune, beauty, spending power, and exciting lives dazzled the film-going public. Writing in 1939 about American film stars, Margaret Thorp defined glamour as "sex appeal plus luxury plus elegance plus romance."

> The place to study glamour today is the fan magazines [she noted]. Fan magazines are distilled as stimulants of the most exhilarating kind. Everything is superlative, surprising, exciting . . . Nothing ever stands still, nothing ever rests, least of all the sentences . . . Clothes of course are endlessly pictured and described usually with marble fountains, private swimming pools or limousines in the background . . . Every aspect of life, trivial and important, should be bathed in the purple glow of publicity.[3]

Although it was forged in the rarefied climate of southern California, glamour took shape at the intersection of political, social, and economic trends. In the Depression years, it was a means whereby privilege and inequality not only could continue to exist in an increasingly democratic and mass world, but also could actually serve to justify it and render it acceptable. It did this by simultaneously creating the impression of distinction and accessibility. This was achieved through spectacle, through the foregrounding of new not inherited wealth, through the display of the pleasures of consumption over production, and consequently of femininity (with its particular associations with beauty, showbusiness, and now consumption) in place of the more obviously power-related masculinity. Instead of envy and class hatred on the one hand or apathetic deference on the other, glamour fostered feelings of desire, aspiration, wonderment, emulation and vicarious identification. In short it fed individual dreams not collective resentments, ostensibly undermining class barriers while in fact reinforcing a hierarchy of status and money.

Glamour, it may be said, is the language of allure and desirability of capitalist society. Its forms change but it is always available to be consumed vicariously by the masses who see in glamour an image of life writ large according to the criteria of a market society. As a language it is a hybrid, in that it mixes luxury, class, exclusivity, and privilege with the sexuality and seduction of prostitution, entertainment, and the commercial world. Aristocratic forms and styles persist within modern glamour but – without the beauty, color and sexual enticements of the popular theater and high-class prostitution – the drama, dynamism, scandal, and feminine display that are central to glamour would be absent. Because it is dedicated to femininity and fashion, as well as sex and display, showbusiness supplies people, stories, modes, and avenues of mobility that are unique.[4] Historically, it also provided the air of scandal and sensuality that were so important in titillating middle-brow morality.

The highly polished, hyperbolic, and manufactured image that characterized the specificity of Hollywood glamour was not an original or, still less, the first modern form of glamour, but it was the most readily recognizable and potent. Film was the only medium that gave rise to extended discussions of the phenomenon and film studies is still the only field in which glamour has in any way been evaluated seriously. Specialists including Richard Dyer, Laura Mulvey, and Annette Kuhn have concentrated on the images produced in movies and stills and highlighted the importance of abstraction and standardization.[5] In an advanced industrial society, in which movies and stars were produced for consumption like automobiles and refrigerators, glamour was a code of allure that necessitated a person (usually a woman) being fetishized as a fictionalized and surveyed object. It also entailed "deception, the interplay between appearance and reality, display and concealment, and ambiguity and role-playing."[6]

In the 1930s, Neal Gabler has shown, Hollywood fictions entered the mainstream; what had been a vision of the United States shaped by newcomers and outsiders became the mythology of urban America.[7] As Americanism became inseparable from consumerism, glamour defined mentalities, behavior, aspirations and patterns of consumption, as well as ideals of beauty and so on.[8] Moreover, from being the lingua franca of a melting pot, it became in the 1940s a powerful tool of American war morale and self-perception as well as a weapon in the United States' armoury against its enemies. The independent producer Walter Wanger probably exaggerated in 1945 when he argued that the United States won the war because it had Tyrone Power and Lana Turner on its side whereas its enemies had only political figures, but the alignment of glamour and power was a seductive one that would serve the United States well in its efforts to persuade Europeans of its virtues and guide them towards a new model of modernization.[9]

Hollywood glamour was a potent force in Europe in the 1940s. People were dazzled by the beauty and sex appeal of the stars and delighted in the dreamworld of prosperity and luxury which they inhabited. But there were filters and factors which meant that Hollywood glamour was never accepted en bloc. Royalty and aristocracy, for example, occupied an important part of the space of glamour, cultivating sensations of loyalty and deference rather than dynamic emulation. Moreover many of the premises of the development of American glamour, like national retail networks, department stores, modern advertising, pronounced individualism etc., were absent. There were also domestic traditions of the representation of the desirable and the sexually alluring which reflected the class structure. Hollywood had the advantage of having incorporated some of these, but its industrial model of glamour was often too big, too commercial, too artificial to sustain simply and positively the conversion of whole societies to new ways of thinking and behaving. Moreover, part of the intention of the European Recovery Program (ERP) and in US postwar policy was to stimulate European societies to develop their own mythologies of capitalism that would cut across, and ultimately displace, political ideologies.

It is in the light of these considerations that the case of postwar Italy needs to be examined.

American Glamour and Postwar Italy

Hollywood glamour arrived in postwar Italy through two means: filmic representations and magazine and newsreel images of American stars in the peninsula. By no means all US films were glamorous; the first to be shown, selected by the Allied Forces' Psychological Warfare Branch, were largely propaganda films justifying the American war effort or, like Chaplin's *The Great Dictator*, satirizing Fascist regimes. It was the first big commercial films which provided the wealth, spect-acle, and sexuality that communicated something new and which matched and expanded the horizon of aspirations that was the consequence of hardship. It is probably misleading to refer to a single film in this context, but King Vidor's 1946 movie *Gilda* was undoubtedly important for the extremely potent image it offered of Rita Hayworth. Hayworth's star image had been forged by Harry Cohn's Columbia Pictures and it presented an unusual mixture of hyperbolic, manufact-ured beauty, perfect fashioning, healthy physicality, vampish behavior, and innocence of spirit. As an image to be consumed, Rita-Gilda offered Italians a powerful taste of the capacity for manufacture of the US film industry. She filled the demand in postwar Italy for a dream of abundance and freedom. With her perfect figure, luxuriant auburn tresses, and the costumes of Jean Louis, she entranced a generation. Posters of the film are being affixed around Rome by the protagonist of *Ladri di biciclette* and Pier Paolo Pasolini produced a memorable account of the film's impact which then appeared in reworked form in his novella *Amado mio*. Gilda's easy sexuality, he wrote, "was like a shout of joy, a sweet cata-clysm that brought down Caorle's cinema."[10] "Gilda speaks a universal language that crosses all frontiers and enters into direct communication with the spectator by means of that special pass that is called *sex appeal*," observed Gion Guida in *Cinemoda*.[11]

Rita Hayworth represented the highest point of glamour manufacture achieved up until that moment in Hollywood. Born Marguerita Cansino and of Mexican origin, she had undergone extensive remodeling to turn her into such a potent symbol of Americanism that her image was affixed by enthusiastic airmen to the first hydrogen bomb to be dropped on Japan. The reaction to the film in Italy and the influence it has had on the collective memory shows that Italians were ready to respond to it, even if the visual codes it employed were unfamiliar to most and it represented a precursor of social and economic developments rather than an integrated part of the development of a new industrialized imagination. Although Rita Hayworth's appeal was enormous and probably unique at the time, it should be seen in relation to the more general effects of the enormous quantity of Hollywood films which poured into Italy in the postwar years.

Hollywood films had been popular with the restricted audiences of the 1930s and before the war a small number of stars had visited Rome to see the newly opened Cinecittà studios. From the late 1940s their visits became more regular and systematic as runaway American film production in Italy became routine following the introduction of protective legislation in 1947 and 1949. Although the impact of the films was very significant and indeed crucial to the overall glamorous impression of the United States as the land of prosperity, sex appeal, and excite-ment, it was ultimately the arrival in Italy of the star lifestyle which had the greater impact on the imagination, customs, and perceptions of glamour. Clearly, the star lifestyle took many forms, but it was always writ large, opulent, excessive, fantastic, and exciting with respect to normal lived lives. Stars were, as Edgar Morin wrote in 1957, beautiful, euphorically happy, healthy, rich, untroubled, leisured, at least in their publicity. Their love lives, weddings, houses, clothes, tastes, favorite haunts and so on were of enormous interest.[12] Illustrated weekly magazines like *Oggi* and *Epoca*, which looked to *Life* as a model, conveyed these images to middle-class Italian families.

The Rome wedding of Tyrone Power and Linda Christian in early 1949 was a defining moment which attracted enormous press attention. Like everything associated with glamour, it was slightly unrespectable. Power's divorce from the French actress Annabella became definitive only on the day of the wedding; the latter was also ostentatious and therefore not in the best of taste. The journalist Ugo Zatterin recounted it in *Oggi* as though it were a publicity stunt. "Tyrone Power has acted in his second wedding," he wrote:

> At the start of the ceremony everything made the Church of Saint Francesca Romana resemble a Hollywood "studio." Mixed groups of people were making a dull, background noise, huge cables snaked between the golden chairs, flashes of neon lighting gave a white glow to the frescoes of the apse and, hidden among the white lilacs of the *prie-dieu*, two cold microphones were waiting to gather the fateful "I do" of Linda and Tyrone for the delight of radio audiences in Italy, France, Switzerland and America. The "shoot" had been prepared in every detail. Since the altar did not lend itself well to the "visibility of the stalls," a substitute was set up at the foot of the statue of Saint Francesca. Even the little organ of the church was deemed inadequate for the musical accompaniment and another, much larger one was temporarily installed.

The spectacle also attracted the attention of the local population:

> The curious and noisy Roman crowd provided the mass audience. People perched with uneasy balance on the ruins surrounding the church, on the arches of the Colosseum and on the fallen pillars of the temple of Venus and of Rome. An entire "Celere" unit, Carabinieri on white horses whirling truncheons, tried to prevent thousands of uninvited spectators from spilling on to the bride and groom and the few genuine guests. An acute, high-pitched, almost hysterical yell from the thousand women stuck behind a gate was the "Action!" that began the shoot. Throughout the whole ceremony the voice of the priest and the solemn tone of the organ were overwhelmed by the distant shouting of the crowd and the closer whirring of the movie cameras.[13]

The wedding showed that American celebrities could be "adopted" by Italy, could be used for internal purposes and could arouse enthusiasm, probably especially among the lower-middle classes, although the lower-class element was also import-ant. Accounts of the day in the newspapers identified schoolgirls, old women, and young workers among those present.[14] It gave the press something to talk about and helped fuel the development of a new type of celebrity photo-journalism. In addition, it had certain political ramifications, in that it was exploited by the elite for use against the Communist opposition. Power had featured on a Christian Democratic poster in the sharply fought 1948 election that proclaimed "Even Hollywood stars are against Communism" and a number of government ministers attended the wedding. Prime minister De Gasperi appeared on the cover of *Oggi* on January 16, 1949 in the company of Linda Christian.

Hollywood stars had enjoyed great social cachet in Europe and their arrival in significant numbers after World War II had the effect of opening up to some extent the closed and stuffy world of the aristocracy. Indeed their prominence in the press and dominance in such areas of traditional aristocratic prerogative as beauty and style led to a displacement of the former. This was especially marked in Italy, where the aristocracy was in any case much less strong than in Britain or even France.[15] The arrival of a new, more attractive, and more public "aristocracy" in Rome created new centers of prestige and exclusivity, new rituals which drew in younger aristocrats, creating a new more visible, open hierarchy of status. The old scenarios and palaces continued to serve a role, but the elite was more open and accessible, it served as a focus not of deference or resentment but of imitation, emulation, and dreams.

In the United States class images of European provenance were extremely useful in the 1950s. European refinement and sophistication could be marketed to a middle class that was seeking history and taste. Although the US government had overridden film industry objections to Italian restrictions on the export of movie profits in order to help the economic recovery of an ally, films set in Rome or Venice (or Paris or London) in fact proved highly marketable at home. They possessed enormous cachet, especially if they were big budget, featured lavish scenery, beautiful people, elegant objects, and big stars. Hollywood studios proved adept not merely at representing European heritage but at appropriating it and remodeling it in their own terms. *Roman Holiday*'s fairytale story of "Princess Anne" (Audrey Hepburn)'s temporary escape from the prison of protocol has been seen as a bold attempt to annexe the image of royalty. The Grace Kelly–Prince Ranier wedding in Monaco in 1956 was the climax of this. But, although nothing staged subsequently would eclipse this, there were other significant marriages too, including Rita Hayworth's to Ali Khan and that of Dawn Addams to Prince Vittorio Massimo in Rome. Such formal liaisons were proof that some parts of the aristocracy and even royalty were reinventing themselves through the language of glamour of Hollywood and that Hollywood could absorb older images of luxury and splendor.[16]

At a time of sharp political divisions, Italian illustrated magazines and newsreels provided star news over hard news, offering images of glamour as part of their recipe.[17] They learned to purvey a dream world that keyed in with other images, of the West as Italy's destiny, the United States as a model society, new consumer products, Christian Democratic government, and scientific and technical progress. The magazines showed old Italian elite centers being taken over or invested once more with allure by the frequentation of a cosmopolitan elite that would shortly become the jet set. Capri, Ischia, Portofino, and other locations were playgrounds of the rich and famous but the undoubted center of this was Rome's Via Veneto, with its cafés, hotels, restaurants, nightclubs. It was here that the celebrity photo-reporter was born.

The key elements of the new glamour were ostentation of wealth, especially of the new variety and sex scandals. In the moralistic official climate of the 1950s, in which the Church was seeking to win support for the reimposition of conventional values, standards were rigid. Sex appeal was something which in postwar Italy was unfamiliar, since sex was either obvious (prostitutes) or very heavily masked (Italian actresses). In the cinema of the 1930s, the entire weight of sexuality had been placed on the shoulders of a handful of homegrown *femme fatales* (Doris Duranti, Luisa Ferida, and Clara Calamai). The vast majority of actresses were sexless girls-next-door. Therefore its routine association with mainstream actors was perplexing. Articles appeared in the film press explaining what it was and it was joked about in musical revues (where it was Italianized as *sessapiglio*). The separation of sexual appeal from commercial sex or sexual favors appeared improbable to Italians. Yet, with Hollywood stars, sex, occasionally illicit, and legitimate wealth seemed to go together. Even the saintly Ingrid Bergman had acquired a sexualized image when she arrived in Italy to begin a scandalous adulterous affair with director Roberto Rossellini.[18]

American stars were perfect consumers. In Hollywood fashion, they were always beautiful, magnificently groomed, and coiffured; moreover they made themselves available for consumption by the public in films and images.[19] For many in postwar Italy, such ideas were unfamiliar and odd. Star sponsorship of products was rare and most entertainers led modest daily lives. Nevertheless, some indication of their economic role was perceptible to all: in the late 1940s, magazines regularly printed Max Factor advertisements featuring Rita Hayworth as Gilda. Through her, Italian women were invited to participate in the beauty secrets that the Max Factor company had revealed to all American women, stars or not. Subsequently, other dimensions were added. Luxury cars and homes, together with leisure, constituted the foremost way in which the new elite offered a material extension of the dreams of the masses in the era of the economic recovery and the miracle.

In comparison to the prewar era, all this was new. Only in the political and economic conditions of the reconstruction and after was there a real possibility of developing the mass consumer market in Italy that was a premise of the deployment of glamour. Yet it remained the case that there was no equivalent of the term "glamour" in the Italian language and there was some hostility to the abstract, standardized qualities it was seen to embody. The women's magazine *Grazia* regarded Hayworth as a vulgarized product of "a monstrous machine that renders everyone equal in appearance and in taste."[20] The nearest Italian term, sometimes used in the press where it was felt the foreign term would not be understood, was "fascino." But *fascino* did not convey the manufactured, exterior, or democratizing aspects of American glamour. Rather it suggested an individual magnetism that was intrinsic rather than manufactured and not at all commercial.

The Development of Italian Glamour

In the postwar years, American glamour and artifice contrasted with Italian grittiness and authenticity. In *Roma città aperta* and other films of the time, elegance and luxury were associated with Nazi collaborators and/or sexual deviance. However, quite quickly, Italy would develop positive models of glamour that no longer had widely shared negative connotations. It will be argued here that Italian glamour could not have occurred without American glamour, that it existed in relation to it and was in some respects a version of it, while also conserving features of its own. The United States brought a widening, democratic influence, a sense of the need to involve the masses in visions of excitement and plenty. Italian glamour developed as both a domestic adaptation of this lesson, taking account of local tastes and culture, and also as a specialist component of it, offering class products and images.

At the end of the war, Italy had little to offer, except a longstanding status as a land of beauty and civilization. It had been nearly destroyed and was searching for self-discovery in cinematic neo-realism. It did however have an industrial base of sorts and was able to take advantage of the opportunities for development that were provided through the ERP. After autarky and war, it was keen to reestablish contact with international currents and win export markets.

At a popular level the return of American glamour keyed in with the proliferation of beauty contests and a more general ostentation of body. The use of beauty to get ahead was prime evidence of the influence of American commercial culture. It derived from the body emphasis of American cinema, the pin-up culture the troops had brought with them and indigenous associations of the body with leisure that in the 1930s had coexisted awkwardly with Fascism's political appropriation of women's bodies. The girls who entered beauty pageants usually aspired to fame and success; they had absorbed the "me too" message of Hollywood, which encouraged the belief that anyone could make it. Unable to imitate the wealth or even afford even modest consumer items invested with star aura, they took on board the message of sex appeal and responded to the invitations of entrepreneurs and impresarios to display their bodies.

Italian cinema could not compete with the sophistication, expense, and skills of the American industry. But it could offer plenty of feminine beauty combined with attractive images of Italian landscapes and lifestyles. For the foreign market, Italy in the 1950s provided a novel and highly attractive input into the international pin-up culture that prospered so widely. The films, from the rice-field melodrama *Riso amaro* (Bitter Rice) to the working-class potboiler *La donna del fiume* (Woman of the River), appealed to art-house spectators in English-speaking countries who found in the wild, dark women of Italian film confirmation of a longstanding northern view of Italy as a primitive land of passion and waywardness. Since the early nineteenth century, writers including De Lamartine, Stendhal, and D.H. Lawrence had cultivated this impression. It found a further extension in the post-World War II writings of authors such as John Horne Burns and Joseph Heller.

The cult of Mediterranean beauty that prospered in Italian films in the 1950s owed something to the global success of neo-realism, with its downbeat yet strong heroines and rejection of the glamorous. But it owed more to the determination of producers and directors to apply some of the lessons of Hollywood as they perceived them. These were successful enough for Hollywood very quickly to seek to insert Italy's female beauties into its own runaway productions. Gina Lollobrigida, Sophia Loren, and others had the advantage of being less stylized than American actresses, they were physical rather than artificial. However, to American eyes, the Italians looked not like stars but starlets since in the United States only the latter exposed their flesh. Actor and director Vittorio de Sica confirmed this view when he declared, in poor English and causing much controversy, that "Italian beauties are all curves . . . Their artistic capabilities really cannot compete with their physical qualities. It is very sad to say it, but the Italian film industry today tends mainly to highlight legs and showy, opulent bosoms."[21]

As they emerged and became successful, winning Hollywood contracts, starlets like Lollobrigida and Loren underwent a process of refashioning. In effect they became absorbed into the styles and codes of Hollywood glamour. They adopted the low-cut gowns, the perfect coiffures, the statuesque qualities, the poses and manners, and the affluent lifestyles of the Hollywood stars with whom they entered into rivalry. For a brief period, Lollobrigida and Loren were seen as direct competitors of Marilyn Monroe; by some they were seen as much sexier, in a less innocent and more adult way. In many American films of this period, Italian actresses played parts which called for them to be prostitutes or ex-prostitutes or to be sexually knowing. For some Italians, however, the addition of sexual allure was problematic. This especially was the case with Lollobrigida who, ever since she had come second in the Miss Italy contest of 1947, had been seen as a typical representative of young Italian womanhood. As *Le ore* wrote in 1954:

> According to the Americans, Gina's beauty is a special beauty. Everyone admits that it is "sexy," i.e. "provocative," but her fiercest supporters have defined her as a "typical Italian brunette," a definition that, understood in the traditional way, should rule out a "sexy" content; rather it is used to refer to types of women whose beauty is serene, pure and a little ingenuous.[22]

In the mid-1950s, Lollobrigida was the leading Italian star. She bought a pink stucco villa on the Via Appia Antica and was frequently featured on magazine covers in full star regalia. She became something of an uncrowned queen, a national representative whose demeanor and manner provoked admiration.[23] For Americans, the glamorous image she and others offered was a variant on the conventional that involved a touch of the Latin exotic. This had various commercial applications, for example by the Revlon Corporation, which tied in the launch of its Fire and Ice range with the Italian stars.[24] It gave Italy a material identity which aided exports too.

To foreigners, the Italian stars were undoubtedly glamorous. But, in fact, there was a significant difference between Italian and American stars. Silvana Mangano (who had been elected Miss Rome in 1946) was the first Italian star to come to the attention of the public through an image. Launched when Rita Hayworth's popularity was at its height, she became known through a famous still photograph from *Riso amaro* which set her in shorts in a rice-field. Released as a promotional device because of the delayed launch of the film, the picture became an internationally celebrated pin-up. But Mangano never acquired in Italy the artificial appeal and manufactured beauty of the Hollywood image. She was too specific and earthy, too individual and familiar. Moreover, she hated her sexy image and did everything possible to throw it off and assert herself as an actress.

With reference to postwar Britain, Paul Swann and Jackie Stacey have separately argued that domestic stars were always seen as less packaged and less overtly sexual than the glamour queens of Hollywood.[25] They had personality and talent rather than looks, and were respectable and reserved. Only American femininity signified excitement and sexuality as well as luxury and abundance. The American stars were awesome and fantastic for ordinary girls. Erica Carter makes some similar points in relation to Germany.[26] In Italy these differences also prevailed, with important distinctions. While Italian stars took on the trappings of glamour more eagerly than some British or German actors, they did not become their defining feature. Moreover, Italian stars were not manufactured or artificial. They never became dehumanized or detached from the realm of the real. They were, it is true, molded by men in a way that took account of the sex appeal of American stars (and sometimes against the instincts and desires of the women themselves) but they retained at least a strong appearance of the natural.

In Italy at the time the body was not fully an object of narcissistic cultivation in a consumerised sense of self, although the female body was certainly subjected to a tendentially modern male gaze.[27] Rather it was mainly perceived as geared to natural functions and to work. Italian stars were often bodies in landscapes; beautiful bodies representing working bodies in real contexts – rice-fields, lagoons, and mountains. Piera De Tassis quotes Carlo Lizzani, who worked as a writer on *Riso amaro*, as saying that Mangano's body in the film assumed a presence and meaning not foreseen in the script. Her body was "offered up for viewing like a natural prodigy, a beautiful animal or a beautiful tree."[28] Because Italy was not yet a fully industrial society, it found its star figures in men and women who were recognizable and real: cyclists, boxers, and shapely women. "In Italy the talents and qualities that are celebrated are absolutely natural and spontaneous, the fruit not of research, study or effort so much as gifts received at birth and cultivated spontaneously which, when they are suddenly revealed, bring the individual to public attention, just like a stroke of luck or a lottery," wrote Silvio Guarnieri in 1956.[29]

Italians wondered at the polished, glossy images of Marilyn Monroe, but many commentators did not find her sexy. Her stylized sexuality was enticing, Oreste Del Buono conceded, "but beneath all the fuss there is the extremely unexciting reality of a small, chubby girl who is almost innocuous and rather dull. In the matter of *sex appeal*, she certainly bears no comparison with our Mangano in *Riso amaro*."[30] Sex appeal was considered by Italians as something imported and curious, an American feature that was constructed rather than natural. Even in the mid-1950s, the term glamour was scarcely used, but some efforts were made to try and understand what it signified in the United States. It tended to be seen as something alien and alienating, the product of "the orderly frigidity of appearances and social relations" in theUnited States.[31]

When Italian magazines depicted Silvana Pampanini and others in regal apparel, almost as though they were queens, they did so not because the external manifestations of royalty had been taken over entirely by the entertainment industry, but because the myth of royalty still exercised considerable fascination for Italians. Lacking a studio system, Italy could not manufacture glamour except by imitation. The ersatz effects of the 1930s' "white telephone" films gave way in the 1940s and early 1950s to a relation with one aspect of glamour – sex appeal – but the neglect of other aspects, including fashion and consumerism, which in the United States gave it a special appeal to women. Fashion spoke to their experiences and desires and provided a utopian element in the construction of images of the ideal self. In Italy this element developed separately and followed a different social trajectory to cinema.

Fashion and Aristocratic Glamour

Italian fashion in the 1930s and 1940s was modest and provincial. The few fashion designers were known only to their almost exclusively local clients. They used good quality materials but offered no originality; Parisian designs to the tastes and pockets of their customers. Simonetta, Antonelli, Biki, Carosa, Galitzine, and others were considered professionals of good standing but there was an abyss between them and the stars of the Paris scene, Chanel, Schiaparelli, and Dior. The latter were both more creative and more practical, more artistic and original and more modern in their efforts to relate fashion to the needs of a broad stratum of well-to-do women. An extreme example of the low standing of Italian fashion was offered in October 1948 when *Oggi* reported that the police had raided the Paris hotel where some Italian designers were staying during the autumn shows and arrested an Italian sketch artist who had copied the Dior collection without permission to sell cut-price to his Italian clients.[32]

The turning point came with the Power–Christian wedding in 1949. One of the great social events of the postwar period, it gave rise to massive publicity which also worked to the advantage of the Fontana sisters, who made Christian's wedding dress. As *Oggi* wrote:

> One hundred and fifty metres of very fine tulle were used by a large Roman fashion house to create an original model with a bodice, a modest *decolletée* and a wide bell-shaped skirt, artistically pleated: this is Linda Christian's wedding dress. *Paillettes* and small pearls add precious touches to the splendid *toilette*. Known as one of the most elegant stars in Hollywood, fanciful in her tastes and impossible to satisfy in fittings, Linda is always arguing with the dress designers even though she is dressed in a furcoat and jewels worth sixty million Lire.[33]

Pictured by numerous magazines in the Fontana sisters' atelier, Christian provided testimony to the skill and quality of the work of Italian professionals.

Italian fashion had been decentralized and largely provincial before the war. In the early 1950s there was a serious attempt to unite it and promote it abroad, by associating it with the traditional attractions of the Italian context. The idea was conceived by Giovan Battista Giorgini, a Florentine trader with excellent contacts among US department stores and the fashion press. The shows he organized in Florence from 1951 are conventionally seen as marking the attempt to break Italian fashion's subordination to Paris and promote it abroad, and especially in America.[34]

The promotion drew attention to the low cost, fine quality materials and simplicity of Italian design, but above all they sought to confer an Italian identity on the work of the designers who joined the shows. This meant that attention was drawn to Italy's artistic and cultural heritage and to the elegance and tradition of good taste of its aristocracy. Photographs appeared first in *Bellezza* and other Italian magazines, and then foreign ones, of young aristocratic ladies wearing elegant clothes in the courtyards and corridors of Renaiassance palaces. Alternatively they were depicted outside, among the monuments of ancient Rome. Because Italian fashion lacked originality, there was much insistence on its image, its staging, with attention being drawn to "the triad of art–craft–aristocracy."[35] Lacking economic and political power, Italy's aristocracy acquired a new prestige abroad through the marketing of its aura. The role of such members of the nobility as Pucci and Simonetta showed that hard-up aristocrats participated in this process.

Aided by organized promotional visits of young ladies and favorable press coverage, Italian fashion made an impression in the United States.[36] As Valerie Steele has argued, Italian fashion became known for its low cost, unusual shapes, bright colors, youthful verve, and playful feel.[37] However, these initiatives did not lead to Italy becoming a regular supplier of quantities of clothing to US department stores. Even boutique fashions such as Pucci's reached only a small clientele. But they did create an image and a desirability that meant that when rich Americans came to Italy, they did not pass up the chance to visit tailors and dress designers and acquire new wardrobes of quality at reasonable prices. In the course of the 1950s, many major film stars took this route as Rome turned into a major international center of film production. By the mid-1950s over 100 films per year were being shot in Italy and a significant proportion of these was American. Audrey Hepburn, Ava Gardner, and Katharine Hepburn were among those who dressed Italian both on and off screen. In films including *Roman Holiday*, *Three Coins in a Fountain*, and *Summer Madness*, an image of Italy was communicated as a land of beauty, charm, elegance, refinement, and nobility. For American stars and for others too Italian glamour did not consist of buxom bodies but rather of class and elegance. Hollywood had always sought to appropriate aspects of European high culture; now Italy was able to contribute specifically to the elaboration of Hollywood glamour by lending it style and associations with history and leisure.

Fashion magazines and fashion pages in Italy paid little attention in the 1950s to Italian film stars like Lollobrigida and Loren. Instead they focused on noble-women and foreign stars of the aristocratic type. Grace Kelly, Deborah Kerr, and Audrey Hepburn were all seen as more appropriate examples by arbiters of taste and by women. It may seem strange that in just the period in which mass culture was taking off, consumerism was beginning to take shape and the old rigidity of the social hierarchy was undergoing erosion, there should have been a flowering in Europe of images so evidently shot through with aloofness and elitist chic. The tall, slim, angular woman, perfectly groomed and cool, proliferated in magazines and advertisements. In fact, although these images were unapproachable for some women, they were not as removed from all as might be thought. First, as Carter has pointed out in her examination of German women's magazines, there was an emancipatory element in that these images often showed women acting in a confident and sophisticated way in public places, unencumbered by family and domestic duties.[38] Second, they portrayed womanhood as fashion, taste, and consumerism, in other words as a process involving pleasures. Third, the upper-class woman was historically the most at home with things that were now coming within the reach of the many: surplus spending, home comforts, domestic help (appliances now, not servants), beautification, fashion. Fourth, images of a model like Lisa Fonssagrives, and by extension those of other models of her type and some "class" film stars, actually "seemed accessible to every woman," David Seidner has written. They offered grace, balance, and reserve, combined with a certain energy "that resonated in the subconscious of generations of women to whom [Fonssagrives'] appeal was irresistible." Such women appeared to be in control and true to themselves. Fonssagrives' "dance experience gave her a sense of theatre so that the elaborate costume never looked mannered or affected – a comfortable masquerade."[39]

The triumph of the "aristocratic type" confirmed the decline of the old upper classes rather than the opposite, for it was not as substance that it acquired resonance but as image, as deracinated look. The image could be promoted by anyone of whatever background provided they possessed the right physique and bearing. The rise of this sort of image in Italy, associated mostly with the haute couture model and later film actress Elsa Martinelli, but also diffused thanks to Lucia Bosè and a physically transformed Silvana Mangano, showed that peasant culture and its associations with the fear of scarcity were being eclipsed.[40]

The influence of fashion culture and its centrality to feminine consciousness was underlined by the way all Italian female stars became more elegant in the mid-1950s. Having won popularity with men by wearing flimsy, revealing costumes that exposed their shapely figures, Loren and Lollobrigida underwent a turn towards elegance in 1955–6. The Neapolitan dressmaker Emilio Schubert, who catered to many foreign stars, provided new inputs into Italian film costume, but importantly he also contributed to the new image of Italy's stars by making spectacular gowns and dresses that they could wear for receptions, festivals, and premières. These were theatrical, geared to the demands of image and flattering. Schubert sought, while preserving the freshness and spontaneity of the stars, to transcend their early images and confer a new look. He persuaded Lollobrigida, who had been "the typical good-looking Italian girl who doesn't really know how she wants to be or should dress," to cut her hair and become more sophisticated: "once she had changed type, the clothes had to change too. No more wide skirts, but instead figure-hugging dresses; no more excessive simplicity, but rather sumptuousness, richness, eye-catching qualities, folds, straps, white, black, pearls and silver."[41]

So equipped, Lollobrigida and Loren were well placed to travel abroad to promote their films and at the same time offer an image of Italian craft and fashion. In Hollywood and more widely in the United States, they would receive admiring comments for the richness and originality of their toilettes. They became objects of admiration and imitation on the part of women of a wide range of social classes the world over. At once different from and part of the star elite that defined and diffused the ideals of Hollywood glamour, they aroused interest and attracted attention.

The "Dolce Vita" Connection

It was not just Italian stars who traveled in the 1950s but the world that came to Rome. While the city underwent population growth and urban expansion, it also became a fashionable city, a cosmopolitan crossroads for the international elite of the rich and famous. Vast numbers of film actors, directors, and personnel acted as a magnet for hangers on, aspirant people, and movers and shakers. In addition rich playboys, idle aristocrats, and bored heiresses made it a vital point in their itinerary. Rome became a center for an international café society that in the 1960s would evolve into the jet set. This cosmopolitan crowd provided a layer of social life that the city had never had before. On top and alongside of the conventional scene, there was another made up of the rich and the beautiful. For a period, Rome became a combination of Paris and Hollywood, and certainly the place that gave rise to the most gossip and scandal. These featured in some of the mainstream press as well as the notorious scandal sheet *Confidential*.

For foreigners Italy had always possessed glamour, in the sense that it presented an enticing image mixing beauty, sexuality, theatricality, wealth (in the form of heritage), and leisure. In the years of the "dolce vita" this was given a new twist as the wealth acquired a contemporary connotation and the beauty and sexuality were associated with fashion and film. Many of the events which appeared in the world's press and were seen to typify the decadent hedonism of the life of the celebrity elite in Rome were not spontaneous but staged by press agents. These included in 1958 Anita Ekberg's night-time dip in the Trevi Fountain and a celebrated impromptu striptease performed at the Rugantino nightclub by Turkish model Aiché Nana. But there were sufficient genuine conflicts between celebrities and press photographers around the Via Veneto to lend an air of authenticity to the phenomenon. Snapshots of illicit celebrity couples and of men kicking and punching photographers in the dead of night turned Rome into a center of modern mythologies featuring aristocrats and movie stars.[42] This added spice to the new image that Italy was acquiring. By the late 1950s, the Italian lifestyle had become fashionable and desirable. The products of Italian design, like the Vespa, Fiat cars, and coffee machines, were no longer featured in films as amusing curiosities (as they had been in *Roman Holiday*) but were seen as stylish and desirable.

Federico Fellini's hit 1960 film *La Dolce Vita* offered a bitter-sweet portrait of a city, and by implication a country, that was caught in the whirl of success and celebrity. The film presented what was already partially a staged reality, probably at a point when it was already in decline, and wrapped it in a mythological aura. The film's exciting depiction of the Via Veneto (in fact recreated in the studio) is said to have killed it off as a chic center and instead brought in the tourists. Following the film, Ugo Gregoretti claimed,

the whole world imagined that Via Veneto was the center of forbidden pleasures. One evening a correspondent of the *Toronto Star*, a freckled "red-head," bumped into me in the street and asked me if I could give him the address of an "orgy." This was the climate, this was the idea that by this time foreigners had of the Via Veneto. In a very short time everyone disappeared.[43]

But if the reality died, the image lived on. In the minds of the public worldwide, Rome was the city of sin and pleasure, of Liz Taylor, Ava Gardner, and Frank Sinatra, of elegance and nightclubs, of Soraya, of aristocrats and Latin lovers, of fast cars and stylish intellectuals.

This image, perpetuated in American films and books, including Irwin Shaw's *Two Weeks in Another Town* and Tennessee Williams's *The Roman Summer of Mrs. Stone*, provided Roman tourist industries and fashion houses with a resource that has lasted down to the present. Roman glamour became Italian glamour for the world. Throughout the 1960s, the city was configured as an adult alternative to the new youth culture which had its center in London. Swinging Rome was not just classy but dangerous in the popular imagination. The surface style and the bright, figure-hugging Brioni men's suits which preceded the flair of London and which featured in so many foreign television films and series of the period were perceived as the tip of a lifestyle that mixed stylishness with decadence and corruption.

Italian glamour combined sex and style for foreigners. The country became an image to be consumed, to be bought into and to be savored in small doses, by means of a film, a vacation, a meal in a restaurant, an item of clothing, or a domestic appliance. The press book for the US release of *La Dolce Vita* encouraged exhibitors to set up tie-ins with local dress shops stocking Italian and continental clothes. Travel agencies and pizza parlors were also deemed suitable sites for window displays promoting the film. Department stores were a source of further such opportunities:

The film's title lends itself to countless tie-ins with stores (in newspaper advertising and in store displays), since there is a certain snob appeal in a foreign title (particularly one that has received such tremendous advance exploitation) and the uninitiated discover that there is an invitation to any number of products in the English translation. Sample copy: LA DOLCE VITA means THE SWEET LIFE. An air conditioner means a sweeter life for your family etc. . . . La DOLCE VITA (The Sweet Life) is not to be missed at . . . theatre . . . The Sweet Life is that much sweeter with . . . chocolates.[44]

This domestication of *La Dolce Vita* says more about 1950s American consumerism and its thirst for continental attributes than it does about Italy. But it was difficult to eliminate totally the film's clear implication that Italy was not merely blandly picturesque; it was a site of scandal too. The movie also marked a transition in the way stars were perceived. In the United States, studio publicity departments were accustomed to exercising complete control over the flow of news about star figures, presenting flawless images that stressed their admirable qualities. In Rome, where there could be no such control, they came down to earth; they became real and were often shown to be flawed. In addition, Rome in the late 1950s (the "dolce vita" reached a head in 1958) saw a certain real renegotiation of the barriers between different elites. With their fall from power, aristocrats were forced to reinvent themselves as personalities for consumption like celebrities, to become part of the alluring landscape of history, tradition, and palaces, or simply to disappear. Certainly, in the world of image where films and illustrated weekly magazines determined who was who, any old distinctions of status ceased to be meaningful. Celebrity, surface, and image triumphed. As had happened in the United States in the 1920s, publicity became an autonomous source of power.[45] Yet, the simultaneous rise of Italian fashion and the development of Rome as a film capital meant that certain distinctions which applied elsewhere did not apply in Italy. "Here in Italy, glamour and elegance were born in the same historical moment, and still today they often overlap – just as they undoubtedly overlap with each other in the image people abroad have of a certain Italy," Italian *Vogue* wrote in 1995.[46]

Towards Mass Consumption

Between the late 1950s and the early 1960s the profile of Italian society changed. Quite suddenly the country found itself to be mainly modern and urban and the values and images of peasant culture, which only a few years previously had appeared to reflect a widespread reality, declined or took on a nostalgic, backward-looking air. It was not the land and the seasons which dominated the thinking of Italians, but rather urban infrastructures, consumer goods, home comforts and conveniences. In this context certain important changes occurred. In the first place the body ceased to be perceived in terms of the Catholic flesh/spirit dichotomy, or the left's idea of it as a tool of work, and became the object of care and attention.[47] The shift was reflected in a more modern idea of beauty and eroticism that no longer arose from the fixed relations of a static, rural society, but was to some extent free-floating in an American way. In the 1960s it became common to see images of glamorous women in advertisements in Italy and for Italian products. Many of these, however, referred directly to an American lexicon. The "blondes" of Perroni beer and the elegant illustrated glamour girls of Vespa scooters (replaced by actresses and live models in the mid-1960s) both stand witness to this. It was the American way of life that provided the framework of Italy's boom and which helped integrate the country in terms of a national cross-class imagined realm.

Combined with this shift there was a tendential move away from archaic ideas of honor, shame and sin. In the 1950s many films were made which featured the word "peccato" (sin) in the title, suggesting simultaneously condemnation and titillation. *La Dolce Vita* was intensely controversial and in many ways a watershed.[48] On the one hand, the film was severely condemned by established and conservative opinion. The presentation of elite life in the eternal city as hedonistic was perceived as subversive and dangerous. But also the hedonism itself was condemned, particularly by religious spokesmen, as being wasteful, immoral, and dissolute. Consumerism was not yet fully accepted as the predominant ethos in society although it was rapidly becoming the economic motor of the country.

On the other hand, the portrayal of the "sweet life" in magazines and then its further mythologization on film provoked widespread fascination. Although it had nothing to do with the way most Italians lived and it had no direct effect on them, it did provoke interest as a spectacle of style, beauty, and consumption. Even small businesspeople, whose wealth was growing in the boom years, aspired to participate in night life, build Hollywood-style villas, and acquire expensive sports cars. The emphasis on fashion in the film (in particular Anita Ekberg's costumes, based on the Fontana sisters' outfits for Ava Gardner including her costumes for *The Barefoot Contessa*) dovetailed with a growing interest in fashion among women and also men. From as early as 1953 *Oggi* increased its fashion coverage, although still most space was given to Paris. However, not all the interest was of this type. Many rushed to see the film because of the strong air of scandal that was associated with it. There is a brief episode in Pietro Germi's satirical comedy *Divorzio all'italiana* (Divorce Italian Style) that depicts the rush in provincial Sicily to see a film reputed to contain "orgies worthy of Emperor Tiberius."

The impact of the film signaled the end of the aristocracy as a class with a meaningful role in Italy. Instead of the aristocratic woman and her surrogate, the "aristocratic type," a more clearly modern image took shape of the elegant woman. Elsa Martinelli passed seamlessly from one type to the other, since it required merely the elimination of a certain 1950s style stuffiness and rigidity. The modern, elegant woman - represented in *La Dolce Vita* by Anouk Aimée (Maddalena) - was not defined by conformity to social norms or by grace and poise, but rather by autonomy, style, travel, wealth. Women of any class, provided they had the looks and determination could, it was implied, take on this role, it was an option not a birthright.

Among the lower and middle classes, it would be wrong to suggest that the great curiosity in royals which flowered in the immediate postwar years was expunged, but there was a qualitative change. Royals were no longer deferred to or admired in a conventional way, as had been the case at the time of the coronation of Queen Elizabeth II in 1953. There was much greater interest in the exteriority of splendor. The change was apparent in the way the Iranian royal family acquired prominence in the magazines in the early 1960s. In 1963 Soraya, the spurned wife of the Shah who became the "sad princess" of the time, undertook her first screen test, arranged by Dino De Laurentis. She passed without difficulty from court life to the nightclubs and the resorts of the jet set. In the same year Gina Lollobrigida visited the Shah in Teheran and escorted the readers of *Oggi* through the magnificence of the royal palaces. Although the actress made all the right deferential noises, it was apparent that she was being treated as an equal by the Shah and Farah Diba and that her clothes were of equal interest as the "enormous stupendous rooms" of the palace.[49]

Yet the provincial connotation remained. Foreign glamour followed by domestic consumerism was insufficient to eliminate a dimension of life that remained firmly rooted in the experience of family, community, and place. In fact Italy gave rise to no domestic glamour in the full sense of the term. The techniques of glamour were often learned, mastered, and employed in designing and marketing products but these took on truly glamorous implications only outside Italy.[50] Elegant clothes, fast cars, and luxury goods provoked desire abroad when combined with Italian natural settings, architectural achievements, and other aspects of the country. At home, however, even cars as romantic and overtly glamorous as Ferraris tended to be seen as products of a craft tradition - the substance counted more than the image. Even in the 1990s, in order to market itself Ferrari employed Sharon Stone or Ivana Trump to add glamour.

Conclusion

In Italy, celebrities eventually became part of the system of consumerism; they endorsed products and offered themselves as consumers and objects of consumption. But they never truly acquired glamour. No one achieved the necessary separation from family, place of origin, and the familiar for even a worked-over and elaborated image to become more than a pale imitation of American glamour. Television personalities, for example, always sought to highlight their down-to-earth qualities even while cultivating an appearance in line with international glamour. Yet, the long-range influence of the American idea of glamour within Italy is evident not just within television, but also in fashion. Italy's most successful export industry in the 1990s, fashion produces jobs, earnings, and image on a grand scale. Yet the imagery of fashion marketing is resolutely American and refers back invariably to the Hollywood golden age. Versace used supermodels who recalled the ice-cool blondes of the 1950s, while Giorgio Armani draws on the masculine tailoring of Hollywood in the 1930s and 1940s. Valentino and Dolce and Gabbana, designers for whom the domestic Italian market is less important, draw on images inspired by *La Dolce Vita* (the celebrated moment of Anita Ekberg's screen dip in the Trevi Fountain – already a re-elaboration of a real-life stunt – was restaged by Valentino in 1996 with Claudia Schiffer in the place of Ekberg) and neo-realism. But this is Italian glamour for export. Italians made their transition to consumerism with the aid of and led by American imagery. Over time they caught up and elaborated original and useful images of glamour for foreign consumption. These conferred a magical aura on the country which still functions to aid tourism and the sale of goods. But informing it all is an idea of American glamour which has never been matched or superseded, only reworked, repositioned, and re-elaborated.

Notes

1. Camille Paglia, *Sexual Personae: Art and Decadence from Nefertiti to Emily Dickinson* (Harmondsworth: Penguin, 1992), pp. 67–8.

2. Some pertinent issues are considered in Reka C.V. Buckley and Stephen Gundle, "Fashion and Glamour," in Nicola White and Ian Griffiths (eds), *The Fashion Business: Theory, Practice, Image* (Oxford: Berg, 2000) and Stephen Gundle, "Mapping the Origins of Glamour: Giovanni Boldini, Paris and the Belle Epoque," *Journal of European Studies* 29 (1999), pp. 269–95. A fuller elaboration of these ideas will be presented in Clino Castelli and Stephen Gundle, *The Glamour System* (in preparation).

3. Margaret Farrand Thorp, *America at the Movies* (New Haven, CT: 1939). Quoted in Jeffrey Richards, *The Age of the Dream Palace: Cinema and Society in Britain 1930-1939* (London: Routledge, 1984), pp. 157–8.

4. For a case study, see Linda Mizejewski, *Ziegfeld Girl: Image and Icon in Culture and Cinema* (Durham, NC: Duke University Press, 1999).

5. Richard Dyer, *Stars* (London: British Film Institute, 1979); Laura Mulvey, *Visual and Other Pleasures* (London: Macmillan, 1989); Annette Kuhn, *The Power of the Image: Essays on Representation and Sexuality* (London: Routledge and Kegan Paul, 1985).

6. Sybil DelGaudio, *Dressing the Part: Sternberg, Dietrich, and Costume* (Rutherford, NJ: Farleigh Dickinson University Press, 1993), p. 21.

7. Neal Gabler, *An Empire of their Own: How the Jews Invented Hollywood* (New York: Anchor, 1989).

8. See Kathy Peiss, *Hope in a Jar: The Making of America's Beauty Culture* (New York: Metropolitan/Holt, 1998), chs 4 and 5.

9. Walter Wanger, "America's Secret Weapon," University of Wisconsin-Madison, State Historical Society, Papers of Walter Wanger/Speeches 36.58. See also Wanger, "Donald Duck and Diplomacy," *Public Opinion Quarterly* (Fall 1950), pp. 443–52.

10. Pier Paolo Pasolini, *Amado mio* (Milan: Garzanti, 1982), pp. 191–2.

11. Gion Guida, "Gilda," *Cinemmoda* (April 6, 1947), p. 7.

12. Edgar Morin, *Les Stars* (Paris: Seuil, 1957).

13. Ugo Zatterin, "Matrimonio in technicolor per Tyrone il buono e Linda la bella," *Oggi* (February 3, 1949), p. 11.

14. For an analysis of the event as reported in the press, see Stephen Gundle, "Memory and Identity: Popular Culture in Postwar Italy," in Patrick McCarthy (ed.), *Italy since 1945* (Oxford: Oxford University Press, 2000), pp. 190–2.

15. For some perceptive observations on postwar Roman aristocracy, see Luigi Barzini, *From Caesar to the Mafia: Sketches of Italian Life* (New York: Doubleday, 1971), pp. 107–10.

16. For a more detailed examination of these issues, see Stephen Gundle, "Il divismo nel cinema europeo, 1945–60," in Gian Piero Brunetta (ed.), *Storia del cinema mondiale*, vol. 1, *L'Europa*, book 1: *Miti, luoghi, divi* (Turin: Einaudi, 1999).

17. On the cultural clashes of the whole Cold War period, see Stephen Gundle, *Between Hollywood and Moscow: The Italian Communists and the Challenge of Mass Culture, 1943–91* (Durham, NC: Duke University Press, 2000).

18. On this episode, see Stephen Gundle, "Saint Ingrid at the Stake: Stardom and Scandal in the Bergman-Rossellini Collaboration," in David Forgacs, Sarah Lutton, and Geoffrey Nowell-Smith (eds), *Roberto Rossellini: Magician of the Real* (London: British Film Institute, 2000).

19. On the stars and consumerism, see Charles Eckert, "The Carole Lombard in Macy's Window," in Christine Gledhill (ed.), *Stardom: Industry of Desire* (London: Routledge, 1991).

20. Ubis, "La Fornarina cede il passo a Rita Hayworth," *Grazia* 404 (1948), pp. 22–3. Cited in Marina Coslovi, "Il Glamour ci viene da Hollywood: l'immagine dell'America in una rivista femminile del dopoguerra," unpublished paper, undated, p. 7.

21. Cited in Cinema Nuovo, "Lo scandalo delle curve" (1953), in Guido Aristarco (ed.) *Il mito dell'attore: come l'industria della star produce il sex symbol* (Bari: Dedalo, 1983), p. 261.

22. Anon., "Lollo degli americani," *Le ore* (February 6, 1954), pp. 12–13.

23. See Reka C.V. Buckley, "National Body: Gina Lollobrigida and the Cult of the Star in the 1950s," *Historical Journal of Film Radio and Television* 20, 4 (2000), pp. 527–47.

24. See Andrew Tobias, *Fire and Ice: The Story of Charles Revson – The Man Who Built the Revlon Empire* (New York: Morrow, 1976), p. 122.

25. Paul Swann, *The Hollywood Feature Film in Postwar Britain* (London: Croom Helm 1987); Jackie Stacey, *Star Gazing: Hollywood Cinema and Female Spectatorship* (London: Routledge, 1994).

26. Erica Carter, *How German is She? Postwar West German Reconstruction and the Consuming Woman* (Ann Arbor, MI: University of Michigan Press, 1987).

27. For a theoretical treatment of the male gaze, see Laura Mulvey, "Visual Pleasure and Narrative Cinema," in Mulvey, *Visual and Other Pleasures*.

28. Piera De Tassis, "Corpi recuperati per il proprio sguardo," *Memoria* 3, 6 (1982), pp. 24–31, here p. 27.

29. Silvio Guarnieri, "Campioni e Dive" (1956), in Aristarco, *Il mito dell'attore*, p. 49.

30. Oreste Del Buono, "Marilyn Monroe" (1953), in Aristarco, *Il mito dell'attore*, p. 66.

31. Nadir Giannitrapani, "'Il glamor' nella società americana," *Cinema* (November 15, 1950), pp. 170–74, here p. 174.

32. Ruggero Gilardi, "A Parigi i sarti italiani hanno conosciuto i poliziotti di Dior," *Oggi* (October 3, 1948), p. 7.

33. Errante, "Le ragazze svengono," *Oggi* (February 3, 1949), p. 11.

34. See Guido Vergani, "La Sala Bianca: nascita della moda italiana," in Giannino Malossi (ed.), *La Sala Bianca: nascita della moda italiana* (Milan: Electa, 1992).

35. Sean Blazer, *Mercanti di moda* (Bergamo: Lubrina, 1997), pp. 32–3.

36. See Nicola White, *Reconstructing Italian Fashion: American and the Development of the Italian Fashion Industry* (Oxford: Berg, 2000).

37. Valerie Steele, "Italian Fashion and America," in Germano Celant (ed.), *The Italian Metmorphosis 1943–1968* (New York: Guggenheim Museum Publications, 1994), pp. 498–9.

38. Carter, *How German is She?*, pp. 209–25.

39. David Seidner, "Still Dance," in Seidner (ed.), *Lisa Fonssagrives: Three Decades of Classic Fashion Photography* (London: Thames and Hudson, 1997), p. 20.

40. See De Tassis, "Corpi recuperati," pp. 29–31. Mangano hated her youthful sexy image and transformed herself into a thin, angular woman of poise and grace.

41. Michele Quiriglio, "Schubert veste le dive," *Cinema* 9, 168 (June 16, 1956), pp. 286–8, here p. 288. See also Bonizza Giordani Aragno (ed.) *Moda romana dal 1945 al 1965* (Rome: De Luca, 1998).

42. See Andrea Nemiz (ed.), *Vita, dolce vita* (Rome: Network, 1983).

43. Cited in Sandro Giulianelli and Antonio Simbolotti (eds), *Via Veneto: un mito e il suo futuro* (Rome: Quaderni di AU - Rivista dell'Arredo Urbano, 1985), page unnumbered.

44. University of Southern California – Film Archives, Advertising, Publicity and Promotion Material for *La Dolce Vita*: An Astor Release.

45. See Cleveland Amory, *Who Killed Society?* (New York: Harper, 1960), p. 143 for a discussion of what the author called "publi-ciety." See also Neal Gabler, *Walter Winchell: Gossip, Power and the Culture of Celebrity* (London: Picador, 1995), esp. p. 81.

46. Anna Gloria Forti and Antonella Amapane, "Glamour italiano," *Vogue (Italia)* (February 1995), pp. 398–402, here p. 398.

47. Luisa Leonini, "Non mi vesto mi travesto," in Cesare Colombo (ed.), *Tra sogno e bisogno* (Milan: Coop-Longanesi, 1986), p. 256.

48. On the impact of the film, see Stephen Gundle, "La Dolce Vita," *History Today* (January 2000), pp. 29–35.

49. Carlo Moretti, "Gina racconta: non credevo che lo scià fosse tanto giovanile e Farah così alta," *Oggi* (March 28, 1963), p. 26.

50. See Giannino Malossi (ed.), *Volare: The Icon of Italy in Global Pop Culture* (New York: Monacelli, 1999).

Index

Adorno, Theodor, 1–2, 4, 5, 8, 19, 21, 75
alcohol, 12–13
    cultural meaning of, 236–7, 244, 247–8
    and the "drink question," 235–6, 239,
      248n3
    pub culture and, 237–9, 245
    scholarship on, 234, 235
    social boundaries and, 247
    see also temperance movement
Alexander, Sally, 269
Altes Museum, 31, 36
Appadurai, Arjun, 19
Aragon, Louis, 73
Arendt, Hannah, 18
art deco, 309
art nouveau, 309
Astley, Philip, 49–50
    and origins of circus, 46
    use of horses by, 46, 48
    see also circuses
Auslander, Leora, 19, 96, 101n86
Autobahn, 12, 218–19
    and "automobile wandering," 220–21,
      222
    and car design, 221–22, 224–5
    and public life, 225–7
    relation to genocide of, 218–19
    and speed, 223–4
    see also automobiles, tourism
automobiles, 11–12
    "airmindedness" and, 229n28
    opposition to, 211n1
    ownership of, 216
    scholarship on, 24n50, 215–17, 227n5,
      227–8n6

social relations and, 12, 192, 221–7
    passim
    see also Autobahn, Michelin Red
      Guides, tourism

Bacall, Lauren, 321–2
Baedeker guides
    Britishness and, 121–23
    compared to Murray's guides, 107–8,
      119–23
    dominance of, 119–23
    literary treatment of, 109
    maps in, 120
    see also tourism
Bailey, Peter, 266–7, 277–8, 282–3, 285
Bakhtin, Mikhail, 47
Balzac, Honoré de, 63–4
Barthes, Roland, 216
Baudelaire, Charles, 65, 66–7, 72
Baudrillard, Jean, 329
Bauman, Zygmunt, 299
Benjamin, Walter, 64–7 passim, 69–70, 75
Bennett, Tony, 37, 38
Berman, Marshall, 27
bicycling, 9, 11, 131–2
    bicycle ownership and, 142, 146n54
    bourgeoisie and, 132–4, 136, 137, 138,
      142–3
    clubs for, 136–41, 142
    cost of, 135
    racing and, 135–6
    working class and, 135–6, 139–43
Bierbaum, Otto Julius, 220
Bond, James, 326
Booth, J.B., 282